Thomas Pynchon and the
Digital Humanities

New Horizons in Contemporary Writing

In the wake of unprecedented technological and social change, contemporary literature has evolved a dazzling array of new forms that traditional modes and terms of literary criticism have struggled to keep up with. *New Horizons in Contemporary Writing* presents cutting-edge research scholarship that provides new insights into this unique period of creative and critical transformation.

Volumes in the series:

Jeanette Winterson's Narratives of Desire, Shareena Z. Hamzah-Osbourne
Transatlantic Fictions of 9/11 and the War on Terror, Susana Araújo
Life Lines: Writing Transcultural Adoption, John McLeod
South African Literature's Russian Soul, Jeanne-Marie Jackson
The Politics of Jewishness in Contemporary World Literature, Isabelle Hesse
Writing After Postcolonialism: Francophone North African Literature in Transition, Jane Hiddleston
David Mitchell's Post-Secular World, Rose Harris-Birtill
New Media and the Transformation of Postmodern American Literature, Casey Michael Henry
Postcolonialism After World Literature, Lorna Burns
Jonathan Lethem and the Galaxy of Writing, Joseph Brooker
The Contemporary Post-Apocalyptic Novel, Diletta De Cristofaro
David Foster Wallace's Toxic Sexuality, Edward Jackson
Wanderwords: Language Migration in American Literature, Maria Lauret
Northern Irish Writing After the Troubles, Caroline Magennis

Forthcoming volumes:

Contemporary Fiction, Celebrity Culture, and the Market for Modernism, Carey Mickalites
Creaturely Forms in Contemporary Literature, Dominic O'Key
Encyclopaedism and Totality in Contemporary Fiction, Kiron Ward

Thomas Pynchon and the Digital Humanities

Computational Approaches to Style

Erik Ketzan

BLOOMSBURY ACADEMIC
LONDON • NEW YORK • OXFORD • NEW DELHI • SYDNEY

BLOOMSBURY ACADEMIC
Bloomsbury Publishing Plc
50 Bedford Square, London, WC1B 3DP, UK
1385 Broadway, New York, NY 10018, USA
29 Earlsfort Terrace, Dublin 2, Ireland

BLOOMSBURY, BLOOMSBURY ACADEMIC and the Diana logo are
trademarks of Bloomsbury Publishing Plc

First published in Great Britain 2022
This paperback edition published 2023

For legal purposes the Acknowledgments on p. xii constitute an extension
of this copyright page.

Cover design: Eleanor Rose and Namkwan Cho

A catalogue record for this book is available from the British Library.

A catalog record for this book is available from the Library of Congress.

ISBN: HB: 978-1-3502-1183-4
PB: 978-1-3502-1187-2
ePDF: 978-1-3502-1184-1
eBook: 978-1-3502-1185-8

Series: New Horizons in Contemporary Writing

Typeset by Newgen KnowledgeWorks Pvt. Ltd., Chennai, India

To find out more about our authors and books visit www.bloomsbury.com
and sign up for our newsletters.

Contents

List of Illustrations viii

Acknowledgments xii

Note on the Texts xiii

Introduction 1

1   Some Formal Overviews of Pynchon's Texts 15

   1.1   Pynchon's Productivity 15

   1.2   Direct Discourse, Narration, and Verse 16

      1.2.1   Songs/Poems Are Decreasing in Pynchon 18

      1.2.2   Direct Discourse Is Increasing in Pynchon 22

      1.2.3   Reading Dialogue and Character in Pynchon 24

   1.3   Formal Overviews: Conclusion 29

2   Archaic Stylistics in *Mason & Dixon* 35

   2.1   Capitalized Nouns 35

      2.1.1   Capitalization in Pynchon: Scholarly Response ... 40

      2.1.2   Querying and Close Reading Pynchon's Irregular
            Capitalization 44

   2.2   Archaic Spelling, Especially <-ick> 48

   2.3   Religious/Profane Censorship 51

   2.4   Archaic Use of Apostrophes 54

   2.5   Archaic Pronouns and Verbs 58

   2.6   Archaic Language and the Sacred/Profane in Pynchon's Texts ... 59

   2.7   Archaic Stylistics in *Mason & Dixon*: Conclusion 64

3   Pynchon, "The Voice of Ambiguity," Quantified 73

   3.1   Ambiguity in Pynchon Studies 74

      3.1.1   "Ambiguous" 76

      3.1.2   "Ambiguity" Queried 79

   3.2   Vagueness Words and Phrases 85

      3.2.1   The Hiller/Hogenraad Vagueness Dictionary 86

      3.2.2   Pynchon's "Preferred" Vagueness Words 97

	3.2.3	A Brief Detour with *Its*	98
	3.2.4	Pynchon's "Preferred" Vagueness Words, Continued	102
	3.2.5	The Least Vague Passages in *Bleeding Edge*	104
	3.3	Ambiguity/Vagueness: Conclusion	107
4		Pynchon's Acronymania	115
	4.1	Acronym Query	116
	4.2	Calculated Overuse of Acronyms	121
	4.3	Acronyms as Parody, Play, and Central Enigma	124
	4.4	Acronymania: Conclusion	128
5		Pynchon's Profanity, Queried and Coded	133
	5.1	Profanity Queries and Changes to Profanity in English	135
	5.2	A Very Brief History of Obscenity Prosecutions of Literature in Twentieth-Century America	142
	5.3	Profanity in Pynchon's Juvenilia and Early Short Stories	144
	5.4	Profanity in *V.* and "The Secret Integration"	152
	5.5	Profanity in *The Crying of Lot 49*	158
	5.6	Pynchon's Profanity: Conclusion	160
6		Pynchon's Ellipsis Marks: Points and Dashes	171
	6.1	A Brief History of Ellipsis Marks in English Literature	173
	6.2	Ellipsis Marks in Pynchon and Comparison Corpora	176
	6.3	Ellipsis Words	181
	6.4	From Frequency to Close(r) Reading	181
	6.5	Ellipsis Marks and Speech	187
	6.6	Ellipsis Marks and Verse	189
	6.6.1	Rilke's Ellipses	190
	6.6.2	Emily Dickinson's Dashes	194
	6.7	Ellipsis Marks: Conclusion	199
Conclusion			207
Appendix I: Corpora, Software, Methods			211
	I.1	Pynchon Corpus	211
	I.1.1	Normalization of *Mason & Dixon*	212
	I.2	Us vs. Them: Comparison Corpora	213
	I.2.1	Influence Corpus	217
	I.3	Software	219

I.4   Statistics   220
I.5   Shared Data   221
Appendix II: Literature Review of Digital Pynchon Studies   227
Bibliography   239
Index   265

Illustrations

Figures

1.1	Narration, direct discourse, and verse in Pynchon corpus	19
1.2	Normalized frequency (per 100k word tokens) of verse in Pynchon corpus	20
1.3	Visualization of songs and poems in Pynchon corpus	21
1.4	Proportion of direct discourse in Pynchon and comparison corpora	23
1.5	Proportion of direct discourse in Pynchon corpus	24
2.1	Query of irregularly capitalized words in *Gravity's Rainbow*	45
3.1	Manfred Pinkal's typology of the indefinite	74
3.2	Normalized frequency of *ambiguous* and its word forms	80
3.3	Normalized frequency of 377 words and phrases from the Hiller/Hogenraad vagueness dictionary	88
3.4	Normalized frequency of Categories 1–9 of the Hiller/Hogenraad vagueness dictionary	89
3.5	Normalized frequency of Category 1 of Hiller/Hogenraad vagueness dictionary	90
3.6	Normalized frequency of Category 2 of Hiller/Hogenraad vagueness dictionary	90
3.7	Normalized frequency of Category 3 of Hiller/Hogenraad vagueness dictionary	91
3.8	Normalized frequency of Category 4 of Hiller/Hogenraad vagueness dictionary	91
3.9	Normalized frequency of Category 5 of Hiller/Hogenraad vagueness dictionary	92
3.10	Normalized frequency of Category 6 of Hiller/Hogenraad vagueness dictionary	92
3.11	Normalized frequency of Category 7 of Hiller/Hogenraad vagueness dictionary	93
3.12	Normalized frequency of Category 8 of Hiller/Hogenraad vagueness dictionary	93

3.13 Normalized frequency of Category 9 of Hiller/Hogenraad
vagueness dictionary 94

3.14 Normalized frequency of Category 10 of Hiller/Hogenraad
vagueness dictionary 94

3.15 Chapter 17 of *Inherent Vice*, with Hiller/Hogenraad vagueness
words highlighted 96

3.16 Normalized frequency of forty-nine vagueness words/phrases
in Pynchon corpus 100

3.17 Normalized frequency of "its" in Pynchon corpus 101

3.18 Normalized frequency of "its" in Pynchon chapters and episodes 101

3.19 Normalized frequency of forty-eight of Pynchon's "preferred
vagueness words" in chapters and episodes 103

3.20 Normalized frequency of forty-eight of Pynchon's "preferred
vagueness words" in chapters of *Bleeding Edge* 107

4.1 Normalized frequency of acronyms in Pynchon corpus 117

4.2 Word cloud of acronyms in Pynchon corpus by frequency 118

4.3 Normalized frequency of types of acronyms in Pynchon corpus 118

4.4 Normalized frequency of acronyms in Pynchon and
comparison corpora 122

4.5 Normalized frequency of acronym types in Pynchon and
comparison corpora 123

5.1 Normalized frequency of "lesser" profanity in Pynchon corpus 137

5.2 Normalized frequency of "lesser" profanity in direct discourse
in Pynchon corpus 137

5.3 Normalized frequency of "lesser" profanity in narration in
Pynchon corpus 138

5.4 Normalized frequency of "greater" profanity in Pynchon corpus 138

5.5 Normalized frequency of "greater" profanity in direct discourse
in Pynchon corpus 139

5.6 Normalized frequency of "greater" profanity in narration in
Pynchon corpus 139

5.7 Normalized frequency of select profanity in Pynchon and
comparison corpora, in chronological order 140

5.8 Normalized frequency of profanity in chapters of *V.* 154

5.9 Textual variation between excerpt of *The Crying of Lot 49* in
Esquire (1965) and the published novel (1966) 160

6.1 Normalized frequency of ellipsis points in Pynchon corpus 176

6.2   Normalized frequency of ellipsis points in Pynchon and
      comparison corpora   177
6.3   Normalized frequency of em dashes in Pynchon corpus   177
6.4   Normalized frequency of em dashes in Pynchon and
      comparison corpora   178
6.5   Normalized frequency of ellipsis phrases   182
6.6   Normalized frequency of ellipsis points in direct discourse and
      narration   187
6.7   Normalized frequency of em dashes in direct discourse and
      narration   188
6.8   Normalized frequency of ellipsis points in verse   190
6.9   Normalized frequency of dashes in verse   190
A.1   Comparing variants of *V.* in the Juxta application   212
A.2   Comparing and classifying edits in variants of *V*   212
A.3   TXM display of query across Pynchon corpus   220
A.4   TXM keyword-in-context (KWIC) view   221

Tables

1.1   Estimate of Pynchon's published word counts by year   17
1.2   Narration, direct discourse and verse in Pynchon corpus   18
2.1   Inconsistently capitalized nouns in *Mason & Dixon* with
      frequency > 100   37
2.2   A selection of noun forms in *Mason & Dixon* with frequency
      > 5 that are both capitalized and uncapitalized   38
2.3   A selection of nouns in a passage from *Mason & Dixon*, with
      frequency of both capitalized and uncapitalized types in the novel   40
2.4   Selection of <-ick> words in *Mason & Dixon*   50
2.5   Frequency of censored/bowdlerized words using dashes in
      Mason & Dixon   52
2.6   Mock-archaic words with <'d> in place of <-ed> with frequency
      ≥ 25, and their equivalents in modern spelling, in *Mason & Dixon*   54
2.7   A selection of mock-archaic words featuring apostrophes in
      Mason & Dixon, with frequency of modern equivalents   55
2.8   A selection of mock-archaic contractions in *Mason & Dixon*,
      with frequency of modern equivalent word groups and contractions   56

2.9   Twelve out of the twenty-five archaic regular verbs ending in
       <-eth> in *Mason & Dixon*, with interpretation of thematic
       associations with the sacred and profane   60
3.1   Examples from the 361 words and phrases in Hiller's vagueness
       dictionary   86
3.2   Words and phrases from the Hiller/Hogenraad vagueness
       dictionary that are significantly more frequent in Pynchon
       corpus than comparison corpora   98
3.3   Raw frequency of words and phrases from the Hiller/
       Hogenraad vagueness dictionary that are significantly more
       frequent in Pynchon corpus than comparison corpora   99
4.1   Frequency of all acronyms in *Mason & Dixon*   120
A.1   Normalized frequency (per 100k word tokens) of "here" and
       "now" in corpora   229

Note on the Texts

The novels and a short story collection by Thomas Pynchon are referenced parenthetically and in figures as:

V.   *V.* New York: Harper Perennial Classics, [1963] 1999.

Lot 49   *The Crying of Lot 49*. New York: Lippincott, 1966.

GR   *Gravity's Rainbow*. New York: Viking, 1973.

SL   *Slow Learner*. New York: Little, Brown, 1984.

Shorts   The short stories published in *Slow Learner*, as well as the uncollected story, "The Secret Integration."

Vine   *Vineland*. New York: Little, Brown, 1990.

M&D   *Mason & Dixon*. New York: Henry Holt, 1997.

ATD   *Against the Day*. New York: Penguin, 2006.

IV   *Inherent Vice*. New York: Penguin, 2009.

BE   *Bleeding Edge*. New York: Penguin, 2013.

Introduction

You guys, you're like the Puritans are about the Bible. So hung up with words, words.

—Thomas Pynchon, *The Crying of Lot 49*, 73

It's quite simple. He proves by algebra that Hamlet's grandson is Shakespeare's grandfather and that he himself is the ghost of his own father.

—James Joyce, *Ulysses*, 18

Thomas Pynchon's style has dazzled and bewildered readers and critics since the 1960s, and this book employs computational methods from the digital humanities to reveal heretofore unknown trends in Pynchon's style and challenge critical assumptions regarding supposedly "Pynchonesque" stylistic features. Pynchon has been the subject of voluminous critical commentary—as early as 1978, William Plater noted "the countless articles and monographs" on Pynchon,[1] and if they were countless then, they are beyond countless now. The best bibliography, Vheissu.net, lists 107 monographs and essay collections, 1,697 articles and book chapters, and this list is ever-growing.[2] Yet despite the extensive output of the "Pynchon industry," relatively few studies focus on stylistics, which are generally discussed briefly within evidence of thematic, generic, and intertextual readings.

This is the first book-length stylistic or computational stylistic examination of Pynchon's oeuvre.[3] As formal and stylistic studies of Pynchon's texts have been fragmented over decades, and across many disciplines and approaches, this book proceeds from the argument that unifying and continuing this work within a common project of scholarship will benefit from fundamental research, a "groundwork" of stylistic experiments and interpretations. The focus of this groundwork is stylistic features which scholars have perceived to be "Pynchonesque," "characteristic" of Pynchon, or at least foregrounded, including ambiguity/vagueness, acronyms, ellipsis marks, profanity, and archaic stylistics in *Mason & Dixon*. Some sections simply present formal descriptions using query, a corpus of Pynchon's texts, and comparison corpora to contextualize results, but most sections follow a mixed-method approach of combining digital experiments with close reading. The following chapters present evidence that some of these stylistic devices are not as unique to Pynchon's texts as previously assumed, while close examination of other devices reveals surprising continuities with stylistics and thematics across Pynchon's career. Such a from-the-ground-up approach can confirm and contest previous readings, provide new knowledge, and contribute at least a few shovelfuls of dirt to a bedrock upon which future digital Pynchon studies may build.

Before going further, what is "style," anyway? Definitions of style have varied considerably for centuries and across many fields.[4] Some leading definitions from the 1960s included "a way of writing"[5] and "an individual's deviations from norms for the situations in which he is encoding."[6] In the influential *Style in Fiction*, Geoffrey Leech and Mick Short warned against placing too much weight on any definition, writing that "we should be wary of becoming slaves to verbal definition [of "style" …] So we shall aim to work *through* definitions towards a richer appreciation of what literary style is."[7] In the 2011 *A Dictionary of Stylistics*, Katie Wales presents five different definitions, but explains that, "although style is invoked very frequently in literary criticism, translation studies, sociolinguistics and especially stylistics it is very difficult to define."[8] Stylisticians seem to have accepted this difficulty as intractable; at least four leading recent handbooks, companions, and surveys of stylistics contain virtually no discussion of how style is or should be defined.[9]

While the definition of style may be elusive, this book follows the operational definition proposed by Herrmann, van Dalen-Oskam, and Schöch in 2015 (hereafter "Revisiting Style" definition).[10] This definition is "an attempt to provide a common ground for both mainstream and literary computational stylistics," which its authors hope "will be put to use by a new generation of computational, quantitative, and empirical studies of style in literary texts."[11] The Revisiting Style definition is: "style is a property of texts constituted by an ensemble of formal features which can be observed quantitatively or qualitatively."[12] A key feature of this definition over some previous ones is that it "conceive[s] of stylistic features as explicitly defined and clearly identifiable."[13] The Revisiting Style definition thus provides common ground for a wide variety of formal description and mixed-method distant and close reading, both of which feature in this book.

Descriptions of Pynchon's style have typically been brief and florid but highlight how little has been claimed with certainty about it. In the first collection of critical essays on Pynchon, George Levine wrote that "[t]here is, obviously, no simple way to characterize Pynchon's prose, and no selection of passages can begin to account for its varieties. It is deliberately unstable, parodic, various, encyclopedic, fragmented (what *are* all those ellipses doing in *Gravity's Rainbow*? why does the narrator, in and later out of Slothrop's consciousness, stutter on 'a-and'?)."[14] While any author will exhibit stylistic variance over the course of a career, Pynchon is an extreme case, especially as a so-called encyclopedic novelist, as Edward Mendelson writes: "Each encyclopedia narrative [like *Gravity's Rainbow*] is an encyclopedia of literary styles, ranging from the most primitive and anonymous levels […] to the most esoteric of high styles."[15] Despite this dizzying variety, many have attempted pithy descriptions of Pynchon's style, often more flowery than formal. Richard Locke's review of *Gravity's Rainbow* noted "the saturnalian density of his prose."[16] Thomas Schaub wrote that in *Gravity's Rainbow*, Pynchon "has developed a prose style that leaches and percolates, seeps and flushes."[17] But while the complexity of Pynchon's prose is often taken as a given, Mark Liberman, an eminent professor of linguistics, disagrees: "I'm puzzled as to why people seem to think that Pynchon's style is complex and difficult. On the contrary, Pynchon's style is generally simple and even colloquial. […] On a sentence-by-sentence or paragraph-by-paragraph basis, Pynchon is more like a genre writer than like a practitioner of High Style."[18] These competing descriptions of Pynchon's style have not begun to be reconciled, as relatively little work explores Pynchon's stylistics rigorously.

Pynchon is not alone in awaiting the extensive stylistic investigation which may be his due. Michael Stubbs, in his digital stylistic analysis of Joseph Conrad's *Heart of Darkness*, writes that "despite a hundred years of critical discussion, there is surprisingly little on the book's linguistic style,"[19] and the same could be said of many widely read and widely studied texts. One explanation for the relative rarity of stylistic Pynchon studies may be that Pynchon's early novels were published and quickly canonized in the 1960s and 1970s, just as stylistics was emerging as a modern discipline. A related explanation is that Pynchon studies, once begun, may have largely confined itself to certain early paradigms in the decade or two following *Gravity's Rainbow*. Earlier Pynchon studies were typically exegeses of plot and themes,[20] motifs, imagery and symbols,[21] the sources and nature of references,[22] and biographical sleuthing,[23] in which Pynchon's texts were quoted as evidence of a reading, but style was rarely the primary object of study, or entry point to further interpretation. The first published book of Pynchon criticism, Joseph W. Slade's *Thomas Pynchon* (1974) is prototypical of early approaches. Slade summarized the plots of Pynchon novels (often too neatly) and explored thematic content but admitted that style was not his focus: "Concentrating on theme and plot will unfortunately not leave much space for dealing with Pynchon's hyperdense metaphors, his felicities of style."[24] Slade's brief and vague commentary on Pynchon's style was limited to a few sentences relegated to his monograph's second-to-last page.[25]

By 1990, Slade had "in many respects set the agenda for subsequent Pynchon studies," a statement by Slade's later editors that Brian McHale confirmed: "and this is so, for better and worse. The recurrent themes and structures of Pynchon's writing that Slade identified—entropy, Preterition, Manichaean dualities and excluded middles [...]—have become *topoi* of Pynchon criticism, as have passages from Pynchon that Slade chose to quote and gloss."[26] A neglected attention to language was high among the list of McHale's criticisms of Slade: "Slade's approach is entirely content-oriented. He commits himself to giving an account of plot, themes, and sources [...] as though language and form were dispensable husks [...] Language has been not so much overlooked as violently effaced."[27] This relative scholarly neglect of Pynchon's style persisted for decades, per Samuli Hägg, writing in 2005: "While Pynchon's textual complexity has in this [thematic] tradition been duly acknowledged and often meditated upon, it has for the most part served as a self-evident, or given, backdrop for thematic interpretations, not as a primary object of study."[28]

McHale attempted to rectify earlier Pynchon studies' neglect of language in a number of articles beginning in 1979 and later collected and updated in *Constructing Postmodernism*, including outstanding analyses of postmodern "erasure," uncertain focalizers, and the odd and ambiguous use of "you," which seems to address the reader, in the narration *Gravity's Rainbow*.[29] A number of other studies from the fields of linguistics, narratology,[30] and literary studies generally have addressed aspects of Pynchon's style in depth. The linguist Robin Lakoff ventured to interpret Slothrop's distinctive use of *that*, as in "She find that kid of hers?" (*GR*, 461).[31] Monika Fludernik's massive study of free indirect discourse in fiction contains examples from *Gravity's Rainbow* as a problematic case.[32] A theoretical work that also pursued some textual approaches (although in a fairly roundabout way) is McHoul and Wills's *Writing Pynchon*, which contains an extensive early catalog of foregrounded stylistic devices in *Gravity's Rainbow*.[33] Stress/meter in Pynchon's prose was touched upon by Robert Ochsner, who proposed a schema for linguistic rhythm in literature in 1985 and included chunks of *Gravity's Rainbow* among his text samples.[34] M. Angeles

Acknowledgments

Thank you to the donor individual or organization, whose identity remains unknown to me, whose extremely generous support fully funded my PhD at Birkbeck, University of London via the Digital Humanities Scholarship. Thanks equally to Martin Paul Eve, PhD supervisor and editor, whose mentorship, friendship, and much-needed whip-cracking turned a three-page outline into the book you now hold in your hands. Thanks to my second dissertation supervisor, Mark Levene, for statistical wisdom. Thanks to Samuel Thomas and Christopher Ohge for criticism and encouragement in the viva. Thanks again to these two gentlemen, as well as one anonymous reviewer, for comments on the book manuscript. Thanks to colleagues at Birkbeck and the University of London at large, especially Joe Brooker for reviewing the *Mason & Dixon* chapter and Martin Steer for ad hoc Python tutoring. *Herzlichen Dank* to the mad geniuses at the Leibniz-Institut für Deutsche Sprache and the CLARIN project for camaraderie and introducing me to the dark arts of corpus linguistics: Andreas Witt, Oliver Schonefeld, Peter Fischer, Norman Fiedler, Peter Fankhauser, Piotr Bański, Paweł Kamocki, and Julia Wildgans. Thanks also to Jens Stegmann, Christof Schöch, and Andreas van Cranenburgh for patiently answering many naive questions on corpus creation and query. Thanks to many in the Pynchon online world, especially Allen Ruch, whose website, The Libyrinth (later The Modern Word), first introduced me to Pynchon many years ago, as well as Laurence Daw, Tim Ware, and the many contributors to *Pynchon Wiki*, known and unknown. Thanks to the fantastic team at Bloomsbury, including Laura Cope, Ben Doyle, and Rachel Walker, as well as Shyam Sunder and the incredible copyediting team at Newgen. Thanks to the British Library, Birkbeck Library, Senate House Library, and Google Books for access to resources. To my mother the aesthete, my father the rationalist, my brother the polyglot, my sister the bibliophile, and M., for everything. Finally, "hymns of thanks" (*V.*, 254) to Thomas Pynchon for writing these "Fictions, folded acceptably between the covers of Books" (*M&D*, 359).

Martínez's "From 'Under the Rose' to *V.*: A Linguistic Approach to Human Agency in Pynchon's Fiction" rigorously compares Pynchon's short story "Under the Rose" with its reworking as chapter three of *V.*, exploring changes in narrative focalizers and transitivity.[35]

Other works could be mentioned,[36] and others will be discussed within the chapters, but even from the summary of studies above, it may strike the reader that stylistically related Pynchon studies, rather than neglected, have actually been rather vibrant and active. And indeed, a wide range of stylistic features in Pynchon's texts have been approached from numerous methodological approaches. But computational stylistics presents an opportunity to unify the stylistic observations from studies such as these, from linguistics, stylistics, descriptive poetics, and narratology. By settling on a definition of style that considers all definable textual features, the many strands of stylistic and formal approaches to Pynchon may finally be brought together in a common comprehensive project, aided by new and ever-improving analysis tools from digital humanities.

With a definition of style chosen, the vastness of Pynchon studies offers a rich vein for digital humanists to confirm, contest, and build upon, as a small selection of stylistic misconceptions may illustrate. Slade interpreted Pierce Inverarity as perhaps embodying "to employ a ubiquitous term in the novel, an Other," yet *Other* as an irregularly capitalized noun appears only three times in *Lot 49*, far from ubiquitously.[37] As another example, McHoul and Wills write that "although we have not tested it empirically, we would hypothesize that, excepting routine words like 'the', 'a', etc., 'death' is the most frequently used word in *Gravity's Rainbow*."[38] But in fact, *death* is only the 160th most frequent word in *Gravity's Rainbow*, or, excluding a stoplist of non-content words (as McHoul and Wills suggest), only the 61st most frequent, well behind *Slothrop*, *white*, *little*, *rocket*, and a bevy of other words.[39] Molly Hite writes that "ellipses are not a stylistic feature of […] *V.*,"[40] but there are more than two hundred by my count. Schaub writes that "the word 'bloom' is one of the most oft-repeated words in" *Lot 49*,[41] yet word forms of *bloom* appear only four times in that novel. Mendelson wrote that "the word 'God' occurs perhaps twenty times in [*Lot 49*] (it appears hardly at all in *V.*)."[42] Mendelson's intuition served him well in one case—*God* appears twenty-nine times in *Lot 49*—but not so well in the other: the frequency of *God* in *V.* is 163, more times, for instance, than the prominent character Esther is mentioned by name. These minor examples could be viewed as nitpicking of parenthetical statements or hyperbole, mostly with little relation to these authors' main theses. And anyway, factual errors can be found in much (perhaps most?) criticism, as McHale reminds us in his review of Slade: "I caught no more than two or three errors of fact […]; how many Pynchon critics could claim as clean a record?"[43]

The capability to contest these assertions and impressions, and the arguments in this book, are, of course, only made possible by advances in technology that were unavailable to earlier scholars. Sitting at our computers in the twenty-first century, it is all too easy to marvel that even in 1990, a Pynchon scholar as distinguished and familiar with Pynchon's texts as McHale could not simply query a particular Pynchon quotation if he wished: "One of [Dale] Carter's epigraphs from *Gravity's Rainbow* is so startlingly unfamiliar to me that I have so far failed to locate it in the text."[44] Writing at a time when the personal computer was in its infancy, McHale even assessed Carter's choice of lesser-known Pynchon quotations as a mark of scholarly excellence: "Of how many literary-critical books about Pynchon could it be said that they found passages worth commenting on that nobody had ever glossed before?"[45]

Far larger claims than the minutiae above will be questioned and contested in this book, but these scholars' minor misunderstandings and the relatively new ability to query Pynchon's texts support the notion that Pynchon studies may at least be aided, and at best improved by computational approaches to stylistics, contextualized by comparison with other texts, and revisited with new or modified interpretations. The ability to query and quantify all of Pynchon's texts also unearths a wealth of fresh texts "that nobody had ever glossed before," the stylistic features hiding in plain sight.

To summarize the following chapters, Chapter 1 begins to build a groundwork of formal and stylistic Pynchon studies starting with the simple number of words Pynchon has published, to reconsider the rate of Pynchon's output and estimate how long it may have taken him to write *Vineland*. The proportion of direct discourse, narration, and songs/poems in Pynchon's texts are then compared, which reveals that song and poems are dramatically decreasing post-*Gravity's Rainbow*, while direct discourse (mostly dialogue) is rising over the course of Pynchon's career, perhaps to add depth to the "unbelievable" or "paper-thin" characters decried by early critics. Chapter 2 turns to the archaic stylistic features of *Mason & Dixon*'s hallucinatory pastiche of eighteenth-century English: irregularly capitalized nouns, archaic spelling and lexis, and religious and profane censorship. A reading that contextualizes these with recorded norms of historical English reveals continuities between the style experiment of *Mason & Dixon* and Pynchon's other texts.

Inspired by Thomas Schaub's claims in *Pynchon: The Voice of Ambiguity* that ambiguity in Pynchon's texts is "the result of an intentional stylistic strategy" and that ambiguity "may well be [Pynchon's] most distinctive achievement as a writer,"[46] Chapter 3 explores conceptual and stylistic ambiguity and its closely related concept, vagueness. By applying an existing measure of quantifying ambiguous/vague words in texts, it turns out that novels by Pynchon score high or highest among all comparison corpora, providing quantitative evidence that Pynchon can indeed be considered "the Voice of Ambiguity." By identifying some of the specific vague words and phrases that Pynchon employs statistically significantly more than other authors, it emerges that Pynchon increases the use of his "preferred" vagueness words over time, doubling down on a stylistic feature with which he is so associated. Ways of reading stylistic vagueness in Pynchon's texts are further explored, including by experimental identification of the "least vague" passage in *Bleeding Edge*, which, it turns out, many critics had previously cited as containing one of the book's most direct (i.e., unambiguous) "messages."

From the definitionally complex subject of linguistic ambiguity/vagueness, I move on to smaller, more definable and queryable stylistic features of Pynchon's texts. Chapter 4 quantifies and interprets acronyms, which critics perceived as ubiquitous in earlier works and, it emerges, are generally increasing in Pynchon's novels over time, with the exception of the historical novels *Mason & Dixon* and *Against the Day*, in which acronyms are greatly reduced. Profanity and "obscenity" in Pynchon's work has generated much commentary and some notoriety, and Chapter 5 presents experiments which demonstrate that Pynchon's texts follow clear trends in American English: low profanity in the 1960s, much higher in the 1970s, and increasing toward recent years, in which profanity has simply become accepted and widespread in American fiction. From these experiments, close reading of Pynchon's seemingly low profanity works from 1959 through the 1960s reveals a pattern of coded profanity, which may be read as sly and rebellious responses to the chilling milieu of government-censored literature in which they were published. Finally, Chapter 6 examines ellipsis marks, specifically ellipsis points (…) and dashes (—), supposedly "characteristic" Pynchonian devices that actually vary greatly from novel to novel, and which may also enrich our understanding of Pynchon's verse and prose poetry. In the conclusion, I draw threads from these chapters together to present evidence for aspects of Pynchon's "late style," as well as suggest avenues for future research.

One aim of this book is to question assumptions by critics who dub certain stylistic features "characteristic" of Pynchon or "Pynchonian" without convincing comparison work (or *any* comparison work). As just one example, James W. Earl, discussing Pynchon's sentence styles, writes that "the simplest kind of Pynchonian long sentence [is] the Whitmanesque catalogue."[47] As an example of such a sentence, Earl cites the catalog of items for sale in a general store in *Against the Day*: "bowlers and deerstalkers, mantillas, lorgnettes, walking sticks, ear trumpets, spats, driving-coats," and so on (*ATD*, 332). Earl writes that this catalogue is "119 words. Does Proust do this, or James, or Joyce, with the long sentences? I do not think so."[48] Although I cannot remark upon lists in Henry James, Earl is mistaken on Joyce and Proust, who both employ 100+ word single-sentence lists/catalogs,[49] and both are included in Umberto Eco's compendium of catalogs in art and fiction, which traces long lists in literary texts back to antiquity.[50] While long catalog lists are certainly present in Pynchon's texts, to dub such sentences Pynchonian (or Whitmanesque, for that matter) goes too far, as comparison work reveals.

To question claims of "Pynchonesque" stylistic features, and simply as good computational stylistic practice, this book's experiments and claims about Pynchon's style are compared, first, to all of Pynchon's fiction and, next, to a number of comparison corpora:

- *Brown Fiction*: Snapshot of American fiction in 1961, The Brown University Standard Corpus of Present-Day American English, fiction subcorpus (~252,000 word tokens).
- *COCA Fiction*: American fiction 1991–2015, The Corpus of Contemporary American English, fiction subcorpus (~100 million word tokens)
- *Pynchon's Peers*: Bespoke corpus, North American postmodern literary fiction, authors roughly contemporary to Pynchon, for example, Don DeLillo and Toni Morrison, published 1959–2013 (~2.4 million word tokens).
- *Popular Fiction*: Bespoke corpus, American popular fiction, authors roughly contemporary to Pynchon, works by Stephen King, Danielle Steel, and James Patterson representing the genres of horror, romance, and thriller, respectively, published 1974–2013 (~1.2 million word tokens).
- *Pynchon Influenced*: Bespoke corpus, American fiction and one literary memoir by younger American authors whom critics have claimed as notable postmodernists or Pynchon-influenced, for example, David Foster Wallace and Richard Powers (~1.6 million word tokens).

The methodology for the selection and creation of these corpora is in Appendix I, along with a description of software and computational methods.

Apart from Pynchon studies, this book draws upon numerous, often overlapping and increasingly converging fields and methodologies. Corpus linguistics has revolutionized nearly all branches of linguistics.[51] Digital Humanities (DH) is a field originating in textually focused computing in the humanities by disciplinary experts, computer scientists, and library and information studies specialists.[52] DH has proven so difficult to define that, for instance, an edited volume has been devoted solely to this task,[53] but put simply, DH encompasses a wide variety of research and methodologies broadly based on data and the humanities. Stylistics has been defined as a subdiscipline of linguistics that is concerned with the systematic analysis of style in language and how this varies by genre, context, historical period, author, and other factors.[54] A more recent definition is that "stylistics uses models of language, analytical techniques and methodologies from linguistics to facilitate the study of style in its widest sense."[55] Stylistics concentrates particularly, although not exclusively, on the analysis of literary texts.[56] One key stylistic concept to mention here is *foregrounding*, which "highlights the poetic function of language, in particular its ability to deviate from the linguistic norm and to create textual patterns based either on parallelism, repetition or deviation from a norm."[57] Narratology is "a humanities discipline dedicated to the study of the logic, principles, and practices of narrative representation," per Jan Christoph Meister,[58] which has "been developing side by side" with stylistics since the 1960s, per Dan Shen, who summarizes the distinction as "stylistics distinguishes between content and style and narratology between story and discourse. On the surface the two distinctions seem to match each other, with 'style' referring to how the content is presented and 'discourse' to how the story is told."[59] Corpus stylistics (or digital stylistics) is a discipline that uses corpora and the tools and methods of corpus linguistics in the study of literary style,[60] while, more broadly, umbrella terms such as computational literary studies, digital literary stylistics, literary data mining, computational criticism, and so on are emerging.[61]

The convergence of digital and hermeneutic approaches, although hardly new, presents challenges that this book must anticipate and address, especially the danger of "leaps" from data to interpretation, as articulated particularly by Stanley Fish. Fish, a vociferous critic of stylistics, argued that by counting word tokens separated from their context, stylisticians are doomed to count essentially meaning objects. The "arbitrariness" of stylistics, Fish suggested, results from "the leap (from the data to a specification of their value [...])", "leaping from […] patterns to the human concerns their procedures exclude," going from data to "readings of the data that are unconstrained by anything in their machinery," and leaps from data to interpretation performed "all too easily, and in any direction one likes."[62] While this book obviously does not subscribe to the full reach of Fish's sweeping denunciations of literary stylistics, navigating the treacherous leap from data to interpretation is a concern that the nascent digital Pynchon studies must take extremely seriously. My solutions throughout this book include a continual skepticism of experimental results, to stress the importance of comparison corpora before presuming "characteristic" stylistic features in Pynchon's texts, and to interrogate my own hypotheses. To quote from John F. Burrows, whose monograph on the style of Jane Austen is another foundational inspiration for this book, "Whether or not [one] make[s] use of computers in gathering their data, they need ask only one concession from their colleagues: that their evidence should not be treated with special deference or special scepticism but that it is taken, case by case, upon its merits."[63] While remaining ever mindful of interpretive leaps, this book follows a mixed-method approach of digital experiments alongside close reading, following J. Berenike Herrmann's suggestion that "DH stylistics should move beyond the dichotomies of 'close vs. distant', 'qualitative vs. quantitative', 'explanatory vs. exploratory', 'inductive vs. deductive', 'understanding vs. explaining'—and, possibly even 'hermeneutic vs. empirical,'" while keeping in mind that, as Herrmann warns, "'moving beyond' here cannot possibly mean resorting to an 'everything-goes' approach that defocuses the nitty-gritty details of difference but an informed perspective that enables scholars to choose particular research designs by their particular objectives."[64]

Any long-form work of scholarship must face the question: who is the audience for this? First and foremost, this is a contribution to Pynchon studies and hopefully of interest to curious nonacademic Pynchon readers, and thus is presented in a manner in which technical and nontechnical audiences alike may follow. To readers who know nothing about coding, I hope that this book may encourage you to learn some, as its computational methods—mostly regular expressions, queries in free and open software, and bits of the Python programming language—are not especially difficult, and there remain plenty of questions in literary studies that even relatively simple digital humanities experiments may inform. Those interested in such authors as David Foster Wallace, Cormac McCarthy, and William Gaddis will find interesting and not-fully-explained findings which warrant further investigation. Readers more focused on corpus linguistics and digital humanities, rather than Pynchon, may be especially interested in Chapter 3 on ambiguity/vagueness, as its methodology can be applied to many texts and explored much further by more sophisticated methods.

Digital Pynchon studies have been a relatively small, but growing body of work, and is reviewed in full in Appendix II. But if the mountain of pre-digital Pynchon studies is any indication, digital Pynchon studies have only just begun.

Notes

1 William M. Plater, *The Grim Phoenix: Reconstructing Thomas Pynchon* (Bloomington: Indiana University Press, 1978), ix.

2 Michel Ryckx, "Thomas Pynchon (1937–): A Bibliography of Secondary Materials," Vheissu.net, accessed September 1, 2019, http://www.vheissu.net/biblio/.

3 Christian Hänggi's *Pynchon's Sound of Music* (Zurich: Diaphenes, 2020) includes data and visualizations of musical references in Pynchon's texts and thus must be considered the first book-length mixed method Pynchon study, but its aims and methods are not generally stylistic. See Appendix II.

4 J. Berenike Herrmann, Karina van Dalen-Oskam, and Christof Schöch, "Revisiting Style, a Key Concept in Literary Studies," *Journal of Literary Theory* 9:1 (2015): 25.

5 Richard Ohmann, "Generative Grammars and the Concept of Literary Style," *Word: Journal of the Linguistic Circle of New York*, 20:3 (1964): 423.

6 Charles E. Osgood, "Some Effects of Motivation on Style of Encoding," in *Style in Language*, ed. T. A. Sebeok (Cambridge: Technology Press of MIT, 1960), 293.

7 Geoffrey N. Leech and Mick Short, *Style in Fiction: A Linguistic Introduction to English Fictional Prose*, 2nd ed. (New York: Pearson Longman, 2007), 9.

8 Katie Wales, *A Dictionary of Stylistics* (Harlow: Pearson Education, 2011), 397.

9 Lesley Jeffries and Dan McIntyre, eds., *Stylistics* (Cambridge: Cambridge University Press, 2010); Peter Stockwell and Sara Whitely, eds., *The Cambridge Handbook of Stylistics* (Cambridge: Cambridge University Press, 2014); Michael Burke, ed., *The Routledge Handbook of Stylistics* (London: Routledge, 2014); Violeta Sotirova, ed., *A Bloomsbury Companion to Stylistics* (London: Bloomsbury, 2016).

10 Herrmann, van Dalen-Oskam, and Schöch, "Revisiting Style," 25.

11 Ibid., 26.

12 Ibid., 44.

13 Ibid.

14 George Levine, "Risking the Moment: Anarchy and Possibility in Pynchon's Fiction," in *Mindful Pleasures: Essays on Thomas Pynchon*, ed. George Levine and David Leverenz (Boston: Little, Brown, 1976), 118.

15 Edward Mendelson, "Gravity's Encyclopedia," in *Mindful Pleasures: Essays on Thomas Pynchon*, ed. George Levine and David Leverenz (Boston: Little, Brown, 1976), 164.

16 Richard Locke, "One of the Longest, Most Difficult, Most Ambitious Novels in Years," *New York Times*, March 11, 1973, http://www.nytimes.com/books/97/05/18/reviews/pynchon-rainbow.html.

17 Thomas Schaub, *Pynchon: The Voice of Ambiguity* (Urbana: University of Illinois Press, 1981), 124.

18 Mark Liberman, comment to "Moar Verbs," *Language Log*, March 14, 2015, http://languagelog.ldc.upenn.edu/nll/?p=18398.

19 Michael Stubbs, "Conrad, Concordance, Collocation: Heart of Darkness or Light at the End of the Tunnel?" (2003), University of Birmingham, May 8, 2003, https://www.uni-trier.de/fileadmin/fb2/ANG/Linguistik/Stubbs/stubbs-2003-conrad-lecture.pdf.

20 E.g., Joseph W. Slade, *Thomas Pynchon* (New York: Warner, 1974).

21 E.g., Kathryn Hume, *Pynchon's Mythography: An Approach to Gravity's Rainbow* (Carbondale: Southern Illinois University Press, 1987).

22 E.g., David Cowart, *Thomas Pynchon: The Art of Allusion* (Carbondale: Southern Illinois University Press, 1980).

23 E.g., Steven Weisenburger, "Thomas Pynchon at Twenty-Two: A Recovered Autobiographical Sketch," *American Literature* 62:4 (1990): 692–7.

24 Slade, *Thomas Pynchon*, 17.

25 Ibid., 247.

26 Brian McHale, "Slade Revisited, or, the End(s) of Pynchon Criticism," *Pynchon Notes* 26–7 (1990): 140.

27 Ibid., 145.

28 Samuli Hägg, *Narratologies of* Gravity's Rainbow (Joensuu: University of Joensuu, 2005), 17.

29 Brian McHale, *Constructing Postmodernism* (London: Routledge, 1992).

30 Stylistics and narratology are different disciplinary approaches, with "superficial similarity and essential difference." Dan Shen, "How Stylisticians Draw on Narratology: Approaches, Advantages and Disadvantages," *Style* 39:4 (2005): 381. When discussing narratological studies relating to Pynchon, this book makes no claims about disciplinary or methodological distinctions between narratology and stylistics but draws upon the definable stylistic features contained within such narratological analyses. This book thus adopts what Shen called the "mild" approach when stylisticians draw upon narratology: "using narratological concepts or models as frameworks for the stylistic investigation of linguistic choices." Ibid., 383.

31 Robin Lakoff, "Remarks on This and That," in *Papers from the Tenth Regional Meeting, Chicago Linguistic Society*, ed. Michael W. La Gary, Robert A. Fox, and Anthony Bruck (Chicago: Chicago Linguistic Society, 1974), 352.

32 Monika Fludernik, *The Fictions of Language and the Languages of Fiction* (London: Routledge, 1993), 5.

33 Alec McHoul and David Wills, *Writing Pynchon* (London: Macmillan Press, 1990), 34–5.

34 Robert Ochsner, "Rhythm in Literature and Low Style," *Style* 19:2 (1985): 258–81. Note that Ochsner's work was based partly on earlier linguistic research in rhythm as a measure of style by Mark Liberman, himself a Pynchonist, as discussed below.

35 M. Angeles Martínez, "From 'Under the Rose' to *V.*: A Linguistic Approach to Human Agency in Pynchon's Fiction," *Poetics Today* 23:4 (2002): 633–56.

36 Maureen Quilligan, *The Language of Allegory: Defining the Genre* (Ithaca: Cornell University Press, 1979), 24. Quoting *Lot 49*, 73; William Logan, "Pynchon in the Poetic," *Southwest Review* 83:4 (1998): 424–37; William Logan, "Back to the Future: On Thomas Pynchon's *Against the Day*," *VQR*, Summer 2007, https://www.vqronline.org/back-future-thomas-pynchon%E2%80%99s-against-day; David Letzler, *The Cruft of Fiction: Mega-Novels and the Science of Paying Attention* (Lincoln: University of Nebraska Press, 2017).

37 Slade, *Thomas Pynchon*, 127.

38 McHoul and Wills, *Writing Pynchon*, 64.

39 Most frequent words calculated with NLTK 3.4 and its 179-word stopword list.

40 Molly Hite, *Ideas of Order in the Novels of Thomas Pynchon* (Columbus: Ohio State University Press, 1983), 138.

41 Schaub, *Pynchon: The Voice of Ambiguity*, 114.

42 Edward Mendelson, "The Sacred, the Profane, and *The Crying of Lot 49*," in *Individual and Community: Variations on a Theme in American Fiction*, ed. Kenneth H. Baldwin and David K. Kirby (Durham: Duke University Press, 1975), 199.

43 McHale, "Slade Revisited," 140.

44 Ibid., 148.

45 Ibid.

46 Schaub, *Pynchon: The Voice of Ambiguity*, ix–x.

47 James W. Earl, "Tom's Longest Sentence," *Literary Imagination* 14:2 (2012): 197.

48 Ibid., 199.

49 Some examples being a 330-word list of "Irish heroes and heroines" and a 314-word list of "saints and martyrs" in the "Cyclops" episode of *Ulysses*, and a 177-word enumeration of the contents of a kitchen dresser opened by Bloom in "Ithaca." For more on lists in "Cyclops," see Marianna Gula, *A Tale of the Pub: Re-Reading the "Cyclops" of James Joyce's "Ulysses" in the Context of Irish Cultural Nationalism* (Debrecen: DU Press, 2012).

50 Umberto Eco, *The Infinity of Lists: From Homer to Joyce* (London: McLehose Press, 2009), 92, 109.

51 Tony McEnery, Richard Xiao, and Yukio Tono, *Corpus-Based Language Studies: An Advanced Resource Book* (London: Routledge, 2006), 4, 7.

52 Susan Schreibman, Ray Siemens, and John Unsworth, "The Digital Humanities and Humanities Computing: An Introduction," in *A Companion to Digital Humanities*, ed. Susan Schreibman, Ray Siemens, and John Unsworth (Oxford: Blackwell, 2004), http://www.digitalhumanities.org/companion/.

53 Melissa Terras, Julianne Nyhan, and Edward Vanhoutte, eds., *Defining Digital Humanities: A Reader* (London: Routledge, 2016).

54 Jeffries and McIntyre, *Stylistics*, 1; Quoting David Crystal and Derek Davy, *Investigating English Style* (London: Longman, 1969), 9; and Geoffrey N. Leech, *Language in Literature: Style and Foregrounding* (London: Pearson Education, 2008), 54.

55 Jeffries and McIntyre, *Stylistics*, 1.

56 Ibid.; Michael Burke, "Stylistics: From Classical Rhetoric to Cognitive Neuroscience," in *The Routledge Handbook of Stylistics*, ed. Michael Burke (London: Routledge, 2014), 1.

57 Michael Burke and Kristy Evans, "Formalist Stylistics," in *The Routledge Handbook of Stylistics*, ed. Michael Burke (London: Routledge, 2014), 41.

58 Jan Christoph Meister, "Narratology," in *The Living Handbook of Narratology*, eds. Peter Hühn, Jan Christoph Meister, John Pier, and Wolf Schmid, University of Hamburg, January 19, 2014, https://www.lhn.uni-hamburg.de/index.html.

59 Dan Shen, "Stylistics and Narratology," in *The Routledge Handbook of Stylistics*, ed. Michael Burke (London: Routledge, 2014), 191.

60 Martin Wynne, "Stylistics: Corpus Approaches," in *The Encyclopedia of Language and Linguistics*, 2nd ed., ed. Keith Brown (Oxford: Elsevier, 2006), 223–5; Martin Wynne, "Review of *Corpus Stylistics in Principles and Practice. A Stylistic Exploration of John Fowles'* The Magus," *Literary and Linguistic Computing* 27:4 (2012); Michaela Mahlberg, "Corpus stylistics," in *The Routledge Handbook of Stylistics*, ed. Michael Burke (London: Routledge, 2014), 378–92.

61 E.g. Fotis Jannidis, "On the Perceived Complexity of Literature. A Response to Nan Z. Da," *Journal of Cultural Analytics*, June 17, 2019, https://culturalanalytics.org/2019/06/on-the-perceived-complexity-of-literature-a-response-to-nan-z-da/.

62 Stanley Fish, *Is There a Text in This Class: The Authority of Interpretive Communities* (Cambridge: Harvard University Press, [1973] 1980), 72, 89, 90.

63 John F. Burrows, "Not Unless You Ask Nicely: The Interpretative Nexus between Analysis and Information," *Literary and Linguistic Computing* 7:2 (1992): 103.

64 J. Berenike Herrmann, "In a Test Bed with Kafka. Introducing a Mixed-Method Approach to Digital Stylistics," *Digital Humanities Quarterly* 11:4 (2017), online.

1

Some Formal Overviews of Pynchon's Texts

the Mellow Sixties, a slower-moving time, predigital, not yet so cut into pieces
— *Vineland,* 38

Pynchon has published over 1.7 million word tokens over six short stories and eight novels published from 1959 to 2013.[1] Some formal overviews of this extensive corpus focusing on word count, proportion of direct discourse, and proportion of songs/poems will support the experiments in the following chapters and add new knowledge to a groundwork of stylistic Pynchon studies. As evidence that such distant reading may aspire to more than formally descriptive trivia, each section is accompanied by a hermeneutic discussion of how the data results may (or may not) inform broader Pynchon studies, and the section separating direct discourse from "narration" will contribute to most chapters in this book.

1.1 Pynchon's Productivity

The first formal metric in Pynchon's texts is simply the number of words, and some observations on Pynchon's productivity may be made based on nothing more than word counts, publication dates, and snippets of biographical data. Given the length of Pynchon's career, varying sizes of his novels, and the years that stretch between their publications, it is difficult to gauge exactly how fast or slow the man has been writing. Pynchon published his first two novels in 1963 and 1966, then his widely acknowledged masterpiece, *Gravity's Rainbow*, in 1973, then did not publish another novel for seventeen years, a period which might be called Pynchon's "wilderness years,"[2] in which Pynchon published only bits of nonfiction. As to what Pynchon was doing for almost two decades, he may have been writing *Mason & Dixon*—which was reportedly mentioned to a friend as early as 1970[3] and rumored since *Gravity's Rainbow*[4]—although the most amusing guess came from David Foster Wallace: "I get the strong sense he's spent twenty years smoking pot and watching TV."[5] After *Vineland* in 1990 and *Mason & Dixon* in 1997, Pynchon published the extremely long *Against the Day* in 2006 and two shorter novels in 2009 and 2013.

It may seem that Pynchon has been unusually productive in recent years, as was voiced by Cornelius Collins in connection with the 2014 MLA conference: "If reports are to be believed, September 2013 will see the publication of a new novel by Thomas Pynchon, marking the third in seven years—a rate of *productivity formerly unprecedented* in this author's closely watched, illustrious, and, by this point, quite long writing career" (emphasis added).[6] Another critic noted how with *Bleeding Edge*, Pynchon "published his third novel in seven years after producing only five in 35 years."[7] Examining the published word counts, however, tells another story. We currently have no way of knowing when Pynchon began most of his works, and biographical snippets unsurprisingly suggest that Pynchon worked on certain novels for years, often overlapping.[8] But conjecturing that Pynchon completed each novel, short story, or nonfiction piece the year before publication (to allow for submission, editing, graphic design, and printing) and began a new novel in a following year, Pynchon's early- and late-career productivity is fairly consistent: an average of 42,000–46,000 words of fiction and nonfiction per year. This simple, counterintuitive estimate, while certainly far from groundbreaking, may readjust the general terms in which Pynchon's early and late career are viewed.

This estimate of Pynchon's per-year output allows us to hazard a guess as to how long it took Pynchon to write *Vineland*. Much about *Vineland* suggests that it was not written over such a long time period: the 1980s subject matter, relatively short length, and arguably its lack of perceived ambition. By this estimate, *Vineland* was composed over 3.2–3.5 years. Until specific biographical and manuscript information is made available, this provides our best current overview of Pynchon's publishing career (Table 1.1). An intriguing suggestion from this estimate is that if Pynchon has been writing at his usual rate since *Bleeding Edge*'s publication in 2013, he may be sitting on over 287,000 words as of 2021, which is more words than *Mason & Dixon*—time will tell.

1.2 Direct Discourse, Narration, and Verse

To estimate the quantity of direct speech/thought/writing (i.e., direct discourse) in Pynchon's texts, I separated the characters within quoted strings—"and"—using

Table 1.1 Estimate of Pynchon's published word counts by year

Early Period

Year	Novel	Short	NF	Total
1958		15,990		15,990
1959		12,623		12,623
1960	59,163	11,436		70,599
1961	59,163			59,163
1962	59,163			59,163
1963		17,279		17,279
1964	24,033			24,033
1965	24,033		4,876	28,909
1966	48,610			48,610
1967	48,610			48,610
1968	48,610			48,610
1969	48,610			48,610
1970	48,610			48,610
1971	48,610			48,610
1972	48,610			48,610
1973	48,610			48,610
Mean (from 1959) =				42,290
Mean (from 1960) =				46,109

"Wilderness Years"

Year	Novel	NF	Total
1974			
1975			
1976			
1977			
1978			
1979			
1980			
1981			
1982		3,224	3,224
1983		10,303	10,303
1984			
1985			
1986			
1987	48,513	2,722	51,235
1988	48,513		48,513
1989	48,513		48,513
1990	38,905	2,801	41,706
Mean =			33,915

Late Period

Year	Novel	NF	Total
1991	38,905		38,905
1992	38,905	2,256	41,161
1993	38,905	3,308	42,213
1994	38,905		38,905
1995	38,905		38,905
1996	38,905	1,984	40,889
1997	50,578		50,578
1998	50,578		50,578
1999	50,578		50,578
2000	50,578		50,578
2001	50,578		50,578
2002	50,578	6,304	56,882
2003	50,578		50,578
2004	50,578		50,578
2005	50,578		50,578
2006	40,981		40,981
2007	40,981		40,981
2008	40,981		40,981
2009	36,835		36,835
2010	36,835		36,835
2011	36,835		36,835
2012	36,835		36,835
Mean =			44,216

Table 1.2 Narration, direct discourse, and verse in Pynchon corpus

Text	Word Tokens	Narration	Narration %	Direct Discourse	Direct Discourse %	Verse	Verse %
Shorts	57,339	43,309	75.5	13,926	24.3	104	0.2
V.	177,490	138,074	77.8	36,678	20.7	2,738	1.5
CoL49	48,065	34,933	72.7	12,359	25.7	773	1.6
GR	340,269	278,813	81.9	54,573	16.0	6,883	2.0
Vineland	145,538	106,701	73.3	37,668	25.9	1,169	0.8
M&D	272,332	140,196	51.5	128,652	47.2	3,484	1.3
ATD	455,199	293,418	64.5	159,923	35.1	1,858	0.4
IV	122,943	69,587	56.6	52,232	42.5	1,124	0.9
BE	147,340	84,345	57.2	62,147	42.2	848	0.6

a script,[9] an approach used by Liberman in exploring the proportion of quoted dialogue in a number of novels.[10] This could identify lifelong trajectories in Pynchon's style and give insight into how individual novels read as a whole, as some are heavier on direct discourse but others feature a greater amount of narration. Once direct discourse and narration are separated into distinct corpora, virtually any stylistic experiment in Pynchon studies could make use of such a division, as I do in certain chapters of this book.

Pynchon also famously intersperses songs/poems throughout his novels, a fact acknowledged by the book jacket description of *Against the Day* (written by Pynchon himself): "Meanwhile, Thomas Pynchon is up to his usual business. Characters stop what they're doing to sing what are for the most part stupid songs." While Pynchon's verse has received much commentary, this literature does not provide any sense of proportion; in other words, how much verse is in Pynchon's texts from novel to novel? To quantify verse in Pynchon's texts, I manually replaced each word token of verse with an arbitrary placeholder token.[11] Table 1.2 presents the data and Figure 1.1 visualizes the percentage of direct discourse, narration, and verse in Pynchon's texts.

1.2.1 Songs/Poems Are Decreasing in Pynchon

Many novelists have inserted songs and poems into their novels—Cervantes, Kipling, Lewis Carroll, to name only a few—and Pynchon is often noted for his substantial and creative use of these forms. Pynchon characters will often burst into (mostly) fictional song, as if in a Broadway musical, or recite (mostly) fictional poems. Pynchon's songs and poems, and music in Pynchon

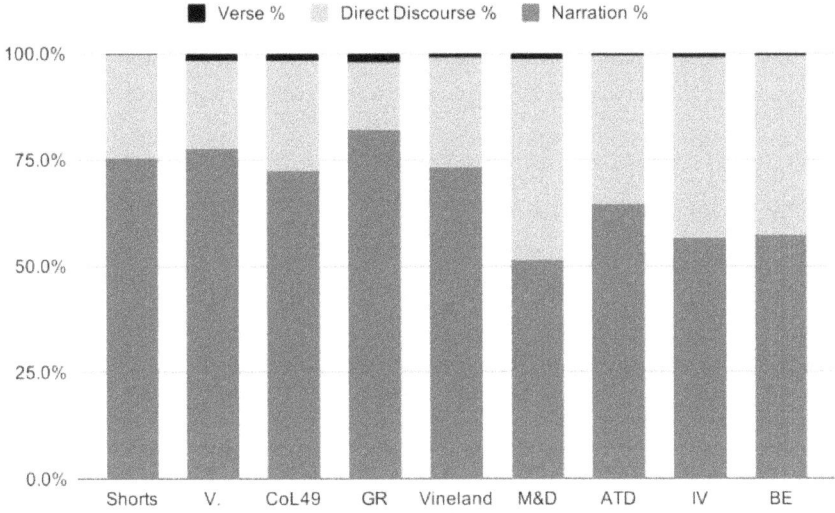

Figure 1.1 Narration, direct discourse, and verse in Pynchon corpus.

more generally, have received extensive critical attention. Writing shortly after *Gravity's Rainbow*'s publication, William Vesterman stated that "poems, and particularly songs, make up a characteristic part of Pynchon's work: without them a reader's experience would not be at all the same."[12] Allusions to music and historical bases for Pynchon's verse have been extensively cataloged and explored.[13] Anahita Rouyan recently argued that in this body of literature, "little attention has been devoted to the songs in Pynchon's texts" and aimed to fill this gap by "a close examination of songs in *Gravity's Rainbow*, focusing on Pynchon's strategies of formal experimentation," including transcription of songs as lyric poems, indication of a song's rhythm or melody in stage directions, phonetic transcription, and punctuation.[14] While the functions of verse in Pynchon's novels have been extensively and convincingly explicated, the formal and linguistic features of the verse texts could be explored much further.

The first data point to consider is simply the total number of words of verse in Pynchon's texts: 18,981. This approaches half as many words as Pynchon's shortest novel (*Lot 49*), but prose works contain many more words than verse. For some context in poetry, Pynchon's verse output is about half the length of Lord Byron's "Childe Harold's Pilgrimage," around 1/20th as long as Ezra Pound's *Cantos*, and approaching the 20,000 to 30,000 words of the complete poems of John Keats. For context in lyrics, Pynchon's verse is about nine times as long as the lyrics to *Pet Sounds* by the Beach Boys (a record Pynchon references and reportedly liked)[15] and 1.76 times as long as an English translation of the libretto to the opera *Das Rheingold* (Wagner being Pynchon's most-referenced musician, per Hänggi, and which takes close to three hours to perform).[16] Pynchon's collected verse, then, could be compared to the length of nine rock albums, or twice the length of a long opera libretto. Printed and bound, it could easily take the form of a two hundred-page book.

This quantifiable volume—18,981 words—and imaginary volume—*Songs and Poems by Thomas Pynchon*, perhaps someday available in bookstores—suggest that it may be time to criticize or merely enjoy Pynchon's verse on its own, separated from its original contexts (an approach that Rouyan, especially, suggests). As a young man, Pynchon had aspirations to write opera librettos; aged twenty-two, he applied for a Ford Foundation fellowship to pursue this, displaying his already wide knowledge of opera and expressing a desire to especially write comic opera and to adapt contemporary science fiction.[17] Around this time, Pynchon also cowrote his aborted science fiction musical/ light opera, *Minstral Island*. Perhaps Pynchon's eventual corpus of poems and songs should be considered as a partial achievement of his youthful aspirations.

The density of verse in Pynchon's texts shows a clear trend: Pynchon's verse is decreasing (Figures 1.2 and 1.3). Pynchon's first three novels virtually teem with verse, especially *Gravity's Rainbow*, but fall by a half, third, or less in the novels following his "wilderness years." *Mason & Dixon* is a relative exception, with a normalized verse frequency approaching Pynchon's early period, perhaps a clue that parts of this novel were authored well before its publication.

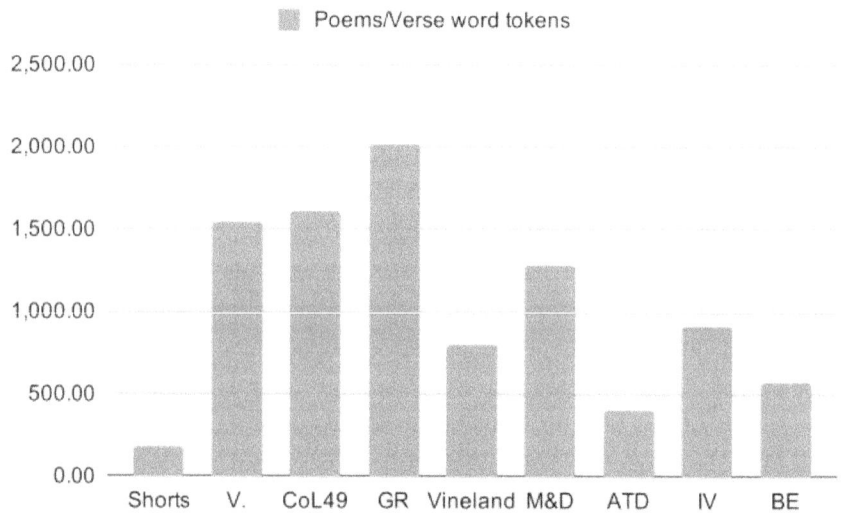

Figure 1.2 Normalized frequency (per 100k word tokens) of verse in Pynchon corpus.

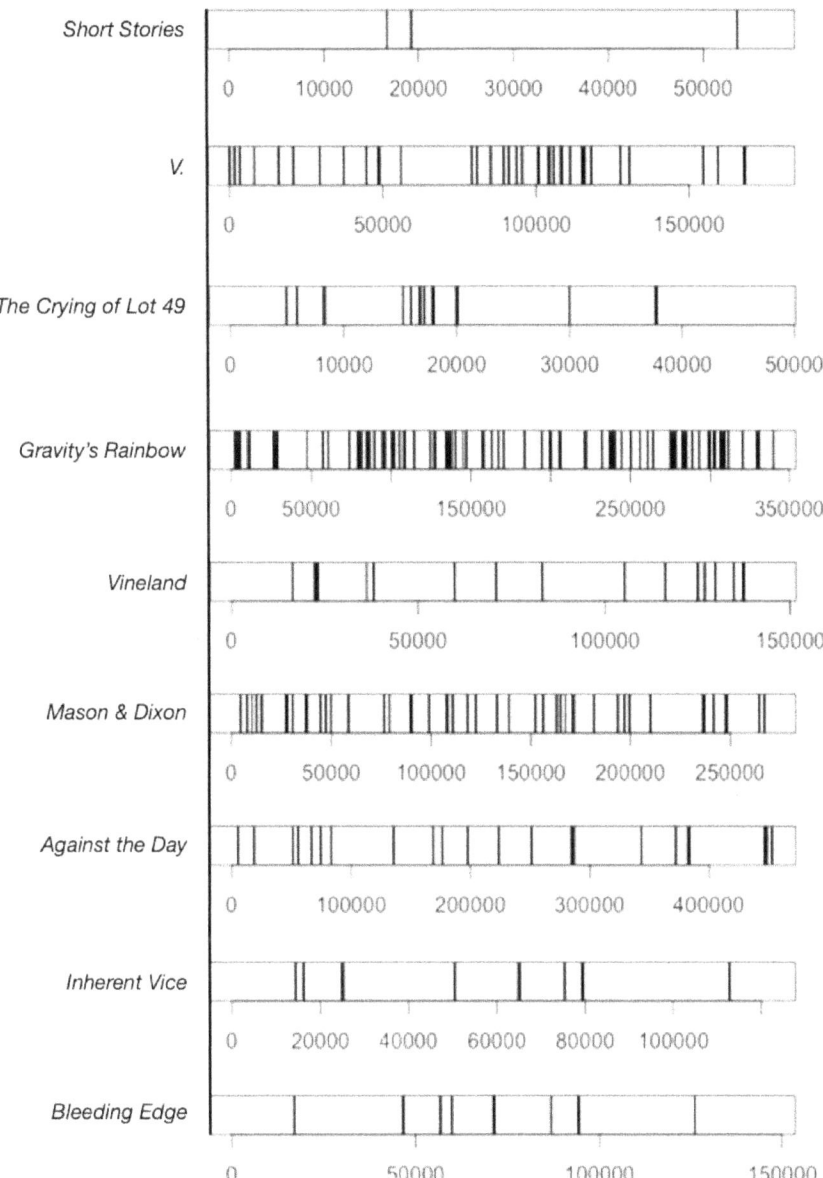

Figure 1.3 Visualization of songs and poems in Pynchon corpus. X-axis indicates word tokens.

1.2.2 Direct Discourse Is Increasing in Pynchon

The percentage of direct discourse in Pynchon's texts may be contextualized by my comparison corpora and earlier results by Liberman. Rule-based measurement of direct discourse can be difficult or impossible depending on the author and novel. For instance, Gaddis, McCarthy, Atwood, and Vollmann do not employ quotation marks at all (in the novels selected), Wallace chose single quotation marks for *Infinite Jest*, a substantial portion of the dialogue in King's *Carrie* is marked not by "Q:" and "A:" and a portion of *The Broom of the System* contains dialogue in the form of a transcript. Accurate measurement of direct discourse in these novels falls beyond the scope of this book, but novels in which direct discourse may be reasonably measured by my chosen method are presented in Figure 1.4.

Liberman writes that a "relatively high proportion of dialogue is a common characteristic of genre novels"—citing examples of 42.54 percent to 60.08 percent—but that there are exceptions, for example, *The Da Vinci Code*, with 29.59 percent estimated dialogue.[18] Liberman found examples of literary fiction as low as 3.27 percent (Woolf's *To the Lighthouse*) but as high as 51.32 percent (*The Great Gatsby*). Liberman provides figures for direct discourse in four of Pynchon's novels, which are very close to my results but not identical.[19] My data at least questions the notion of high proportion of dialogue being a "common characteristic of genre novels," as King's *IT* and a James Patterson thriller are around 20 percent, although, as Liberman suggests, many more data points will be required to test such a correlation. At the least, it can be stated here that the proportion of direct discourse in literary texts is highly variable, and the range of quoted dialogue in Pynchon's texts—16.04 percent to 47.24 percent—is by no means unusual: similar percentages are found in a variety of novels across genres.

Again, one observation from my data is clear: the proportion of direct discourse is much higher in later Pynchon (Figure 1.5).

One curious hypothesis for increasing direct discourse could be that writers tend to write more dialogue as they age, a tendency noted by Liberman in select novels by Agatha Christie, Elmore Leonard, and Pynchon, as well. My findings confirm and complete the results for Pynchon's oeuvre, and lend additional data to Liberman's statement that "this small sample suggests that a trend towards more dialogue over the course of an author's career is not implausible."

For Pynchon scholars, this trend of increasing dialogue suggests new avenues for reading the novels. What formal qualities of *Gravity's Rainbow* make it

Direct discourse

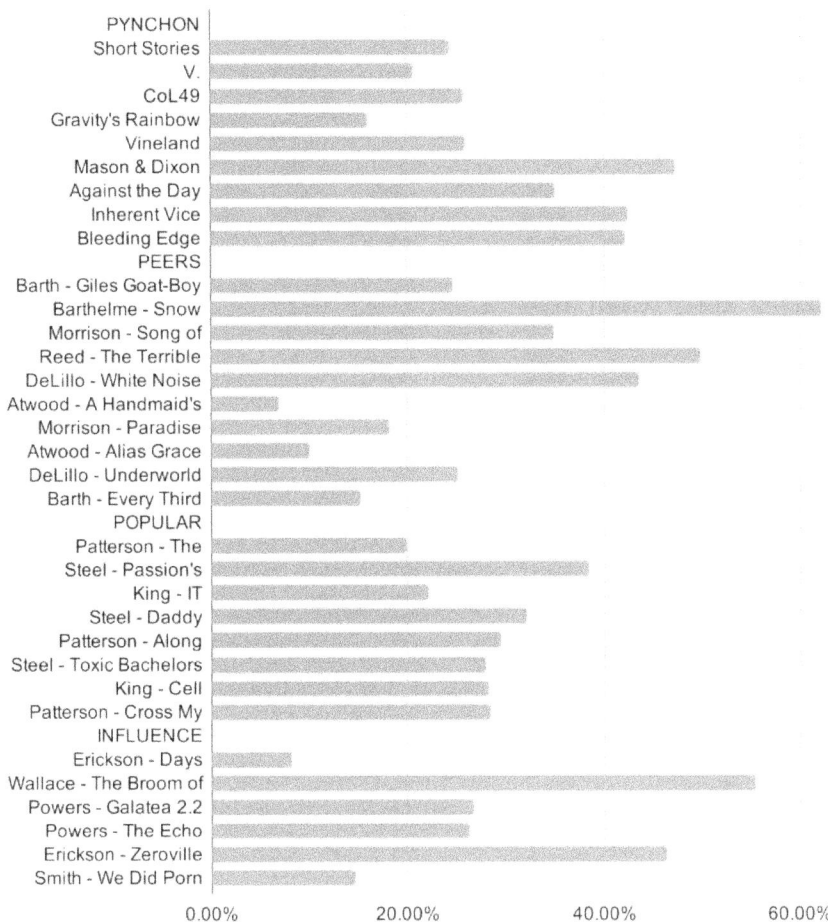

Figure 1.4 Proportion of direct discourse in Pynchon and comparison corpora.

Pynchon's lowest direct discourse novel, at only 16.04 percent? This may be one explanation why *Gravity's Rainbow* reads as Pynchon's most aggressively experimental text, as Pynchon's formal experiments tend to go further in narration than in dialogue. It is another irony that *Gravity's Rainbow*—Pynchon's most heavily narrated novel—features no clear narrator, while *Mason & Dixon*, which is narrated ostensibly by Wicks Cherrycoke, conversely features the most quoted discourse. Does the relatively rare dialogue in *Gravity's Rainbow* serve different functions than the more profuse, conversational dialogue of later Pynchon? Although whether a high proportion of dialogue is correlated with popular genres remains an open question, it is possible that Pynchon's increase

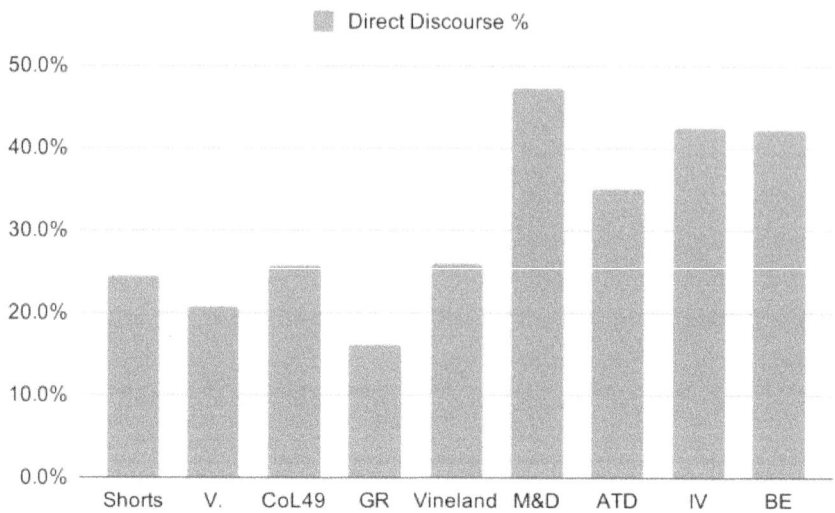

Figure 1.5 Proportion of direct discourse in Pynchon corpus.

in direct discourse may be some effect of the later novels' pastiches of popular genres. Pynchon's earlier novels contain many such pastiches, but these tend to be episodic or subsumed within the kaleidoscope of these novels' tendency to modulate modes and voices. Lindsay Indeherberg describes *Inherent Vice* "as a pastiche of hard-boiled detective fiction" and notes that narrative tempo in that genre is fast-paced.[20] Perhaps the increased direct discourse in later Pynchon is a way to imitate the fast-paced tempo of detective stories and the presumably dialogue-heavy genres of boys' fiction, westerns, and adventure stories ironically mimicked by *Against the Day*.

1.2.3 Reading Dialogue and Character in Pynchon

The increase in direct discourse (mostly dialogue) in Pynchon's texts may be related to an increased attention to rendering characters. Dialogue is voiced by characters, which is important because the rendering of characters in Pynchon has drawn significant criticism. Decades of book reviewers and general readers have judged Pynchon's characters as thin, unbelievable, poorly rendered, interchangeable, or merely allegorical ciphers, criticisms that began with Pynchon's *V.*, in which a protagonist is named, appropriately enough, Stencil. Locke's contemporary book review of *Gravity's Rainbow* is illustrative: "Pynchon doesn't create characters so much as mechanical men to whom a manic comic impulse or a vague free-floating anguish can attach itself."[21] Kathryn Hume echoes such responses—"Thinness of character in *Gravity's Rainbow* disquiets even the book's partisans. Pynchon confounds us with an opulent Ulyssean world but denies us the filigrain complexity of Joyce's psychological portraits"[22]—and summarizes critical responses to the question of "thin" characters in *Gravity's Rainbow*:

> Pynchon's admirers have tried to explain away this "fault" in two fashions. One consists of redefining the genre: if *Gravity's Rainbow* is a satire rather than a novel, argues Alfred MacAdam, we can expect flat figures. Much the same goes for calling it an encyclopedic narrative, a menippea, a jeremiad, or a gothic novel. The other consists of invoking postmodernism by any of several definitions. The intermapping between characters destroys conventional individuality (Brian McHale) or creates prismatic figures, without "core or identifiable inner self" the absent center beloved of deconstructors (Carol Richer).[23]

Pynchon's increase of direct discourse since *Gravity's Rainbow* may possibly correlate with changes to Pynchon's approach to character. Perhaps all of this dialogue serves to "flesh out" characters in renderings favored by realism.

Numerous critics have suggested that Pynchon does, indeed, bring greater depth to certain characters in later novels. In his reception study of *Mason & Dixon*, Douglas Keesey surveys the novel's early reviews:

> reviewers almost all agree on one thing: they love the characterization of *Mason and Dixon*. Even critics flummoxed by other aspects of the book find in Pynchon's delineation of the title characters something they can understand and appreciate. Mason and Dixon are called "endearing" (Eder) and "curiously touching" (Abbott); they possess "emotional amplitude" (Kakutani) and "psychological complexity and depth" (Mooney); they are "extremely real" (Pelovitz), "anything but cartoons" (Sante). In short, critics find the characters realistic and moving [...].[24]

As for later novels, Bernard Duyfhuizen writes that in *Against the Day*, Pynchon's "characters this time are much more nuanced and in many ways more human than some of their predecessors."[25] Bill Millard repeats and expands this when discussing *Inherent Vice*: "The steady attainment of greater self-awareness by Sportello [...] indicates that Pynchon is capable of considerable psychological nuance when he puts his mind to it. [...] [In] *Against the Day*, the extended Cyprian Latewood plot [...] presents a decisive response to Wood's charges of chronic immaturity, superficiality, and overtheatricality."[26] Maxine Tarnow in *Bleeding Edge* may be Pynchon's most critically admired character, as far as depth of character is concerned. Sean M. Carroll is impressed by the characterization in *Bleeding Edge*: "There is a colourful cast of memorable personalities," and Maxine "is a rich, believable character, and we are fortunate to be privy to her wry commentary on the rogue's gallery of characters who cross her path."[27] Diana Benea describes Maxine as "a mix of Pynchon's previous female protagonists, *The Crying of Lot 49*'s Oedipa Maas and *Vineland*'s Frenesi Gates, albeit one endowed with more agency than her predecessors."[28] The trend of growing direct discourse in Pynchon could be an important stylistic component of this increased and more sustained character development.

A trend of increasingly "deep" Pynchon characters should not be overstated, as a chorus of the old criticism persists. William Logan, writing after *Mason & Dixon*, states that "Pynchon loathes the idea of character," and a "novel may need neither plot nor character alone [...] It's difficult for a novel, even a novel everywhere touched by brilliance, to offer so little of either."[29] James Wood, in an extended argument for a realism based on portrayal of character, argued that novels by Pynchon and others "are profligate with what might be called inhuman stories: 'inhuman' not because they could never happen, but because they are not really about human beings."[30] In his review of *Against the Day*, Wood continued this line of argument: "everyone [in the novel] is ultimately protected from real menace because no one really exists."[31] Duyfhuizen qualified his above assessment of "much more nuanced" characters with "It is a fair criticism, especially from readers whose tastes tend toward realism, that with a broad cast of major characters [...] Pynchon still falls short of developing his characters as fully as they deserve."[32]

Many of the critics who read an increased depth in Pynchon's characters may also be perpetuating a longtime trend of Pynchon criticism, readings that uncover a "redemptive new humanism" in Pynchon. This began with Slade in 1974, McHale contends:

> Since Slade, this has become [...] a sanctioned move of Pynchon criticism, whereby Pynchon is redeemed from charges of 'nihilism' (whatever that might be) by a recuperative appeal to the humanist tradition and the recovery of a fully human subject [...] This same old tired rabbit of humanism has been produced from the same old hat more times than one can easily count in the years since 1974.[33]

This should only bring more skepticism to the hypothesis that an increase in word tokens of dialogue may be related to a more "humanistic" Pynchon.

The hypothesis that increased dialogue = more "believable" characters is also undermined by the fact that novels render "humanistic," "real," or "believable" characters not only through dialogue but narration as well, and narration may often be the more important contributor. "Interiority" has long been discussed as a central concept in the history of the novel as mode,[34] and interiority has been championed as a defining aspect of the novel by, for instance, the editors of *N+1* magazine, who claim that the "novel is unexcelled at one thing only: the creation of interiority, or inwardness."[35] In stylistics, the textual creation of such interiority is partly explored through *attribution theory*, the study of how attributions of states of mind are made in texts, and Alan Palmer's reading of a passage of *Lot 49* demonstrates that Pynchon can explore the interiority of his characters far more through narration than dialogue.[36] Palmer explicates a passage in which Oedipa knows that her husband Mucho has been sleeping with young girls:

> She knew the pattern because it had happened a few times already, though Oedipa had been most scrupulously fair about it, mentioning the practice only once, in fact, another three in the morning and out of a dark dawn sky, asking if he wasn't worried about the penal code. "Of course," said Mucho after awhile, that was all; but in his tone of voice she thought she heard more, something between annoyance and agony. She wondered then if worrying affected his performance. Having once been seventeen and ready to laugh at almost anything, she found herself then overcome by, call it a tenderness she'd never go quite to the back of lest she get bogged. It kept her from asking him any more questions. Like all their inabilities to communicate, this too had a virtuous motive. (*Lot 49*, 38–9)

Palmer discusses how the mental state of characters can be interpreted not only through descriptions of inner states but actions as well, and that often "the mental and physical sides of action and behavior coexist and interpenetrate to the points where they are difficult to disentangle."[37] Here, Oedipa takes an action (she closes her mouth, does not ask a question), and this is accompanied by a *reason word* (in this case, "*It kept her*") that explains these actions. Oedipa's mental state is thus conveyed by a combination of action and mental state description, which is typical of novels, Palmer writes: "Novels tend to contain few action descriptions that simply describe only the surface of physical behaviour. [...] the accompanying mental event is often made part of the action description, rather than left implicit."[38] In this passage, almost all of the mental state of Oedipa, Mucho, and what Oedipa *thinks about* Mucho are conveyed via narration. Mucho's dialogue—"Of course"—may be the least revealing words in the passage, as far as his mental state. This passage emphasizes that direct discourse is hardly the only—or even primary—vehicle of rendering "believable" characters, and that counting direct discourse tokens can, at best, hint at the issue.

Despite all of these cautions, a correlation of increased dialogue and depth of character need not be absolute, and the increased dialogue in Pynchon's later texts probably does play a role in the more believable, humanistically rendered characters welcomed by many critics. I leave further exploration of this to future work, but Maxine's dialogue in *Bleeding Edge*, for instance, often showcases her idiosyncratic wit, and the constancy and volume of Maxine's witty dialogue, even when the character is under fire, portrays her uncommonly unflappable character. Although it may be found in free indirect discourse, as well, Maxine's clever dialogue (and the large amount of it) does add considerable depth to the character.

Moving on from character depth, another hypothesis is that increased direct discourse in Pynchon is related to the timeframe of each novel. Duyfhuizen writes that "because the scope of *Against the Day* is so broad, the reader follows the main characters over many years and sees the evolutions of their personalities. As in *Mason & Dixon*, this novel's chronology forces the characters to undergo changes as the world itself changes. In Pynchon's first three novels, the primary chronologies were limited to roughly a single year."[39] Yet in Pynchon, no correlation can be observed between novel timeframe and dialogue percentage. If this book were written following *Against the Day*, this might seem to be the case, but the proportion of direct discourse is higher in *Inherent Vice* and *Bleeding Edge*—which both take place within a year—than *Against the Day*, which spans from 1893 through the First World War.

Another way to interpret the increase in direct discourse in Pynchon is that it simply makes the texts more readable, as certain later novels are considered "lighter" or less challenging, "Pynchon Lite," as Michiko Kakutani dubbed *Inherent Vice*.[40] Dialogue strikes readers as a welcoming aspect of reading fiction, even when the content of speech is ambiguous or vague, as in Pynchon. My results complement an impression that *Gravity's Rainbow*, which contains the least amount of direct discourse, with long passages of dense, dialogue-free blended narration, is Pynchon's most "difficult" text. The convergence of these threads is suggested by Duyfhuizen's review of *Against the Day*, which he states is "in many ways a character-driven novel" and that "the knock against the style of *Against the Day* may be that it is too accessible."[41] Aspects of the *style* of *Against the Day* may be relatively accessible for Pynchon, then; it is mostly the novel's length, profusion of subplots and characters, and the struggle to consider it as a "whole" that provide the novel's real challenges.

1.3 Formal Overviews: Conclusion

This chapter has yielded some clear findings: verse is decreasing in Pynchon's texts, while direct discourse is increasing. Other results must remain speculative, especially regarding Pynchon's output, which will only be factually established once manuscripts and biographical information reveal precisely whether and when Pynchon began and worked on *Mason & Dixon* and *Against the Day* during his "wilderness years."

Future digitally informed work on Pynchon's verse could consider comparing verse density with frequency of a related topic or semantic group, such as music, comparison with other novelists who intersperse verse, and computational linguistic analysis of formal poetic features and phonetic rendering in verse. It is also an open question whether Pynchon's waning interest in verse is reflected in the verse's reception. While the closing song of *Gravity's Rainbow* remains oft-quoted, I doubt that many readers value the faux pop songs in *Bleeding Edge* as highly.

An unexplored explanation for the increased direct discourse in Pynchon's texts is his perhaps increasing attention to rendering accent (pronunciation), dialect (pronunciation, grammar, and vocabulary), and idiolect (speech habits peculiar to a particular person). Close attention to accent/dialect/idiolect is present in Pynchon's earliest published stories,[42] and Pynchon's introduction to *Slow Learner* affirms his continuing interest in *improving* his rendering of accents: "Equally embarrassing is the case of Bad Ear to be found marring much of the dialogue [...]. My sense of regional accents in those days was primitive at best." Liberman, a leading authority on phonetics, once claimed (facetiously or not) to reread *Inherent Vice* "for purely phonetic reasons,"[43] and analyzed *inter alia* the phonetics of Pynchon's rendering of a New York dialect.[44] One reviewer of *Against the Day* highlights Pynchon's rendering of speech as one of the saving graces of the novel:

> There are, of course, great things in *Against the Day*. Pynchon's ear for vernacular accents and dialects [...] is peerless. Whether he is writing the precious, periphrastic literary twaddle of 19th-century boys' books, or the vernacular of the miners and anarchists on the Colorado frontier or the perfect phonetic approximations of all the *mitteleuropa* speech he imitates, he makes us hear what we can never have heard at all.[45]

Without confirming the hypothesis (which might require a separate book), Pynchon's interest in phonetics may partly explain his increase in dialogue.

The two clear findings of this chapter, when considered together, may also inspire additional future work: is there some overarching explanation as to why verse decreases *as* dialogue increases in Pynchon's texts, or why Pynchon's output increasingly prioritizes speech over verse? Although I present and attack the hypothesis that increase in dialogue may neatly correlate with increased attention to character, it is worth considering whether some of the previous functions of verse in Pynchon—"for character development and aspiration, for verisimilitude, for formal order, for thematic development," per John Joseph Hess[46]—are largely taken over by Pynchon's dialogue (or narration?) in later novels.

Many other distant, formal overviews of Pynchon's texts are left to be uncovered. In *Close Reading with Computers*, Martin Eve suggests the analogy of a microscope for digital methods which support close-reading interpretations,[47] and in the next chapter, I trade my telescope, so to speak, for such a microscope and examine arguably the most striking and sustained stylistic experiment in Pynchon's career.

Notes

1 Different software produces different word counts. These and other word counts in this book rely on AntWordProfiler 1.4.1., which shows 1,766,515 word tokens. NLTK using RegexpTokenizer shows 1,768,923. LancsBox 5.1.2 shows 1,700,430.

2 Boris Kachka, "On the Thomas Pynchon Trail," *New York Magazine*, August 25, 2013, http://www.vulture.com/2013/08/thomas-pynchon-bleeding-edge.html.

3 Ibid.

4 Brian Edwards, "Surveying 'America': In the Mnemonick Deep of Thomas Pynchon's *Mason & Dixon*," *Australasian Journal of American Studies* 23 (2004): 21.

5 Ibid.

6 Cornelius Collins, "A Discussion of Thomas Pynchon's New Novel at MLA 2014," *Pynchon at the Bleeding Edge*, August 20, 2013, https://bleedingedge.mla.hcommons.org/2013/08/20/panel-description/.

7 Michael Nelson, "Pynchon's *Bleeding Edge*: A Challenging, Rewarding Read," *Post and Courier*, February 15, 2014, http://www.postandcourier.com/features/arts_and_travel/pynchon-s-bleeding-edge-a-challenging-rewarding-read/article_8f5ae3f1-27fb-5f57-a836-15103f9a424a.html.

8 E.g.: Mel Gussow, "Pynchon's Letters Nudge His Mask," *New York Times*, March 4, 1998, http://www.nytimes.com/1998/03/04/books/pynchon-s-letters-nudge-his-mask.html; Tore Rye Andersen, "Mapping the World: Thomas Pynchon's Global Novels," *Orbit: A Journal of American Literature* 4:1 (2016): 20–1.

9   Python code by myself and Martin Steer as part of a separate project. An important
    step in preprocessing these texts was to correct instances where a left quotation
    mark is not matched by a right quotation mark, e.g., where the same character
    continues direct discourse across paragraph breaks. These were manually
    corrected via a regular expression, "([^"])+?". Code available at https://github.com/
    erikannotations/TPDH.

10 Mark Liberman, "Proportion of Dialogue in Novels," *Language Log*, December 29,
    2017, http://languagelog.ldc.upenn.edu/nll/?p=35968. For an advanced methodology
    to automatically detect direct speech, indirect speech, and other categories in
    the German language, see Annelen Brunner, "Automatic Recognition of Speech,
    Thought, and Writing Representation in German Narrative Texts," *Literary and
    Linguistic Computing* 28:4 (2013); Annelen Brunner, *Automatische Erkennung von
    Redewiedergabe: Ein Beitrag zur quantitativen Narratologie* (Berlin: De Gruyter, 2015).

11 I chose "YYYYY" because this does not otherwise appear in Pynchon's texts and, to
    support visualization, five Ys are chosen because the average number of letters in
    English words in texts has been estimated to be 4.79. Peter Norvig, "English Letter
    Frequency Counts: Mayzner Revisited or ETAOIN SRHLDCU," accessed September
    1, 2019, http://norvig.com/mayzner.html.

12 William Vesterman, "Pynchon's Poetry," in *Mindful Pleasures: Essays on Thomas
    Pynchon*, ed. George Levine and David Leverenz (Boston: Little, Brown, 1976), 101.

13 Cowart, *Thomas Pynchon: The Art of Allusion*, 77; Steven Weisenburger, *A Gravity's
    Rainbow Companion*, 2nd ed. (Athens: University of Georgia Press, 2006); J. O.
    Tate, "Gravity's Rainbow: The Original Soundtrack," *Pynchon Notes* 13 (1983): 3–24;
    Robert L. McLaughlin, "Movie Music in *Gravity's Rainbow*," *Pynchon Notes* 28–9
    (1991); Tim Ware et al., *Pynchon Wiki*, https://www.pynchonwiki.com; Kathryn
    Hume and Thomas J. Knight, "Pynchon's Orchestration of *Gravity's Rainbow*,"
    Journal of English and Germanic Philology 85:3 (1986): 367; Charles Clerc, Mason
    & Dixon & Pynchon (Lanham, MD: University Press of America, 2000), 116. John
    Joseph Hess, "Music in Thomas Pynchon's *Gravity's Rainbow*," *Orbit: A Journal of
    American Literature* 2:2 (2014): 1–36. Hänggi, *Pynchon's Sound of Music*.

14 Anahita Rouyan, "Singing Thomas Pynchon's *Gravity's Rainbow*," *Journal of
    Literature and the History of Ideas* 15:1 (2017): 118.

15 Jules Siegel, "Who Is Thomas Pynchon … and Why Did He Take Off with My
    Wife?" *Playboy*, March 1977.

16 Hänggi, *Pynchon's Sound of Music*, 215. English translation of Das *Rheingold* by
    Frederick Jameson, *DM's Opera Site*, accessed September 1, 2019, http://www.
    murashev.com/opera/opera.php?opera_id=35. Character names removed, stage
    directions left intact for calculation of 10,788 word tokens.

17 Weisenburger, "Thomas Pynchon at Twenty-Two."

18 Liberman, "Proportion of Dialogue in Novels."

19 I attribute this to my additional separation of verse, which is sometimes marked by quotation marks, and the different results that various word token counting tools provide.

20 Lindsay Indeherberg, "What You Cannot Avoid: Thomas Pynchon's *Inherent Vice* as a Pastiche of Hard-boiled Detective Fiction," master's thesis, University of Antwerp, 2015, 7.

21 Locke, "One of the Longest, Most Difficult, Most Ambitious Novels in Years."

22 Kathryn Hume, "Repetition and Construction of Character in *Gravity's Rainbow*," *Critique: Studies in Contemporary Fiction* 33:4 (1992): 243.

23 Ibid.

24 Douglas Keesey, "*Mason & Dixon* on the Line: A Reception Study," *Pynchon Notes* 36–9 (1996): 174.

25 Bernard Duyfhuizen, "'The Exact Degree of Fictitiousness': Thomas Pynchon's *Against the Day*," *Postmodern Culture* 17:2 (2007), online.

26 Bill Millard, "Pynchon's Coast: *Inherent Vice* and the Twilight of the Spatially Specific," in *Pynchon's California*, ed. Scott McClintock and John Miller (Iowa City: University of Iowa Press, 2014), 86.

27 Sean M. Carroll, "Review of *Bleeding Edge*," *Nature* 501 (2013): 312–13.

28 Diana Benea, "Post-modernist Sensibility in Thomas Pynchon's *Bleeding Edge*," *British and American Studies* 21 (2015): 144.

29 William Logan, "Pynchon in the Poetic," *Southwest Review* 83:4 (1998): 425, 437.

30 James Wood, *The Irresponsible Self: On Laughter and the Novel* (London: Jonathan Cape, 2004), 148.

31 James Wood, "All Gravity, No Rainbow," *New Republic*, March 5, 2007, https://newrepublic.com/article/63049/all-rainbow-no-gravity.

32 Duyfhuizen, "The Exact Degree of Fictitiousness."

33 McHale, "Slade Revisited," 146.

34 See e.g., Elaine McGirr, "Interiorities," in *The Cambridge History of the English Novel*, ed. Robert L. Caserio and Clement Hawes (Cambridge: Cambridge University Press, 2012).

35 Editors, "The Novel: The Way Out Is In," *N+1* 2 (2005), https://nplusonemag.com/issue-2/the-intellectual-situation/way-out/.

36 Alan Palmer, "Attribution Theory: Action and Emotion in Dickens and Pynchon," in *Contemporary Stylistics*, ed. Marina Lambrou and Peter Stockwell (New York: Continuum, 2007).

37 Ibid., 85.

38 Ibid.

39 Duyfhuizen, "The Exact Degree of Fictitiousness."

40 Michiko Kakutani, "Another Doorway to the Paranoid Pynchon Dimension," *New York Times*, August 3, 2009, https://www.nytimes.com/2009/08/04/books/04kaku.html.

41 Duyfhuizen, "The Exact Degree of Fictitiousness."

42 In "The Small Rain": "the angular edges of [Levine's] Bronx accent had been dulled and softened into a modified drawl" (*SL*, 28); "a Virginia accent said" (28); "a precise, dry Beacon Hill accent" (33); Dugan "pronounced 'out' like 'oot' " (29). In "Mortality and Mercy in Vienna," Harvey Duckworth's Alabama accent is rendered so thickly that the protagonist, Siegel, cannot understand it: " 'Mayun ah said whay's Lewpayskew,' the sailor said."

43 Mark Liberman, "The Price of Wisdom," *Language Log*, December 16, 2014, http://languagelog.ldc.upenn.edu/nll/?p=16498.

44 Mark Liberman, "The Syntonic Phonetics of Pynchon's Pitchuhv," *Language Log*, January 9, 2007, http://itre.cis.upenn.edu/~myl/languagelog/archives/004023.htmlhttp://languagelog.ldc.upenn.edu/nll/?p=16498.

45 Terrence Doody, "*Against the Day* by Thomas Pynchon," *Houston Chronicle*, December 3, 2006, https://www.chron.com/life/books/article/Against-the-Day-by-Thomas-Pynchon-1560368.php.

46 Hess, "Music in Pynchon's *Mason & Dixon*," 2.

47 Martin Paul Eve, *Close Reading with Computers* (Stanford: Stanford University Press, 2019), 18–20.

2

Archaic Stylistics in *Mason & Dixon*

*"[…] Twas but a Representation," they explain'd, repeatedly, till I quite lost
count, having also ceas'd to know what the word meant, anyway.*
—*Mason & Dixon*, 186

As stylistically rich as all of Pynchon's novels are, *Mason & Dixon* could be
Pynchon's most radical and sustained stylistic experiment. *Mason & Dixon* is a
historical novel written entirely in mock-archaic prose that evokes the style of
mid-/late-eighteenth-century English, via archaic spelling (*Musick, Atlantick*),
apostrophes and elision (*learn'd, match'd*), pronouns (*thee, thy, ye*), contractions
(*thah's, ye'd*), and censored religious and profane words (*G-d* for *God*, *D——l* for
Devil). Within Pynchon's career, the style experiment of *Mason & Dixon* might
seem *sui generis*, but this chapter demonstrates how these mock-archaic features
take part in a continuum of stylistic experimentation across Pynchon's texts.

A stylistic analysis of Pynchon's mock-archaic or invented English in *Mason
& Dixon* might fill a book by itself, but as no such book yet exists, this chapter
contributes groundwork on some of the most salient archaic aspects of its
style. The overarching questions are: what archaic stylistic devices did Pynchon
employ in *Mason & Dixon*? Are these used consistently? How do these relate to
recorded eighteenth-century English, if at all? How do these relate to Pynchon's
oeuvre? The stylistic devices in *Mason & Dixon* explored are orthographic
(including capitalized nouns, archaic spelling, and archaic use of apostrophes
and contractions), lexical (including pronouns and verbs), and censored words.

2.1 Capitalized Nouns

Pynchon capitalizes thousands of nouns (as well as some verbs and adjectives)
in *Mason & Dixon*, for example, "He can smell the Town upon the Wind, the

Smoke and Muck-Piles, long before he sees it" (*M&D*, 175). *The Cambridge Encyclopedia of the English Language* provides a history of the rise and fall of capitalization in eighteenth-century orthography:

> [Sixteenth-century spelling reformer John] Hart recommended his readers to use a capital letter at the beginning of every sentence, proper name, and important common noun. By the 17th century, the practice had extended to titles (Sir, Lady), forms of address (Father, Mistris), and personified nouns (Nature). Emphasized words and phrases would also attract a capital. By the beginning of the 18th century [...] this practice [was] extended still further (e.g. to the names of the branches of knowledge), and it was not long before some writers began using a capital for any noun that they felt to be important. Books appeared in which all or most nouns were given an initial capital (as is done systematically in modern German)—perhaps for aesthetic reasons, or perhaps because printers were uncertain about which nouns to capitalize, and so capitalized them all.
>
> The fashion was at its height in the later 17th century, and continued into the 18th. The manuscripts of Butler, Traherne, Swift, and Pope are full of initial capitals. However, the later 18th-century grammarians were not amused by this apparent lack of discipline in the written language. In their view, the proliferation of capitals was unnecessary, and causing the loss of a useful potential distinction. Their rules brought a dramatic reduction in the types of noun permitted to take a capital letter.[1]

Historical capitalization of nouns in English thus followed broad rules for a time but descended into wide inconsistency. This inconsistency is also found in *The Journal of Charles Mason & Jeremiah Dixon*, written by the historical figures from 1763 to 1768,[2] which Pynchon must have drawn upon, as Charles Clerc convincingly argues.[3]

This raises a question: what rules, if any, did Pynchon set for himself in capitalizing nouns in *Mason & Dixon*, and how rigorously did he follow these rules? An initial impression is that nouns are capitalized inconsistently in *Mason & Dixon*, but to experimentalize the inquiry, I queried the two most common forms of noun as defined by the part-of-speech tagger TreeTagger, NN (noun, singular or mass), and NNS (noun, plural). Manually inspecting the over 1,400 capitalized words identified by this method, the capitalization patterns of nouns with frequencies greater than one hundred strongly indicate that Pynchon capitalizes nouns inconsistently in *Mason & Dixon* (Table 2.1).[4] Capitalized words at the beginning of sentences were not counted for these experiments.

Table 2.1 Inconsistently capitalized nouns in *Mason & Dixon* with frequency > 100. Italics indicate greater frequency

Type	Frequency	Type	Frequency
time	*473*	Time	114
way	*363*	Way	18
day	*246*	Day	164
line	32	Line	*220*
something	*180*	Something	3
night	*157*	Night	102
world	41	World	*142*
years	*141*	Years	23
moment	*134*	Moment	34
others	*117*	Others	4
nothing	*114*	Nothing	2
side	*111*	Side	20
end	*110*	End	19
thing	*106*	Thing	6
earth	9	Earth	*103*

Although some of these include adjectival forms (e.g., *nothing more*), the pattern—inconsistency—stands. More precisely, this method identifies 206 nouns that Pynchon capitalized inconsistently in *Mason & Dixon*. One good example is *zone*, which appears only thrice in the text:

> We have passed, tho' without comment, out of the *zone of influence* of the western mountains... (*M&D*, 354)

> they fetch up against the flank of the North Mountain, having enter'd the personal *Zone of Influence* of Capt. Evan Shelby. (*M&D*, 499)

> The Worm continues to enlarge its *Zone of emptiness*, but with a change of Center. (*M&D*, 590; emphases added)

Not only is the noun *zone* capitalized inconsistently, but noun phrases beginning with *zone*, as well. This inconsistency also applies when word derivatives are considered (Table 2.2).

It is possible that close reading the sentences in which these nouns appear might suggest patterns in Pynchon's capitalization. Clerc asserts that "all generalized nouns [in *Mason & Dixon*] and even some adjectives are capitalized,"[5] but this is clearly incorrect, insofar as "generalized noun" is not a common term in modern linguistics, and is, where used, synonymous with a "common noun." As just one counterexample:

Table 2.2 A selection of noun forms in *Mason & Dixon* with frequency > 5 that are both capitalized and uncapitalized

Type	Frequency	Type	Frequency
animal	9	direction	21
Animals	11	Direction	7
animals	8	directions	8
Axmen	37	Friend	21
axmen	6	friends	12
Axman	5	Friends	7
beauty	6	Ghosts	19
Beauty	8	ghosts	8
certainty	8	History	37
Certainty	5	history	18
Death	50	instrument	5
death	23	Instruments	27
deaths	5	knowledge	11
Despair	6	Knowledge	14
despair	5		

But the boy had watched her out on the Fell, riding so fast that *her amazing hair* blew straight back behind her, the same Wind pressing *her Eyelids* shut and *her Lashes* into a Fan, and forcing *her Lips* apart. … Long on a personal basis with the horses the Earl had given her to ride, Dixon sought their company now in the stables at night (*M&D*, 416; emphases added)

Why is *her amazing hair* uncapitalized when, later in the sentence, *her Eyelids* and *her Lashes* are? The primary linguistic difference is that, here, *Eyelids* and *Lashes* are direct objects of a verb. Perhaps *Mason & Dixon* only capitalizes nouns when they are direct objects? Yet in the next sentence, "Dixon sought their company," *company* remains uncapitalized despite being a direct object. The best possible explanation, then, is that the boy in the quotation, a young Jeremiah Dixon, was particularly drawn to the Eyelids, Lashes, and Lips of the woman (a young Lady Lepton), rather than to her hair. In this example, Pynchon thus capitalizes for foregrounding or poetic emphasis. William B. Millard supports poetic emphasis as one explanation for capitalization in *Mason & Dixon*: Pynchon "create[s] useful distinctions between ordinary terms and those attracting a shade more attention. He deploys capitals artfully and unpredictably, attaching them not to the more conventionally important nouns but to those whose *ad hoc* contextual importance appears to require momentary emphasis."[6] In a sense, this is consistent with historical English capitalization of nouns post-Hart, as mentioned above: "writers began using a capital for any noun that they felt to be important." Perhaps a difference is that, for Pynchon, what is "important" or not seems entirely up to the ever-changing whims of the author. More generally, this also places capitalization, as a poetic device, within the purview of scholars who see Pynchon's writing as moving between poetry and prose.[7]

One passage in *Mason & Dixon* which could illustrate a pattern in the novel's capitalization strategy is discussed by Millard, a conversation involving George Washington that Millard interprets as displaying "sharp contrasts" in capitalization. In this passage, Millard suggests that Pynchon capitalizes "more trivial and transient items" to "reflec[t] Pynchon's tropisms toward the things, ideas, and personages that are customarily subordinated":[8]

> "Here," the Col$^{\rm o}$ beams, "more *fame* attaches to the Transits,—Observers station'd all 'round the *world*, even in Massachusetts,—*Treasuries* of all *lands* pouring forth *gold*,—ev'ry Astronomer suddenly employ'd,—and all to find a true *value* for the 'Earth's Parallax.' Why, most of us here in Virginia wouldn't know a Parallax from a *Pinwheel* if it came on up and said how-d'ye do."

> "Yet, what a *Rage* it was! the Transit-of-Venus Wig, that several *women* were seen wearing upon Broad Street, *Husband*, do ye remember it? a dark little round *Knot* against a great white powder'd *sphere*,—"

> "And that Transit-of-Venus Pudding? Same thing, a single black Currant upon a Circular Field of White,—." (*M&D*, 283; emphases added)

Millard writes that "the observant reader will have noticed that the terms 'fame,' 'world,' 'lands,' 'gold,' 'value,' 'women,' and 'sphere' do *not* appear capitalized. It is the more trivial and transient items, the dark little knowns rather than the larger white spheres, that receive the emphatic capital here." Millard does not assert that Pynchon *often* does this or *always* does this. He merely, and correctly, identifies one passage where Pynchon's capitalization strategy exhibits contrasts and one where the capitalization strategy (capitalize certain transient nouns) seems to echo the thematic subject matter (the astronomical event, the Transit of Venus).

This passage Millard highlights raises a tantalizing possibility: that Pynchon may tend to capitalize subordinate, trivial, or transient things. Perhaps there is some method to Pynchon's capitalization madness? But my data consistently discounts this, as does close reading of the passages that the data identify. Even in the passage Millard quotes above, there are counterexamples to the sharp contrasts he identifies: *women* and *Husband* do not easily align with a "capitalize the subordinate" pattern, while *Treasuries*, a locus of power, remains

Table 2.3 A selection of nouns in a passage from *Mason & Dixon*, with frequency of both capitalized and uncapitalized types in the novel

Type	Frequency	Type	Frequency
fame	2	Fame	0
world	41	World	142
lands	15	Lands	6
gold	10	Gold	18
value	6	Value	4
women	36	Women	39
sphere	4	Sphere	6
transits	1	Transits	10
observers	3	Observers	6
treasuries	0	Treasuries	1
astronomer	1	Astronomer	36
pinwheel	0	Pinwheel	1
rage	6	Rage	7
wig	1	Wig	34
Husband	9	Husband	26
Knot	0	Knot	2

capitalized. Query also reveals that the uncapitalized words in the passage that Millard identifies as dominant (*fame, world, lands, gold, value, sphere*) are, on the contrary, more often capitalized in *Mason & Dixon* than not (Table 2.3). The passage Millard singles out, while notable, is thus in no way exemplary of Pynchon's capitalization strategy in *Mason & Dixon*.

What may be claimed about capitalization of nouns in *Mason & Dixon*: eighteenth-century English texts capitalized nouns inconsistently, and so does Pynchon. Given the hundreds of examples, this inconsistency should be read *as* the stylistic strategy. Capitalization in *Mason & Dixon* can be interpreted as motivated, at least sometimes, as poetic emphasis. But to better understand capitalization in *Mason & Dixon*, capitalization among the other mock-archaic stylistic devices in the text and irregular capitalization in Pynchon's oeuvre should be considered.

2.1.1 Capitalization in Pynchon: Scholarly Response

"So many capital letters," Mondaugen protested. (V., 256)

Scholars have briefly commented on capitalization primarily in *Gravity's Rainbow*, in which some central thematic concepts are famously capitalized: *Us,*

They, *Zone*, *Rocket*, and so on. Millard, addressing capitalization before *Mason & Dixon*, writes that Pynchon

> has long treated certain nouns or phrases in this manner, elevating them out of their ordinary lexical functions and rendering them perceptibly public and substantial, sometimes with a comic touch, and recognizable as proper nouns for deities or brand names. While *Gravity's Rainbow* confers such a capital on the *War*, an obviously significant choice for this treatment, the ostensibly minor detail of Beaver/Jeremy's Pipe also continually appears with such an anomalous capital P (49, 148). It marks this personal effect with the sign of the generic and this produces an effect of impersonality, just as the lieutenant himself is so much less a defined personage than his rival Roger Mexico. In the Luddism essay, the salient features of the Badass — that he is "Big" and that he is "Bad"—take on additional scale and menace by virtue of their blatantly brobdingnagian Bs.[9]

Millard thus highlights some effects of capitalization in Pynchon's texts: to form a proper noun (War), to evoke the common subjects of proper nouns (including brand names and deities), to inflate and magnify (Badass), sometimes ironically (Jeremy's Pipe). Pynchon's capitalization-as-deification has been echoed by Alan Ramón Clinton, who argues that capitalizing *Rocket* "emphasizes both its holy status and its metonymic relation to postwar culture."[10] The connection between capitalization and deification is explicit in *Gravity's Rainbow*: riding a motorcycle through the ruins of the Zone in Germany, Enzian experiences "an extraordinary understanding" or epiphany on the nature of war, elites, and technology, that

> the War was never political at all, the politics was all theatre, all just to keep the people distracted … secretly, it was being dictated instead by the needs of technology … by a conspiracy between human beings and techniques […] The real crises were crises of allocation and priority, not among firms—it was only staged to look that way—but among the different Technologies, Plastics, Electronics, Aircraft, and their needs which are understood only by the ruling elite …
>
> Yes but Technology only responds …, "do you think we'd've had the Rocket if someone, some specific somebody with a name and a penis hadn't *wanted* to chuck a ton of Amatol 300 miles and blow up a block full of civilians? Go ahead, capitalize the T on technology, deify it if it'll make you feel less responsible—but it puts you in with the neutered, brother, in with the eunuchs keeping the harem of our stolen Earth for the numb and joyless hardons of human sultans, human elite with no right at all to be where they are—" (*GR*, 520–1)

Here, the capitalization of Technology within its context has manifold effects: the formation of an individual proper noun Technology, so individual that it even speaks, albeit in the first-person plural (we), and deified and magnified. It is somewhat ironic that in the passage above, in damning those who would capitalize *Technology*, a narrator of *Gravity's Rainbow* presents a damning criticism of a stylistic technique that Pynchon employs profusely in his texts. The ironic use of irregular capitalization in Pynchon's texts—for example, Jeremy's Pipe—also hints at a much broader reading: do Pynchon's texts frustrate or dismantle their own stylistic strategies, the way, as many scholars have discussed, Pynchon's texts frustrate forms of order? The stubborn inconsistency of capitalization in *Mason & Dixon* is one example.

The relation of Pynchon's capitalization with "the abstraction of the literal" was earlier discussed by Schaub:

> The abstraction of the literal is the technique by which Pynchon develops meaningfulness in his labyrinthine plots, and is analogous to Benny Profane's assimilation of street experience: "Profane had grown a little leery of streets, especially streets like this. They had in fact fused into a single abstracted Street, which come the full moon he would have nightmares about" (2). The literal "street," […] is eventually capitalised, which is the typographical transformation of meaningless detail into meaningful symbol.[11]

Schaub highlights the semantic effect of some capitalization in Pynchon's texts: to move from literal or individual to abstract concept, the opposite of how proper nouns are defined (again, as an *individual* person, place, organization, etc.). This richness of uses of capitalization is an example of what commentators mean when they state that Pynchon's style is constantly shifting. For example, observe the capitalization in one of the most quoted passages of *Mason & Dixon*:

> Who claims Truth, Truth abandons. History is hir'd, or coerc'd, only in Interests that must ever prove base […]. She needs rather to be tended lovingly and honorably by fabulists and counterfeiters, Ballad-Mongers and Cranks of ev'ry Radius (*M&D*, 350)[12]

Here the reader is confronted with the considerable task of interpreting not only the words but each capitalization in turn: Truth as abstract concept magnified and perhaps deified, Interests as abstract but possessing sinister individual agency, Ballad-Mongers and Cranks perhaps rendered larger and legendary, and Radius, not only a novel metaphor for *variety* but also basking in some of the magnifying, deifying glow of the words earlier in the sentence.

Charles Hohmann, a linguistically informed Pynchon scholar, provided a reading of capitalization in *Gravity's Rainbow*:

> Capitalization in *Gravity's Rainbow* is a hyperbolic device and therefore one of the means that push discourse toward the metaphorical pole. According to Thomas Schaub its function is to transform "meaningless detail into meaningful symbol," a process we have come to qualify as obnoxious in *Gravity's Rainbow*. Its evil nature is made explicit in the novel when a narrator exclaims: Go ahead, capitalize the T on technology, deify it if it'll make you feel less responsible [...].[13]

While some capitalization in *Gravity's Rainbow* does indeed evoke the "obnoxious" and "evil"—*Technology, They, System,* even *Rocket*—there are many counterexamples to Hohmann's claim here, including *Creation, Soul, World, Love,* and others discussed below. But the way that capitalization can "push discourse toward the metaphorical pole," as Hohmann observed in *Gravity's Rainbow*, would multiply in *Mason & Dixon*.

Another way to consider capitalization is its evocation of the language of 1960s politics and counterculture. Herman and Weisenburger note how in "*Gravity's Rainbow*, as in sixties counterculture discourse, 'the System' is always much more than the military-industrial complex, though that's a core reference," while "the Man," in the counterculture sense, appears in the novel, as well.[14] This raises the question of whether these and similar political/countercultural terms from the long 1960s can be read in other, less obvious, capitalizations in Pynchon's texts, such as bodies of authority or power in *Gravity's Rainbow*: System, Us, They, Counterforce, and so on.

Finally, a contributor to *Pynchon Wiki* writes that "all nouns are capitalized in German. Worth noting because the country, language and history loom so large in *Gravity's Rainbow* as well as Pynchon's first two novels, so much so that Pynchon scholar David Cowart refers these novels as Pynchon's 'German period.'"[15] Capitalization, then, could be (or have begun as) a means of evoking the German language and culture. The presence of a variety of creative capitalization as early as Pynchon's short stories, however, which contain far less of the "German-ness" of the early novels would argue against this connotation.

Here, then, are different effects of capitalization in Pynchon's texts: to coin a proper noun, that is, to transform a class of entities (common noun) into an individual (proper noun), that is, transform from abstract to concrete; conversely, to transform the literal to the abstract; for mock-archaic effect; to transform from the literal to a single, abstracted concept; as a device that pushes discourse toward metaphor; for poetic emphasis; to inflate, magnify, or even deify, as parody or extension of 1960s political discourse, for example, *the Man*, *the System*; to connote or evoke the German language.

2.1.2 Querying and Close Reading Pynchon's Irregular Capitalization

To locate the words Pynchon capitalizes for stylistic purposes (i.e., irregularly), I first queried words in TXM with certain part of speech tags that are *not* proper nouns (especially common nouns and pronouns), isolated the ones that are capitalized, excluded capitalized words that begin a sentence or quotation,[16] then manually inspected the results. Although many false positives were included in the results, due to incorrect tagging by the TreeTagger part of speech tagger, the KWIC visual interface of TXM allowed me to quickly disregard them as well as further inspect results within their textual context. This methodology shows promising results, as demonstrated in Figure 2.1, where the query alone (before any manual sifting) located numerous instances of the famously capitalized *They* in *Gravity's Rainbow*.

This query is challenged by the fact that classifying words as capitalized for stylistic effect (i.e., irregular) or due to an established capitalization rule (i.e., regular) involves some subjectivity.[17]

The brief, but insightful, scholarly attention to capitalization in Pynchon's texts has focused on *Gravity's Rainbow* and *Mason & Dixon*, with a small amount on *V*. Yet in Pynchon's short stories (1959–64), one finds, *da capo*, numerous instances of lifelong Pynchon capitalization habits. Here are capitalizations in the form of

- coining proper nouns: "only then did he realize that the isolated system— galaxy, engine, human being, culture, whatever—must evolve spontaneously toward the Condition of the More Probable" (*SL*, 87). To this day, the only results for the query "Condition of the More Probable" in Google and Google Book Search are for Pynchon.[18]
- mock-archaic, mock-Biblical effect: "he had lived by a golden rule of Screw the Sergeant before He Screweth Thee" ("Mortality and Mercy in Vienna").
- parody of political terms: "it occurred to him insanely, discuss the Midget Problem or something" (*SL*, 74). Although the term "the negro problem" dates from earlier than the 1960s, its place in 1960s discourse is exemplified in, for instance, *The Fire Next Time* by James Baldwin.[19] More to the point, Pynchon's editor, Cork Smith, reportedly suggested that Pynchon cut parts

text_id	Left context	Keyword	Right context
P4	The Night Rog and Beaver Fought Over Jessica	While She	Cried in Krupp's Arms, and drool over
P4	us. We will help legitimize Them,	though They	don't need it really, it's another dividend
P4	the Earth it "strikes" No But	Then You	Never Really Thought It Was Did You
P4	strikes "No But Then You Never Really	Thought It	Was Did You Of Course It Begins Infinitely
P4	But Then You Never Really Thought It Was	Did You	Of Course It Begins Infinitely Below The
P4	Never Really Thought It Was Did You Of	Course It	Begins Infinitely Below The Earth And
P4	They can't keep us from dying,	so They	lie to us about death. A cooperative structure
P4	.A cooperative structure of lies. What	have They	ever given us in return for the *trust,*
P4	—we' re supposed to owe Them?	Can They	keep us from even catching cold? from
P4	2 of Swords What will come: The	World He	appears first with boots and insignia
P4	an ex-scientist now, one who'll never get	Into It	far enough to start talking about God
P4	hold on—hold each voice, each hum or	crackle—He	thinks of their love in illustrations for
P4	if song must find you, here's	one They	never taught anyone to sing, a hymn

Figure 2.1 Query of irregularly capitalized words in *Gravity's Rainbow*.

of *V.* featuring the character McClintic Sphere, a black jazz musician, as "Cork somehow thought the McClintic Sphere material angled the book unhelpfully in the direction of a 'Protest novel' on 'the Negro Problem' and suggested it be cut."[20]

In Pynchon's short story "Under the Rose," later rewritten and incorporated in *V.*, we also see early examples of common nouns elevated, magnified from their everyday definition to connote powerful, abstract enemies: "When had he stopped facing an adversary and taken on a Force, a Quantity?" (*SL*, 135). Developing this elevation further, "Under the Rose" introduces the capitalized form of "The Situation," which appears in unremarkable contexts in the short story, but which *V.* greatly expands upon, rendering "The Situation" as the first of many capitalized, vaguely defined concepts in Pynchon to keep the scholars in business. In *V.*, "The Situation," described as a force that drives men mad, beyond space and time,[21] and the magnitude and unknowable nature of "The Situation" are aptly described by Tina Käkelä-Puumala: "a political or historical situation, in which several intelligence services gather information for their own purposes," and "The Situation is something beyond chaos and order: it cannot be reduced to any kind of conceptual order and yet it has elements that are connected with each other."[22] *V.*, then, marks an important evolution in Pynchon's capitalization, where capitalization is first harnessed in the creation of a (relatively) Big Ambiguous Pynchonian Enigma.

Irregular capitalization in *V.* blossoms overall, and there are even early signs of inconsistent capitalization. The word *balloon* is uncapitalized twenty-one times in *V.*, except for once: "Maijstral, leery like any Maltese of the Balloon's least bobbing" (*V.*, 483). While there are no irregularly capitalized pronouns in the short stories, Pynchon begins to play with capitalized pronouns in *V.*, for example, "He Who Looks for V." and "His Ghostly Magnificence" (*V.*, 239, 500). *Lot 49* contains little irregular capitalization apart from the central device of W.A.S.T.E. A notable mention of archaic capitalization itself takes place where Oedipa is handed an antique tome when researching the Tristero:

> "Wharfinger, like Milton, kept a commonplace book, where he jotted down quotes and things from his reading. That's how we know about Blobb's *Peregrinations*."
>
> It was full of words ending in e's, s's that looked like f's, capitalized nouns, y's where i's should've been. "I can't read this," Oedipa said.
>
> "Try," said Bortz. (*Lot 49*, 152)

Oedipa, whom the text introduces as an average suburban housewife, "can't read" a book whose stylistics resemble *Mason & Dixon*. Obviously, archaic orthography is difficult for later readers, but this raises a small point: that capitalization in *Mason & Dixon* may be inconsistent because to capitalize every last noun, as some books of the seventeenth and eighteenth century did, would overwhelm modern readers even further. As extreme as the style of *Mason & Dixon* sometimes seems, Pynchon might have made it even *more* extreme (by, say, including the "s's that looked like f's").

On capitalization in *Gravity's Rainbow*, much has already been written, by myself and previous scholars. Suffice it to repeat that the frequency and variety of capitalization was radically increased. Creative capitalization continued in *Vineland*, notably in its expanded use of political terms from 1960s countercultural discourse, for example, *the Man, the State, the Revolution, Red Slave State,*

"American Martyr in the Crusade Against Communism," *Ordinary American*, "back with the rest of the American Vulnerability" (251, 346). This makes sense, as scholars have assessed *Vineland* as Pynchon's most overtly political novel.[23] Also of note is the capitalization of another Overarching Pynchonian Symbol, "The Tube," a colloquial term that Pynchon employs for television. McHale, in his extensive analysis of the Tube, notes a number of Tube-related neologisms (*Tubal, non-Tubal, Tubefreeks,* and so on) and discusses how "such neologisms are clear evidence of how deeply TV has penetrated the discursive medium of this text. TV in *Vineland* in effect constitutes a kind of secondary language, a code supplementary to the linguistic codes of American English."[24] Sean Carswell notes how *Vineland* portrays "a site of resistance against Empire: a society so hypnotized by television that they barely notice the neoliberal revolution taking place around them."[25] Television and politics, two related themes in *Vineland*, are thus afforded the special designation of Pynchonian capitalization.

In *Against the Day*, the most notable capitalization is yet again a central symbol/theme/metaphor, namely Time. *Time* appears irregularly capitalized 71 times, and uncapitalized a staggering 965 times (in a novel of 1,085 pages). When grammatical words (i.e., function words) are removed, *time* is actually the most frequent lexical word in *Against the Day*, as measured by the frequencies in WMatrix, an online corpus linguistic analysis tool.[26] Some examples:

> it wasn't that much of a radical step even the first *time* (*ATD*, 92)
>
> no, it is more of an ongoing Transgression, accumulating as the days pass, the invasion of *Time* into a timeless world. (*ATD*, 223)
>
> but I might need some *time* on that (*ATD*, 358)
>
> Among the many superstitions inside this mountain was a belief that the tunnel was "neutral ground," exempt not only from political jurisdictions but from *Time* itself. (*ATD*, 654; emphases added)

Unlike in *Mason & Dixon*, however, the capitalization of *Time* in *Against the Day* is largely grammatically regular: *Time* is capitalized when it is used as a proper noun, a singular thing. Despite this contrast with the manifold capitalization strategy of *Mason & Dixon*, *Time* in *Against the Day*, which has attracted considerable scholarly attention,[27] could be read as a continuation of a now-lifelong stylistic feature in Pynchon's texts.

Pynchon's creative capitalization is muted in *Inherent Vice* and *Bleeding Edge*, although one finds, some fifty years after his short stories, a similar parody of 1960s political discourse:

> Bigfoot's scripts featured a relentless terror squad of small children, who climbed all over the model-home furniture […] and hollered and pretended to shoot Bigfoot down, screaming 'Freak Power!' and 'Death to the Pig!'" (*IV*, 9)

In these latest novels, however, Pynchon seems to have lost his predilection for the abstract made singular (or vice versa) through capitalization. While it is difficult to quantify, given the debatable nature of many capitalizations (is this noun regularly or irregularly capitalized?), it appears that Pynchon's shorter novels employ creative capitalization far less than his longer novels and that *Mason & Dixon* largely ended Pynchon's love affair with the capital letter. This lends some poignancy to the lone references to capitalizations from Pynchon's earlier novels, Tube and Time, in *Bleeding Edge*:

> Maxine picks up Otis and Fiona, who are soon in front of the living-room Tube about to watch *The Aggro Hour* (*BE*, 32)

> Time travel, as it turns out, is not for civilian tourists, […] and navigating Time is an unforgiving discipline. (*BE*, 242)

These could be read as nostalgic Ghosts of Capitalizations Past, perhaps, or selections from the jukebox of Pynchon's Greatest Capitalization Hits.

When considering Pynchon's influence on younger generations of writers, a number of supposedly "Pynchonesque" novelists have taken up capitalization for stylistic effect, most notably David Foster Wallace ("the capitalization-prone Wallace," as a writer for *Newsweek* called him).[28] If Pynchon's influence is read in Wallace's capitalization, Pynchon may be one of the most important links between the lost capitalization of eighteenth-century English and the present day. A capitalization revivalist, so to speak.

2.2 Archaic Spelling, Especially <-ick>

all took time to appreciate the musick of Voices from far away, yet already, unmistakably, American. (*M&D*, 570)

In *Mason & Dixon*, Pynchon's use of archaic spelling, especially words normally ending in <-ic> spelled with <-ick>, such as *Musick* and *Topick*, is, alongside capitalized nouns, one of the most salient stylistic devices. The use of <-ick> spelling is conspicuous in *Mason & Dixon* because it is conspicuous in eighteenth-century written English, and reading early editions of, say, Jonathan

Swift (1667–1754), Alexander Pope (1688–1744), and Samuel Johnson (1709–1784), the two most obvious, notable differences compared with twentieth-century English are the use of the *long s* (ſ) and <-ick> spelling. It is unclear, however, if such spelling exists in the original *Mason/Dixon Journal*, as only a modernized spelling transcription of the full manuscript has been published.[29]

The historic use of <-ick> spelling is explained by D. G. Scragg in his *History of English Spelling*:

> By 1700 the stabilisation [of English spelling] was complete. The relatively few changes which have taken place in spelling since then have affected only a small number of words […], or minor developments involving a group of words such as the loss of the final <k> from <-ick> in such words as *music* and *comic* […].[30]

In the only detailed study on the appearance and disappearance of <-ick> spelling, Andreas Fischer and Peter Schneider analyzed a corpus of English newspapers from 1671 to 1791, finding that the <-ick> spelling dominated in the early decades of the 1700s, followed by a transition period from 1731 to 1751 where <-ic> began to gain prominence, then <-ic> dominating the second half of the century, so that by 1791, <-ick> was found only occasionally in their corpus.[31] Throughout the seventeenth century, however, the spellings were used inconsistently, with the same newspapers often employing both spellings and Samuel Johnson, for instance, consistently writing *musick* but also *musical*.[32]

To query <-ick> spelling in *Mason & Dixon*, I simply queried the string and manually corrected results.[33] As with capitalization of nouns, Pynchon is inconsistent in his use of <-ick> spelling for mock-historical effect, as a selection demonstrates (Table 2.4). For example, Pynchon sometimes writes *musick*, but other times *music*.

Interestingly, the two most frequent <-ick> words in Fischer and Scheider's corpus of eighteenth-century English newspapers are the second and third most frequent <-ick> words in *Mason & Dixon*: *publick* and *musick*.[34] This is evidence that the orthography in *Mason & Dixon* was influenced by actual historical texts.

As should be expected, Pynchon employs <-ick> in wordplay through invented mock-historical adjectives:

> There are *Germanickal* Mystics who live in Trees. (*M&D*, 481)

> the Kings, the Enterprisers, the Adventurers Charter'd and *Piratickal*. (*M&D*, 524)

> " 'Flower of Light'? Light, hey? Sounds *Encyclopedistick* to me, perhaps even Masonick," says Mason. (*M&D*, 688;[35] emphases added)

Table 2.4 Selection of <-ick> words in *Mason & Dixon*

Type	Frequency	Type	Frequency
Topick	47	Topic	0
Topick	4	topic	3
Musick	25	Music	8
Musick	5	music	10
Publick	15	Public	4
Publick	9	public	10
Traffick	13	Traffic	2
Traffick	2	traffic	1
Panick	11	Panic	4
Panick	1	panic	2
Atlantick	9	Atlantic	3
Gigantick	1	Gigantic	0
Gigantick	9	gigantic	7
Magnetick	9	Magnetic	3
Magnetick	2	magnetic	0
Mystickal	1	Mystical	0
Mystickal	9	mystical	2

I could locate no examples of these in historical corpora, but some of the <-ick> words that a reader might guess are Pynchon inventions, on the other hand, are surprisingly present in actual period texts, such as *Mnemonick* and *frolicksome*.

While <-ick> words may be the most salient orthographic feature in *Mason & Dixon*, other mock-archaic spellings are present. For example, *joak* and its derivatives appear twenty times, although *joke* appears six times. *Smoak* and its derivatives appear twenty-six times, meaning both to exhale smoke and "to figure out," an archaic definition (*smoke* meanwhile, appears sixty-five times). Also, *Lanthorn* for lantern, *phiz* for face, and *damme* for *damn*, all of which appear in actual historical sources. Nouns ending in <-ack> also appear in *Mason & Dixon*, for example, *Almanacks, insomniack, zodiack*.

Unlike capitalization, Pynchon has not employed archaic spelling much outside of *Mason & Dixon*. Querying <-ick> spellings in the Pynchon corpus reveals two instances of *traffick*, although published thirty-six years apart:

[Tchitcherine:] "Are you really this evil, or is it just an act? Are you really trafficking in pain?"

[Wimpe, a German IG salesman:] "Doctors *traffick* in *pain* and no one would dream of criticizing their noble calling. (*GR*, 349)

[A portrait of Thomas Jefferson on a large plastic nickel hung on the wall of a diner] turned quickly to Doc, and said, "So! the Golden Fang not only *traffick* in *Enslavement*, they peddle the implements of Liberation as well."

"Hey ... but as a founding father, don't you get freaked out a little with this black apocalypse talk?"

"The tree of Liberty must be refreshed from time to time with the blood of patriots and tyrants," replied Jefferson. "It is its natural Manure." (*IV*, 294; emphases added)

Traffick is actually a not uncommon transitive form of *trafficking*, so these passages should not necessarily be read to contain archaic orthography, but this hallucinatory scene in *Inherent Vice*, in which Thomas Jefferson speaks to Doc through stylistics reminiscent of *Mason & Dixon* (capitalized nouns and <-ick> words), could perhaps be read, as with Pynchon's references in *Inherent Vice* to the Tube and Time, as a nostalgic self-reference.

2.3 Religious/Profane Censorship

Another stylistic device Pynchon deploys in *Mason & Dixon* is the use of em dashes and en dashes non-punctuationally to replace letters in sacred and profane words, primarily *God*, *Devil*, and *damned*, such as:

Some Captain!—step away from a Privateer, by G-d. (*M&D*, 32) → *God*

I would say, the D——l take it (*M&D*, 328) → *Devil*

and d——'d if I'll share any more (*M&D*, 346) → *damned*.

As Table 2.5 shows, Pynchon once again deploys a stylistic device inconsistently in the case of *Devil*, sometimes employing *D——l*, other times *Devil* or *De——l*, with *d——'d*, *damn'd*, *damn*, and derivatives in abundance.

In historical English, this practice seems largely confined to the eighteenth and nineteenth centuries and was common—if inconsistently applied—in the texts that Pynchon must have consulted when researching *Mason & Dixon*. Broad trends can be guessed at from entries in the *Oxford English Dictionary*. In its selection of quotations, *devil* was first censored in this manner in 1710, in an issue of a periodical called the *British Apollo* (although in another issue from the same year, the word was printed in full).[36] In *OED*-cited works by Jonathan Swift ranging 1711–38, *Devil*, *D——l*, *D——*, and *Dev'l* all appeared. *Devil* seems to be thus censored in the *Mason/Dixon Journal*.[37] Eighteenth-century works by Laurence Sterne, James

Table 2.5 Frequency of censored/bowdlerized words with dashes in *Mason & Dixon*

Type	Frequency	Type	Frequency
G-d	9	God	44
G-dawful	3	godawful	2
D——1	12	Devil	6
De——1	1	—	—
d——'d	10	Damn'd/damn'd	49
—	—	D/damme	42
—	—	damned	0
—	—	Damn/damn	10
—	—	Damnation	3
—	—	damnable	2

Boswell, and other less famous names, meanwhile, employed *Devil* uncensored. As for *damned*, the first censored quotation is from Fielding's *Tom Jones* (1749, which meanwhile printed *Devil* in full), while eighteenth-century works by other authors featured a mix of *damn'd*, *d——m'd*, and *Damned*.[38] Such censorship persisted well into the Victorian era, with *Devil* and especially (as indicated by *OED* quotations) *damned*, which was censored in works by Thackeray, Fielding, and various newspapers. Inconsistency continued to reign: the first London edition of an 1859 novel by Trollope leaves *damn* and *Devil* uncensored,[39] yet the first New York edition of another Trollope novel from 1875 censors *d——d* but not *Devil*.[40] This chaos is exemplified by an 1866 edition of *Robinson Crusoe*, which features *damn'd*, *D—n 'em*, and *G—d Damme* all on a single page.[41]

A notable Victorian who railed against this form of censorship was Charlotte Brontë, who, in an editor's preface to the 1850 edition of her late sister Emily's masterpiece, *Wuthering Heights*, denounced the practice and chided those genteel readers who

> will suffer greatly from the introduction into the pages of this work of words printed with all their letters, which it has become the custom to represent by the initial and final letter only—a blank line filling the interval. I [... deem it] a rational plan to write words at full length. The practice of hinting by single letters those expletives with which profane and violent persons are wont to garnish their discourse, strikes me as a proceeding which, however well meant, is weak and futile. I cannot tell what good it does—what feeling It spares—what horror it conceals.[42]

Brontë published this preface pseudonymously (under her longtime pen name Currer Bell), a reminder of the subversive nature of her opinion. The final

OED quotations with censored *D——l* or *d——'d* were from 1857 and 1865, respectively. In the Victorian era, this practice even led to the use of *dash* as a euphemism for profanity, such as in an 1883 memoir by a member of Parliament: "Who the Dash is this person whom none of us know? and what the Dash does he do here?"[43] Pynchon has used *dash* in this sense as well: "I mean, dash it" (*V.*, 210), "Dash it all" (*ATD*, 829, 859).

Pynchon's use of this censoring device in *Mason & Dixon* should perhaps not be overstated or overinterpreted. It existed in eighteenth-century literature, Pynchon borrowed it and used it thirty-six times (for the most commonly censored words) in a rather long novel. It is employed inconsistently in period texts and inconsistently in *Mason & Dixon*, as well. But a few interpretations could be ventured. First, the censored words in *Mason & Dixon* are notable simply for being an extremely minor stylistic device that nonetheless invokes a number of major Pynchon themes: meaning and who controls that meaning, censorship and power, and the sacred and profane. Second, censored words in *Mason & Dixon* add to the exploration of both censorship *in* Pynchon and censorship *and* Pynchon. As shown in Chapter 5, Pynchon's early texts contain a pattern of coded profanity, through non-English words and by slipping hidden profanity past unsuspecting editors. *D——l* and *d——'d* in *Mason & Dixon* could be read as, simply, more examples of such coded profanity, but also metafictive commentary on Pynchon's prior use of coded profanity, as the words which *D——l* and *d——'d* deign to conceal are so transparently evident. As also shown in Chapter 5, which queries profane lexis across the Pynchon corpus, *Mason & Dixon* happens to be Pynchon's lowest-profanity post-1960s novel. This self-censorship by Pynchon, albeit in a knowing transaction with the reader, could be read as another instance of Pynchon frustrating his own stylistic choices. Censorship-via-dashes also invokes anonymity, as such dashes were used historically to anonymize names in texts (names that readers would nonetheless recognize). Jonathan Swift, for instance, wrote, "We are careful never to print a man's name out at length; but, as I do, that of Mr. St—le, although everybody alive knows who I mean."[44] This form of censorship is thus historically a device that constantly frustrates itself—a censored word that everyone nonetheless understands—comparable to Pynchon frustrating his own stylistic choices in *Mason & Dixon*. Finally, dashes are another perceived Pynchon stylistic trademark, as discussed in Chapter 6, and the use of em dashes in the censored words in *Mason & Dixon* is a novel way that Pynchon plays one of his favorite instruments, so to speak.

2.4 Archaic Use of Apostrophes

Mock-archaic use of apostrophes is also widespread in *Mason & Dixon*. Like *damn'd*, words ending in <-ed> are often written <-'d>, for example, *coax'd*, *inscrib'd*, *honor'd*. The frequency of such words is over four thousand times in the text: 207 types with frequency ≥ 5 and roughly 1,400 types in all. The majority of these <-'d> words are simple past verbs, with some adjectives, as well. To detect these, I ran a simple query[45] and removed commonly used modern contractions from the results (Table 2.6).[46]

Unlike some of the other mock-archaic stylistic features examined in this chapter, Pynchon was relatively consistent in ending words with <-'d>. The low frequencies of such words with modern spelling tend to suggest authorial or editorial errata, rather than an intentional strategy of inconsistency. Oddly, all three instances of *happened* (rather than the novel's usual use of *happen'd*) occur within two pages of one another (*M&D*, 356–58) while two instances of *supposed* occur within one paragraph (*M&D*, 24), indicating brief lapses in editing or proofing, perhaps.

Table 2.6 Mock-archaic words with <'d> in place of <-ed> with frequency ≥ 25, and their equivalents in modern spelling, in *Mason & Dixon*

Type	Frequency	Type	Frequency
damn'd	45	damned	0
happen'd	45	happened	3
seem'd	45	seemed	1
pass'd	41	passed	7
allow'd	38	allowed	3
learn'd	37	learned	0
oblig'd	35	O/obliged	5
us'd	35	used	4
wish'd	35	wished	1
suppos'd	34	supposed	7
imagin'd	33	imagined	1
turn'd	32	turned	1
call'd	31	called	3
arriv'd	30	arrived	2
believ'd	25	believed	0
observ'd	25	observed	1
styl'd	25	styled	1

Table 2.7 A selection of mock-archaic words featuring apostrophes in *Mason & Dixon*, with frequency of modern equivalents. Frequencies include both capitalized and uncapitalized types

Type	Frequency	Type	Frequency
ev'ry	194	every	37
thro'	192	through	125
ev'ryone	91	everyone	14
ev'rywhere	63	everywhere	11
ev'rything	59	everything	16
'Pon	25	upon	1204
cap'n	14	captain	105
th'	13	the	14,627
ev'rybody	12	everybody	2
ev'ryday	10	everyday	0
m'self	9	myself	45
wand'ring	6	wandering	7
o'er	5	over	382
ne'er	5	never	327

Another use of mock archaic apostrophes are instances where the apostrophe replaces letters via elision, for example, *ev'ryplace, She's a wonderful woman, 's Hepsie, thro'out,* and so on, as well as a gaggle of archaic contractions: *'twas, 'twill, 'twere, 'tis, 'twere, 'twill, 'twould, 'twas, ye're, ye'd, ye've, tha'd, tha're, tha've, thah, thah's, thro',* and so on. To detect this in the corpus, I ran a query and removed modern words from the results.[47] Selection of frequencies of mock-archaic words with single-word modern equivalents are in Table 2.7 and word group modern equivalents in Table 2.8.

The highest frequency words are fairly few: forms of *ev'ry (ev'ryone, ev'rywhere, ev'rything), thro',* and contractions of *it ('tis, 'twas, 'twould, 'twill).* These are present in the voices of the narrator and numerous characters, but some of the lower frequency words, especially forms of *tha* for *thou,* are spoken primarily by Jeremiah Dixon, to portray his Northern English accent.[48] The apostrophe entered the English language in the mid-sixteenth century, and historically was largely used for the elision of vowels.[49] Pynchon's mock-archaic uses of apostrophes mostly take this form.

Before querying similar archaic apostrophe words in the Pynchon oeuvre, the most frequent word in Table 2.7, *ev'ry,* immediately recalls the final poem of

Table 2.8 A selection of mock-archaic contractions in *Mason & Dixon*, with frequency of modern equivalent word groups and contractions. Frequencies include both capitalized and uncapitalized types

Contraction	*Frequency*	Word Group	Frequency	Modern Contraction	Frequency
'tis	*435*	it is	176	—	—
'twas	171	it was	62	—	—
'twould	51	it would	13	—	—
'twill	47	it will	18	it'll	4
ye've	16	you have	58	you've	59
d'ye	15	do you	61	d'you	5
'twere	14	it were	5	—	—
thah's	13	that is	108	that's	117
tha've	12	you have	58	you've	59
ye're	10	you are	70	you're	141
ye'll	10	you will	15	you'll	60
ye're	10	you are	70	you're	141
tha'd	10	you would	25	you'd	57
tha're	9	you are	70	you're	141
ye'd	9	you would	25	you'd	57
tha're	9	you are	70	you're	141
Ah'm	5	I am	142	I'm	152
tha'll	5	that will	12	that'll	2

Gravity's Rainbow, probably the most cited Pynchon passage to contain mock-archaic language:

> There is a Hand to turn the time,
> Though thy Glass today be run,
> Till the Light that hath brought the Towers low
> Find the last poor Pret'rite one …
> Till the Riders sleep by *ev'ry* road,
> All through our crippl'd Zone,
> With a face on *ev'ry* mountainside,
> And a Soul in *ev'ry* stone.…

Now everybody—(*GR*, 760; emphases added)

Although *ev'ry* and *Pret'rite* could include apostrophes to achieve poetic meter, the (inconsistently) capitalized nouns and mock-archaic apostrophes in this oft-quoted poem clearly anticipate the style of *Mason & Dixon*.

A few facts from Pynchon's biography raise the possibility that this is not mere coincidence, and that Pynchon had begun *Mason & Dixon* while writing

Gravity's Rainbow. In a 1964 letter, Pynchon discussed four fictional projects he had in progress; Herman and Weisenburger guess that one was *Lot 49*, one was *The Secret Integration*, the third became *Gravity's Rainbow*, while the "fourth project is anyone's guess. It might well have been a discarded text, or early sketches that wound up in *Mason & Dixon.*"[50] In a 1965 letter, Pynchon declined an invitation by the literary critic and educator Stanley Edgar Hyman to teach literature at Bennington College, "explaining that he had resolved, two or three years earlier, to write three novels at the same time. Pynchon hinted that it was not going well, and called the decision 'a moment of temporary insanity.' But he also said he was 'too stubborn to let any of them go, let alone all of them.' "[51] We may never know which novels Pynchon was referring to in 1965, but it is unlikely that *Vineland*, so reliant on 1980s pop culture and politics, was one of them. Rumors of *Mason & Dixon* were making the rounds as early as 1990, when *Vineland* was published, as confirmed by Salman Rushdie,[52] and, as mentioned, Kachka reports that "a friend remembers [Pynchon] bringing up the subject of 1997's *Mason & Dixon* in 1970."[53] It is, at least, possible that Pynchon wrote the final page of *Gravity's Rainbow* with *Mason & Dixon*'s style already in mind.

On the other hand, querying the Pynchon corpus for *ev'ry* reveals that Pynchon uses it and related words—*ev'rybody, ev'rything*—almost exclusively in songs/poems (in *Gravity's Rainbow*, *Vineland*, and *Inherent Vice*). These poems, moreover, are characterized by numerous stylistic devices meant to evoke vocalized speech (or song), especially informal, idiomatic American English:

> Buggy-whip rigs for just a dollar down, / Hey come along *ev'rybody*, headin' for the Jubi-lee! (*GR*, 378)

> They're *ev'ry* … / Place that ya go, / Down *ev'ry* / Row that ya hoe, / Somehow, ya /

> Just ne-ver know, say it ain't so, (*Vineland*, 224)

> Good-bye and cheeri-o / To my ol' stere-o! / Wohh, / The repossess man, he / Never will be / Hap-py, / Till he's got *ev'rything* I need that / Gets me through. (*IV*, 51; emphases added)

As stated above, *Mason & Dixon* contains hundreds of words with an apostrophe for the elision or deletion of an *e* in <-ed> words, for instance *damn'd, happen'd, seem'd*. Such words are virtually absent in the rest of Pynchon's oeuvre,[54] but the handful of exceptions all appear in songs or immediately following them, for instance:

> Where is the hand of mercy, / Where is the kindly face, / Where in this heedless slaughter / Find we the *promis'd* place? (*ATD*, 50)

> Let him that vizard keep unto his grave, / That vain usurping of an *honour'd* name.; (*Lot 49*, 65; emphases added)

There is, then, at the very least, a textual link between certain forms of archaic words and Pynchon's verse, which in turn often consists of idiomatic, spoken, American English. Aspects of *Mason & Dixon*'s style could therefore be considered within the context of Pynchon's numerous poems, which appear in all of his novels, as well as scholarly discourse that reads Pynchon's prose as verse (discussed in Chapter 6).

2.5 Archaic Pronouns and Verbs

Mason & Dixon is littered with archaic pronouns, with the following frequencies: including *ye* (160), *thee* (109), *thy* (89), *thou* (23), *thine* (7). In addition, there are a handful of archaic irregular verbs: *hath* (12), *hast* (3), *doth* (4).

To provide a very brief history of second person pronouns—*thou, thee, thy*—the distinction between *you* and *thou* emerged during Middle English and developed through Early Modern English.[55] *Thou* often expressed intimacy, solidarity, and/or social equality (similar to French *tu*, German *du*), while *you* encoded power, status, and formality (similar to French *vous*, German *Sie*), although this development was loose, unstable, and pragmatically subtle (unlike the rigid, hierarchical systems of certain European languages). From the late fourteenth century and increasing into the seventeenth century, *you* gradually became the neutral term of singular address, while *thou* was increasingly marked by affectivity (i.e., expressing emotion or feeling). By the end of the seventeenth century, "non-users [of *thou*] outnumber users, and *thou* [wa]s not really a living option in ordinary usage in the eighteenth century."[56] Although *ye* originally meant *you* plural (cf. German *ihr*, English *y'all*), by the sixteenth century, *you* and *ye* were nearly interchangeable.[57] Pynchon's extensive use of *thee, thy*, and *thou* in *Mason & Dixon*, therefore, would seem to be a bit of an anachronism, examples of what the novelist David Mitchell dubbed "bygone-ese," or language which evokes historical English that is "modern enough for readers not to stumble over it, but it's not so modern that the reader kind of thinks this could be out of *House* or *Friends* or something made for TV."[58]

Archaic regular verbs could end in <-est> and <-eth>, for example, *thou needest* and *she needeth*, so I also queried these,[59] and found that *Mason & Dixon* contains twenty-five mock-archaic regular verbs, all ending in <-eth> (i.e., the third person indicative form). During the sixteenth century, there was considerable variation in <-s> and <-th> at the end of verbs,[60] as illustrated by a line from *Henry VI, Part 2*: "With her, that hat*eth* thee and hate*s* us all." Linguists are uncertain as to when, after the 1630s, <-th> verbs died out in speech, as <-th> forms seem to have been written long after it ceased to be commonly spoken.[61] The use of regular archaic verbs ending in <-th> in the time period in which *Mason & Dixon* takes places would again, therefore, be a bit of an anachronism.

Examining the passages in *Mason & Dixon* in which these verbs—for example, *knoweth, keepeth, cometh*—appear, I observe a recurring thematic presence. Over half of the archaic (regular) verbs in this novel occur in sentences invoking God, Biblical quotation, discussion of religious topics, or arguable association with a sacred or profane theme. See Table 2.9.

This proximity between archaic language and sacred/profane thematic language could have many explanations. First, most American writers of Pynchon's generation would obviously associate archaic English with Biblical language. Second, perhaps the sacred/profane theme is spread so widely throughout *Mason & Dixon* that it will appear in proximity to many kinds of words, not only archaic ones. Third (and related), *Mason & Dixon* is narrated by a preacher, Reverend Wicks Cherrycoke, a character who functions much as the biographer James Boswell famously did for Dr. Samuel Johnson. It is possible that the choice of a clergyman narrator leads to an overall increase in religious themed language. Another conjecture is that pairing archaic language with sacred/profane is simply part of Pynchon's greater strategy of opposites. In summary, the most obvious associations with archaic English are the *Bible*, Shakespeare, great books of the past—sacred, grand things. One seemingly notable aspect of Pynchon's style is the pairing of opposites[62] (which should be explored by future computational stylistic Pynchon studies), and the opposite of sacred, grand things is the profane.

2.6 Archaic Language and the Sacred/Profane in Pynchon's Texts

Following these possible connections between archaic verbs, the sacred/profane, and Biblical language in *Mason & Dixon*, I queried a variety of archaic language across all of Pynchon's fiction, and discovered evidence that this is a lifelong

Table 2.9 Twelve out of the twenty-five archaic regular verbs ending in <-eth> in *Mason & Dixon*, with interpretation of thematic associations with the sacred and profane

Type	Context	Thematic Association
runneth	"Piss *runneth* downhill"	Profane
cometh	"with confession apt to flow like the 'water that *cometh* down out of the country' noted in ancient Maps of this place"	Confession (Sacred)
freezeth	"and y' knaah I'd love to sit about and talk of Religion till Hell *freezeth* oahver"	Sacred/Profane
goeth	"*goeth* likewise under the protection of a superior Power,— not, in this case, God, but rather, Business"	Sacred
hangeth	"[God] stretcheth out the north over the empty place, and *hangeth* the earth upon nothing"	Sacred. Direct quotation from Job 25:7, *King James Bible*
knoweth	"*who* but the Time-Keeper *knoweth*?"	Sacred
lendeth	"even as [God] raiseth the storm at sea, *lendeth* the Weather-gage to the dark Dromonds of Piracy"	Sacred
maketh	"*maketh* the involuntary American more than once bless his Exile"	Sacred
provoketh	"even as [God] raiseth the storm at sea, lendeth the Weather-gage to the dark Dromonds of Piracy, *provoketh* theMohawk against the Trader's Post"	Sacred
raiseth	"even as [God] *raiseth* the storm at sea"	Sacred
speaketh	"Serpent, Worm, or Dragon, 'tis all the same to It, for It *speaketh* no Tongue but its own."	Profane
stretcheth	"[God] *stretcheth* out the north over the empty place, and hangeth the earth upon nothing"	Sacred. Direct quotation from Job 25:7, *King James Bible*

trend in Pynchon's writing. Pynchon played with archaic language as early as his juvenilia and short stories. His high school newspaper piece, "Ye Legend of Sir Stupid and the Purple Knight," features a few *thees* and *thous* and "up spake Sir Bushwack." Later, in "Mortality and Mercy in Vienna," *thee* appears once:

> In the army [Siegel] had lived by a golden rule of *Screw the Sergeant before He Screweth Thee*; later in college he had forged meal tickets, instigated protest riots and panty raids, manipulated campus opinion through the school newspaper; and this was the part of him inherited from a mother who at the age of 19 had struggled with her soul one night in a railroad flat somewhere in Hell's Kitchen and, half-drunk on bootleg beer, had ended up refuting Aquinas and quitting the Roman church. ("Mortality and Mercy in Vienna"; emphasis added)

Note how this sentence imitates archaic/Biblical language that incorporates profanity, capitalized pronouns (*He*, in this case, meaning not God but the Sergeant), and, later in the sentence, invokes an infernally named locale, Hell's Kitchen, as well as the Roman Church (neither of which are mentioned elsewhere in the story), and caps it off with refuting a saint and apostasy. It is almost as though the deliberate use of archaic/Biblical stylistic elements somehow conjured further, unrelated sacred/profane associations.

In *V.*, *thy* and *thine* appear five times, in one sacred context and a number of profane and sexual contexts. *Thy* is used in the translation of an Egyptian phrase, again invoking Biblical language: "My own mother is alive and well. God willing will continue so. But if she is to be taken from me (or me from her) *ikun li trid Int*: Thy will be done" (*V.*, 341). *Thy* also appears in the translation of another Egyptian phrase, by a young woman, which inspires the Egyptian anarchist scoundrel Yusef to think some kind of sexual thought about her:

> "Oh," she smiled: "Oh thank you. Leltak leben." May thy night be white as milk.
>
> As thy belly … enough. She bobbed off […]. (*V.*, 64)

Later, the most overtly profane character in the novel, Pig Bodine, appears to assault the character Paola and, when pulled off of her, succinctly pairs archaic English with profanity: " 'Up thine,' snarled Pig, 'with turpentine' " (*V.*, 400). *V.* also contains an archaic verb in a Biblical quote.[63]

Gravity's Rainbow continues the trend of pairing archaic language with the sacred/profane. A few *thee*s and *thou*s appear in the direct speech, or in proximity, of a character who perhaps exceeds Pig Bodine in profanity, Major Duane Marvy, who twice exclaims, "What in thee hell" (*GR*, 606–7). Here, *thee* is the phoneticization of Marvy's thick American accent, not, on the face of it, a Biblical or Shakespearean *thee*, but *thee*'s repeated pairing with *hell*, in the context of Pynchon's many pairings of archaic language with sacred/profane themes, raises eyebrows. A character named Clayton Chiclitz, who rides along with Marvy, also yells from their shared car, "Fuck not with the Kid, lest instead of fucker thou become fuckee," (*GR*, 559), closely mirroring the line from "Mortality and Mercy in Vienna" cited above. A parody of a wedding vow, "unto thee I pledge my trough," is delivered when Slothrop, dressed in a pig costume, believes for a moment that he will be forced to marry a sow (*GR*, 576). Finally, archaic language paired with the sacred/profane appears in some of the novel's most opaque passages, after Slothrop "has begun to thin, to scatter," and forget things immediately after experiencing them:

> No, but even That only flickers now briefly across a bit of Slothropian lobe-terrain, and melts into its surface, vanishing. So here passes for him one more negligence … and likewise *groweth* his *Preterition* sure…. (*GR*, 509; emphasis added)

However this is read, here again is an archaic verb paired with the religious theme of preterite/elect.

In *V.*, *Lot 49*, and *Gravity's Rainbow*, archaic pronouns and verbs appear in pastiche poems/songs/plays that mimic archaic modes, and some of these passages relate to the sacred/profane/Biblical. In *V.*, in the patriotic poem of a Maltese poet, "Britain and Crown, we join *thy* swelling guard / To drive the brute invader from our strand." (*V.*, 328; emphasis added throughout this paragraph). In *Lot 49*, all instances of *thee*, *thy*, and *hath* are in a song and lines from the fictional play "The Courier's Tragedy." Yoyodyne employees sing a company song "to the tune of 'Aura Lee'": "Yoyodyne, Yoyodyne, / Contracts flee *thee* yet. / DOD has shafted *thee*, / Out of spite, I'll bet" (77). "Aura Lee" was an American Civil War song about a maiden that contains archaic language such as *spake*, *thine*, and *thy*. "The Courier's Tragedy," a pastiche of Jacobean revenge theatre, includes a macabre scene where Ercole captures and tortures Domenico and tears his tongue out:

> sets the tongue aflame and waving it around like a madman concludes the act by screaming,
>
> > *Thy* pitiless unmanning is most meet,
> > Thinks Ercole the zany Paraclete.
> > Descended this malign, Unholy Ghost,
> > Let us begin *thy* frightful Pentecost. (*Lot 49*, 61; emphases added)

Once again, archaic language is paired with the sacred turned profane, the Holy Ghost made Unholy, the Christian holiday of Pentecost transformed into a time for barbaric acts. The sea chanty of the black market ship captain Frau Gnahb in *Gravity's Rainbow* is yet another example:

> I'm the Pirate Queen of the Baltic Run, and nobody fucks with me—
> And those who've tried are bones and skulls, and lie beneath the sea.
> And the little fish like messengers swim in and out their eyes,
> Singing, "*Fuck ye not* with Gory Gnahb and her desperate enterprise!"
> I'll tangle with a battleship, I'll massacre a sloop,
> I've *sent a hundred souls to hell* in one relentless swoop— (*GR*, 497; emphases added)

Here again, archaic language is paired with profanity, followed closely by the sending of souls to hell. The few examples of archaic language in *Vineland* again display this pattern:

> Roy kept a prop Bible on his desk, useful when he needed to get along with the born-agains in the Agency. He opened it and pretended to read. "*Harken* unto me, read *thou* my lips, for *verily* I say that wheresoever the CIA *putteth* in its meathooks upon the world, there also are to be found those substances which God may have created but the U.S. Code *hath* decided to control." (*Vineland*, 354; emphases added)

Roy is referring to drugs, in mock-Biblical language, from a prop Bible—Pynchon, impishly blasphemous.

These many examples provide evidence that *Mason & Dixon* continued and expanded what had been a lifelong stylistic-slash-thematic trend in Pynchon's writing: to pair the stylistic elements of archaic, often Biblical English with profanity and the theme of sacred/profane. After *Mason & Dixon*, Pynchon continued to associate archaic English with the sacred/profane, although there are only six passages across *Against the Day* and *Bleeding Edge* that contain similar archaic pronouns and verbs (*Inherent Vice*, as far as I can detect, contains zero). In *Against the Day*, in addition to a handful of *thou, hast, hath* when invoking Biblical themes, I locate only one archaic regular verb, *bringeth*, in the novel's first pages, which could be read as a spilling over of the style of Pynchon's previous novel, *Mason & Dixon*. As the airship flies over Chicago in 1893, archaic language again is immediately followed by sacred imagery:

> the buildings of the leagues of city lying downwind retreated, like children into sleep which *bringeth* not reprieve from the day. In the Stockyards, workers coming off shift, overwhelmingly of the Roman faith, able to detach from earth and blood for a few precious seconds, looked up at the airship in wonder, imagining a detachment of not necessarily helpful angels. (*ATD*, 10; emphasis added)

Bleeding Edge employs archaic pronouns and verbs in a scant two passages. First, where Pynchon parodies the language of the Ten Commandments when describing Maxine's use of hacker tools, paired with a sacred/profane dichotomy: "not exactly falling within Generally Accepted Accounting Practices, such as thou shalt not hack into anybody's bank account, thou shalt leave that sort of thing for the FBI" (*BE*, 173). The second passage occurs when Maxine pretends to be an employee of internet security firm Hashslingrz. While on the phone, Maxine invokes the "guardian spirit" of an old high school drama teacher:

> Mrs. Plibbler, *high-school drama teacher from hell*, once again must Maxine *invoke thee* here as guardian spirit of fraud police accredited and otherwise. "Oh hi, I'm calling from hashslingrz? Is this Mr. Larday?" (*BE*, 216; emphasis added)

Note how the archaic pronoun *thee* is paired in the same sentence, as in "Mortality and Mercy in Vienna" (published some fifty-five years before) with an infernal reference that is a completely extraneous detail. Here, the drama teacher, who is never mentioned before or after in *Bleeding Edge*, is "from hell," just as in Pynchon's short story, discussed above, *thee* was paired with an unnecessary reference to Hell's Kitchen.

2.7 Archaic Stylistics in *Mason & Dixon*: Conclusion

In summary, Pynchon has employed creative use of capitalization throughout his career, to achieve a wide variety of effects, and my survey of capitalization challenges some existing scholarly commentary. The capitalization throughout *Mason & Dixon* should be considered within this wider context of capitalization in Pynchon's oeuvre, both for critical purposes and in terms of how to normalize the novel for corpus stylistic study. Many iconic concepts in Pynchon's writing—*V.*, *The Situation*, *W.A.S.T.E.*, *Rocket*, *Us/Them*, the *Tube*, *Time*—should be considered as aspects of the writer's lifelong use of capitalization for stylistic purposes.

Mason & Dixon toys with alternate histories and alternate worlds, and numerous scholars have explored aspects relating to time and the way the ostensibly historical novel plays with speculation and invention. Douglas Keesey, surveying the novel's reception, noted that "Pynchon's novel shimmers between 'anachronism' and 'chronicle' as between alternative and official histories, with 'what could have been' or 'might yet be' challenging 'the way it way' and 'must be.' "[64] McHale explored this extensively by highlighting the importance of subjunctive passages in *Mason & Dixon* and the subjunctive as theme. The subjunctive mood, in linguistics, is the verb form used to express a wish, suggestion, or a condition that is contrary to fact, a hypothetical rather than an actual situation, for example, "if only I *were* a better basketball player," or "it was suggested that she *wait* until next week." Subjunctive sentences, McHale argues, build upon one another in *Mason & Dixon* to achieve a portrayal of "the American West as subjunctive space, the space of wish and desire, of the hypothetical and the counterfactual, of speculation and possibility."[65] Chapter 73, for instance, is one long hypothetical, speculating on what might have happened had Mason and Dixon continued journeying West.

Above, I traced how some of the archaic stylistic devices are themselves, for the time period *Mason & Dixon* is set in, anachronistic. Many commentators have named and interpreted the novel's more explicit anachronisms, references from *Star Trek* to James Brown to string theory. Keesey writes that "what first appear to be comical anachronisms may turn out to be factual pointers to alternative histories."[66] Elizabeth Jane Wall Hinds argues that "with the pervasive anachronisms, Pynchon further disrupts [...] the Enlightenment project of regularising, measuring, and ordering."[67] *Mason & Dixon*'s style itself, then, can be added to the subjunctive spaces of *Mason & Dixon* that Keesey mentions and that McHale and others explore, as stylistic markers of a hypothetical, counterfactual English. Perhaps every invented, mock-archaic word and usage could be read to evoke the counter-Enlightenment theme.

More generally, the inconsistencies and anachronisms of *Mason & Dixon*'s archaic stylistic devices fit into the greatest Pynchon theme of all: order frustrated, systems shown as false, "the rage for order is persistently denied," as Schaub put it.[68] In *Mason & Dixon*, inconsistent capitalization could be read as Pynchon intentionally frustrating his own stylistic device, while inconsistent use of <-ick> spelling for mock-historical effect (sometimes writing *musick*, while other times *music*) and the censored words that nonetheless reveal their meaning (such as *d——'d* for *damned*) are further examples. Tracing the use of mock-archaic apostrophes in *Mason & Dixon* and the Pynchon oeuvre reveals a connection with Pynchon's poetry. Closer readings of the archaic words in Pynchon's texts, meanwhile, reveals a correlation with the sacred/profane theme. Finally, this chapter demonstrates that query may prove effective, if imperfect, in locating instances of irregular capitalization, archaic words and spelling across over 1.7 million word tokens in the Pynchon corpus.

Having presented the first extensive analysis of style in *Mason & Dixon*, within the context of Pynchon's oeuvre, future work may wish to further contextualize these stylistic devices within the history of English fiction. Pynchon's stylistic experiment in *Mason & Dixon* could be compared with, for instance, the most-mock-historical prose of William Golding's *The Inheritors*, Mitchell's *Cloud Atlas*, Alan Moore's *Voice of the Fire*, or many others: which rules authors set for themselves, with what rigor, and how archaic spelling, lexis, and punctuation function in these texts in comparison with Pynchon's.

Two potentially fruitful comparisons are from the canon of encyclopedic narratives introduced by Mendelson: *Ulysses* and *Moby-Dick*.[69] The "Oxen of the Sun" episode in Joyce's *Ulysses* famously narrates the birth of a child in successive pastiches of periods of historical English, and Mendelson compellingly contrasts Joyce's and Pynchon's portrayals of diachronic change in language:

> Joyce provides a history of language in terms of an historical embryology of style in his "Oxen of the Sun" chapter of *Ulysses*. His vision of linguistic history is deterministic and pessimistic, treating the development of language as unconscious and unchosen. Pynchon provides a *political* history of language, an account of the deliberate introduction by Soviet authorities of a written alphabet for the Kirghiz language in central Asia, a language which had earlier been spoken.[70]

Without commenting on these claims, a larger scope of inquiry could be explored. The handful of pages in which the Kirghiz alphabet is treated in *Gravity's Rainbow* are rich interpretive territory, but interpreting Pynchon's conception of language and its history may be better examined via the language of Pynchon's oeuvre, which just so happens to evoke or parody large swathes of historical American English: eighteenth century (*M&D*), c. 1900 (*ATD*), the Second World War era (*GR*), 1950s (short stories, parts of *V.*), 1960s (*Lot 49, IV*), 1980s (*Vineland*), and post-2000s (*BE*). If Pynchon had actually written a rumored novel on the Civil War,[71] his oeuvre would even more closely approach a survey—or "birth" and "life"—of the history of American English, not dissimilar to Joyce's "genealogy" of British and Irish English in "Oxen of the Sun." In a recent paper, I argued that Pynchon references Joyce extensively in *Gravity's Rainbow*—including possible references to the "Oxen" episode"[72]—and the archaic language discussed in this chapter would play an important role in any comparison of Joyce's and Pynchon's histories of English.

   Like *Ulysses*, Melville's *Moby Dick* is among the novels most often mentioned in scholarly and popular[73] commentary on *Gravity's Rainbow*, and extensive intertextual readings of Melville's and Pynchon's *magnum opera* have focused on not only the encyclopedic genre, but, *inter alia*, comparison of narrative structure and the treatment of history.[74] Archaic language washes in and out of Melville's *Moby Dick*, and Captain Ahab's foregrounded use of archaic speech has often been noted, although a full accounting of how the "archaic Elizabethan rhetoric Melville has put in Ahab's mouth," in the words of Thomas Woodson,[75] departs or contrasts with the language of Ahab's crewmen, Melville's other fiction and nonfiction, and literary English of the mid-nineteenth century or prior has yet to be written. As with Pynchon, I am surprised by how relatively little stylistic attention has been paid to Melville's texts, but in a 1960 reading of *Moby Dick*, (the somewhat Pynchonesquely named) Merrel D. Clubb Jr.

traced the novel's use of the second personal pronoun—*you, thou, ye*—finding that "the usual definite is *you* in all ordinary description and narration" but that "by far the common usage of metaphysical or symbolic discussions is *thou*."[76] Melville's use of *thou* in elevated metaphysical and symbolic discussions presages Pynchon's use of archaic spelling in relation to the sacred and profane, even if the likely explanation—the fact that most American authors' first and most formative acquaintances with archaic language have long been *The Bible* and Shakespeare—is obvious.

Although the archaic language in *Mason & Dixon* could extensively be compared and contrasted with many texts, my third and final suggestion for future work is Barth's *The Sot-Weed Factor*, with which it bears a number of similarities: both are postmodern, historical, parodic, encyclopedic fictions featuring Transatlantic adventure and employ archaic lexis, syntax, and punctuation. The archaic stylistic devices that Barth employs—period slang, elision via apostrophe, *Thou* and *'Twas* and *ye*—are far less extensive than in *Mason & Dixon*, but all of the stylistic devices examined in this chapter may be found in *The Sot-Weed Factor*. Intertextual readings have been explored by critics, most thoroughly by Amy J. Elias, who notes that these novels "cover roughly the same historical territory," and that "both recuperate an eighteenth-century context that metafictionally rebounds to the cultural politics of the present, and [...] both are self-reflexive about the First World colonial gaze."[77] Earl Rovit claims to vouch for the rigor of Barth's stylistic adherence to historical English: Barth "elects to write his novel in the eighteenth-century manner, using no words, images, illusions, metaphors, or other figures of speech not current and available to the English novelist writing in Fielding's time. It is possible that here again there may be minor transgressions, but I did not find any."[78] It would be interesting to confirm this via, for instance, Eve's method of detecting anachronistic words in historical fiction.[79] Barth's novel is inspired by the life and works of the minor English poet Ebenezer Cooke—the title is taken from one of Cooke's poems—and Manfred Pütz notes that "many passages in [Barth's] novel are either repetitions of, or more frequently, elaborations on the material presented in the [Cooke's] poem."[80] While scholars have unearthed many of these through close reading, locating these borrowings would be an ideal application for text reuse detection software. Although critical and popular interest in Barth's texts has waned in recent years (with *The Sot-Weed Factor* now out of print in the United States), the text provides plenty of material for future comparison with *Mason & Dixon*'s style.

Mason & Dixon repeatedly plays with the subjunctive—*might* and *may*—vague words which will be mentioned in the next chapter, which considers Pynchon's oeuvre in terms of ambiguity and vagueness.

Notes

1 David Crystal, *The Cambridge Encyclopedia of the English Language*, 2nd ed. (Cambridge: Cambridge University Press, 2003), 65.

2 A. Hughlett Mason, *The Journal of Charles Mason and Jeremiah Dixon* (Philadelphia: American Philosophical Society, 1969).

3 Clerc, Mason & Dixon *& Pynchon*, 60–74.

4 Words are only included in these results when the word is used as a noun and not another part of speech, as verified manually.

5 Clerc, Mason & Dixon *& Pynchon*, 90.

6 William B. Millard, "Delineations of Madness and Science: *Mason & Dixon*, Pynchonian Space and the Snovian Disjunction," in *American Postmodernity: Essays on the Recent Fiction of Thomas Pynchon*, ed. Ian D. Copestake (New York: Peter Lang, 2003), 103–4.

7 E.g., John O. Stark, *Pynchon's Fictions, Thomas Pynchon and the Literature of Information* (Athens: Ohio University Press, 1980), 37.

8 Millard, "Delineations of Madness and Science," 104.

9 Ibid., 103.

10 Alan Ramón Clinton, *Intuitions in Literature, Technology, and Politics* (New York: Palgrave MacMillan, 2012), 42.

11 Schaub, *Pynchon: The Voice of Ambiguity*, 15.

12 For more on *Truth*, see Margaret Lynd, "Situated Fictions. Reading the California Novels against Thomas Pynchon's Narrative World," in *Pynchon's California*, ed. Scott McClintock and John Miller (Iowa City: University of Iowa Press, 2014), 17. ("The very idea of a capitalized 'Truth' is precisely what all of Pynchon's work undermines in multiple ways").

13 Charles Hohmann, *Thomas Pynchon's* Gravity's Rainbow, *A Study of Its Conceptual Structure and of Rilke's Influence* (New York: Peter Lang, 1986), 374–5. Reprinted in Charles Hohmann, *Angel and Rocket: Pynchon's* Gravity's Rainbow *and Rilke's* Duino Elegies (Norderstedt: Books on Demand GmbH, 2009), 125.

14 Luc Herman and Steven Weisenburger, Gravity's Rainbow, *Domination, and Freedom* (Athens: University of Georgia Press, 2013), 61–2.

15 Ware et al., "Pages 3–7," *Pynchon Wiki*, accessed May 12, 2017, http://gravitys-rainbow.pynchonwiki.com/wiki/index.php?title=Pages_3-7. Referencing David

Cowart, *Thomas Pynchon and the Dark Passages of History* (Athens: University of Georgia Press, 2011).

16 Sample CQP query: [word!="[\.!:;\?;,"()\[\]—""\"*]"][enpos="PP" & word="[A-Z] [a-z]+"].

17 As just one example, in *V.*, jazz fans who miss the great Charlie Parker say, as well as write in graffiti, "Bird Lives" (*V.*, 56). Since an invented slogan, especially a written one, could be expected to be capitalized, I did not consider this an example of irregular capitalization.

18 For critical issues regarding Google Books, see e.g., Mark Liberman, "The Google Books Settlement," *Language Log*, August 28, 2009, http://languagelog.ldc. upenn.edu/nll/?p=1698; James Somers, "Torching the Modern-Day Library of Alexandria," *The Atlantic*, April 20, 2017, https://www.theatlantic.com/technology/ archive/2017/04/the-tragedy-of-google-books/523320/.

19 James Baldwin, *The Fire Next Time* (New York: Vintage International, 1993), 89–90.

20 Gerald Howard, "Pynchon From A to V: Gerald Howard on *Gravity's Rainbow*," *Bookforum* 12:2 (Summer 2005), http://www.bookforum.com/archive/ sum_05/ pynchon.html.

21 Schaub, *Pynchon: The Voice of Ambiguity*, 8; Simon de Bourcier, *Pynchon and Relativity: Narrative Time in Thomas Pynchon's Later Novels* (London: Continuum Literary Studies, 2012), 188; Mario Faraone, "Traveling and Spying into Baedeker's Land," in *Dream Tonight of Peacock Tails: Essays on the Fiftieth Anniversary of Thomas Pynchon's* V., ed. Paolo Simonetti and Umberto Rossi (Newcastle upon Tyne: Cambridge Scholars, 2015), 69.

22 Tina Käkelä-Puumala, *Other Side of This Life: Death, Value and Social Being in Thomas Pynchon's Fiction* (Helsinki: Yliopistopaino, 2007), 76–7.

23 Shawn Smith, *Pynchon and History: Metahistorical Rhetoric and Postmodern Narrative Form in the Novels of Thomas Pynchon* (New York: Routledge, 2005), 98; Fran Mason, *Historical Dictionary of Postmodernist Literature and Theater*, 2nd ed. (New York: Rowman & Littlefield, 2017), 377.

24 McHale, *Constructing Postmodernism*, 119–20.

25 Sean M. Carswell, "The *Vineland* Guide to Contemporary Rebellion," *Orbit: Writing Around Pynchon* 1:1 (2012): 4.

26 Paul Rayson, "Matrix: A Statistical Method and Software Tool for Linguistic Analysis through Corpus Comparison," PhD diss., Lancaster University (2003). Paul Rayson, "Wmatrix: a Web-Based Corpus Processing Environment, Computing Department" (Lancaster: Lancaster University, 2009).

27 Inger H. Dalsgaard, "Readers and Trespassers: Time Travel, Orthogonal Time, and Alternative Figurations of Time in *Against the Day*," in *Pynchon's Against the Day: A Corrupted Pilgrim's Guide*, ed. Jeffrey Severs and Christopher Leise (Newark: University of Delaware Press, 2006), 115–37; Justin St. Clair, "Borrowed

Time: Thomas Pynchon's *Against the Day* and the Victorian Fourth Dimension," *Science Fiction Studies* 38:1 (2011): 46–66; de Bourcier, *Pynchon and Relativity*; Jeeshan Gazi, "Mapping the Metaphysics of the Multiverse in Pynchon's *Against the Day*," *Critique: Studies in Contemporary Fiction* 57:1 (2016): 80–93.

28 Alexander Nazaryan, "The Turbulent Genius of David Foster Wallace," *Newsweek*, January 8, 2015, http://www.newsweek.com/2015/01/16/turbulent-genius-david-foster-wallace-297688.html. For a critique of Wallace's prescriptive grammarianism that includes capitalization, see Steve Dodson, "David Foster Wallace Demolished," *Language Hat*, accessed September 1, 2019, http://languagehat.com/david-foster-wallace-demolished/. ("Sure, it's a minor matter that [Wallace] misuses a capital letter in 'Wedgied'—except that the only point of his using it (since nobody else ever has or ever will, unless they foolishly copy it from him) is to make a point of his extreme accuracy in the tiniest of matters … and he gets it wrong.")

29 "A few geographical and other terms have been modernised" in the transcription published by the American Philosophical Society, so it is unclear if <-ick> words are present in the manuscript, held at the National Archives in Washington, DC, Mason, *The Journal of Charles Mason and Jeremiah Dixon*, 1.

30 D. G. Scragg, *A History of English Spelling* (Manchester: Manchester University Press, 1974), 80.

31 Andreas Fischer and Peter Schneider, "The Dramatick Disappearance of the <-ick> Spelling," in *Text Types and Corpora: Studies in Honor of Udo Fries*, eds. Andreas Fischer, Gunnel Tottie, and Hans Martin Lehmann (Tübingen: Gunter Narr Verlag, 2002), 147. As to *why* <-ick> spelling disappeared, Fischer and Schneider question prevailing scholarly opinion that American spelling reformer Noah Webster (1758–1843) was somehow responsible.

32 Ibid., 149.

33 CQP query: [word=".*ick.*"].

34 Fischer and Schneider, "The Dramatick Disappearance of the <-ick> Spelling," 142.

35 Some additional examples include "Some twenty or thirty musicians, by the sound of it,—new music, advanced music, as far from the Oboick Reveries of [Baroque composers]" (*M&D*, 413); "Thoughts that in my Line of work are too often denounc'd as 'Stukeleyesque,' or at the least 'Stonehengickal'" (*M&D*, 595).

36 "devil, n.," *OED Online*, Oxford University Press, accessed April 30, 2017, http://0-www.oed.com.catalogue.libraries.london.ac.uk/view/Entry/51468?rskey=ROxxpX&result=1&isAdvanced=false.

37 Mason, *The Journal of Charles Mason and Jeremiah Dixon*, 67.

38 "damned, adj.," *OED Online*, Oxford University Press, accessed April 30, 2017, http://0-www.oed.com.catalogue.libraries.london.ac.uk/view/Entry/47071?redirectedFrom=damned.

39 Anthony Trollope, *The Bertrams*, volume III (London: Chapman & Hall, 1859), 118, 122, 143, 275, 278.

40 Anthony Trollope, *The Way We Live Now* (New York: Harper & Brothers, 1875), e.g., 99, 152, 171, 181.

41 Daniel Defoe, *Robinson Crusoe* (London: MacMillan, 1866), 356.

42 Charlotte Brontë, "Editor's Preface to the New Edition of *Wuthering Heights*," *Wuthering Heights* (Edinburgh: Turnbull and Spears, 1850), xxiv.

43 Keith Houston, *Shady Characters: Ampersands, Interrobangs and Other Typographical Curiosities* (London: Particular Books, 2013), 158.

44 Quoted and discussed in Lisa Getelman, *Paper Knowledge: Toward a Media History of Documents* (Durham: Duke University Press, 2014), 27.

45 CQP query: [word=".*'d.*"%c].

46 *I'd, you'd, he'd, you'd, we'd, they'd*, etc., as well as *tha'd* and *ye'd*, which are measured separately.

47 CQP query: [word=".*'.*"%c & word!=".*'d"%c & word!=".*'s"%c & word!=".*'ve"%c].

48 Contractions of *tha* (*tha're, tha'll, tha've*) in Jeremiah Dixon's dialogue, for instance, may be found in such historical sources of Northern English as Richard Blakeborough, *Wit, Character, Folklore and Customs of the North Riding of Yorkshire* (London: Henry Frowde, 1898).

49 Vivian Salmon, "Orthography and Punctuation," in *The Cambridge History of the English Language*, volume III, ed. Roger Lass (Cambridge: Cambridge University Press, 2008), 40.

50 Herman and Weisenburger, Gravity's Rainbow, *Domination, and Freedom*, 18.

51 Scott Lemee, "You Hide, They Seek," *Inside Higher Ed*, November 15, 2006, https://www.insidehighered.com/views/2006/11/15/you-hide-they-seek.

52 Salman Rushdie, "Still Crazy after All These Years," *New York Times*, January 14, 1990, http://www.nytimes.com/books/97/05/18/reviews/pynchon-vineland.html.

53 Kachka, "On the Thomas Pynchon Trail."

54 CQP query: [word=".*'d"%c & word!="I'd"%c & word!="you'd"%c & word!="he'd"%c & word!="she'd"%c & word!="they'd"%c & word!="there'd"%c & word!="who'd"%c & word!="it'd"%c].

55 This paragraph summarizes Roger Lass, "Phonology and Morphology," in *The Cambridge History of the English Language*, Volume III, ed. Roger Lass (Cambridge: Cambridge University Press, 2008), 149–53.

56 Ibid., 153.

57 Ibid., 154.

58 David Mitchell, "Interview with David Mitchell," interview by Carolyn Kellogg, *Goodreads*, July 5, 2019, https://www.goodreads.com/interviews/show/537.David_Mitchell.

59 CQP queries: [word=".*est"], [word=".*eth"].

60 Lass, "Phonology and Morphology," 163.

61 Ibid.

62 This stylistic tendency is discussed most extensively in Schaub, *Pynchon: The Voice of Ambiguity*.

63 "Scrawled on the walls were occasional quotes from the Gospels, Latin tags (Agnus Dei, qui tollis peccata mundi, dona nobis pacem—Lamb of God, who taketh away the sins of the world, grant us peace)" (*V.*, 123).

64 Keesey, "*Mason & Dixon* on the Line: A Reception Study," 171.

65 Brian McHale, "Mason & Dixon in the Zone or, a Brief Poetics of Pynchon-Space," in *Pynchon and Mason & Dixon*, ed. Brooke Horvath and Irving Malin (Newark: University of Delaware Press, 2000), 44.

66 Keesey, "Mason & Dixon on the Line: A Reception Study," 171.

67 Elizabeth Jane Wall Hinds, "Sari, Sorry, and the Vortex of History: Calendar Reform, Anachronism, and Language Change in *Mason & Dixon*," *American Literary History* 12:1–2 (2000): 197–8.

68 Schaub, *Pynchon: The Voice of Ambiguity*, x.

69 Edward Mendelson, "Encyclopedic Narrative: From Dante to Pynchon," *MLN* 91:6 (1976): 1267.

70 Ibid., 1273.

71 Rushdie, "Still Crazy after All These Years."

72 Erik Ketzan, "Clash of the Modern/Postmodern Titans? James Joyce in *Gravity's Rainbow*," *English Studies* 101:3 (2020): 333–56.

73 Ed Finn, "The Social Lives of Books: Literary Networks in Contemporary American Fiction," PhD diss., Stanford University, 2011, 63.

74 E.g., Richard Hardack, "'From Whaling to Armaments to Food': Melville's, Pynchon's, and Wedde's Economies of the Pacific," *Critique: Studies in Contemporary Fiction* 54:2 (2013).

75 Thomas Woodson, "Ahab's Greatness: Prometheus as Narcissus," *ELH* 33:3 (1966): 351–69.

76 Merrel D. Clubb, Jr., "The Second Personal Pronoun in *Moby-Dick*," *American Speech* 35:4 (1960): 256.

77 Amy J. Elias, *Sublime Desire: History and Post-1960s Fiction* (Baltimore: Johns Hopkins University Press, 2001), 232, 223.

78 Earl Rovit, "The Novel as Parody: John Barth," *Critique: Studies in Contemporary Fiction* 6:2 (1963): 82.

79 Eve, *Close Reading with Computers*.

80 Manfred Pütz, "John Barth's *The Sot-Weed Factor*: The Pitfalls of Mythopoesis," *Twentieth Century Literature* 22:4 (1976): 462.

3

Pynchon, "The Voice of Ambiguity," Quantified

"Let me be unambiguous," [Pynchon] said. "I prefer not to be photographed."
—statement to CNN by Thomas Pynchon[1]

In *Pynchon: The Voice of Ambiguity*, Thomas Schaub argued that Pynchon's use of ambiguity is "the result of an intentional stylistic strategy," and that ambiguity "may well be [Pynchon's] most distinctive achievement as a writer."[2] Deborah L. Madsen writes that Schaub's text "is still an essential resource because ambiguity remains the single greatest obstacle for the reader of Pynchon. That is to say, ambiguity characterizes every aspect, formal and thematic, of Pynchon's narrative project."[3] Any groundwork of Pynchon's style, then, must begin to contend with Pynchon's stylistic ambiguity (and its closely related concept, vagueness), which this chapter approaches via close and distant reading. Working "from the ground up," this chapter begins with the query and close reading of the word *ambiguous* in Pynchon's texts and comparison corpora. This reveals that Pynchon employs *ambiguous* and its word forms more frequently than four comparison corpora, and, turning to close reading, the word *ambiguous* is used more broadly semantically than in the comparison texts. Following this context, I query vagueness words, primarily via the methodology of Robert Hogenraad, which quantifies ambiguity/vagueness in texts by querying an existing dictionary of hundreds of (presumably) vague and ambiguous words and phrases. From these experiments, it emerges that by numerous measures, Pynchon's texts are indeed higher in vague/ambiguous lexis than all or almost all comparison texts, a result which confirms the attention to ambiguity in Pynchon's texts by critics, exemplified by Schaub's moniker for Pynchon as "the Voice of Ambiguity." These experiments also provide evidence of a trend in Pynchon's "late style": by certain measures, Pynchon's use of vague lexis (especially Pynchon's "preferred" vague

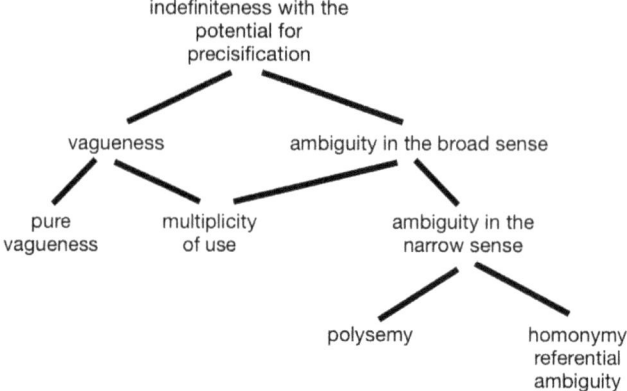

Figure 3.1 Manfred Pinkal's typology of the indefinite.

lexis, or vague words Pynchon uses significantly more often than all comparison texts) is clearly increasing.

Examining ambiguity/vagueness in literary texts is a difficult task for many reasons, not least because the scholars who most closely engage with the topic, linguists, may conceive of ambiguity/vagueness more broadly than literary scholars such as Schaub. Linguists have suggested definitions and complex typologies,[4] for instance Manfred Pinkal, who proposed a typology of the indefinite that formally distinguishes ambiguity and vagueness (Figure 3.1).[5]

Pinkal also writes that "semantic indefiniteness and contextual fluctuations of sense are essential, omnipresent properties of natural language."[6] In other words, an exhaustive linguistic analysis of ambiguity and vagueness in Pynchon would not only have to wrestle with the finer gradations of "precisification," but would be an endless task, as even the simplest and most common words—"omnipresent" words such as *he, she, green, fast*—are inherently "vague" and "ambiguous" as these terms are defined by some linguists. When Schaub labeled Pynchon "The Voice of Ambiguity," however, he employed "ambiguous" differently—more narrowly—than linguists might define it, so that one could argue distinctions between "linguistic ambiguity" and "literary ambiguity."

3.1 Ambiguity in Pynchon Studies

Critical to Schaub's *The Voice of Ambiguity* is the assertion that "Pynchon's stylistic devices [...] have specific thematic goals, and both are inseparable from each other."[7] These thematic goals include political, moral, semantic, and epistemological ambiguity, eschewing discrete concepts for vague or ambiguous shades of gray; "The confidence of unity," Schaub writes, "has been suddenly replaced by a bewildering 'multiplicity.' "[8] Schaub discusses how these thematic goals are effected by repeated use of ambiguous/vague stylistic devices, including pronouns, verb tense, and conditional words (such as "seemed," "as is," "perhaps," and "either … or"), and the latter will be investigated closely in this chapter. Not all writers are strongly associated with a particular rhetorical strategy. As Harold Bloom writes, "we do not associate Shakespeare with any particular rhetorical trope, unlike Marlowe, who is synonymous with hyperbole."[9] Yet just as Marlowe is synonymous with hyperbole and Rabelais is so known for list-making that scholars refer to "Rabelaisian lists,"[10] this chapter proceeds from the assumption that, following Schaub and Madsen, ambiguity/vagueness is a fundamental device of Pynchon's style.

Schaub described Pynchon's ambiguity with numerous terms: "Pynchon seeks a form of expression that conforms to *the lack of formal certainties* in the world he is describing; Pynchon's books […] establish for the reader *an intentional and strict uncertainty*" (3, 4; emphases added). Schaub's description of ambiguity in Pynchon generally follows the dictionary definition: Sense 1 of AMBIGUOUS adj. in the *OED* is defined as "doubtful, questionable; indistinct, obscure, not clearly defined."[11] Yet Schaub also sees contradictions as an important component of ambiguity: Pynchon's "fiction aspires to the condition of simultaneity, in which contradictory possibilities co-exist,"[12] which Schaub wrote in 1981 but which presciently describes *Against the Day*, which plays extensively with bilocations and multiple worlds.

In other Pynchon studies, Schaub's emphasis on the political and moral dimensions of ambiguity has been echoed by, for example, Joanna Freer, who summarizes the political and moral effects of Pynchon's "ambivalence" as a "refusal to endorse any single viewpoint without qualifications, […] an important reflection of his anarchic political philosophy, and indeed functions as a structural principle in his narratives. All of Pynchon's commentaries have an open-ended quality; there are very few, if any, final judgements in his work. Rather than asserting one or another particular perspective, Pynchon promotes habits of critical thought."[13] In addition, Pynchon's ambiguity lies at the heart of many aspects of the postmodernism ascribed to him by scholars. McHale, for instance, notes that "Pynchon's fiction relentlessly questions and undermines all of the West's master narratives" and discusses the double-coding, irony and pastiche, figurative worlds, and contradictions of postmodernism and postmodernity evident in Pynchon's texts.[14] McHale's general thesis in *Postmodernist Fiction* is that the "dominant" of postmodernist fiction is ontological, relating to multiple worlds and multiple realities, and ambiguity underlies most of these: ambiguity wielded against declarative statements, narratives, and single worlds, as well as ambiguity that embraces contradictions.

While Schaub mentions specific linguistic/stylistic devices which Pynchon deploys to achieve ambiguity, stylistic ambiguity/vagueness in Pynchon's texts can be explored much further by mixed-methods computational and close reading analyses, especially as Schaub's commentary was limited to Pynchon's novels published at the time of his study, 1981.

3.1.1 "Ambiguous"

Pynchon creates ambiguity through, most obviously, the use of the word *ambiguous*. Sense 2 of *ambiguous* in the *OED* refers to "words or other indications," and Pynchon sometimes uses *ambiguous* in this sense: "an ambiguous footnote" (*Lot 49*, 153); "had seen no definite trace of him, though plenty of ambiguous ones" ("The Secret Integration"); "When backs were left uncovered and chores undone, when words got too ambiguous" (*Vineland*, 198); "the Tense is ambiguous between present and future" (*M&D*, 486). Love itself is an ambiguous word in an early story:

> Tell a girl: "I love you." No trouble with two-thirds of that, it's a closed circuit. Just you and she. But that nasty four-letter word in the middle, that's the one you have to look out for. Ambiguity. Redundance. Irrelevance, even. Leakage. All this is noise. Noise screws up your signal, makes for disorganization in the circuit. ("Entropy")

In this passage, ambiguity is evoked through one scientific concept of entropy (in a short story entitled, appropriately enough, "Entropy"), and while entropy in Pynchon has attracted much scholarly attention,[15] I suggest that entropy is merely one of many scientific metaphors Pynchon employs in relation to ambiguity, a de-emphasis that follows, for instance, David Cowart, who wrote in 1980 that "the most abused of these critical 'keys' to Pynchon is the concept of entropy."[16] In addition, the prominence of entropy in early Pynchon works has not continued in the five novels that follow *Gravity's Rainbow*,[17] so that Schaub's assertion in 1981, that "Pynchon's use of entropy as a metaphor of decline underlies all of his fiction,"[18] is no longer supported by as much textual evidence.

Sense 3 of *ambiguous* in the *OED* is "of doubtful position or classification, as partaking of two characters or being on the boundary line between," and

Pynchon's texts have used *ambiguous* in this sense, in the postmodern habit of breaking down structures and order. Examples include, "People were always mistaking him for the only kinds of probable outlander—French Canadian or Italian—and you felt he enjoyed that easy ambiguity" ("The Secret Integration"); "In '36 he came to England to work for Imperial Chemicals, in a status that was never to be free from ambiguities" (*GR*, 630); "toward a beleaguered coast ambiguous as to the disposition of land and sea" (*ATD*, 551). Ambiguity between genders and their qualities are a notable example of this sense: "It did bring up, however, an interesting note of sexual ambiguity. What a joke if at the end of this hunt [for V., ostensibly a woman] he came face to face with himself" (i.e., a man) (*V.*, 240); "a line of young women in black [...] hair swept up tightly and pinned so close to the head that they could be ambiguous boys" (*ATD*, 502); a noted ruffian, Piet Woevre, is gender-bending: "There were suggestions of a time-consuming daily toilette, including lip-rouge and a not unambiguous cologne. But Woevre was indifferent to most of the presumptions and passwords of everyday sexuality." (*ATD*, 540). This also demonstrates the continued blending of genders that, for example, Mark. D. Hawthorne analyzed in *V.*[19]

Perhaps most telling is that Pynchon describes humans, and fictional characters when well crafted, as fundamentally ambiguous; in his review of *Love in the Time of Cholera*, Pynchon discusses its protagonist, Florentino: "like the best fictional characters, he insists on his autonomy, refusing to be anything less ambiguous than human."[20]

Semantically, most uses of *ambiguous* in Pynchon's texts follow dictionary definitions, but Pynchon's use of *ambiguous* as a euphemism for drugs and alcohol appears semantically novel. For instance, marijuana is referred to as "a thin cigarette of ambiguous odor" (*GR*, 254), and "the last stragglers entered the room in a cloud of ambiguous smoke" (*Vineland*, 136). Questionable alcoholic drinks: "Somebody handed Siegel an ambiguous mixture in an old-fashioned glass" ("Mortality and Mercy"); "with a cigarette in one hand and a paper cup of something ambiguous in the other" (*BE*, 219). Similarly, Pynchon has used *ambiguous* as a euphemism for sex and amor: "Chick Counterfly, as the most worldly of the company, and thus spokesman by default in fair-sex encounters that might turn in any way ambiguous" (*ATD*, 246).

In Pynchon's early novels, ambiguity is something that can spread out, as if taking on form or even a life of its own: "His efforts at the code [...] didn't succeed in keeping back the nightfall of ambiguity that filled his room progressively as time [...] went by" (*V.*, 273). When Oedipa receives her final phone call from

Pierce Inverarity, the ambiguity of his final words over the phone line somehow extends to subsume her memories of Pierce:

> That phone line could have pointed any direction, been any length. Its quiet ambiguity shifted over, in the months after the call, to what had been revived: memories of his face, body, things he'd given her, things she had now and then pretended not to've heard him say. It took him over, and to the verge of being forgotten. (*Lot 49*, 3)

The fictional play "The Courier's Tragedy" seems to undergo a transformation midway into greater ambiguity: "It is at about this point in the play, in fact, that things really get peculiar, and a gentle chill, an ambiguity, begins to creep in among the words" (*Lot 49*, 65).

Unsurprisingly for a writer known for eschewing directness, Pynchon makes precious little use of the word *unambiguous* and its word forms, which appear only five times in his oeuvre, all in *Against the Day*, and three of these are negated, rendering them, semantically, as *ambiguous*.[21] Of the remaining uses, one describes a sexual act, "the tip of whose toe she now placed unambiguously against his penis," while the other describes Lew Basnight, who, "achieving this self-clarity, at that time and place a mortal sin, got himself just as unambiguously dynamited." (*ATD*, 721, 1057)

Pynchon's lifelong commitment to thematic and stylistic ambiguity provides the context for a quote he released to a journalist in 1997, among the only statements to the media that Pynchon has made. During the release of *Mason & Dixon*, the news network CNN sent a camera crew to, paparazzi-style, surreptitiously film Pynchon walking the streets of Manhattan. The author subsequently spoke with CNN over the telephone "to strongly request that he not be pointed out to viewers in any videotape (a request which, after much debate, CNN opted to honor)."[22] The accompanying online article contained the video, as well as three statements by Pynchon to CNN, including "'Let me be unambiguous,' [Pynchon] said. 'I prefer not to be photographed.'" The fact that there are only two unnegated uses of *unambiguous* in the entire Pynchon corpus lend this statement—"Let me be unambiguous"—a profound significance.

Pynchon's introduction to Jim Dodge's novel *Stone Junction* could be read as a reference to the CNN incident and was published in the same year. This frames "resistance" in terms of ambiguity:

> Writers since have been obliged to acknowledge and deal with the ubiquitous cyber-realities that come more and more to set, and at quite a finely chopped-up

scale too, the terms of our lives, not to mention calling into question the very traditions of a single author and a story that proceeds one piece after another—a situation Jim Dodge back then must have seen coming [...] because the novel, ever contrarian, keeps its faith in the persistence of at least a niche market—who knows, maybe even a deep human need—for modalities of life whose value lies in their having resisted and gone the other way, against the digital storm—that are likely, therefore, to include pursuits more honorable than otherwise.

One popular method of resistance was always just to keep moving—seeking, not a place to hide out, secure and fixed, but a state of dynamic ambiguity about where one might be at any given moment, along the lines of Heisenberg's uncertainty principle. Modern digital machines, however, managed quickly enough to focus the blurred hyper-ellipsoid of human freedom down to well within Planck's Constant.[23]

These passages position "ubiquitous cyber-realities" (perhaps like the website of CNN) that set "the terms of our lives" in conflict against a quality Pynchon ascribes to Dodge's work, faith in the "deep human need—for modalities of life whose value lies in their having resisted and gone the other way, against the digital storm." Pynchon laments that one way to resist the "digital storm"—to "keep moving," "seeking [...] a state of dynamic ambiguity, along the lines of Heisenberg's uncertainty principle"—is now over, as the cyber realities have won over this aspect of human freedom, just as CNN won over Pynchon's long attempt to remain un-photographed by the media. Again, so much attention has been drawn to Pynchon's avoidance of the media, and here Pynchon seems to assign it a name, one that echoes his overriding stylistic and thematic habit: "a state of dynamic ambiguity."

In summary, Pynchon's texts describe humans, fictional characters, genders, identity, scents, names, words, geography, and a few dozen other things as *ambiguous*, while ambiguity is a force or form that can fill rooms, subsume memories, and "creep in among words." In his nonfiction, Pynchon may have referenced his own avoidance of the media, framed as an author resisting "ubiquitous cyber realities" by constantly keeping on the move, as "a state of dynamic ambiguity." Pynchon, voice of ambiguity, indeed.

3.1.2 "Ambiguity" Queried

The Pynchon corpus contains *ambiguity* and related word forms (hereafter, *ambig**) forty-three times, and while each of Pynchon's books only contains 1–11 instances, this is a frequency higher (at a very highly significant statistical measure) than four comparison corpora: Brown Fiction, Peers, Popular, and COCA Fiction (Figure 3.2).[24]

While cautioning that these compare very low frequencies across all corpora, some observations include the following: Pynchon's novels tend to contain more use of *ambig** than contemporary fiction, Pynchon's texts which employ *ambig** most frequently are the short stories and *Lot 49*, the use of the word *ambig** is decreasing in Pynchon, and Pynchon's two most recent novels contain a mere single use, each.

"Ambiguous" and word forms

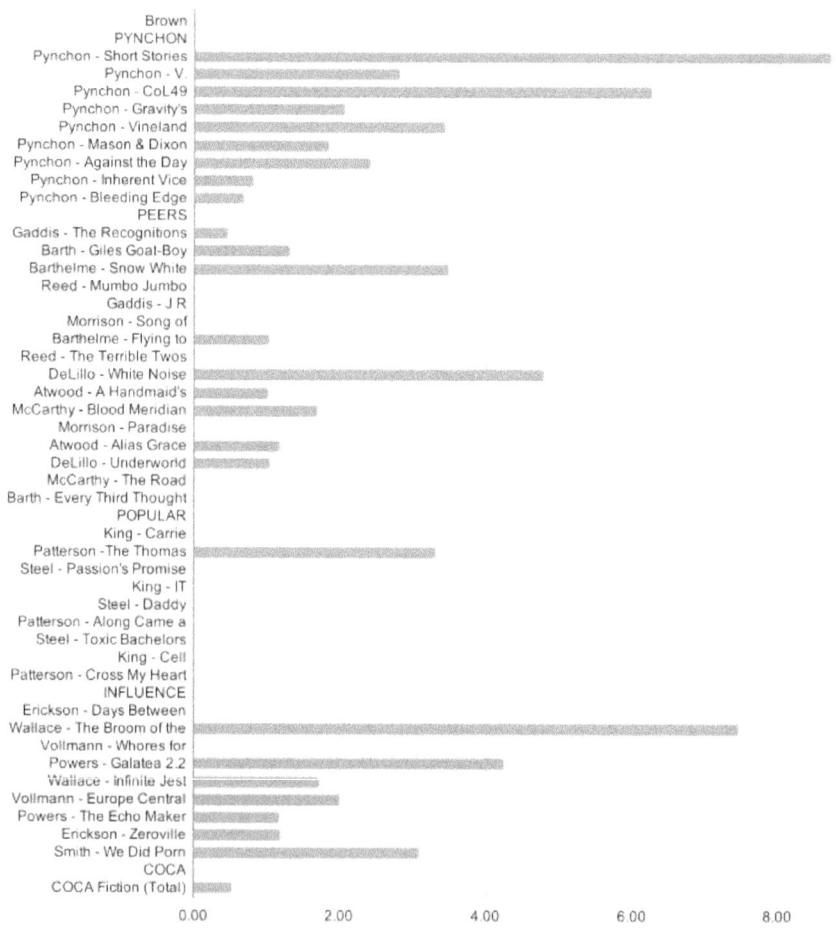

Figure 3.2 Normalized frequency (per 100k word tokens) of *ambiguous* and its word forms.

Pynchon's Peers include the word *ambig** 0–5 times per novel tested. Reed and Morrison eschew the word completely, Gaddis, Barth, and McCarthy employ it in one novel only, while DeLillo and Atwood use the word in both novels analyzed. Most of the instances of *ambiguity* by the Peers are semantically unsurprising and not of particular poetic noteworthiness: "the ambiguous clause" (Barth), "he emits an ambiguous h'm" (Atwood), "ambiguous thunder to the east" (DeLillo). Most of the Peers texts do not explicitly explore the concept of ambiguity in depth, but two notable exceptions are DeLillo and, on one occasion, McCarthy:

> It was the judge and the imbecile. They were both of them naked and they neared through the desert dawn like beings of a mode little more than tangential to the world at large, their figures now quick with clarity and now fugitive in the strangeness of that same light. Like things whose very portent renders them ambiguous. Like things so charged with meaning that their forms are dimmed. (*Blood Meridian*, 297)

Here is *ambiguity* in the sweeping sense evoked by Pynchon, in close proximity to prose that invokes related concepts of opposites, indirectness, and uncertainty: figures "tangential to the world at large," "now quick … now fugitive," and fundamentally ambiguous characters. DeLillo, more than any of the Peers Corpus texts (although still second to Pynchon), explores *ambiguity* in wider breadth and depth:

> The plot was hard to follow. There was no plot. Just loneliness, barrenness, men hunted and ray-gunned, all happening in some netherland crevice. There was none of the cross-class solidarity of the Soviet tradition. No crowd scenes or sense of social motive—the masses as hero, colossal crowd movements painstakingly organized and framed, and this was disappointing to Klara. She loved the martial architecture of huge moving bodies, the armies and mobs in other Eisenstein films, and she felt she was in some ambiguous filmscape somewhere between the Soviet model and Hollywood's vaulted heaven of love, sex, crime and individual heroism, of scenery and luxury and gorgeous toilets. (*Underworld*, 430–1)

Here, *ambiguous* is no mere adjective for speech or a gesture but lies at the fulcrum of two elaborately described *milieux*: Eisenstein films contrasted with Hollywood. DeLillo also explores the self-conscious ambiguity of affect and identity in a bravura description of college professor Murray Jay Siskind:

> Murray is able to produce a look that is sneaky and frank at the same time. It is a look that gives equal credence to disaster and lecherous success. He says that

in the old days […] he believed there was only one way to seduce a woman, with clear and open desire. He took pains to avoid self-depreciation, self-mockery, ambiguity, irony, subtlety, vulnerability, a civilized world-weariness and a tragic sense of history—the very things, he says, that are most natural to him. Of these he has allowed only one element, vulnerability, to insert itself gradually into his program of straightforward lust. He is trying to develop a vulnerability that women will find attractive. He works at it consciously […] But his efforts so far have produced only this half sneaky look, sheepish and wheedling. (*White Noise*, 20–1)

Yet another exchange in DeLillo's *White Noise* associates *ambiguity*, perhaps ironically, with "stilted language":

"Are you saying the printout shows the first ambiguous signs of a barely perceptible condition deriving from minimal acceptable spillage exposure?"
Why was I speaking in this stilted fashion?
"The magnetic scanner is pretty clear," he said. (*White Noise*, 266)

That *ambiguous* can be characterized as "stilted language" may explain why *ambig** appears only twice in the ~1.2 million words of the Popular Fiction Corpus, in an early James Patterson thriller. One instance illustrates the *un*ambiguous way a typical popular fiction character sees the world: "Morality had never been ambiguous with the woman and she highly disapproved of a party held there the night before." The second *ambiguous* describes the relationship between a murdered man and his potential killer in the novel's whodunit, one of the few ambiguous aspects of any typical thriller: "Poole had an ambiguous and inconsistent attitude toward Jimmie Horn."[25] Ambiguity is a key discriminator between so-called popular fiction and literary fiction, as Anita Gandolfo summarizes: "For the average reader, the accessibility of popular fiction is its major virtue. The reader is not looking for ambiguity or metaphoric allusions so much as escapism."[26] In his study of popular fiction, Ken Gelder writes that "students are supposed to read Literature precisely *because* of its complexities, its 'ambiguities,' its depth of character, its refusal to solve difficulties, and so on."[27] Ambiguity, in concept and word, is thus perceived to be avoided in popular fiction.

The difference of frequency of *ambiguity* in Pynchon and the Influence corpus was not statistically significant, hinting that perhaps the Influence writers are explicitly concerned with ambiguity around as much as Pynchon and certainly more than the Peers (although again, the low frequencies across all corpora would caution against much interpretation). More importantly, the query of *ambiguity* leads to passages in the Influence writers which may be read as responses to ambiguity in the texts of Pynchon, DeLillo, and no doubt others. The first sentence of Richard Powers's *Galatea 2.2* is a statement of essential ambiguity—"It was like so, but wasn't."—perhaps referring to the partly autobiographical, partly fictional nature of the novel. Some of the greatest first sentences in the canon encapsulate the theme or worldview of the book which follows, and one might expect that a Pynchon-influenced Powers would maintain this ambiguous state of affairs in *Galatea 2.2*. But on at least two occasions, *Galatea 2.2* foregrounds the concept of ambiguity *gone too far*, in the realms of linguistics and academic theory. Powers's narrator invokes ambiguity among a summary of critical theory concepts:

> I watched [the English professors] up close, our opponents, the curators of the written language. I moved about among them, a double agent. I listened around the mailboxes, in the coffee room. Criticism had gotten more involuted while I was away. The author was dead, the text-function a plot to preserve illicit privilege, and *meaning an ambiguous social construction* of no more than sardonic interest. Theory had grown too difficult for me, too subtle. (*Galatea 2.2*, 191; emphasis added)

Here, the previous generation's "involuted" "difficult theory," promulgated by "our opponents" the English professors, has become *too* ambiguous, text and meaning too critically and skeptically interrogated by ambiguity run amok. Powers, who seems well versed in linguistics, again invokes the paralyzing consequences of too much ambiguity in a scene in which a scientist, Lentz, trains an artificial intelligence named H.:

> Lentz loved to torture […] H. He spent hours inventing hideous diagramming tasks such as, "Help set implied precedents in *sentences with ambiguous parts*." A simple story like "The trainer talked to the machine in the office with a terminal" could keep H paraphrasing all evening. (*Galatea 2.2*, 173; emphasis added)

Powers, in these scenes, hints at the limits and dangers of lit-crit ambiguity, arguably exemplified by Pynchon—the end of crisp meaning and the bottomless holes that unbridled ambiguity can create—and also suggest a reading of anxiety of influence vis-à-vis Pynchon.

Yet ambiguity is not all serious theory, as for some of the Influence writers, ambiguity is the locus of creative intellectual play. After Pynchon's short stories, the novel which features the highest frequency of *ambig** is Wallace's *The Broom of the System*, which has been noted for its heavy debt to Pynchon (see Appendix II). There, Wallace employs *ambiguity* in attempts at humor, at times genuinely clever ("the poor insecure ambiguously dimensional woman is in no shape to resist," 427), other times rather less so ("Lenore Beadsman's foot- and shoe-fixations occur and exist within a disordered hygiene-network thoroughly infected with membrane ambiguity," 348). Yet the treatment of *ambig** in Wallace's texts is nowhere near as far-reaching as in Pynchon texts. In *The Broom of the System*, *ambiguous* is most often paired with relations, between two characters, or between characters and their geographic surroundings.[28] In *Infinite Jest*, however, *ambig** (frequency: 10) displays a wider variety of semantics and associations. Fictional films in the novel achieve ambiguity through unexpected artistic choices: "Low-budget celluloid horror films created ambiguity and possible elision by putting? after THE END" (234), "all intercut with ambiguous shots of a human thumb's alterations in the interference pattern of a plucked string" (989). Ambiguity is a dreamlike state: "The city's aggregate nighttime lights lightened the sky through the room's window to the same dark rose shade you see when you close your eyes, adding to the dream-of-dream-type ambiguity" (830). Ambiguity is invoked in a sentence which questions whether a human or machine is in control: "The situation is ambiguous between whether it's the Moms steering the Rototiller or vice versa" (1041). This echoes the ambiguous, dominating technological systems in, for instance, *Lot 49* and *Gravity's Rainbow*. Similarly to Powers, Wallace once associates *ambiguity* with the critical/postmodern literary theory that preceded his writing career:

> And, as we have observed thus far in our class, we, as a North American audience, have favored the more Stoic, corporate hero of reactive probity ever since, some might be led to argue "trapped" in the reactive moral *ambiguity* of "post-" and "post-post"-modern culture. (*Infinite Jest*, 142; emphasis added)

This is a further indication, perhaps, that ambiguity has become, to the Influence generation, associated with literary theory and a source of anxiety (as well as anxiety of influence).

In *Infinite Jest*, there is some indication of an essentially ambiguous character, as in the Pynchon and DeLillo passages quoted above, in the late Orin Incandenza: "The fact that Orin was our one and only source for data shrouded the whole thing in further ambiguity, as far as I was concerned. Pinpoint accuracy had never been Orin's forte" (901). A more thorough example appears in Smith's *We Did Porn*, in a footnote to an apparently real script for a pornographic film that Smith appeared in but which was written and directed by a director whom

Smith refers to as "Osbie Feel" (appropriately enough, a character in *Gravity's Rainbow*):

> there is also a footnote at the bottom of the original script: *Every emotion Lucy expresses is ambiguous.* Is she really scared, or is she just faking it? Is it lust or just opportunity? Her lifetime of elaborate scams, coupled with the opportunistic nature of junkie day-to-day survival, have left her true motivations enigmatic even to herself. She has embraced the mind-set of a hive insect: capable of always putting the most sympathetic face forward, but never truly in touch with one's own desires. She would make an excellent spy, a sociopathic agent for shadow governments. She could trick herself into passing a polygraph test (*We Did Porn*, 445; emphasis added)

This passage (even though ostensibly written by someone other than Smith) is, except for Pynchon and DeLillo, unmatched in these corpora in the extent to which ambiguity suffuses a specific character.

The query of *ambiguous* in these corpora thus reveals that *ambig** appears zero times in the Brown Fiction corpus, is used infrequently in the COCA Fiction corpus and even less frequently in the Popular Fiction corpus, perhaps related to the theory that ambiguity is inherently a distinguisher between popular and literary fiction. Pynchon's explicit use of *ambig** is greatest in frequency and breadth, yet there are indications that, among his Peers, Don DeLillo especially explores the concept of ambiguity and displays some evidence of salient use of ambiguity-related stylistic devices. Finally, there is some evidence that for the Influence writers, ambiguity, associated with academic literary criticism and perhaps Pynchon's long shadow, has become a source of anxiety.

3.2 Vagueness Words and Phrases

"Pick some words," said Bortz. "Them, we can talk about." (*Lot 49*, 146)

Naturally, Pynchon does not only use the word *ambiguity* to achieve ambiguity, but words and phrases that effect ambiguity and vagueness. After *ambiguous* and its word forms, the next related word to investigate might be *vague* and its word forms, yet rather than conduct a comparative explication of *vague**, a stylistic investigation of ambiguity in Pynchon's texts will benefit from the query of wider groups of vagueness words.

In a much-cited digital exploration of Conrad's *Heart of Darkness*, Michael Stubbs traced frequencies of words suggesting vague impressions or unreliable knowledge, a "major theme of the book."[29] For context, Stubbs obtained frequencies for about two dozen vague words and phrases: *vague, something, somebody, kind of, seemed*, and so on. Stubbs also looked at lexico-grammatical patterns, including repetitiveness ("the air was warm, thick, heavy, sluggish"), an abstract noun plus an adjective with a negative prefix ("the aspect of an unknown planet"), words relating to negation (*no, not, never, nothing, nobody*, etc.), and frequent n-grams.[30] Following Stubbs, I examine words related to ambiguity/vagueness in my corpora, but on a much larger scale. But which words to choose? The words identified by Stubbs as well as, say, *inexplicable, ambivalent*, and *ineffable* could be candidates. Computational query of collocates, that is, words that appear in close proximity to *ambiguity* would be an option, but this yields few helpful results.[31] These approaches thus seem rather limited. A more robust examination of vagueness words is called for.

3.2.1 The Hiller/Hogenraad Vagueness Dictionary

> Any deviations into jealousy, metaphysics, vagueness would be picked up immediately (*GR*, 417)

In the late 1960s, Jack Hiller et al. investigated how the frequency of vague words in student essays correlated with grades assigned by teachers.[32] By 1971, Hiller refined and formalized his method using a list of 361 vague words and phrases to query (Table 3.1).[33]

Table 3.1 Examples from the 361 words and phrases in Hiller's vagueness dictionary

Category	Words	Examples
1. Ambiguous designation	50	something, whatever, somebody, somehow, stuff
2. Negated intensifiers	57	not just, not quite, not really, not exactly, doesn't seem
3. Approximation	35	almost, kind of, sort of, just a, nearly
4. Bluff and recovery	53	you know, of course, actually, I mean, anyway
5. Admission of error	20	maybe, I think, sorry, not sure, I don't know
6. Indefinite amount	29	some, most, a little, few, a lot
7. Multiplicity	35	things, many, several, age, various
8. Probability and possibility	33	might, sometimes, may, perhaps, probably
9. Reservations	35	seemed, seems, apparently, appeared, basically
10. Anaphors	14	he, it, she, her, this, him, they, them
Total	361	

For decades, Hiller's dictionary has been used and cited primarily in educational research, but a recent paper by Robert Hogenraad adapted Hiller's dictionary, by removing some duplicates and adding twenty-one more words and phrases (for a total of 377),[34] to detect ambiguity/vagueness (Hogenraad employs the terms more or less interchangeably) in political speeches and literary texts by Henry James and Gustave Flaubert.[35] Hogenraad used this modified dictionary of vagueness words to trace the rate of vagueness across the progression of each text. Hogenraad reported that James's *The Bostonians*, for instance, begins with more vagueness words, but this vagueness steadily decreases as the novel goes on. Hogenraad interpreted this result by stating that "high scores of blurriness characterize the first chapters" of *The Bostonians* and that "the novelist, controlling ambiguity by slowly releasing specifics, keeps the reader in suspense as long as possible. Letting the fog at the start of the intrigue to lift with time is deliberate transformation."[36] Below, I challenge aspects of Hogenraad's method and thus this interpretation.

As a first step, I queried the Hiller/Hogenraad dictionary as-is across my corpora, as a preexisting (not to say "objective") method which may be less susceptible to preconceived notions and selection bias than the small sample of vagueness words investigated by Stubbs in *Heart of Darkness* (Figure 3.3).[37]

This figure demonstrates a major criticism of Hogenraad's method for "tracing ambiguity in texts": the vast majority of results are due to Category 10, titled "Anaphors,"[38] and the vast majority of results for Category 10 derive from the many commons pronouns in the category. The full list of Category 10 in the Hiller/Hogenraad dictionary is *former, other, he, she, her, such, him, them, it, they, its, this, latter, those*.

Thus when Hogenraad used this dictionary to trace "ambiguity" across the texts of Henry James and Flaubert, the majority of his results derive from common pronouns, such as *he, she*, and *they*, which greatly outnumber the hundreds of other vague words and phrases in the dictionary, such as *not exactly* or *sometimes*. Linguists consider pronouns to be vague, and the inclusion of these pronouns made sense for Hiller's original goal of tracing vagueness in student essays. But they are highly problematic for a general measure of *literary vagueness*, as pronouns are typically semantically unambiguous in fiction. In most novels, readers most often know whom *he* or *she* refers to. Yes, ambiguous pronouns exist in fiction, especially modernist and postmodern texts. Pynchon has made use of ambiguous pronouns,[39] which are often a feature of stream-of-consciousness modernist texts, for example, Joyce and Woolf, and Gaddis in particular features no doubt hundreds of ambiguous pronouns, and further

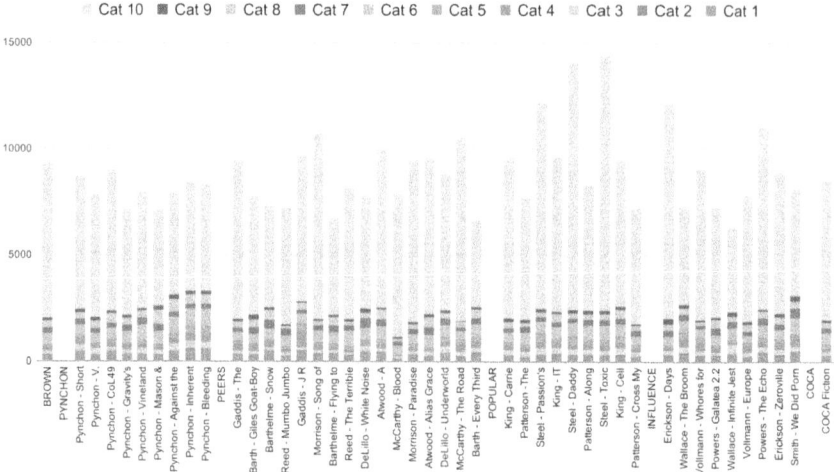

Figure 3.3 Normalized frequency of 377 words and phrases from the Hiller/
Hogenraad vagueness dictionary (per 100k word tokens). The largest value for each
text is Category 10 in light gray on top.

notable examples exist in my corpora.[40] But as a measure of ambiguity/vagueness
in *fiction generally*, this method is severely deficient, as the frequency of pronouns
in the Hiller/Hogenraad dictionary overwhelms the other nine categories.
Certainly, a novelist such as Flaubert, whom Hogenraad analyzes by this
method, uses pronouns unambiguously as a rule. Apply the Hiller/Hogenraad
dictionary to my corpora, it emerges that popular romance novels by Danielle
Steel—*Passion's Promise*, *Daddy*, and *Toxic Bachelors*—would demonstrate the
most "ambiguity/vagueness" using Hogenraad's method, mostly due to common
pronouns, which are almost never, if ever, ambiguous in Steel's romances.

While applauding Hogenraad's aim to trace vagueness/ambiguity in texts, his
method could be improved much further.[41] I would prefer to modify the Hiller/
Hogenraad dictionary in many ways, but to do so in a volume devoted to the
texts of a single author could risk the accusation of cherry-picking results. For
now, the results of Categories 1–9 and 10 should be visualized and interpreted
separately to account for the overwhelming frequency of Category 10 pronouns
in literary texts (Figures 3.4–3.14).[42]

In combined Categories 1–9, the highest results are Pynchon's latest three
novels and Smith's Pynchon-influenced *We Did Porn*. Compared to Brown
Fiction and COCA Fiction, these results are very highly significant.[43]

Novels by Pynchon, "The Voice of Ambiguity," do indeed score high or
highest among all corpora in numerous categories of the Hiller/Hogenraad

Categories 1-9 (352 words and phrases)

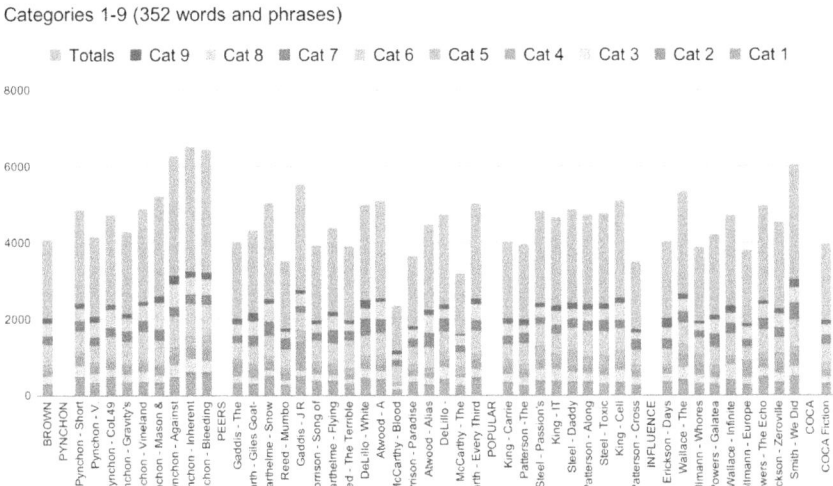

Figure 3.4 Normalized frequency of Categories 1–9 of the Hiller/Hogenraad vagueness dictionary (per 100k word tokens), with *OK* and *okay* removed.

vagueness dictionary. When Category 10 (and its frequent pronouns) is removed, Pynchon's latest three novels score highest overall; a novel by Pynchon has the highest result in four categories; a novel by Pynchon has both the first and second highest results in four categories; a late novel by Pynchon has the first, second, third, and fourth highest results in Category 6; and in Category 2, Pynchon scored first, second, and fourth.

Although Schaub's monograph, *Pynchon: The Voice of Ambiguity*, inspired this experiment, the highest results are, interestingly, highest for Pynchon's novels published *after* Schaub's book in 1981. Also, the novel most discussed by Schaub is *Gravity's Rainbow*, which does not score particularly highly in most categories. In numerous categories Pynchon's results also increase over time, indications of (at least some elements of) a "late style," an increasing use of vague and ambiguous lexis. Pynchon's "late style" will be revisited in this book's conclusion, but if one were to investigate a particular category more closely based on the high frequency of these terms in Pynchon's texts, the most likely candidates for future research would be Categories 2 (negated intensifiers), 6 (indefinite amount), and 8 (probability and possibility). In the previous chapter, I discussed how critics have given considerable attention to the alternate histories and worlds of *Mason & Dixon*, effected stylistically via the subjunctive mood (of *may* and *might*), and Category 8 seems to detect this, with *Mason & Dixon* scoring highest among all texts.

Category 1: Ambiguous Designation (52 words and phrases)

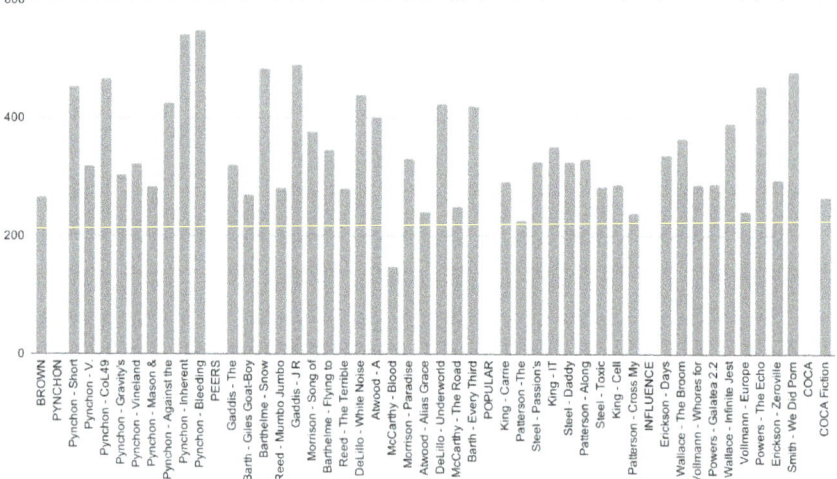

Figure 3.5 Normalized frequency of Category 1 of Hiller/Hogenraad vagueness dictionary (per 100k word tokens).

Category 2: Negated Intensifiers (55 words/phrases)

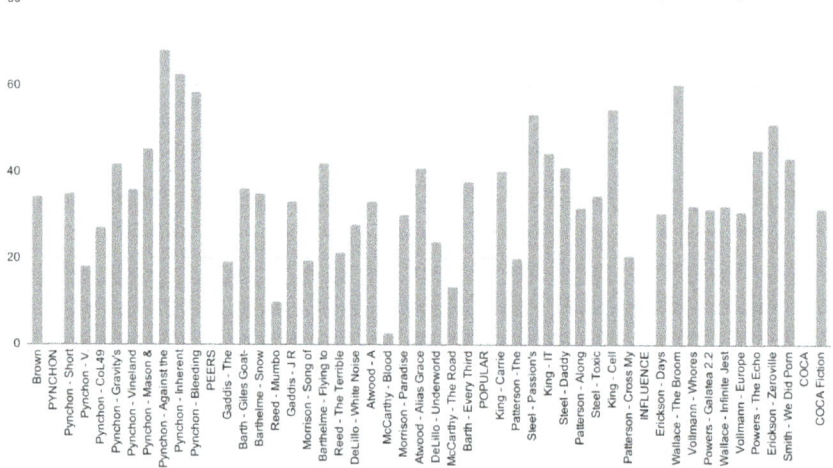

Figure 3.6 Normalized frequency of Category 2 of Hiller/Hogenraad vagueness dictionary (per 100k word tokens).

Category 3: Approximation (37 words and phrases)

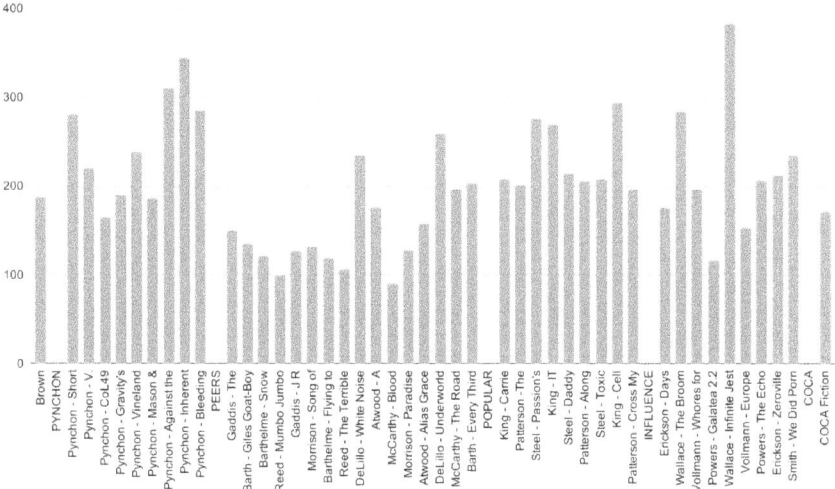

Figure 3.7 Normalized frequency of Category 3 of Hiller/Hogenraad vagueness dictionary (per 100k word tokens).

Category 4: Bluff and Recovery (51 words and phrases)

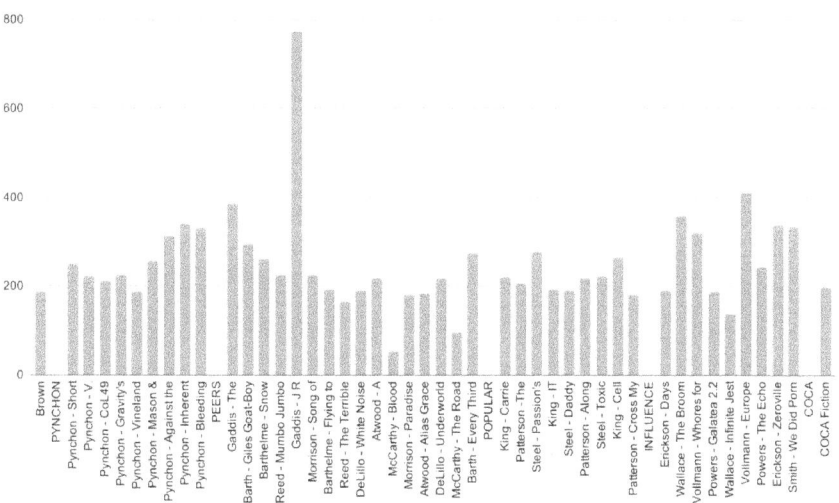

Figure 3.8 Normalized frequency of Category 4 of Hiller/Hogenraad vagueness dictionary (per 100k word tokens), with *OK* and *okay* removed.

Category 5: Admission of Error (19 words and phrases)

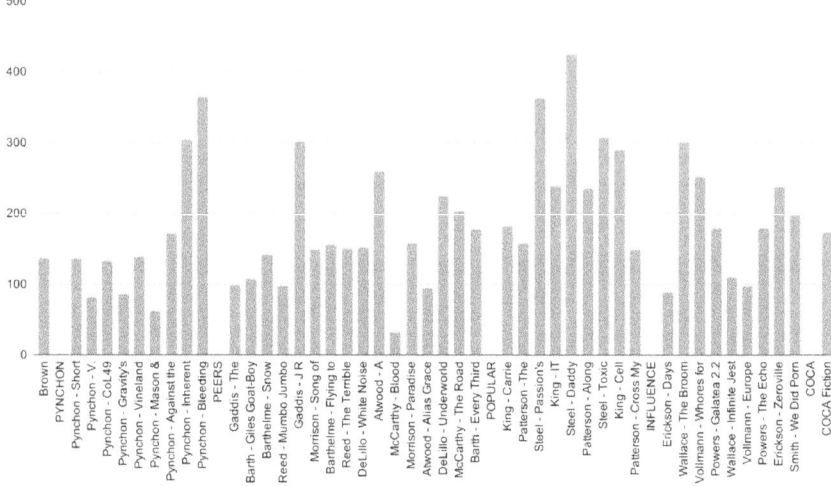

Figure 3.9 Normalized frequency of Category 5 of Hiller/Hogenraad vagueness dictionary (per 100k word tokens).

Category 6: Indefinite Amount (38 words and phrases)

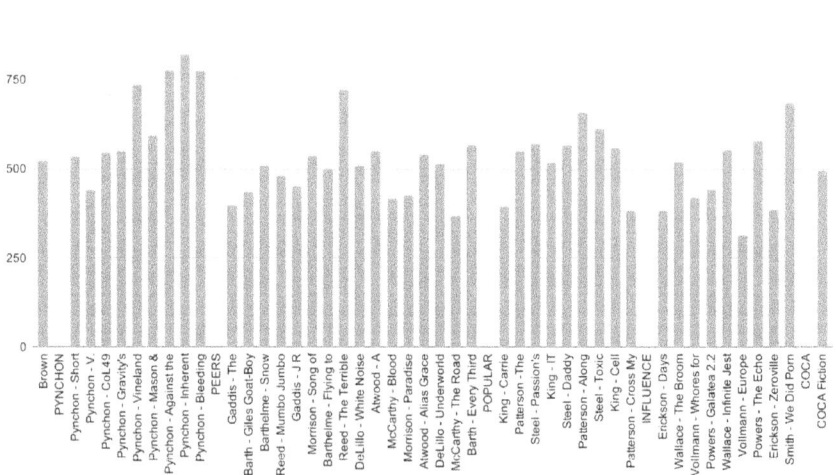

Figure 3.10 Normalized frequency of Category 6 of Hiller/Hogenraad vagueness dictionary (per 100k word tokens).

Category 7: Multiplicity (31 words and phrases)

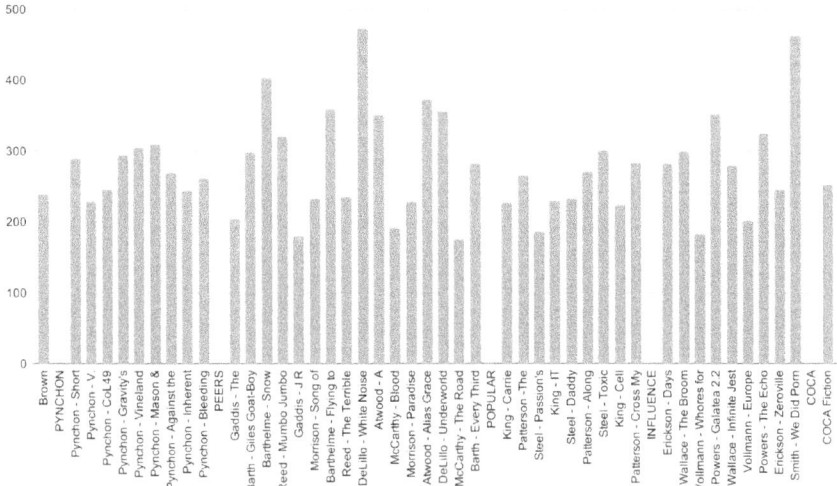

Figure 3.11 Normalized frequency of Category 7 of Hiller/Hogenraad vagueness dictionary (per 100k word tokens).

Category 8: Probability and Possibility (32 words and phrases)

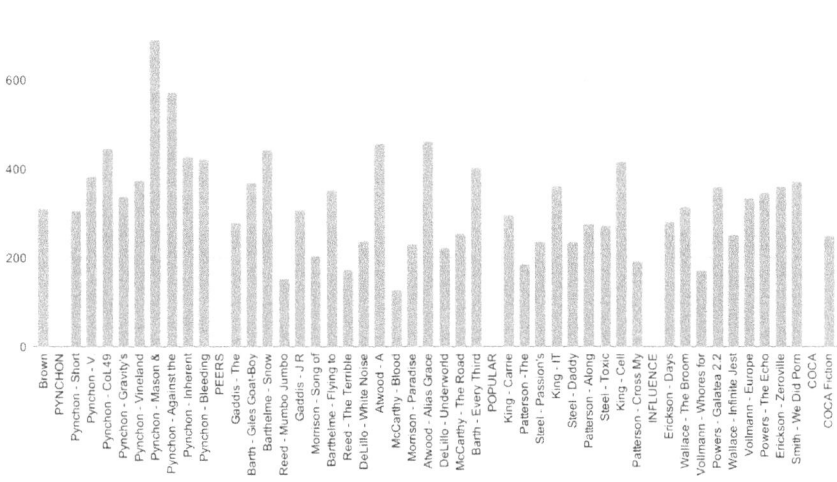

Figure 3.12 Normalized frequency of Category 8 of Hiller/Hogenraad vagueness dictionary (per 100k word tokens).

Category 9: Reservations (37 words and phrases)

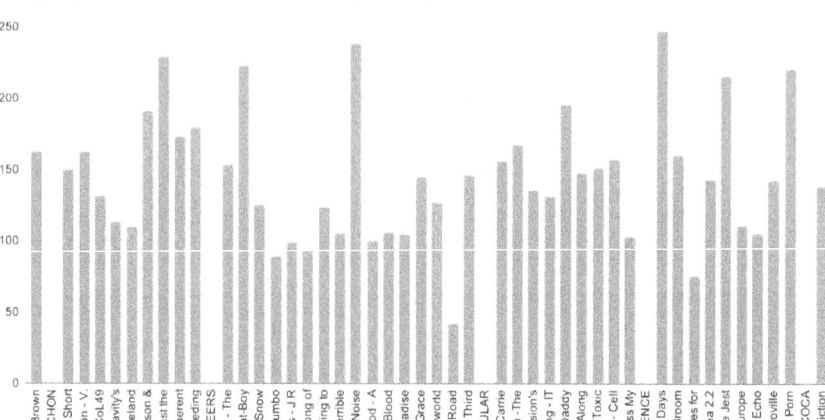

Figure 3.13 Normalized frequency of Category 9 of Hiller/Hogenraad vagueness dictionary (per 100k word tokens).

Category 10: Anaphors (14 words and phrases)

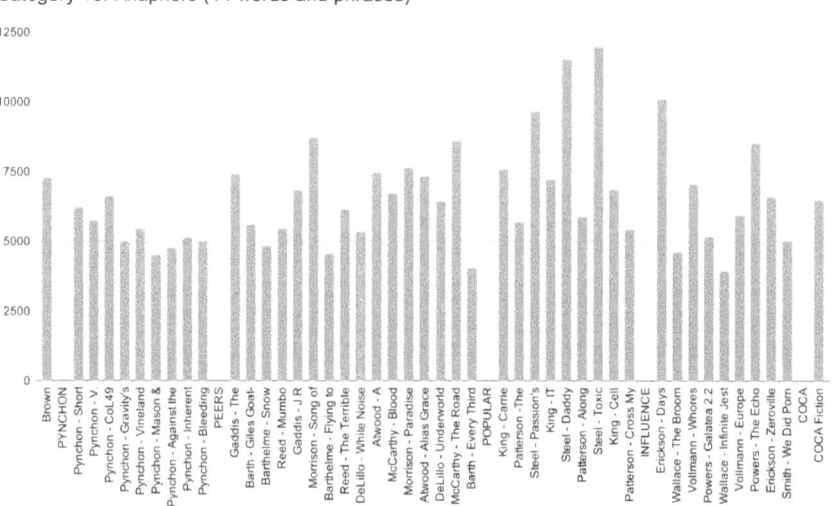

Figure 3.14 Normalized frequency of Category 10 of Hiller/Hogenraad vagueness dictionary (per 100k word tokens).

Pynchon aside, this experiment may serve the future study of certain other authors. A novel by Cormac McCarthy placed absolutely lowest in 8 out of 10 categories, which may be unsurprising, as McCarthy often writes in dramatically unambiguous prose, with one extreme example being: "He ate the last of the eggs and wiped the plate with the tortilla and ate the tortilla and drank the last of the coffee and wiped his mouth and looked up and thanked her."[44] Readers "are unanimous in recognizing" McCarthy "as a great stylist," per John Rothfork,[45] and these results add new data points to the burgeoning digital humanities interest in McCarthy's texts.[46] Next, the outsized result of Gaddis's *J R* in Category 4 (bluff and recovery) is the greatest outlier across all categories, which Gaddis scholars may wish to investigate. In addition, Smith's *We Did Porn* placed among the highest results in four categories, although it cannot be excluded that this is because, unlike the comparison corpora, Smith's text takes the generic form of a memoir. Finally, the stylistic use of vague language in David Foster Wallace's texts has already been noted by critics. Geoff Dyer complains about the "contrived sloppinesses of all those 'sort ofs' and 'kind ofs',"[47] while Maud Newton notes that "Wallace's nonfiction abounds with qualifiers like 'sort of' and 'pretty much'."[48] Interestingly, all three of these phrases—*sort of, kind of, pretty much*—are contained in Category 3, in which *Infinite Jest* scores higher than all tested novels, followed by two of Pynchon's later novels. This is yet another indication that Wallace's stylistic use of vague lexis may have been Pynchon-influenced.

This experiment suggests a new way of reading Pynchon's texts: simply to be aware of the stylistic use of vagueness words. A reading of Pynchon could proceed via careful attention to which dialogue, narration, concepts, and characters the text renders vaguely and which more crisply. As an example of how vagueness words may litter Pynchon's texts, see Figure 3.15.

This visualization demonstrates the frequency with which vagueness words may surface in Pynchon's texts, and a reader who pays close attention to vague words and phrases will find many examples per page. The pervasiveness of vague language uncovered in these experiments reinforces the *Weltanschauung* of Pynchon's texts, a worldview which eschews clarity and binary thinking. But again, the Hiller/Hogenraad dictionary is a general approach to vagueness words which is open to much criticism in the literary context, and Pynchon employs many other lexical and syntactic devices to achieve vagueness which this dictionary does not detect.

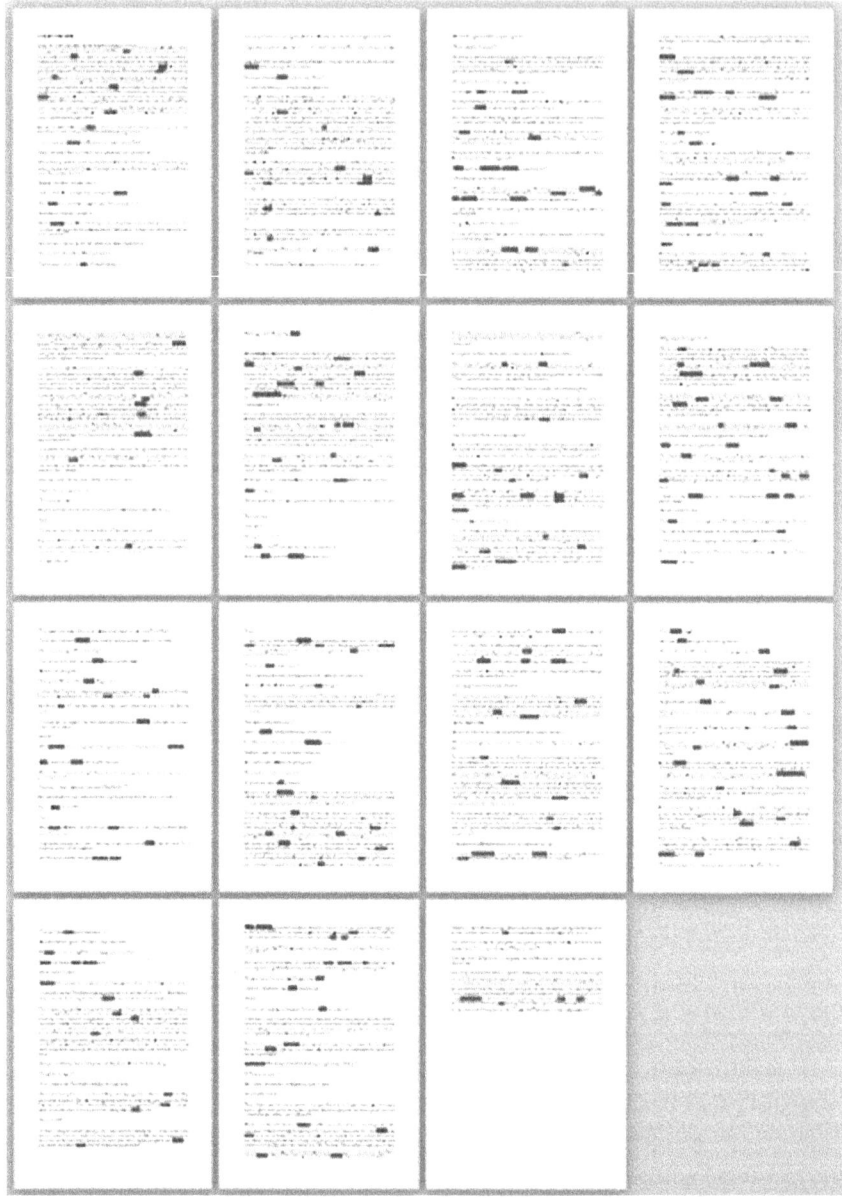

Figure 3.15 Chapter 17 of *Inherent Vice*, with Hiller/Hogenraad vagueness words highlighted.

3.2.2 Pynchon's "Preferred" Vagueness Words

To narrow the inquiry, I isolate the vague words and phrases from the Hiller/ Hogenraad dictionary which Pynchon employs significantly more than other writers. By statistical comparison of the word frequencies using log-likelihood, there are fifty-one words and phrases that are significantly more frequent (p < 0.05) in the Pynchon corpus than Brown Fiction, Peers, Popular, and COCA Fiction (Tables 3.2 and 3.3).[49]

These, then, are the vagueness words that could be called characteristic of Pynchon's style based upon the chosen comparison corpora, the most frequent being *some* and *many* (rather than a defined quantity or specific concept), *its* (describing the qualities of inanimate objects or animals), and *might*, *may*, and *perhaps* (the hypothetical or subjunctive). Figure 3.16 visualizes these results, with the exclusion of *ok* (as already discussed) and *seems*, which varies greatly depending on the tense of the novel.[50]

These vagueness words increase observably over time in the Pynchon corpus, suggesting a stylistic trend. To explain how this impacts the texts on a per page basis, the early Pynchon stories contain about 1 vagueness word/phrase per 100 words (or 10 per 1000, or 100 per 10,000), while the later novels increase to approximately 1.5 per 100 words. Yet when comparing the full sum of these words per novel, the log-likelihood value of later novels versus *Gravity's Rainbow* as a baseline is very highly significant. A page of *Gravity's Rainbow* is roughly 500–750 words, depending on how much dialogue each contains, which suggests a rough increase of 2–4 additional vagueness words and phrases per page in later novels. While this increase is relatively minor, it is nonetheless a small, observable aspect of Pynchon's "late style." This also contrasts with the chronological decline of the word "ambiguous" in Pynchon's texts, discussed above, perhaps suggesting that rather than name ambiguity, Pynchon increasingly *shows* ambiguity.

While Pynchon has been lauded as a master of complex, "high" literary style, it is interesting how many of these vagueness words would be considered markers of "bad" writing by prescriptive writing manuals. How many composition teachers would *not* use a red pen to strike out "and so forth" or "sooner or later" in student essays? As William Strunk and E. B. White state in their widely read *The Elements of Style*, "use definite, specific, concrete language. Prefer the specific to the general, the definite to the vague, the concrete to the abstract,"[51] which suggests one more reading of vagueness in Pynchon's prose: yet another act of rebellion.

Table 3.2 Words and phrases from the Hiller/Hogenraad vagueness dictionary that are significantly more frequent in Pynchon corpus than Brown Fiction, Peers, Popular, and COCA Fiction corpora. Asterisk refers to lemma/word forms

---

Category 1: Ambiguous designation
    a certain, a particular, and so forth, somebody, somehow, somewhere, whatever
Category 2: Negated intensifiers
    not all, not always, not exactly, not necessarily, not quite
Category 3: Approximation
    a while, form of, kind of, less and less, more and more, nearly, not as, one or two, sooner or later, sort of
Category 4: Bluff and recovery
    actually, in fact, more of a, ok
Category 5: Admission of error
    [no results]
Category 6: Indefinite amount
    a bit, any number of, some
Category 7: Multiplicity
    complex, complicated, kinds, many, not so much, numbers, points, various, ways
Category 8: Probability and possibility
    likely, may, might, now and then, often, ordinary, perhaps, suppose.*,usually
Category 9: Reservations
    appear.*, basically, seems, tend, tending
Category 10: Anaphors
    its

3.2.3 A Brief Detour with *Its*

In identifying Pynchon's "preferred" vagueness words, it emerges that *its* is significantly more frequent in the Pynchon corpus than all comparison corpora. This frequency of *its* invites interpretation by Pynchon scholars, first, as Pynchon's attention to the inanimate (beyond common anthropomorphism) has attracted numerous commentators, at least as early as Richard Poirier's 1963 review of *V.*: "The insistent grotesqueness of this novel—literally of confusing human, animate and inanimate things—is Pynchon's way of showing a world in which gestures of human warmth, kindness or love are barely visible."[52] Brian Stonehill later explored how "the line between the animate and the inanimate is frequently blurred in Pynchon," providing such examples as the human refugees in the opening pages of *Gravity's Rainbow*, who are "stacked about among the rest of the *things* to be carried out to salvation" (3; emphasis added), and Tchitcherine, "who is more metal than anything else" (337).[53] Hume focused particularly on the blurring of human and machine, or "immachination."[54]

Table 3.3 Raw frequency of words and phrases from the Hiller/Hogenraad vagueness dictionary that are significantly more frequent in Pynchon corpus than Brown Fiction, Peers, Popular, and COCA Fiction corpora. Asterisk refers to lemma/word forms

Word/Phrase	Frequency (Raw)	Category
some	5265	Cat 06
its	2242	Cat 10
might	2068	Cat 08
may	1391	Cat 08
many	1049	Cat 07
Perhaps	1036	Cat 08
appear.*	718	Cat 09
suppose.*	717	Cat 08
kind of	704	Cat 03
somebody	693	Cat 01
a while	657	Cat 03
sort of	648	Cat 03
actually	639	Cat 04
whatever	610	Cat 01
somehow	609	Cat 01
often	563	Cat 08
seems	477	Cat 09
somewhere	476	Cat 01
in fact	450	Cat 04
nearly	420	Cat 03
now and then	350	Cat 08
usually	329	Cat 08
likely	299	Cat 08
a certain	275	Cat 01
a bit	272	Cat 06
ok	205	Cat 04
ways	193	Cat 07
and so forth	189	Cat 01
points	167	Cat 07
not quite	143	Cat 02
various	130	Cat 07
more and more	123	Cat 03
not as	121	Cat 03
not exactly	119	Cat 02
form of	116	Cat 03
sooner or later	103	Cat 03
not so much	102	Cat 07
kinds	100	Cat 07
complex	76	Cat 07
more of a	71	Cat 04

Table 3.3 Continued

Word/Phrase	Frequency (Raw)	Category
not always	69	Cat 02
any number of	67	Cat 06
basically	67	Cat 09
complicated	66	Cat 07
not all	63	Cat 02
ordinarily	61	Cat 08
a particular	53	Cat 01
tend	52	Cat 09
tending	36	Cat 09
not necessarily	26	Cat 02
less and less	21	Cat 03

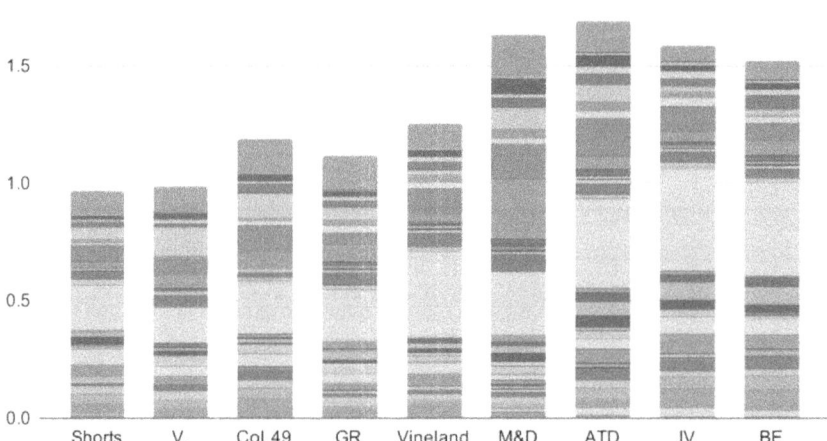

Pynchon's "preferred" vagueness words

Figure 3.16 Normalized frequency (per 100 words) of forty-nine vagueness words/ phrases in Pynchon corpus.

Ted Underwood recently reported that the possessive pronoun *its* is notably frequent in science fiction and that his computer model of genre "strongly (and persuasively) misclassifies" Pynchon's *Lot 49* as science fiction.[55] Underwood did not connect these two observations, but my results suggest a novel hypothesis: *Lot 49* may have been automatically classified as science fiction by a computer model partly because the text contains *its* more than many comparison corpora.

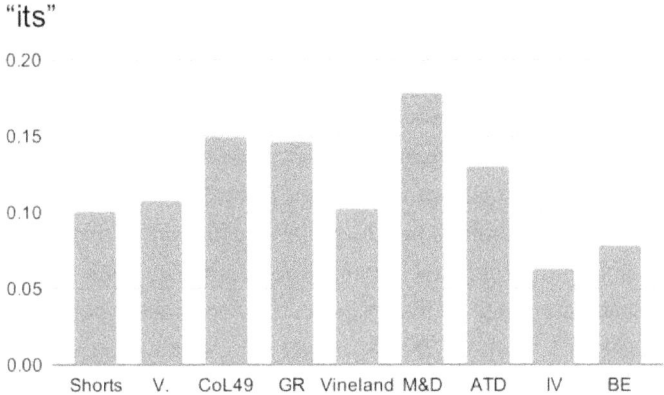

Figure 3.17 Normalized frequency (per 100 words) of "its" in Pynchon corpus.

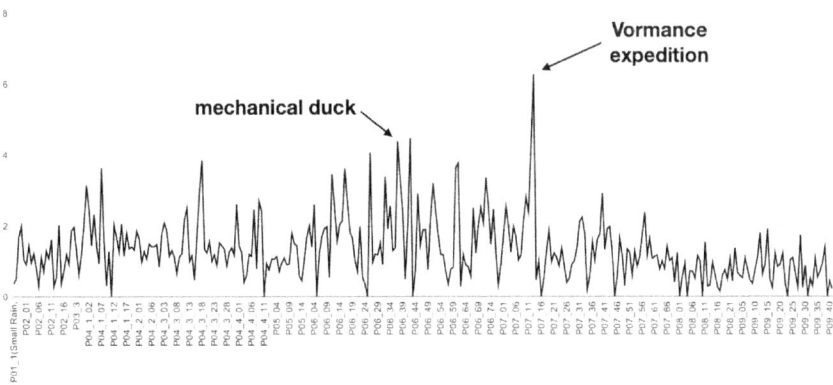

Figure 3.18 Normalized frequency of "its" in Pynchon chapters and episodes, per 1,000 word tokens.

The frequency of "its," or any single word, has many limitations in informing readings of Pynchon's attention to the inanimate, not least because Pynchon's texts have described the inanimate without employing this pronoun. The most famous example of the inanimate made animate in Pynchon's texts is the "Byron the Bulb" sequence in *Gravity's Rainbow*, about the "life" of a sentient lightbulb, but Byron is consistently referred to as "he," not "it." Given these limitations, the frequency of *its* in the Pynchon corpus is presented in Figures 3.17 and 3.18 as exploratory experiments.

Figure 3.17 suggests a reduction of "its" in Pynchon's most recent two novels,[56] an impression reinforced when the query is separated by chapter/ episode in the novels in Figure 3.18. Differing chapter lengths affect this query (as the longer the chapter, the less likely that a cluster of "its" will be high on average), but the first and third highest spikes in the graph correspond with two of the most prominent instances of Pynchon's engagement with the inanimate made animate: the unnamed giant creature in the Vormance expedition chapter of *Against the Day* and the mechanical duck in *Mason & Dixon*, a machine so lifelike that it flies, attacks humans, and even defecates.[57]

This exploratory experiment may help contextualize the Vormance expedition chapter, a much-praised and much-commented upon high point in an otherwise long and exhausting novel. In this chapter, "the Vormance expedition has been commissioned by Scarsdale Vibe to recover a mysterious, ancient and, in its unspecified, abstract nature of colossal power, mythically structured, entity from the Icelandic wastes," as summarized by Eve.[58] The giant, mysterious creature, referred to as "it," rampages through "the city" Godzilla-like, causing mass death and destruction, which many have read as evocative of 9/11.[59] Minor phrases and attention to the inanimate continue to populate Pynchon's texts (as with much fiction), but following *Against the Day* (which also contains a brief contrivance of a sentient, speaking ball lightning named Skip), these—an oversized coin bearing the image of Thomas Jefferson hallucinatorily speaking to Doc in a diner (*IV*, 294), an undeposited check in Maxine's purse "laughing at her" (*BE*, 67), a haunted elevator "rumored to possess a mind of its own" (*BE*, 142)—do not address a single subject for longer than a few sentences. While throughout this book I caution against too much interpretation based on the query of single words, in this case, this simple graph, supplemented by cursory close inspection of words in context, suggests that the Vormance episode constitutes a high water mark of Pynchon's extended and concentrated exploration of an inanimate/animate figure. This hints at one aspect of Pynchon's style in the final two novels, which seem to eschew sustained attention to an inanimate subject. Combined with the increase of dialogue in later Pynchon novels and reception which sometimes applauds the increasingly "deep" characters, this raises a hypothesis (for future exploitation) that the stylistic subject matter in Pynchon's latest two novels has turned from a mix of human and the inanimate toward an author more focused on human characters.

3.2.4 Pynchon's "Preferred" Vagueness Words, Continued

Returning to the rest of Pynchon's "preferred" vagueness words, the frequency of these words/phrases across the chapters/episodes of the Pynchon corpus is in Figure 3.19.

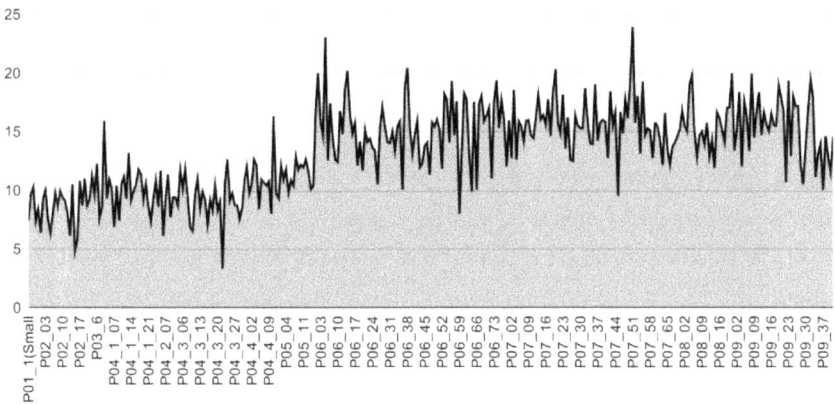

Figure 3.19 Normalized frequency of forty-eight of Pynchon's "preferred vagueness words" in chapters and episodes, per 1,000 word tokens. *Seems, ok,* and *its* have been excluded from the list of fifty-one above.

The beginning of *Mason & Dixon* (P06 in Figure 3.19) begins a sustained increase in Pynchon's preferred vagueness words, and the chapter with the greatest density of these vagueness words happens to be episode 2 of part 4 of *Against the Day*. In that chapter, Cyprian returns to Vienna and amorously encounters Yashmeen, who is then subjected to an interrogation. Selections from this chapter illustrate the frequent and often subtle ways that the text makes concepts and situations more vague:

> "So!" cried Ratty with *a certain* forced joviality, "here we all are again. Yashmeen still in the picture, I see." He seemed to Cyprian *not so much* puzzled as curious in a professional way.
>
> "*Not quite* as she was." [...]
>
> "*More of a* sibyl these days. Deeper than maths, but that's as far as I can see. *Perhaps* because of *some* rogue psychic gift, *perhaps* only the secular gravity of whatever her father is up to out in Inner Asia [...]" (*ATD*, 846)

————————————

> "*Whatever* they had expected of me in Buda-Pesth, I had failed them. But that *might* have been separate from this other matter of the departures. Could I borrow a cigarette from *somebody*?" (*ATD*, 850)

————————————

> "*Perhaps somebody* 'saw' something? [...]" (*ATD*, 849; emphases added)

In these examples, Pynchon's "preferred" vagueness words and phrases have been italicized, and the final example is a consummately vague sentence: three out of the four words are vague, and while *saw* is a relatively unambiguous verb, here, it is ambiguated by apostrophes. Every word in "Perhaps somebody 'saw' something?" is both linguistically vague and, more narrowly, "literarily vague."

The lowest frequency of "preferred" vagueness words in one of Pynchon's chapters, meanwhile, happens to be episode 22 of part 3 of *Gravity's Rainbow*. This episode nevertheless teems with vague imagery ("Clouds, a dozen shades of gray, go scudding along the sky," 528) and situations, especially at the end of the chapter where Slothrop, in the engine room of the Anubis, is attacked in the dark by *someone*, and, as Weisenburger summarizes, "Slothrop discovers, or hallucinates that he discovers, the dead body of Bianca Erdmann."[60] *Gravity's Rainbow* here— and later in the novel—denies the reader firm knowledge of whether Bianca is simply alive or dead, an example of what Duyhuizen discusses in his essay on Bianca as a "reader-trap": "stylistic and thematic techniques that on the one hand court the conventional readerly desire to construct an ordered world within the fictional space of the text, but that on closer examination reveal the fundamental uncertainty of postmodern textuality."[61] Then why does this episode score lowest in Pynchon's "preferred" vagueness terms in the entire Pynchon oeuvre? It is difficult to hypothesize omissions, but one possibility is that parts of this episode adopt the mode of high-seas adventure stories, a subgenre of popular fiction. Slothrop, Otto, and Der Springer, aboard Frau Gnahb's ship, ram into the Anubis and board it in language evoking pirate or adventure stories: "Up the slippery ladder goes salty and buccaneering Slothrop, hefting his grappling hook, letting out line, keeping an eye on that Otto" (529). Similarly to this sentence, some passages describing physical action tend to eschew Pynchonian ambiguity:

> "Springer is already up on the yacht's main deck. Slothrop tucks Luger in belt and follows." (*GR*, 530)

> "Just as he touches the deck, all the lights go out. Air blowers whine down to stillness. The engine room is down one more deck." (*GR*, 530)

As to why this fairly ambiguous episode scores lowest amongst all chapters in Pynchon's oeuvre for "vagueness," it is probable that "Pynchon's preferred vagueness words" remains a crude and incomplete measure, and querying the texts at the chapter/episode level is too imprecise.

3.2.5 The Least Vague Passages in *Bleeding Edge*

To narrow the inquiry further, the longest strings in Pynchon's novels where *none* of Pynchon's "preferred" vagueness words appear were queried.[62] This attempts to locate textual oases of unambiguity (or *crispness*, as linguists dub the opposite of vagueness)[63] in Pynchon's texts.

The "least vague" or "most crisp" continuous section of *Bleeding Edge* identified by this method is 688 words occurring late in the novel, or about 2.5 pages, on pages 420–2 of the novel's 476 pages.[64] These happen to contain some of the novel's most-cited passages, in which Ernie, Maxine's father, delivers what Edwin Turner describes as an "elegy for the internet."[65]

> "Yep, and your Internet was their invention, this magical convenience that creeps now like a smell through the smallest details of our lives, the shopping, the housework, the homework, the taxes, absorbing our energy, eating up our precious time. And there's no innocence. Anywhere. Never was. It was conceived in sin, the worst possible. As it kept growing, it never stopped carrying in its heart a bitter-cold death wish for the planet […]."
>
> "Call it freedom, it's based on control. Everybody connected together, impossible anybody should get lost, ever again. Take the next step, connect it to these cell phones, you've got a total Web of surveillance, inescapable […] handcuffs of the future. Terrific. What they dream about at the Pentagon, worldwide martial law." (*BE*, 420)

This dialogue strikes the reader as direct, perhaps uncommonly direct for Pynchon, and free from vagueness words such as *some, might, may, somehow*, and *kind of*, which proliferate in this novel. Ernie's brief monologues are polemical and unambiguous, and can easily be read as lecturing both Maxine and the reader that the Myth of the Free Internet is a lie. Numerous critics have cited these passages in book reviews and scholarship, while the sentence, "Call it freedom, it's based on control" is cited in well over a dozen book reviews of *Bleeding Edge* revealed after only a cursory search. These passages emphasizing the malicious origins of the internet are also among the most frequently highlighted by readers of *Bleeding Edge* on Amazon's Kindle e-book reader.[66] Clearly, passages from the "least vague" 2.5 pages of *Bleeding Edge* have resonated with readers of the novel. Could the reason be that here, amidst Pynchon's sea of vagueness, is a welcoming island of clarity and directness, a clear "message" to distill the novel, an unambiguous "takeaway" that the reader can confidently underline?

More than a few commentators have read Ernie's skewering of the Internet Myth as an unmediated, unironic stand-in for empirical author Thomas Pynchon. Citing the first passage quoted above, Michael Jarvis writes that "this is the unrepentant Luddite in Pynchon, the one who warned in his 1984 essay of 'a permanent power establishment.'"[67] Jason Siegel, quoting from the same lines, writes that "it seems that *Pynchon wants us to take his words at face value* because Ernie's predictions had proven to be prophetic by the time the novel was published" (emphasis added).[68] Nathaniel Rich writes that, "Maxine's father, a curmudgeonly intellectual approximately Pynchon's age, seems to come closer than any other character to articulating the novel's conscience."[69] McHale has cautioned against naively reading the empirical author Thomas Pynchon as *ever* addressing the reader (as when a narrator of *Gravity's Rainbow* employs the second person singular you).[70] Without fully succumbing to the temptation to read Ernie's warnings about the internet as evidence of Pynchon dropping his ironic mask and addressing the reader— "Allow me to be unambiguous," for once?—it is possible that readers may be more likely to interpret such authorial messages in passages with direct and low-vagueness language. Relatedly, and it is also possible that crisp sentences in Pynchon texts are more likely to be cited by book reviewers or critics, or underlined by readers.

Discussing the later part of *Bleeding Edge*, Luc Herman observes that "after the terrorist attacks take place ([on page] 316), *Bleeding Edge* becomes much more explicit. Pynchon largely drops his crime spoof in order to deliver social commentary," via fiction that "give[s] up on irony" and that "the narrator doesn't hesitate to let us in on a number of truths, including those that pertain to the internet."[71] Pynchon has such a strong lifelong association with irony and obliqueness that Herman seems reluctant to accept an irony-free Pynchon in these later sections of *Bleeding Edge*: "I would prefer to explain this turn as a wish on the author's part to illustrate what fiction is going to be like if we give up on irony […] rather than concede that [Pynchon] is going soft."[72] The "least vague" passages in *Bleeding Edge*, which appear late in the novel, seem to be instances of what Herman is referring to: "truths … that pertain to the internet," delivered in a direct manner which "give[s] up on irony."

If Herman is correct that *Bleeding Edge* features reduced irony from page 316 on (the beginning of chapter 29), this may thus be correlated with stylistic vagueness. And indeed, chapters 29–41 of *Bleeding Edge* are slightly lower in average density of Pynchon's "preferred" vagueness words (Figure 3.20).[73]

Figure 3.20 is presented merely as exploratory evidence that the later chapters of *Bleeding Edge* reduce the amount of "irony," as textual irony in both literary studies and linguistics involves far more than a dictionary of vagueness words. But here is evidence that a number of later chapters of *Bleeding Edge* are, at the least, more stylistically crisp.

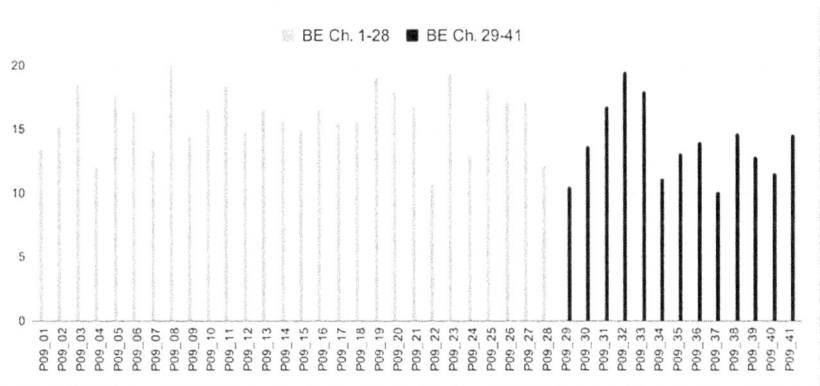

Figure 3.20 Normalized frequency of forty-eight of Pynchon's "preferred vagueness words" in chapters of *Bleeding Edge*, per 1,000 word tokens.

3.3 Ambiguity/Vagueness: Conclusion

Applying the Hiller/Hogenraad dictionary to Pynchon's texts has thus resulted in tantalizing but incomplete results. Pynchon's novels do indeed score highest or high in many categories of the Hiller/Hogenraad dictionary, compared with thirty-three novels across genres, as well as the entire Brown Fiction and COCA Fiction corpora. In most instances, however, the novels that score highest are post-*Gravity's Rainbow*, in other words, after Schaub had dubbed Pynchon "the Voice of Ambiguity." In a number of experiments, vagueness words are increasing and/or highest in Pynchon's three latest novels: *Against the Day*, *Inherent Vice*, and *Bleeding Edge*, suggesting an aspect of Pynchon's "late style."

Future studies could explore the interpretation of stylistic vagueness, Pynchon's "preferred" vagueness words, and the fact that they increase over time. A reader could simply revisit passages with an eye toward stylistic vagueness, for instance:

> *Sometimes* I wanna go back north, to Humboldt County—
> *Sometimes I think* I'll go back east, to see my kin …
> *There's times I think* I *almost could be* happy,
> If I knew you thought about me, *now and then*… (*GR*, 740. Hiller/Hogenraad vagueness words italicized)[74]

Any interpretation of this memorable passage can be enhanced by the knowledge that the text is brimming with vagueness words, that these are a Pynchonesque stylistic feature, and that this stylistic feature is associated in Pynchon's texts with a considerable amount of thematic weight, Pynchon's wide-ranging treatment of ambiguity.

One unresolved contradiction is that Pynchon's latest two novels are considered his easiest to read and understand—"Pynchon Lite"—but also highest in vagueness words. While the proliferating instances of *kind of* and *somehow* and *perhaps* perpetually underscore Pynchon's eschewal of binaries, in what ways do they function textually, other than to blanket Pynchon's worlds within a kind of druggy haze?

> "He's allowed to talk about what he does?"
> "Perhaps not. We're never sure. It's … it's Lloyd, you see."
> "Y— Well, not exactly." (*BE*, 351)

Here, even a simple affirmative "yes" is cut off for "not exactly," a "preferred" Pynchon vagueness phrase that so encapsulates the concept of vagueness that a leading expert on linguistic vagueness, Kees van Deemter, titled one of his books, *Not Exactly: In Praise of Vagueness*.

The longest passage in *Bleeding Edge* with none of Pynchon's "preferred" vagueness words has been noted by critics for its irony-free directness, and readers have associated these passages as messages from Thomas Pynchon, empirical author. Future work could explore the modulation of stylistic vagueness in Pynchon's texts much further, including in character dialogue. For instance, it is possible that the characters Duyfhuizen dubbed Pynchon's "unambiguous villains,"[75] such as Scarsdale Vibe, Brock Vond, and Gabriel Ice, might speak in crisp, unambiguous dialogue. But while some direct speech by Gabriel Ice displays a notable crispness ("Are you on a secure line?," 136; "You despise me, right?," 137), vagueness words creep into Ice's speech, as well:

> "[…] Thing to do," Ice proclaims, "is to go north, set up server farms where heat dissipation *won't be so much* of a problem, take your power from renewables like hydro or sunlight, use surplus heat to help sustain *whatever* communities grow up around the data centers." (*BE*, 310, vagueness words italicized)

Vagueness/ambiguity in Pynchon's texts—and literary texts at large—is a vast topic which may sustain a wealth of future digital stylistic investigation, which could dig deeper into vagueness at the sentence, phrasal, and syntactic levels, as well as closer investigations of individual topics revealed by the Hiller/Hogenraad categories in which Pynchon was high, including negated intensifiers, indefinite amount, and probability and possibility. If nothing else, a sustained awareness of vagueness in Pynchon's texts enhances our understanding of his stylistics and that there are, perhaps, somehow, various times in which Pynchon drops his mask of ambiguity and, now and then, may address the reader in the manner in which he addressed CNN: "Let me be unambiguous."

The rest of this book turns to more reliably operationalized queries of other stylistic features of Pynchon's texts: acronyms, profanity, and ellipsis marks. Some aspects of these features relate to vagueness/ambiguity and provide further observations regarding Pynchon's elusive and so far undefined "late style," which will be revisited in the conclusion.

Notes

1 Uncredited, "Where's Thomas Pynchon?" *CNN.com*, June 5, 1997, http://edition. cnn.com/US/9706/05/pynchon/.

2 Schaub, *Pynchon: The Voice of Ambiguity*, ix–x.

3 Deborah L. Madsen, "Ambiguity," in *Thomas Pynchon in Context*, ed. Inger H. Dalsgaard (Cambridge: Cambridge University Press, 2019), 298.

4 E.g., Kees van Deemter, *Not Exactly: In Praise of Vagueness* (Oxford: Oxford University Press, 2010).

5 Manfred Pinkal, *Logic and Lexicon* (London: Kluwer Academic, 1995), 110.

6 Ibid.

7 Schaub, *Pynchon: The Voice of Ambiguity*, 107.

8 Ibid., 3.

9 Harold Bloom, *The Anxiety of Influence: A Theory of Poetry*, 2nd ed. (Oxford: Oxford University Press, 1975), xxxii.

10 E.g., Hans Eichner, *"Romantic" and Its Cognates: The European History of a Word* (Toronto: University of Toronto Press, 1972), 176.

11 "Ambiguous, adj.," *OED Online*, Oxford University Press, accessed January 22, 2018, http://0-www.oed.com.catalogue.libraries.london.ac.uk/view/Entry/6145?redirected From=ambiguous.

12 Schaub, *Pynchon: The Voice of Ambiguity*, 4.

13 Joanna Freer, *Thomas Pynchon and American Counterculture* (Cambridge: Cambridge University Press, 2014), 7.

14 Brian McHale, "Pynchon's Postmodernism," *The Cambridge Companion to Thomas Pynchon*, ed. Inger H. Dalsgaard, Luc Herman, and Brian McHale (Cambridge: Cambridge University Press, 2012), 98.

15 For the most scientifically rigorous study of entropy in Pynchon's "Entropy," see David Letzler, "Crossed-Up Disciplinarity: What Norbert Wiener, Thomas Pynchon, and William Gaddis Got Wrong about Entropy and Literature," *Contemporary Literature* 56:1 (2015): 23–55.

16 Cowart, *Thomas Pynchon: The Art of Allusion*, 2.

17 *Vineland*, *Mason & Dixon*, and *Inherent Vice* contain no explicit invocation of *entropy*, while *Bleeding Edge* contains only one. Although see e.g., David Thoreen, "The Economy of Consumption: The Entropy of Leisure in Pynchon's *Vineland*," *Pynchon Notes* 30–1 (1992). Entropy is mentioned explicitly in *Against the Day*.

18 Schaub, *Pynchon: The Voice of Ambiguity*, 5.

19 Mark D. Hawthorne, "A 'Hermaphrodite Sort of Deity': Sexuality, Gender, and Gender Blending in Thomas Pynchon's *V.*," *Studies in the Novel* 29:1 (1997): 74–93.

20 Thomas Pynchon, "'The Heart's Eternal Vow,' review of *Love in the Time of Cholera*, by Gabriel García Márquez," *New York Times Book Review*, April 10, 1998, 47.

21 "Repeatedly failed to provide an unambiguous result" (*ATD*, 112); "a not unambiguous cologne" (*ATD*, 540); "Without an unambiguous go-ahead from home" (*ATD*, 763).

22 Uncredited, "Where's Thomas Pynchon?"

23 Thomas Pynchon, "Introduction," in Jim Dodge, *Stone Junction* (Edinburgh: Rebel, 1997), vii–xii.

24 Pynchon corpus compared with Brown Fiction (10.7 LL, $p < 0.001$), Peer Corpus (16.76 LL, $p < 0.0001$), Popular Fiction Corpus (33.49 LL, $p < 0.0001$), Influence Corpus (0.02 LL, not significant), COCA Fiction (62.4 LL, $p < 0.0001$).

25 James Patterson, *The Thomas Berryman Number* (New York: Little, Brown, [1976] 2006), 47, 200.

26 Anita Gandolfo, *Faith and Fiction: Christian Literature in America Today* (London: Praeger, 2007), 130.

27 Ken Gelder, *Popular Fiction: The Logics and Practices of a Literary Field* (London: Routledge, 2004), 35.

28 In a brief magical realist story described in the novel—about a man who falls in love too easily and a woman with a frog who lives nestled in her neck—Wallace oddly uses *ambig** six times in six pages. David Foster Wallace, *The Broom of the System* (New York: Penguin Classics, [1987] 2016), 188–94. This frequent use of *ambiguous* in a handful of pages could be read to evoke the repetitious language of fairy tales, which the story-within-a-story resembles. Tentative corpus query also suggests that Wallace makes more frequent use of the same repeated adjectives compared to other writers, an avenue for future research.

29 Michael Stubbs, "Conrad in the Computer," *Language and Literature* 14:1 (2005): 9.

30 For a different approach, Mahlberg has noted that certain clusters (n-grams) in Dickens's characters' speech contained repeated vague phrases. Michaela Mahlberg, *Corpus Stylistics and Dickens's Fiction* (London: Routledge, 2013), 279–87.

31 Word forms that collocate with "ambig*" in the Pynchon corpus with frequency of at least five are *and*, *in*, *an*, and *any*. As calculated by the *Cooccurrences* feature in TXM to query collocated lemmas within a span of ten words to the left, ten words to the right of *ambig**.

32 Jack H. Hiller, Donald R. Marcotte, and Timothy Martin, "Opinionation, Vagueness, and Specificity-Distinctions: Essay Traits Measured by Computer," *American Educational Research Journal* 6:2 (1969): 271–86.

33 Jack H. Hiller, "Verbal Response Indicators of Conceptual Vagueness," *American Educational Research Journal* 8:1 (1971): 151–61.

34 Hogenraad removed five duplicates from Hiller's vagueness dictionary, changed a few entries from word-to-word form, and added twenty-one words and phrases (category in parenthesis): *all people* (1), *all the time* (1), *less and less* (3), *more and more* (3), *off the top of* (3), *overall* (3), *beyond doubt* (4), *plus or minus* (9), *seemed* (9); and the following in category 6: *aggregate, as much as, bulk, caboodle, flock, give or take, heap, majorit*(y), mass, mess, muddle, volume**.

35 Robert Hogenraad, "Smoke and Mirrors: Tracing Ambiguity in Texts," *Digital Scholarship in the Humanities* 33:2 (2018): 297–315.

36 Ibid., 306, 308.

37 Technical steps: In addition to preprocessing already described, I removed ellipsis marks (hyphens and ellipsis points) from the corpora, as they tend to cause errors in TXM results, and converted the texts to lower case (so that queries have combined results, rather than separate frequencies for e.g. *Almost* and *almost*). I then ran regular expressions to query the Hiller/Hogenraad dictionary categories, outputted as .csv files, then performed comparison and statistical analysis in a spreadsheet application and Rayson's log-likelihood calculator.

38 Anaphors are defined as "a pronoun or similar element that must be understood in relation to an antecedent." P. H. Matthews, *The Concise Oxford Dictionary of Linguistics*, 2nd ed. (Oxford: Oxford University Press, 2007), 19.

39 See e.g., McHale, *Constructing Postmodernism*, 79 ("ambiguous pronoun references help smooth the transition"); de Bourcier, *Pynchon and Relativity*, 65 ("the odd switch of pronouns, the ambiguity of 'we,' all help to make the final sentence an ending but not a resolution").

40 E.g., the final sentences of Toni Morrison's *Song of Solomon* feature ambiguous *he* and *his*: "it did not matter which one of them would give up his ghost in the killing arms of his brother. For now he knew what Shalimar knew: If you surrendered to the air, you could ride it." On this, Morrison stated in an interview, "the ambiguity is deliberate because it doesn't end, it's an ongoing thing." Christina Davis and Toni Morrison, "Interview with Toni Morrison," *Présence Africaine* 145 (1988): 149.

41 Some issues with using the Hiller/Hogenraad dictionary in experiments for literary vagueness are some words are queried as lemmas, others as a number of words forms, seemingly in an arbitrary fashion; numerous words have debatably vague/ambiguous semantics in the literary mode (e.g., *flock, mass, mess, age, fields, involved*), while others are spoken formalities that will vary greatly in novels with greater or less amounts of direct speech (e.g., *sorry, you know*).

42 As a minor modification to the Hiller/Hogenraad vagueness dictionary, I also exclude results for *OK* and *Okay* (in Category 4), as the dictionary does not include *O.K.*, which could skew results given the high frequency of this word in certain texts.

43 Log-likelihood for *Against the Day* cf. Brown Fiction (LL 68.77), *Against the Day* cf. COCA Fiction (LL 26,033.43), *Inherent Vice* cf. Brown Fiction (LL 1602.11), *Inherent Vice* cf. COCA Fiction (LL 20,752.62), *We Did Porn* cf. Brown Fiction (LL 2,006.57), *We Did Porn* cf. COCA Fiction (LL 20,049.84).

44 Cormac McCarthy, *The Crossing* (New York: Vintage, 1995), 354.

45 John Rothfork, "Cormac McCarthy as Pragmatist," *Critique: Studies in Contemporary Fiction* 47:2 (2006): 201.

46 Brigham Young University has launched a Cormac McCarthy Corpus Project providing metadata and access to the texts via certain interfaces. Phillip A. Snyder, Delys W. Snyder, and Jeremy Browne, "All Novels 1.0 in Sentence Structure Search (Experimental)," *The Cormac McCarthy Corpus Project*, accessed September 9, 2019, http://cmcp.byu.edu/index.php/corpus-and-tool/ all-novels-in-sentence-structure-search/.

47 Geoff Dyer, "My Literary Allergy," *Prospect*, March 23, 2011, https://www.prospectmagazine.co.uk/magazine/ geoff-dyer-david-foster-wallace-pale-king-literary-allergy.

48 Maud Newton, "Another Thing to Sort of Pin on David Foster Wallace," *New York Times*, August 19, 2011, https://www.nytimes.com/2011/08/21/magazine/another- thing-to-sort-of-pin-on-david-foster-wallace.html?src=tp.

49 As Pynchon's style may have influenced the authors in the Influence corpus, I exclude these for this experiment.

50 For instance, *seems* occurs 103 times in the present-tense novel *Bleeding Edge*, but only 18 times in the preceding, past-tense novel *Inherent Vice*. The frequency of these words still rises over time in the Pynchon corpus if *seems* is included.

51 William Strunk Jr. and E. B. White, *The Elements of Style* (New York: Macmillan, 1959), 15.

52 Richard Poirier, "Cook's Tour," *New York Review of Books*, June 1, 1963, https:// www.nybooks.com/articles/1963/06/01/cooks-tour/.

53 Brian Stonehill, "Pynchon's Prophecies of Cyberspace," *Pynchon Notes* 34–5 (1994): 13–14.

54 Hume, *Pynchon's Mythography*, 91–4.

55 Ted Underwood, *Distant Horizons: Digital Evidence and Literary Change* (Chicago: University of Chicago Press, 2019), 59.

56 Using *Gravity's Rainbow* as a baseline, all subsequent novels significantly differ in frequency of *its*, over minimum 95th percentile, $p < 0.05$, using log-likelihood.

57 The second highest spike, meanwhile, occurs in chapter 42 of *Mason & Dixon*, which includes lengthy descriptions of a rifle and an electric eel.

58 Martin Paul Eve, *Pynchon and Philosophy: Wittgenstein, Foucault and Adorno* (Basingstoke: Palgrave Macmillan, 2014), 107.

59 E.g., Michael P. Maguire, "September 11 and the Question of Innocence in Thomas Pynchon's *Against the Day* and *Bleeding Edge*," *Critique: Studies in Contemporary Fiction* 58:2 (2017): 95–107.

60 Weisenburger, *A* Gravity's Rainbow *Companion*, 2nd ed., 277.

61 Bernard Duyfhuizen, "'A Suspension Forever at the Hinge of Doubt': The Reader-Trap of Bianca in *Gravity's Rainbow*," *Postmodern Culture* 2:1 (1991), https://muse.jhu.edu/article/27320.

62 Query performed using Python code by Andreas van Cranenburgh which queries the longest string in text which excludes a list of "taboo" words: https://github.com/andreasvc/longestnontabooseq.

63 van Deemter, *Not Exactly: In Praise of Vagueness*.

64 This "least vague" string runs from "even took their own lives" (*BE*, 420) through "You'd come back from school, history classes" (*BE*, 422).

65 Edwin Turner, "Blog about Thomas Pynchon's Novel, *Bleeding Edge*," *Biblioklept.org*, May 8, 2020, https://biblioklept.org/2020/05/08/blog-about-thomas-pynchons-novel-bleeding-edge/.

66 These passages are the third and sixth most highlighted passages by readers in the Kindle version of *Bleeding Edge*. The passage including "Yep, and your Internet" is highlighted 121 times, and the "Call it freedom" passage is highlighted 89 times.

67 Michael Jarvis, "Pynchon's Deep Web," *Los Angeles Review of Books*, September 10, 2013, https://lareviewofbooks.org/article/pynchons-deep-web/.

68 Jason Siegel, "Meatspace is Cyberspace: The Pynchonian Posthuman in *Bleeding Edge*," *Orbit: A Journal of American Literature* 4:2 (2016).

69 Nathaniel Rich, "The Thomas Pynchon Novel for the Edward Snowden Era," *The Atlantic*, October 2013, https://www.theatlantic.com/magazine/archive/2013/10/losing-the-plot/309450/.

70 McHale, *Constructing Postmodernism*, 96.

71 Luc Herman, "Reading Pynchon in and on the Digital Age," in *The New Pynchon Studies*, ed. Joanna Freer (Cambridge: Cambridge University Press, 2019), 204.

72 Ibid.

73 The frequency of Pynchon's "preferred" vagueness words in chapters 1–28 is statistically significantly higher than in chapters 29–41, log-likelihood 14.26, $p < 0.001$.

74 "There's times" is not in the dictionary but "at times" is.

75 Bernard Duyfhuizen, "'God Knows, Few of Us Are Strangers to Moral Ambiguity': Thomas Pynchon's *Inherent Vice*," *Postmodern Culture* 19:2 (2009), https://muse.jhu.edu/article/366239/.

4

Pynchon's Acronymania

4

Pynchon's Acronymania

> *"It's W.A.S.T.E., lady," he told her, "an acronym, not 'waste,' and we had best not go into it any further."*
>
> —*The Crying of Lot 49*, 81

To transition from vague language to the more clear, or at least, more clearly defined and queryable, this chapter provides a stylistic analysis of acronyms in Pynchon's texts. Comic, parodic, and often invented acronyms are a memorable feature in Pynchon's fiction, from absurdly named organizations (ACDC for "Alameda County Death Cult") to fictional conditions (THO for "Teen Hair Obsession") to central enigmas which underlie the fragmented narratives (above all, W.A.S.T.E. in *Lot 49*). Scholars and especially book reviewers tasked with introducing a Pynchon text to readers invariably mention creative acronyms as characteristic of Pynchon's style. As Duyfhuizen summarized after the publication of *Against the Day*, "we have come to expect so-called 'Pynchonesque' features in his work, such as thematic concerns with paranoia, […] wacky character names […] and organizations with wacky acronyms (T.W.I.T., I.G.L.O.O., and L.A.H.D.I.D.A., for instance)."[1] Pynchon's "wacky" acronyms are considered so characteristic of his style and influence that critics have mentioned, for instance, the use of "Pynchoneseque acronym[s]" in *Infinite Jest*.[2]

Via distant and close reading, this chapter investigates the frequency, variety, and semantics of acronyms in Pynchon's texts and the comparison corpora, to add formal knowledge, confirm or challenge critics' assumptions and update the most extensive study on the subject, Manfred Pütz's "The Art of the Acronym in Thomas Pynchon" (1991), which explored how this seemingly ubiquitous stylistic device relates to broader thematic strategies in Pynchon's texts. Pütz summarized the history of acronyms in literature, stressed Pynchon as a "notable exception" in their use, teased broader interpretations from "bizarre acronyms [which] at first seem to point to mere playfulness," and concluded that "the frequent and almost provocative use of acronyms in the novels of Thomas Pynchon marks a stage of development where playing with this form of words is turned into a literary art with sophisticated functions and effects."[3] Pütz also posed some questions for future scholars: "one might wonder whether [Pynchon's] acronymania will prove to be a constant feature of his literary works, and also whether it will spread [...] from his novels to the works of other contemporary authors with similar orientations." These questions are now eminently addressable using my corpora.

As it turns out, Pynchon's acronymania did *not* prove to be a constant feature of his works, at least in terms of frequency, as acronyms are greatly reduced in *Against the Day* and especially *Mason & Dixon*, in which the "zany Pynchonesque acronyms" are reduced to merely a handful. Some possible explanations for this stylistic shift are explored below, most obviously as these novels are written in (often parodic) pastiches of historical English. But when Pütz spoke of Pynchon's "acronymania," he was concerned not only with frequency and the effect of such "calculated overuse" but also with a wider variety of "sophisticated effects," especially Pynchon's acronyms as parody, play, and central enigma.

Through close reading contextualized by the queries, I update Pütz's study by examining acronyms in Pynchon's post-1991 novels and provide evidence that a number of contemporaries, especially John Barth, should be included in any discussion of acronyms in postmodernism at large. Finally, when Pütz wondered whether Pynchon's acronymania would spread to later writers' works, my corpora show that the answer is yes, although only in certain authors, especially David Foster Wallace. While the profusion and absurdity of acronyms in especially *Infinite Jest* is noticeable to any reader, the quantification of acronym types and tokens underscores the degree to which Wallace attempted, in the words of critic Dale Peck, to "out-*Gravity's Rainbow Gravity's Rainbow*."[4]

4.1 Acronym Query

To query acronyms in the corpora, I used simple regular expressions and examined the output in TXM's KWIC (keyword in context) display.[5] Although scholars are advancing the automatic detection of acronyms,[6] I opted for this more labor-intensive method to sift out the numerous initials of names, for example, FDR, JFK, the character DL in *Vineland*, and words from sentences and paragraphs capitalized for effect. Some additional initial criteria were to only include capitalized acronyms (ignoring common abbreviations such as *e.g.*

Acronyms

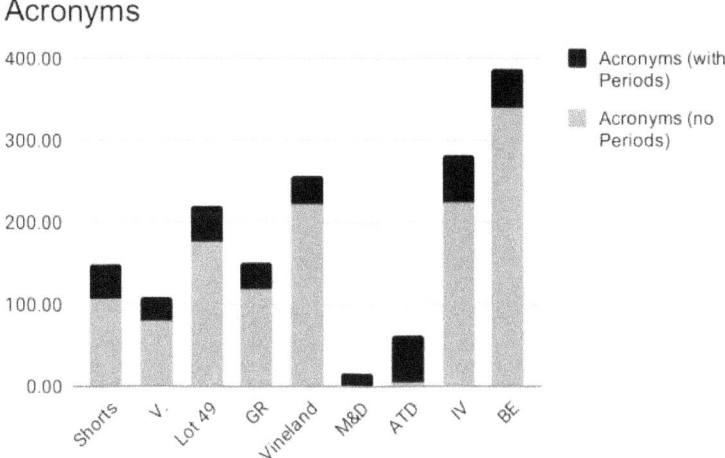

Figure 4.1 Normalized frequency (per 100k word tokens) of acronyms in Pynchon corpus.

and *i.e.*) as well as excluding uncapitalized acronyms that have become common parlance as words, such as *radar* or *laser*. Some of these methodological choices are arbitrary by necessity, as definitions of an acronym vary in linguistic literature; as Heidi Harley notes, "the terms abbreviation, initialism, and acronym have not been used consistently by scholars."[7]

By this method, I count 519 types of acronyms in Pynchon's fiction, with a total frequency of 2,515 (1,809 with no periods, e.g., *RAF*, and 706 with periods, e.g., *M.B.A.*). See Figure 4.1.

Observing the most frequent acronyms in Pynchon's texts suggests that these results may be skewed by some frequent common acronyms, such as *O.K.*, *U.S.*, and *TV*. (Figure 4.2).[8]

As an experiment, I excluded the words with frequency > 20 which seem least indicative of acronym as creative choice: place names (*U.S.*, *L.A.*, *D.C.*), the time indicators *A.M.* and *P.M.*, as well as *T.V.* and *O.K.*. But the resulting trend is essentially the same as in Figure 4.1 (for data and visualization, see the online data appendix). Acronyms in Pynchon's texts trend upward through *Gravity's Rainbow*, followed by a large decline in *Mason & Dixon* and *Against the Day*, then rise to new heights in Pynchon's latest two novels. The frequency of acronyms by type (i.e., the variety of different acronyms) are in Figure 4.3.

The data on types of acronyms should be considered with caution, as type increases based upon the length of the text, as studies of type/token ratios in texts have shown.[9] The longer the text, the more likely that new and different

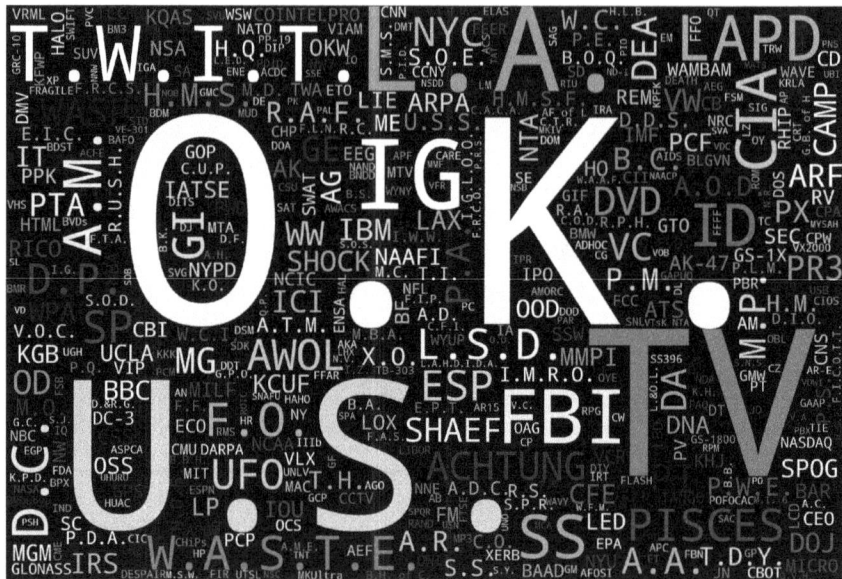

Figure 4.2 Word cloud of acronyms in Pynchon corpus by frequency (combining acronyms with and without periods).

Acronyms (types)

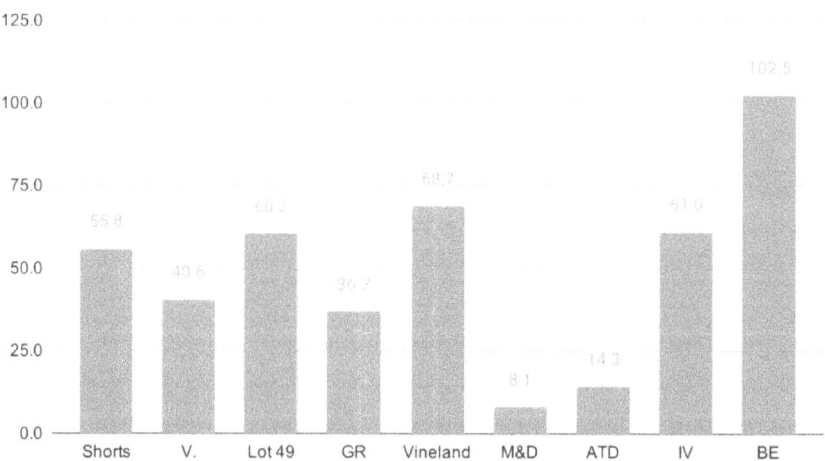

Figure 4.3 Normalized frequency (per 100k word tokens) of types of acronyms in Pynchon corpus.

words and acronyms will appear as the plot progresses. Nonetheless, the results for Pynchon's fiction do not readily evince this tendency; quite the contrary, as Pynchon's shorter novels feature a greater variety of acronyms per page than his longer novels.

These results add formal detail on the abundance of acronyms in Pynchon's oeuvre. A narrator in *Bleeding Edge* once invokes a "universe" of acronyms: "Maxine never imagined that Driscoll's universe of three-letter acronyms might include 'LBD […]'" (*BE*, 232). And by my count, Pynchon's texts contain 130 or almost 20 percent of the 676 possible combinations that can be made from two letters (AA, AB, AC, etc.) and 240 or 1.5 percent of the possible 15,600 combinations of three-letter acronyms. This is a substantial charting of the acronymic universe, by any measure.

These results reveal some surprises in Pynchon's novels that follow Pütz's 1991 investigation. First, although *Gravity's Rainbow* seems so notable in acronym use, it is not a high watermark of early Pynchon acronymania when one considers page counts, and especially not when one considers type rather than frequency. Despite Pütz's description of a "veritable pandemonium of acronymania" in *Gravity's Rainbow*,[10] *V.*, *Lot 49* and even Pynchon's short stories exceed the variety of acronym use by various measures, per page. Next, Pütz wondered "whether [Pynchon's] acronymania will prove to be a constant feature of his literary work," but acronyms declined dramatically in the next two novels published after Pütz's study, *Mason & Dixon* and *Against the Day*. Following these, acronyms shot up again in the two most recent novels, *Inherent Vice* and *Bleeding Edge*, to record levels of frequency in Pynchon's texts. *Bleeding Edge* almost doubles the density of acronyms in *Gravity's Rainbow* and almost triples its variety of acronyms.[11]

The low number of acronyms in *Mason & Dixon* and *Against the Day* has a few possible explanations. One speculative possibility is that Pynchon simply (if temporarily) tired of a stylistic device he had employed profusely for decades. A better explanation is that acronyms are reduced because these are historical novels written in pastiche (of eighteenth-century English and 1893-First World War English, respectively), and acronyms were found far less in written English of those time periods, per Pütz: "The use of abbreviations, sometimes prematurely considered to be a modern phenomenon, has a tradition of long standing," but "the term *acronym* allegedly was coined in the 1940s, and linguists seem to agree that the most productive period of the rise of 'Alphabetic Shortening' and acronyms was from WWI on."[12] If so, this highlights an important aspect of Pynchon's stylistics: Pynchon is not always chained, so to speak, to continuous use of certain tools from his stylistic bag of tricks, as may sometimes seem to be the case (for instance, in the case of Pynchon's incorrigible use of silly and unusual character names). While any writer's style will display manifold variations over fifty years, acronyms provide a clear indication that Pynchon is willing to tone down "Pynchonian" stylistic devices when the setting of a novel calls for it.

Creative acronyms are such an established *topos* of Pynchon's style that critics came to expect them in later novels. But after close attention to the acronyms in *Mason & Dixon*, it emerges that most of them may actually be found in eighteenth-century texts, with only a handful being creatively coined by Pynchon, suggesting a certain rigor to Pynchon's acronymic pastiche (Table 4.4).

Table 4.1 Frequency of all acronyms in *Mason & Dixon*. Italics indicate apparent inventions by Pynchon

Acronym	Note	Frequency
A.R.	Astronomer Royal	8
B.C.	Before Christ	4
H.M.S.	His/Her Majesty's Ship	4
E.I.C.	East India Company	3
R.S.	Royal Society	3
A.M.	Time	2
D.I.O	"Damme, I'm Off!"	2
V.O.C/O.C	Dutch: *Verenigde Oostindishe Compagnie* (Dutch East India Company)	2
R.P.H.	*Red Public Hair*	2
B. of L.	Board of Longitude	2
A.M.	Ante meridiem	2
A.D.	Anno Domini	1
B.D.	*Black Dog*	1
B.H. of C.	*Black Hole of Calcutta*	1
F.A.S.	Fellow in our America Society	1
H.M.	His/Her Majesty's	1
L.E.D.	*Learned English Dog*	1
O.O.	Once Over	1
Q.E.D.	Quod erat demonstrandum	1
S.N.S	*Simply Not Suitable*	1
SSE	South-South-East	1
SSW	South-South-West	1
W.G.P.	*Weird Geordie Powers*	1
S. of J.	Society of Jesus	1
C. of E.	Church of England	1

Even some of the acronyms which a reader might assume are Pynchon's creations appear in period texts, for instance *D.I.O.* for "Damme, I'm Off!," included in *A Classical Dictionary of the Vulgar Tongue* (1788), which might have appealed to Pynchon's occasional predilection for acronymic profanity (such as "GNASH, the Global Network of Anecdotal Surfer Horseshit" in *Inherent Vice*).[13] Pynchon does coin a few acronyms in *Mason & Dixon*, such as an egregiously unscientific unit of measurement, "the width of a Red Pubick Hair or R.P.H." (296), as well as in some comic dialogue by Dixon, a self-identified Geordie: "If it's Weird Geordie Powers they wish, why W.G.P.'s they shall have" (301). But nowhere in *Mason & Dixon* are the "Pynchonian" parodic acronyms of invented organizations, and creative acronyms are rare instances in a fairly long novel. Overall, Pynchon's acronymania is at its most subdued in *Mason & Dixon* (which, naturally, only serves to foreground the rare exceptions).

Acronyms in *Against the Day* are relatively low, probably—again—in deference to the mock-historical style of the novel, but this novel marks a return of some of Pynchon's acronymic patterns discussed by Pütz, for instance in elaborately satirical inventions such as L.I.S.P. (Lieutenants of Industry Scholarship Program) and M.6I. (Modern Imperial Institute for Intensive Instruction In Idiotics).

4.2 Calculated Overuse of Acronyms

Pütz claims of a "calculated overuse" of acronyms in Pynchon's texts can be tested by querying the comparison corpora (Figures 4.4 and 4.5).

These results suggest that Pynchon's texts are indeed high in frequency and variety of acronyms, supporting Pütz's impression of a "calculated overuse" of acronyms. The comparably high acronym types and tokens in *Along Came a Spider*, a "lowbrow" thriller by James Patterson—due to genre- and subject matter-specific acronyms such as FBI (frequency 84), EMS (Emergency Medical Services, 8), and S.I.T (Special Investigator Team, 6)—underscores the limits of query, however. Pütz suggested Joseph Heller and David Lodge as notable acronymic experimenters, and my data suggest that texts by Barth, Barthelme, Wallace's *Infinite Jest*, and Smith's *We Did Porn* could be added in any survey of postmodern acronymania, but, again, the example of Patterson's thriller serves as a reminder of the necessity of close reading. Barth's texts, for instance, provide plenty of evidence of acronymic and absurd wordplay, as well as parodies of contemporary English via an overuse of acronyms. In *Giles Goat-Boy*, "Hedda of the Speckled Teats" is referred to as "Hedda O.T.S.T." (619, 684), repetitions

Acronym frequency

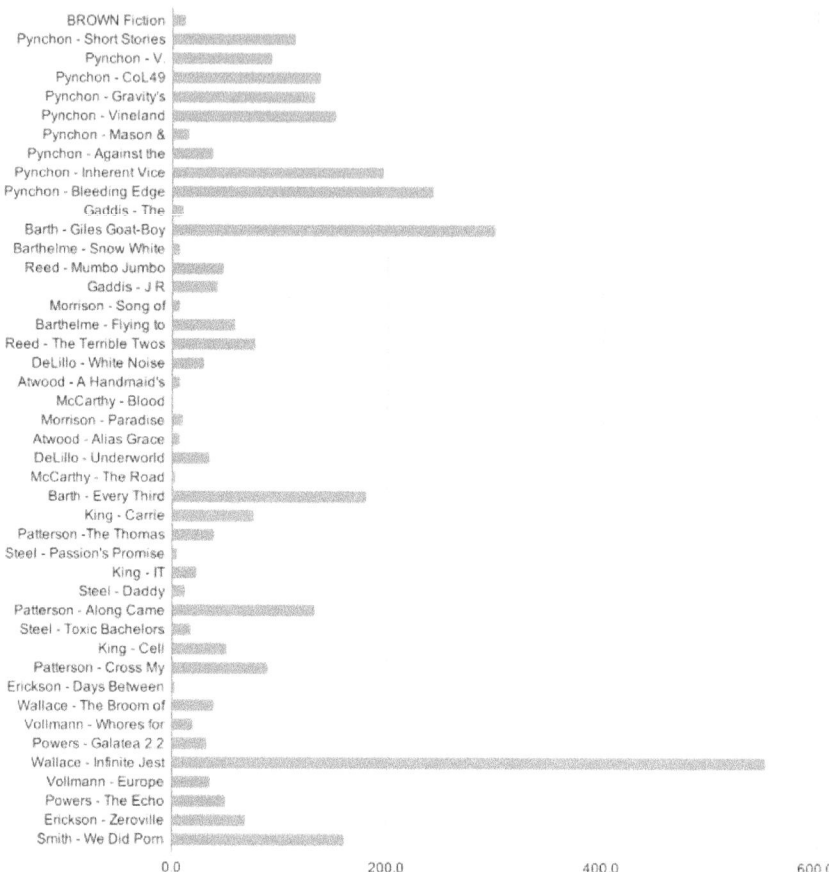

Figure 4.4 Normalized frequency (per 100k word tokens) of acronyms in Pynchon and comparison corpora, with seven common acronyms removed (O.K., U.S., T.V., L.A., D.C., A.M., and P.M.).

include "the P.-G.'s in the P.P.F.O., sir" (514), while a deer implausibly named "Tommy's Tommy's Tom" is referred to as "Triple-T" and T.T.T. and subject to even more convoluted wordplay: "seeing it was not I, T.'s T.'s Tom lowered horns and charged" (695). These examples demonstrate how, at times, Barth's acronymania may be even more surreal than Pynchon's.

Pütz wondered whether Pynchon's acronymania "will spread [...] from his novels to the works of other contemporary authors with similar orientations," and close and distant reading suggest that the answer is yes, in the case of Wallace and Smith. *Infinite Jest* contains 453 different acronyms, over triple the variety of

Types of acronyms

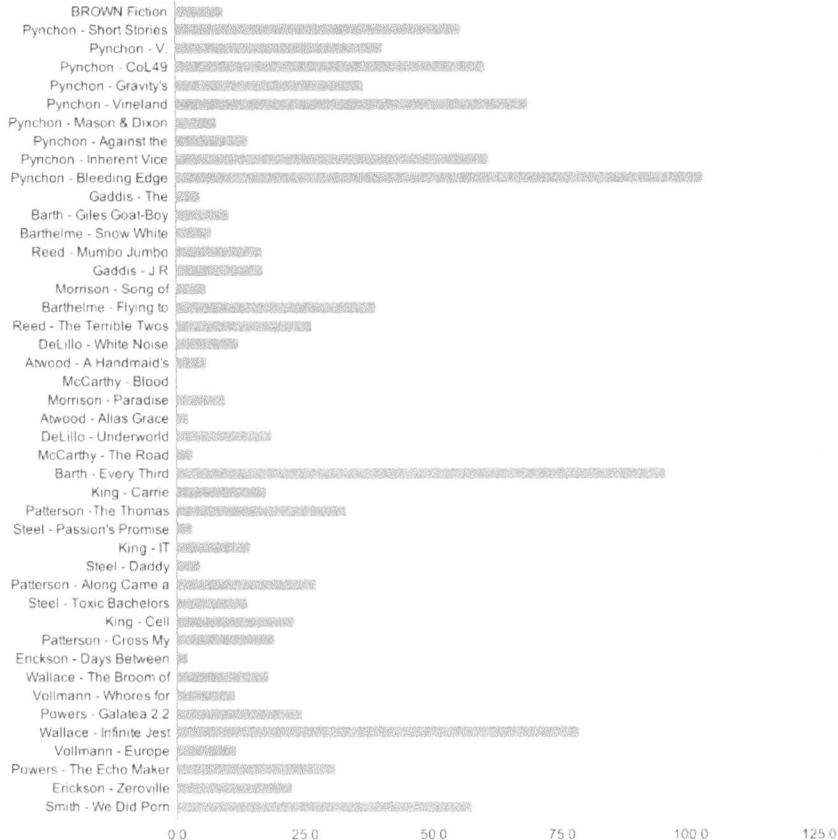

Figure 4.5 Normalized frequency (per 100k word tokens) of acronym types in Pynchon and comparison corpora, with same exclusions as Figure 4.4.

acronyms in *Gravity's Rainbow*. Although, again, some increase is to be expected due to the greater length of *Infinite Jest*, an over 300 percent increase is surely an example of Wallace attempting to "out-*Gravity's Rainbow Gravity's Rainbow*," as Peck put it, in conspicuous acronym overuse. As with Pynchon, the acronyms in *Infinite Jest* have spawned the creation of acronym guides in book and wiki form.[14] Some acronyms occur over a hundred times throughout the text, such as ETA (for Enfield Tennis Academy), AA (Alcoholics Anonymous), and TP (Teleputer, an imagined device merging television and computer). Wallace's "calculated overuse" of acronyms manifests in sentences comically overloaded with them, as in Barth, for example, "way more powerful than mescaline or MDA or DMA or TMA or MDMA or DOM or STP or the I. V.-ingestible DMT"

(170). Smith's *We Did Porn*, meanwhile, contains some similar sentences, for instance when describing Osbie Feel's collection of acronymically named toy robots: "I crash at Osbie's while he stays at his girlfriend or ex-girlfriend's place, along with an RGM79 (G) GM, two RX-75s, and RX-77, an MS-06J (or C?), an MS-07-B3, and MS-09, and MSM-03C, and, Osbie being hopelessly sentimental, an RX-78-2" (298). A reading of Pynchonian influence is hardly a stretch in this sequence, particularly as Osbie Feel is a character name plucked from *Gravity's Rainbow*.

A final consideration of Pynchon and others' overuse of acronyms is that acronyms are clearly increasing in modern English. Obviously, "new abbreviations continually come into use," as Larkey et al. note.[15] Gale's original *Acronym Dictionary* (1960) contained only 1,200 entries, while the forty-ninth edition from 2015 runs over six thousand pages.[16] In the field of cardiology, for instance, acronyms grew almost exponentially between 1992 and 1994 alone, reports Tsung O. Chen.[17] And the internet is increasing this acronym saturation, via "Netspeak" littered with LOL, OMG, and many others. As David Crystal writes, "acronyms are so common [in Netspeak] that they regularly receive critical comment."[18]

This increase of acronyms in English certainly may be observed in the acronyms chosen by Influence corpus authors and Pynchon's latest two novels. The most frequent acronyms in *Inherent Vice* relate either to power and control (LAPD, FBI, PI, DA, ID, CIA) or 1960s counterculture (LSD, ESP, OD). *Bleeding Edge* includes numerous technology-related acronyms of relatively recent coinage (DOS, LM hash, VC, LED, CCTV, etc.) and textually engages with concentrated acronym overuse at times: "wearing a green glow-in-the-dark T-shirt reading UTSL, which Maxine at first takes for an anagram of LUST or possibly SLUT but later learns is Unix for 'Use The Source, Luke'" (69). The acronyms are appropriate for the settings of these novels, but their frequencies reveal an aspect of Pynchon's "late style," even if acronyms are increasing in the style of many (or most?) American authors.

4.3 Acronyms as Parody, Play, and Central Enigma

To turn from frequencies and "overuse" of acronyms to other functions of acronyms in Pynchon's texts, a close reading suggests that, *Mason & Dixon* aside, the nature of the acronym parody and play in Pynchon's later novels largely follows patterns identified by Pütz. Pütz discussed how acronyms, historically associated with the First and Second World Wars, government agencies, and bureaucratic bodies, in Pynchon's texts "infest"

> practically all forms of communication from private to public discourse, from idiolects to everyday speech […]. The calculated blurring of such distinctions, which parallels the blurring of fact and fiction in Pynchon, leads over to an ironic and a satirical dimension in the acronym games played by the author.[19]

Pütz notes how "the paradox that the mindless overproduction of abbreviations, allegedly meant to facilitate communication, eventually brings about the opposite effect" and that acronyms are deployed in Pynchon's larger strategy of satirizing the sources of domination and control, totalitarian and technocratic authorities: "the author satirises the language uses of those he detests and fears in order to satirise the users themselves in a more efficient way."[20]

In novels by Pynchon post-1991, the parody of organizational and bureaucratic names continues: T.W.IT. for "True Worshippers of the Ineffable Tetractys" (*ATD*, 255); WAMBAM for "Warriors Against the Man Black Armed Militia" (*IV*, 292); DESPAIR for "Disgruntlement Employee Simulation Program for Audit Information and Review" (*BE*, 87). Fresh examples of acronym play which touches on the homonymic, ambiguous nature of acronyms may be found, for example, "Phipps Epperdew, better known as Vip because he always looks like he's just emerged from a Lounge or flashed a Discount Card with that acronym on it" (*BE*, 88). Perhaps as minor evidence of Pynchon's increasing attention to acronyms in later novels, *Bleeding Edge* also includes Pynchon's longest acronymic absurdity: "a little operation downtown calling itself hwgaahwgh.com, an acronym for Hey, We've Got Awesome And Hip Web Graphix, Here" (42).

This chapter presents the opportunity to very briefly identify examples of acronymic parody and play in the comparison corpora, to supplement the data and interpretation above. A comic acronym for a society is found in Gaddis's *J R*: "group calling itself the Modern Allies of Mandible Art […] MAMA" (672), and as *J R* was published two years after *Gravity's Rainbow*, this raises an open question as to whether Gaddis may have drawn acronymic influence from Pynchon. Reed and Morrison, like Pynchon, riffed on the acronym as ambiguous homophone: "A little trip down to the C.A.D., you cad" (*Mumbo Jumbo*, 108); The protagonist of *Song of Solomon* is named Macon "Milkman" Dead, and his mother "hinted strongly that he ought to consider going to medical school. He'd foisted her off with 'How would that look? M.D., M.D. If you were sick, would you go see a man called Dr. Dead?'" (*Song of Solomon*, 69). Barthelme once engages in acronym wordplay, as well: "even though I ain't a A.B., I am a B.A., and maybe in the dimness the one thing will be taken for the other" (*Snow White*, 95). These are, however, rare examples in the chosen works of these authors.

DeLillo, like Pynchon and Heller, parodies military language via acronyms in *Underworld*, which employs the word *acronym* more (ten times) than any of Pynchon's novels or Pynchon contemporary analyzed. In a section of *Underworld* portraying a military pilot, the connection between acronyms and war technology is explored at length:

> You can't fight a war without acronyms. This is a fact of modern combat, according to Louis T. Bakey.
>
> And where do these compressed words come from?
>
> They come from remote levels of development, from technicians and bombheads in their computer universe—storky bespectacled men who deal with systems so layered and many-connected that the ensuing arrays of words must be atomized and redesigned, made spare and letter-sleek.
>
> But acronyms also come from the ranks, don't they, at least occasionally? Look at old Louis [...] in the lower deck of the forward fuselage, going through the checklist. And the crews in alert barracks worldwide waiting for the klaxons to sound. [...]
>
> And this is why the high-altitude bomber sitting on the ramp out there, crew of six including Louis, a great, massive, swept-winged and soon-to-soar B-52— this aircraft is known as a BUFF to tens of thousands of men throughout the command, for Big Ugly Fat Fuck. (*Underworld*, 606–7)

As *Underworld* was published in 1997, this passage could be read as, if not Pynchon- influenced, at least echoing a number of Pynchon's stylistic and thematic interests, especially in *Gravity's Rainbow*: acronyms as features of military/war, paranoia, scientist-elites vs. rank-and-file soldiers, aviation technology, and profane acronyms. DeLillo also employs acronyms to parody military logic: "The bombs fluttered down on the NVA [army of North Vietnam] and the ARVN [army of South Vietnam] alike, because if the troops on both sides pretty much resemble each other and if their acronyms contain pretty much the same letters, you have to bomb both sides to get satisfactory results" (*Underworld*, 612). As discussed above, the high frequency and variety of acronyms in Barth's texts underscore the notability of his creative acronym use, and Barth also deploys acronyms to parody military system and language, and computer technology more generally, most conspicuously via the sentient computer WESCAC and its menacing EAT ability in *Giles Goat-Boy*.

Acronymic wordplay and comedy are almost entirely absent from the popular fiction corpus, with the only noteworthy exception being a passage from a James Patterson thriller:

"I think he's legitimately VFC."

"What the hell is VFC?" Scorse asked. "I don't know VFC. You've lost me."

"It's a common enough psych term," I told him. "All of us shrinks talk about VFC when we get together. Very fucking crazy, Gerry."

[…] "Very fucking funny, Alex," Scorse finally said. "That's VFF." (*Along Came a Spider*, 211)

This suggests that acronym wordplay is largely confined to "literary" fiction. As acronymic wordplay foregrounds textual style, perhaps popular fiction tends to avoid it in furtherance of reader entertainment.

One might expect copious examples of acronyms as parody and play in the Pynchon Influence corpus, but with the major exception of Wallace, examples are isolated. In Powers's *The Echo Maker*, the ambiguous essence of acronyms is played upon: "That probation kid from Poquott who we were getting employment letters for mistook the UPS man for a SWAT team" (122). Smith engages in stream-of-consciousness word association play based on acronyms: "Over the hiss of heat or drone of the AC, we listen to Alice Cooper, or the racing bands of sustained static hum coming across the lonely traffic" (471). Here, *AC* (air conditioning) suggests the rock musician *Alice Cooper* to the author, while *static hum* may be suggested by yet another form of *AC*, alternating current. Again, however, these are exceedingly rare examples in the Influence corpus.

In *Infinite Jest*, the extreme profusion of acronyms includes voluminous examples of acronyms as parody and play. In the novel's near-future setting, the United States, Canada, and Mexico have merged into O.N.A.N., the "Organization of North American Nations," appearing 160 times in the text and which, as Mary K. Holland interprets, "signals the intense narcissism that permeates the culture of this novel far beyond political practice, as well as, perhaps, the masturbatory technique of the novel itself."[21] In place of A.D. for *anno domini*, calendar years in Wallace's imagined future are marked Y.D.A.U. for "Year of the Adult Depend Undergarment" (frequency forty-two). The ambiguous and bewildering nature of acronyms is invoked via acronyms that are sometimes not defined for the reader until hundreds of pages after being introduced, for example, "'ALGOL' is anybody's guess, unless it's not an acronym but some actual Québecois term, 'l'algol'" (1037). Comic political group names are present, as well, for example,

FOPPP, for "Female Objectification Prevention And Protest Phalanx outside the Pizzitola Athl. Center's main gates right at game-time, two FOPPPs per motorcycle" (929). Many other examples may be found.

Again, Pütz notes how in *Lot 49*, "the acronym WASTE also becomes the central enigma of the whole novel which, as usual in Pynchon, deals in enigmas of quasi metaphysical proportions."[22] This issue of acronym as central enigma, in the texts of Pynchon and others, deserves an update since Pütz's article. As discussed in Chapter 2, Pynchon has a history of marking important, ambiguous, central concepts in his novels with selective capitalization: V., the Zone, Us, Them, the Tube, the Line, and so on. Yet while Pynchon's acronymania in later novels has oscillated, Pynchon has not truly repeated the use of acronym as a central enigma.

An acronym as central, ambiguous concept may be found in certain works by Pynchon's contemporaries and the Influence corpus writers. The sentient computer WESCAC and its EAT ability are comparable examples that run throughout Barth's *Giles Goat-Boy*, published the same year as *Lot 49* (1966). In Reed's *Mumbo Jumbo* (1972), the central plot follows an international conspiracy, the Wallflower Order, seemingly working with the Knights Templar, as they seek to eradicate the "Jes Grew" virus, which is carried by black artists, the "J.G.Cs," or "Jes Grew Carriers." Just as WASTE does, these examples draw on and foreground the essentially ambiguous semantics of the acronym form.

In the Influence corpus, the most notable instance of acronym-as-central-concept is once again Wallace. In *The Broom of the System*, the characters in 1990 Cleveland reside in the vicinity of a man-made desert called the Great Ohio Desert (or G.O.D.) "meant to restore a sense of the sinister to Midwestern life. The confused heroine is 24-year-old Lenore Stonecipher Beadsman who, despite her proximity to the sinister G.O.D., has a ridiculous life," as summarized by Caryn James.[23] This allows Wallace to add layers of ambiguity and theological philosophy to such superficially straightforward statements as, for example, "he said he didn't think Lenore should go to the G.O.D." (415) Although not necessarily the *central* enigma of *The Broom of the System*, how G.O.D. may be interpreted (and what it is doing in Ohio, of all places) is certainly reminiscent of the enigmatic essence of WASTE.

4.4 Acronymania: Conclusion

Acronyms have a long linguistic history of association with technology, and Pynchon's extensive engagement with technology is certainly one of many causes for his acronymania. Among novelists, Pynchon is eminently qualified to incorporate science into his fiction, due to his scientific training (briefly as an engineering undergraduate) and work experience (as a technical writer at Boeing). Pynchon's role in pioneering the insertion of scientific concepts into literary fiction has also been acknowledged, for instance by Tom LeClair: "Although the Pynchon of *V.* displayed a precocious familiarity with history, geography, and multiple literary forms, what set him apart was his scientific knowledge."[24] A quotation from *Mason & Dixon* hints at a tantalizing association of acronyms with a particular aspect of scientific knowledge, namely mathematical/scientific variables: "Coffee is an art, where precision is all,—Water-Temperature, mean particle diameter, ratio of Coffee to Water or as we say, CTW, and dozens more Variables I'd mention" (467). This allows a reading that Pynchon may be drawn to acronyms because the capital letters of acronyms resemble the capital letters of scientific variables, and all of the acronym play thus evocative of the shuffling and reordering of variables in a mathematical equation or proof.

This chapter revealed great variation in the frequency of acronyms within Pynchon's later texts, adds insight into the milieu in which Pynchon's postmodern use of acronyms developed (with Pynchon at the forefront), and finds that some, but by no means all, of the presumably Pynchon-influenced authors imitate aspects of Pynchon's acronymic overuse, parody, and play. Acronyms throughout Pynchon's and other authors' texts are parodied as the detritus of bureaucracy, military, and power systems, and the next chapter turns to one conspicuous target of such systems: profanity.

Notes

1 Bernard Duyfhuizen, "'The Exact Degree of Fictitiousness': Thomas Pynchon's *Against the Day*," *Postmodern Culture* 17:2 (2007), online.

2 E.g., Robert L. McLaughlin, "Wallace's Aesthetic," in *The Cambridge Companion to David Foster Wallace*, ed. Ralph Clare (Cambridge: Cambridge University Press, 2018), 166.

3 Manfred Pütz, "The Art of the Acronym in Thomas Pynchon," *Studies in the Novel* 23:3 (1991): 371, 375.

4 Dale Peck, *Hatchet Jobs* (New York: New Press, 2004), 42.

5 Sample CQP and grep queries: [word="[A-Z][A-Z].*"], [word="[A-Z]\.[A-Z].*"], [A-Z]\.[A-Z]\.

6 E.g., Stuart Yeates, "Automatic Extraction of Acronyms from Text," in *Proceedings of Third New Zealand Computer Science Research Students' Conference* (Hamilton,

New Zealand, 1999); Dana Dannells, "Automatic Acronym Recognition," in *EACL '06 Proceedings of the 11th Conference of the European Chapter of the Association for Computational Linguistics* (Stroudsburg: Association for Computational Linguistics, 2006).

7 Heidi Harley, "Why Is It *The* CIA but Not *The NASA? Acronyms, Initialisms, and Definite Description," *American Speech* 79:4 (2004): 397.

8 Visualization created with the Python module wordcloud by Andreas Muller: https://amueller.github.io/word_cloud/index.html.

9 E.g., David L. Hoover, "Another Perspective on Vocabulary Richness," *Computers and the Humanities* 37 (2003): 157.

10 Pütz, "The Art of the Acronym," 374.

11 Using *GR* as a baseline comparison, the frequencies of acronyms in short stories, *Lot 49*, and *Vineland* are not statistically significant (above p < 0.05). The difference in acronyms between *GR* and the other novels is highly significant. Critical values for the comparison: short stories (1.26 LL, less than 95th percentile); *V.* (16.43 LL, p < 0.0001); *Lot 49* (0.12 LL, less than 95th percentile); *Vineland* (2.71, less than 95th percentile); *Mason & Dixon* (303.51 LL, p < 0.0001); *Against the Day* (220.15 LL, p < 0.0001); *Inherent Vice* (23.07 LL, p < 0.0001); *Bleeding Edge* (70.48 LL, p < 0.0001). Calculated using Rayson's Log-likelihood and Effect Size Calculator, http://ucrel. lancs.ac.uk/llwizard.html. Excluded acronyms: O.K., U.S., T.V., L.A., D.C., A.M., and P.M.

12 Pütz, "The Art of the Acronym," 372.

13 Francis Grose, *A Classical Dictionary of the Vulgar Tongue*, 2nd ed. (London: S. Hooper, 1788), unnumbered pages, at "P." The entry for D.I.O. for "Damme, I'm Off!" first appears in this second edition.

14 Robert Bell and William Dowling, *A Reader's Companion to* Infinite Jest (Self-published: 2005); Tim Ware, Andrew E. Mathis, et al., *Wallacewiki*, accessed September 1, 2019, http://www.wallacewiki.com.

15 Leah S. Larkey, Paul Ogilvie, M. Andrew Price, and Brenden Tamilio, "Acrophile: An Automated Acronym Extractor and Server," *DL '00 Proceedings of the Fifth ACM Conference on Digital Libraries* (New York: Association for Computing Machinery, 2000), 205.

16 Kristen Mallegg, ed., *Acronyms, Initialisms & Abbreviations Dictionary*, 49th ed. (Detroit: Cengage Gale, 2015).

17 Tsung O. Chen, "Acronymophilia: The Exponential Growth of the Use of Acronyms Should Be Resisted," *BMJ: British Medical Journal* 309:6956 (1994): 683–4.

18 David Crystal, *Language and the Internet*, 2nd ed. (Cambridge: Cambridge University Press, 2006), 89.

19 Pütz, "The Art of the Acronym," 375.

20 Ibid., 376–7.

21 Mary K. Holland, *Succeeding Postmodernism: Language and Humanism in Contemporary American Literature* (London: Bloomsbury, 2013), 88.

22 Pütz, "The Art of the Acronym," 378.

23 Caryn James, "Wittgenstein Is Dead and Living in Ohio," *New York Times*, March 1, 1987, https://www.nytimes.com/1987/03/01/books/wittgenstein-is-dead-and-living-in-ohio.html.

24 Tom LeClair, "The Prodigious Fiction of Powers, William Vollmann, and David Foster Wallace," *Critique* 38:1 (1996), 13.

5

Pynchon's Profanity, Queried and Coded

"How many times," continued Lindsay Noseworth, […] "have you been warned, Suckling, against informality of speech?" […] [H]e flipped Darby upside down, and held the flyweight lad dangling by the ankles out into empty space […] proceeding to lecture him on the many evils of looseness in one's expression, not least among them being the ease with which it may lead to profanity, and worse.
—*Against the Day*, 5

Pynchon provides an interesting case study for stylistic use of profanity for a number of reasons: profanity is a foregrounded stylistic feature in Pynchon's texts, Pynchon's early works were published within tumultuous years for the legal banning and prosecution of "obscene" literature, and Pynchon's publications span years in which profanity in written English was rapidly changing. Critical attention has focused on profanity and offensive content in *Gravity's Rainbow*, which was reportedly denied a Pulitzer Prize because some members of the Pulitzer board found the book to be "'unreadable,' 'turgid,' 'overwritten' and in parts 'obscene.'"[1] But as with so many inquiries in Pynchon studies, there is much to be learned by expanding the scope beyond *Gravity's Rainbow* alone.

This chapter queries profane lexis in the Pynchon and comparison corpora, finding that in terms of frequency and choice of profanity words, Pynchon's texts are fairly typical of American fiction. As the early phase of Pynchon's oeuvre is least illuminated by these profanity trends, I turn to close reading of profanity in the early short stories and novels, revealing a pattern of "coded" profanity and veiled references to banned works of literature. By contextualizing these textual patterns with some history of "obscene" literature prosecution in the United States, this chapter contributes a stylistic groundwork of profanity in Pynchon's texts and adds a reading of Pynchon's earliest acts of opposition to governmental control over language.

Profanity in *Gravity's Rainbow* has been explored in two excellent studies, the first being "Power and the Obscene Word: Discourses of Extremity in Thomas Pynchon's *Gravity's Rainbow*" by Christopher Ames.[2] Ames argued that profanity in *Gravity's Rainbow* may be read as oppositional language and gestures directed against power and its unambiguous truths: "The obscene utterance—borne through gesture, shout, or graffito—becomes the purified language of the Preterite, the not completely powerless cry of the dispossessed."[3] Ames highlighted the scene in which Slothrop whispers "Fuck you" to the empty casino room, a "profane oath directed at a target […] a cry of outrage at the ubiquity of the enemy," as well as when Mexico and Pig Bodine ("the crown prince of obscenity," per Ames) disrupt the banquet via disgusting and profane descriptions.[4] Writing in 1990, Ames surveyed the relatively limited literature on profanity in American speech and fiction, including a study on the rhetorical strategies of antiwar and black power groups in the 1960s, in which J. Dan Rothwell identified how obscenity "expresses a profound contempt for society's standards, a revolt against authority, and an irreverence for things sacred," as well as how "the use of obscenity is an effective rhetorical technique for channeling anger in an oppressed group."[5] In the decades since Ames wrote his article, linguistic studies have further explored profanity as language directed against authority. As Tony McEnery writes, "the ultimate basis of any political mandate is linguistic," and "to subvert that linguistic mandate [through profanity] is akin to undermining the foundations of a building."[6]

The next important work on profanity in Pynchon's texts is *Gravity's Rainbow, Domination, and Freedom* by Herman and Weisenburger, which situates the novel within the history of the counterculture, war protests, the civil rights movements of the "long sixties," and governmental acts to contain these.[7] Herman and Weisenburger contend that obscenity prosecutions in the United States by state and federal authorities, to silence and persecute underground presses and counterculture voices, "is the contentious, tumultuous historical context for reading *Gravity's Rainbow*, which Pynchon criticism cursorily acknowledges but otherwise leaves quite unexamined."[8] Within this legal/historical context, the authors argue that *Gravity's Rainbow* would have been a risky book for its author and publishers to release even a few years prior, and propose a "thought experiment," wondering "what scenes and narrative practices would have brought the heat down on *Gravity's Rainbow*?"[9] A scene they suggest is the infamous orgy aboard the *Anubis*, which they argue can be read "as a deliberately scripted, in-your-face challenge to existing obscenity and pornography laws, a resistance to governmental dominion over speech."[10]

Herman and Weisenburger also highlight Slothrop's "fuck you" in the casino, which "enables us to read Slothrop's 'Fuck You!' and his fugitive status in the terms of a compelling philosophical dialogue on nonviolent resistance to imperial aggression."[11]

This chapter adds to these studies by a consideration of profanity in not only *Gravity's Rainbow* but all of Pynchon's fiction, through digital experiments and updated context from corpus linguistic studies of profanity in English. While *Gravity's Rainbow* was published in a relatively liberal time for profanity and offensive content in American fiction, due to landmark court decisions on obscenity law, Pynchon's earlier texts, from his short stories through *Lot 49*, were published in much more legally restrictive times. Any "resistance to governmental dominion over speech" in these earlier Pynchon stories, if any such resistance exists, must have thus been more oblique. Through close reading of Pynchon's early fiction, this chapter provides a prehistory of Herman and Weisenburger's analysis of profanity in *Gravity's Rainbow*, following their approach of discussing notable bannings and court cases but focusing instead on the late 1950s and early 1960s. By contextualizing Pynchon's earlier texts with this history of profanity *contra* censorship, this chapter reveals a pattern of *coded* profanity, typically disguised profanity via foreign languages and absurd names. While critics have noted some references to banned literature (e.g., Nabokov and Henry Miller) in early Pynchon stories, the trend of coded profanity suggests new readings of Pynchon's early textual resistance to government censorship. While focusing on the stylistic use of profane lexis, the other, arguably dominant aspect of obscenity, namely depictions of sex—depictions challenging whatever readers and authorities consider as sexual norms—must be considered. While sex in Pynchon's texts has been much more fully explored elsewhere,[12] the degree of vagueness in sexual depictions, or how clearly or obliquely sex is described in the texts, will inform readings of explicit and coded profane language.

5.1 Profanity Queries and Changes to Profanity in English

"I pass, I intersect, I articulate, I do not count."—Roland Barthes, *S/Z*[13]

The first step in querying profane lexis in Pynchon's texts is simply to decide which words to include, which the literature on profanity demonstrates is fairly methodologically subjective. In their study of *fuck* in the British National Corpus, Tony McEnery and Zhonghua Xiao write that "bad language may be related to religion, sex, racism, defecation, homophobia (e.g. *queer*) and other matters."[14] McEnery's later book-length *Swearing in English* queries a similar list of "bad language words" or *BLWs* "partly guided by claims within the literature, partly by my own intuition."[15] Luis von Ahn has assembled a dictionary of 1,300+ "offensive/profane words,"[16] but this is overinclusive for my purposes, as many of the words are often or mostly non-offensive in context, for example, *yankee* or *period*. In a computational analysis of Raymond Chandler's style, Lee Sigelman and William Jacoby queried the terms "*bastard, bitch, damn, hell*, and *shit*, and their compounds e.g., *bullshit* and *horseshit*,"[17] but this, in contrast, seems limited. As a pragmatic approach, I begin with common profanity terms from a 2015 PhD dissertation looking at profanity in novels by J. D. Salinger and Robert Cormier[18] and add common terms for corporeal profanity. Racist and homophobic epithets are not included, as these should be explored by future work informed by the extensive scholarship on racism and homophobia in Pynchon's texts.[19] Religious profanity raises complex semantic issues when the name of a religious figure is included: for instance, if a character utters, "Oh, God!," the determination of profane intent involves some assessment of the religious belief system portrayed by the character. I thus limit religious profanity queried to *hell* and *damn* (and include *Goddamn* simply as a compound of *damn*).

As a first step, I query twelve words of corporeal and sexual profanity (*ass, bastard, bitch, cock, crap, cunt, dick, fuck, piss, pussy, screw, shit*) and two words of religious profanity (*damn, hell*). The queries include word forms and compounds (e.g., not only *fuck*, but *fucking, motherfucker*, etc.) and common misspellings and phonetizations (e.g., *goddam, sonnuvabitch*). Some words may simply be queried with confidence of profane semantics (e.g., *fuck*), but many require manual inspection of results to exclude literal and/or non-profane uses (e.g., *screw* meaning a metal nail with a helical thread). For this task, TXM is once again beneficial, as it allows convenient inspection of query results with context from the source texts via a KWIC interface. Visualizations that separate such "lesser" and "greater" profanity might be helpful, if inevitably subjective, especially because of diachronic changes in English (i.e., words widely perceived as offensive in 1960 are often less so now).[20] Profanity thus separated is shown in Figures 5.1 through 5.6.[21]

Again, while no claims are being made on the methodology of dividing "greater" and "lesser" profanity, this facilitates a closer look at data and trends.

Interpretation of these results must be contextualized by trends in profanity in written English from 1959 to 2013, a topic which scholars of the subject admit has only begun to be addressed.[22] First, as all of us know, profanity has become

"Lesser" profanity

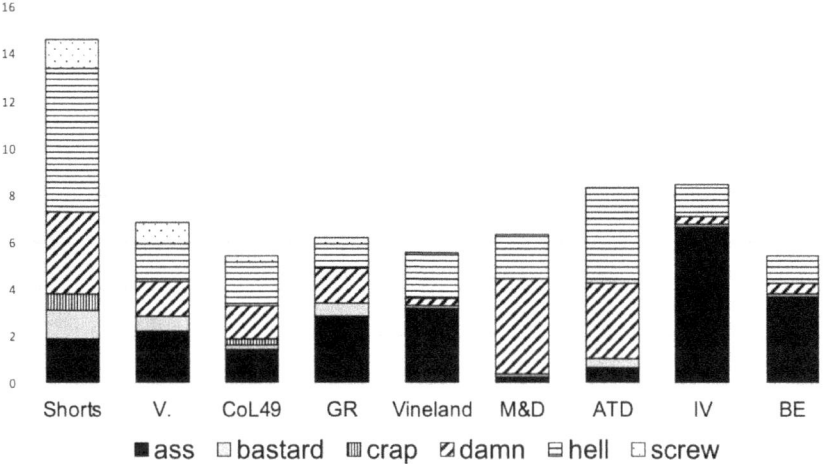

Figure 5.1 Normalized frequency of "lesser" profanity in Pynchon corpus (per 10k word tokens), including word forms and compounds.

"Lesser" profanity in direct discourse

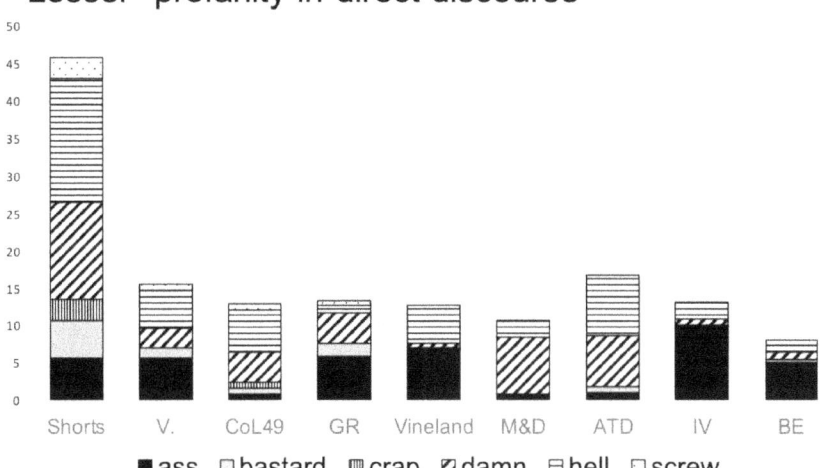

Figure 5.2 Normalized frequency of "lesser" profanity in direct discourse in Pynchon corpus (per 10k word tokens), with songs/poems removed, including word forms and compounds.

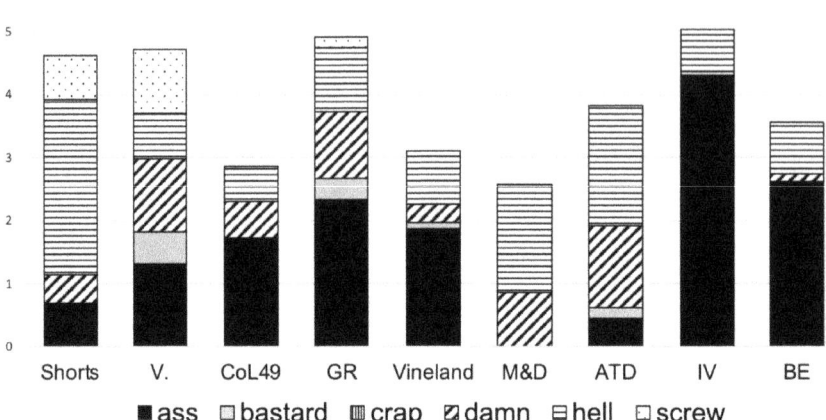

Figure 5.3 Normalized frequency of "lesser" profanity in narration in Pynchon corpus (per 10k word tokens), with songs/poems removed, including word forms and compounds.

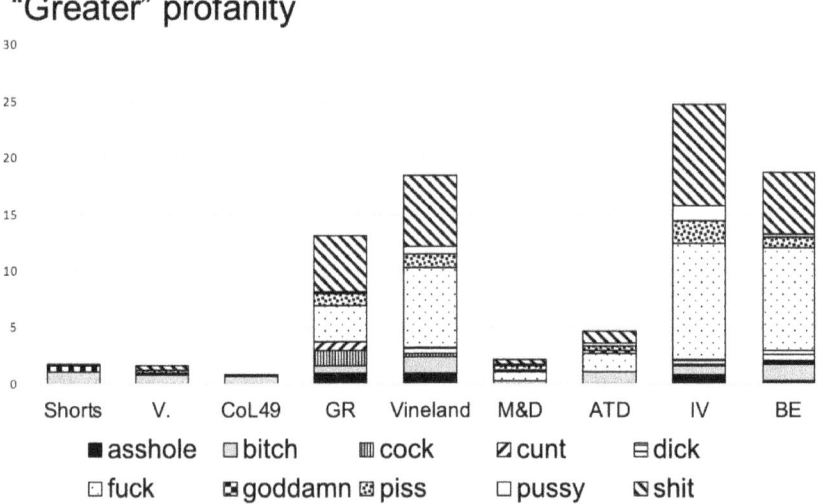

Figure 5.4 Normalized frequency of "greater" profanity in Pynchon corpus (per 10k word tokens), including word forms and compounds.

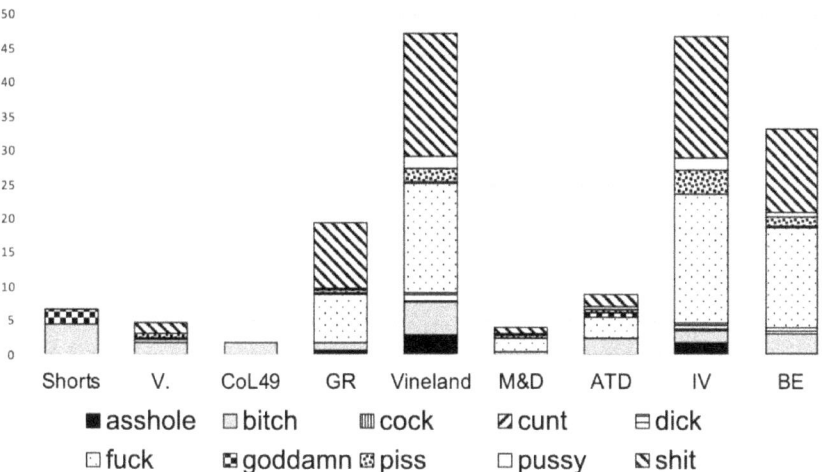

Figure 5.5 Normalized frequency of "greater" profanity in direct discourse in Pynchon corpus (per 10k word tokens), with songs/poems removed, including word forms and compounds.

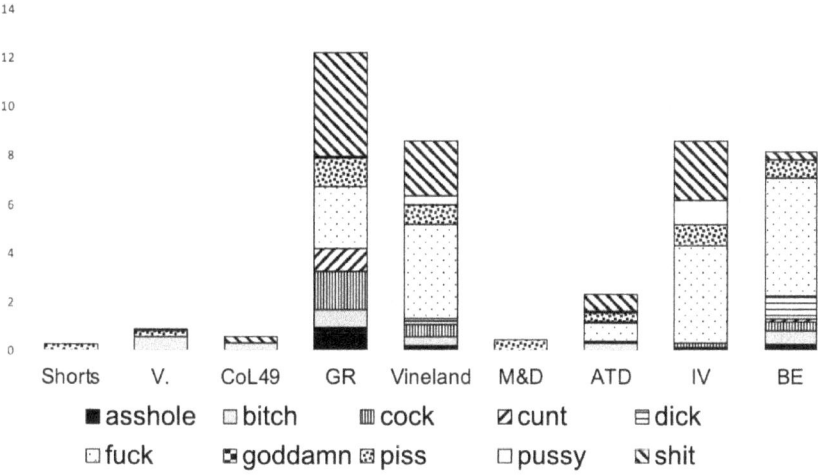

Figure 5.6 Normalized frequency of "greater" profanity in narration in Pynchon corpus (per 10k word tokens), with songs/poems removed, including word forms and compounds.

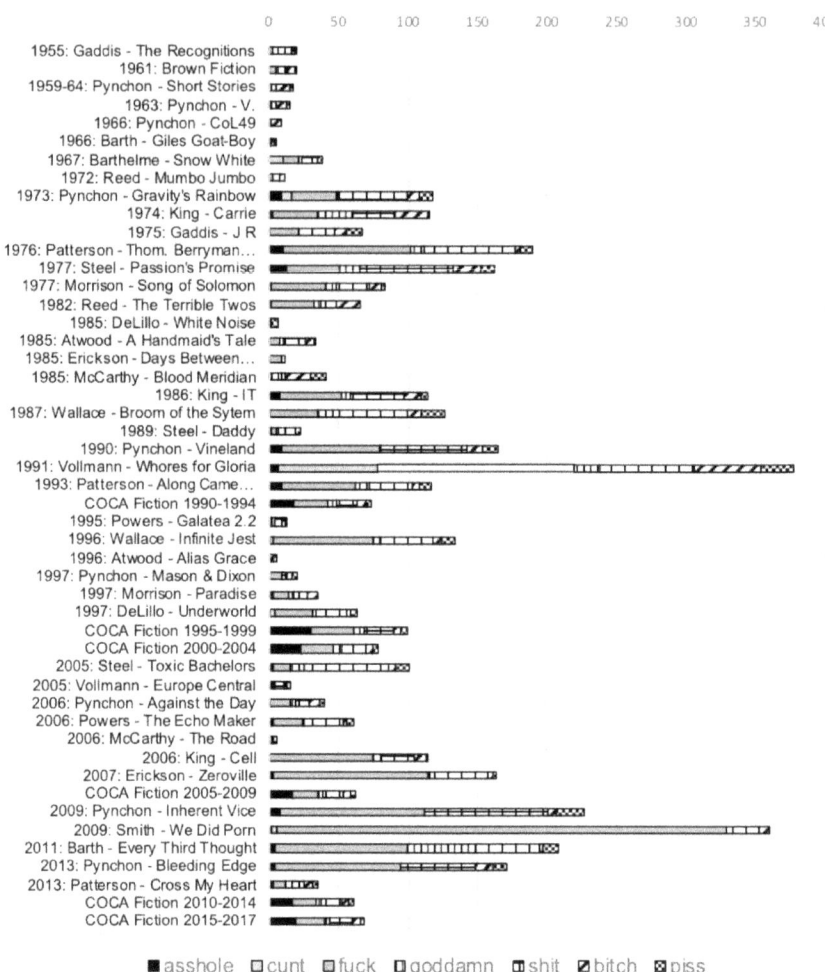

Figure 5.7 Normalized frequency of select profanity (per 100k word tokens) in Pynchon and comparison corpora, including word forms and compounds, in chronological order.

far more abundant, commonplace, and socially acceptable in recent decades. As Michael Adams wrote in 2016, "the profanity taboo has weakened almost—not completely—out of existence."[23] The watershed period is, as Geoffrey Hughes notes in his history of profanity, "from 1950 to 1970, [when] a radical shift in attitudes occurred" in the conventions of swearing in the United States and that "in the course of the 1960s, the floodgates opened."[24]

In Pynchon's texts and comparison corpora, the first substantial rise in profanity in American fiction is the early 1970s, when publishers were probably emboldened by the 1966 *Naked Lunch* case and *Miller v. California* in 1973, as discussed below. While a plethora of "lesser" profanity and a smattering of "greater" profanity may be found in the Brown Fiction Corpus (1961) and 1960s texts by Pynchon, Barth, and others, the 1970s mark a true sea change in the amount of "greater" profanity such as *fuck* and *shit* (Figure 5.7).

Google n-gram data add further nuance by evidence of a marked increase in *fuck* and *shit* beginning in the late 1960s through the early 1980s, followed by a slower increase, then a sharp increase in the late 1990s through 2004.[25] There is also some evidence in my corpora that authors who employed profuse profanity in 1970s novels later reigned in this tendency; 1970s novels by Patterson, Steel, and Morrison employ considerable profanity, especially *fuck* and *shit*, but their later novels are lower in profanity, sometimes dramatically so. Future work could explore whether following the "floodgates" of permissive profanity in the 1970s, authors, editors, and/or the reading public ceased to be as titillated by this novel taboo-breaking, or otherwise engaged in some societal backlash (e.g., the conservative Reagan years) against the sudden rise of profanity in American fiction in the 1960s/1970s.

Returning to Pynchon, "greater" profanity explodes in *Gravity's Rainbow*, which no doubt attracted the attention of Ames, Herman, and Weisenburger, but in terms of frequency alone, this data suggests that profanity in *Gravity's Rainbow* is typical of 1970s American fiction. In later novels, Pynchon employs profanity in increasing quantities, but the exceptions are, once again, *Mason & Dixon* and *Against the Day*. Just as these novels feature few acronyms, the relative dearth of profanity in these novels is probably due to the same reason: excessive profanity would excessively jar readers historical pastiche. Another historical novel in my comparison corpora, Atwood's *Alias Grace*, also features low profanity. Pynchon's *Vineland*, *Inherent Vice*, and *Bleeding Edge* are high in profanity (largely due to extensive use of *fuck* and *shit*), but not excessively higher than certain contemporary comparisons, suggesting that the frequency of swearing in these later Pynchon novels is also fairly characteristic of the times in which they were published.

To conclude the interpretation of queries and comparisons, profanity in *Gravity's Rainbow* has already been comprehensively analyzed by Ames, Herman, and Weisenburger, and the profusion of profanity in *Vineland*, *Inherent Vice*, and *Bleeding Edge* may be credibly explained by the simple rise of profanity in written American English. Certainly, further work on profanity across Pynchon's texts could be performed, but for the rest of this chapter, I focus on profanity in Pynchon's early works from 1959 and the 1960s, on the basis that Pynchon's use of profanity in these times is the least explored in existing scholarship and least illuminated by queries and diachronic change in English. Close reading of these early Pynchon texts within the context of government censorship of the times reveals a pattern of *coded* profanity (disguised via foreign languages and absurd names, rather than mere euphemism) alongside references to banned authors, such as Henry Miller and Faulkner, who were pushing the boundaries of acceptable literature at the time.

5.2 A Very Brief History of Obscenity Prosecutions of Literature in Twentieth-Century America

Reading profanity in Pynchon's early texts will be informed by a brief summary of obscenity law in the United States, which begins with the *Hicklin* test in Victorian England, handed down by Lord Chief Justice Cockburn: "The test of obscenity is this, whether the tendency of the matter charged as obscenity is to deprave and corrupt those whose minds are open to such immoral influences, and into whose hands a publication of this sort may fall."[26] The pamphlet in that case contained no words that would commonly be considered profanity today.[27] Even though the pamphlet's intent was "to expose the errors of the Roman Catholic religion," not to "deprave the public mind," the court nonetheless found the work to be obscene, as it might fall into the hands of people "of a mischievous and demoralizing character" and thus "corrupt" them.

The *Hicklin* test "was imported into the United States and was used immediately to prohibit the publication and distribution of a variety of books and periodicals," per Haig Bosmajian, although the doctrine had considerably weakened by the obscenity trial of *Ulysses* in New York in 1933.[28] There, Judge Woolsey held that the obscenity standard is not the effect upon the young or "abnormal" but a "normal" person "with average sex instincts" and that the *entirety* of a book's "tend[ency] to excite sexual impulses and lustful thoughts" should be considered, not mere selections.[29] Applying this standard, Woolsey held that *Ulysses* was not obscene, and although sex was the dominant focus of the obscenity holding, profane lexis was mentioned by Woolsey as well: "The words which are criticized as dirty are old Saxon words known to almost all men and, I venture, to many women, and are such words as would be naturally and habitually used, I believe, by the types of folks whose life, physical and mental, Joyce is seeking to describe." While some profane lexis in *Ulysses* denotes actual sex ("Ill let him know if thats what he wanted that his wife is fucked," 764, *sic* throughout), it mostly appears as expletives and intensifiers, for example, "I'll wring the neck of any fucker says a word against my fucking king" (579) and "I don't give a shit for him" (586). Woolsey's ruling was affirmed by the United States Court of Appeals for the Second Circuit in 1934, which upheld that the legal test for obscenity is the work's "dominant effect," that *Ulysses* "as a whole is not pornographic," and that even though in "not a few spots it is coarse, blasphemous, and obscene, it does not, in our opinion, tend to promote lust."[30]

These (for the times) liberal rulings, however, were not binding precedent on most courts in the United States due to jurisdictional issues in American common law, and publishers, literary authors, and booksellers across much of the nation had good reason to fear prosecution and banning in the following decades. In 1944, a New York court, even while noting the *Ulysses* rulings, held D. H. Lawrence's *Lady Chatterley's Lover* to be "clearly obscene," stating that the "author's central theme and the dominant effect of the whole book is that it is dangerous to the physical and mental health of a young woman to remain continent" (i.e., not engage in sex).[31] But this obscenity ruling was based more on sexual content than language, and the judge implied that style alone was neither evidence of obscenity nor necessary in finding it: "it is easy to imagine a book, let us say, by another Oscar Wilde, clever, scintillating, even brilliant in its writing and utterly foul and disgusting in its central theme and dominating effect." In 1949, a number of books including Faulkner's *Sanctuary* were ruled not obscene by a Pennsylvania court.[32] Nabokov's *Lolita*, printed in Paris in 1955, was initially banned by the French government in 1956,[33] yet another example of the divergence of obscenity and profanity, as *Lolita* contains few profanity words but obviously controversial subject matter. Henry Miller's *Tropic of Cancer*, published in Paris in 1934, was banned from import in the United States, a ban upheld by a federal district court as well as the Ninth Circuit Court of Appeals in 1953.[34] *Tropic of Cancer* and Faulkner's *Sanctuary* would later be referenced explicitly in Pynchon's early texts, while scholars have also read numerous oblique references to Nabokov and *Lolita*.

In 1957, the Supreme Court weighed in decisively on obscenity's scope under the First Amendment in *Roth v. United States*, which finally replaced the *Hicklin* test with a new test for obscenity: "Whether to the average person, applying contemporary community standards, the dominant theme of the material taken as a whole appeals to the prurient interest."[35] To a degree, this only created more uncertainty, as defining these terms "remained only partially answered in scores of concurring and dissenting opinions written by different justices who had their different views on obscenity and speech," per Bosmajian.[36] The earliest lower court application of the *Roth* standard was the 1957 obscenity trial of Allen Ginsberg's beat poem *Howl*, in which a bookseller and *Howl*'s publisher Lawrence Ferlinghetti had been arrested.[37] Judge Clayton W. Horn ruled that *Howl* was not obscene, citing *Roth* in stating that "unless a book is entirely lacking in 'social importance' it cannot be held obscene."[38] Judge Horn's opinion was also liberal and pragmatic on the matter of profane words: "There are a number of words used in *Howl* that are presently considered coarse and vulgar in some circles of the community, in other circles such words are in everyday use. It would be unrealistic to deny these facts. The author of *Howl* has used those words because he believed that his portrayal required them as being in character."[39]

This was the state of obscenity prosecution and banning of literature in 1959, the year Pynchon published his first story, "The Small Rain." Although literature had achieved some historic wins in courts, these victories often came at high costs: time, money, arrest, fear, and the chilling effect of paranoia. Pynchon knew the works of many of these persecuted writers well: as a young man, Pynchon was an avid reader of Faulkner and the Beats, including Ginsberg,[40] Nabokov taught English at Cornell while Pynchon was enrolled there, and Joyce references have been read in an early Pynchon short story.[41] As the following sections demonstrate, the young Pynchon was probably keenly aware of some of the victories and losses in the ongoing war by authorities on creative writing.

5.3 Profanity in Pynchon's Juvenilia and Early Short Stories

Both profanity *contra* power and the coding of profanity began in Pynchon's juvenilia, short humorous pieces published in his high school newspaper,[42] which feature implied profanity involving authority figures. In "The Voice of the Hamster," the school chums prank their teacher, Mr. Faggiaducci: "For Christmas our 'trig' class gave Mr. Faggiaducci a necktie with an inscription that lights up in the dark. The first day after Christmas vacation, Mr. Faggiaducci came into class with a large red mark across his face, but he refused to tell us what had happened." The narrator also states that

> nobody seems to know why they call the place Hamster High, other than the highly debatable rumor that its founder, J. Fattington Woodgrouse, had a strong liking for the fuddy little creatures. There is a statue of J. Fattington Woodgrouse in front of the school. He is a little bald-headed man with a pot belly […] Last

Hallowe'en someone wrote on this statue a very nasty word in bright orange
paint. There was a big scandal. I was suspended for four weeks.

In both instances, the boys ridicule and defy their teachers and school by
profanity (left for the reader to imagine), corporeally affixed to the literal and
symbolic bodies of their authority figures, while the graffito presages the "graffito
[...] the purified language of the Preterite" in *Gravity's Rainbow* discussed
by Ames.[43] It is difficult not to read *Faggiaducci*, although the first of many
exaggerated Italian surnames in Pynchon (e.g., Squalidozzi in *GR*), as encoding
the derogatory profanity *faggot*, a reading aided by the line "Sometimes I think
that Mr. Faggiaducci is—but never mind." Pynchon later offered an apologia for
the "unacceptable level of racist, sexist, and proto-Fascist talk" in a later short
story (*SL*, 11), his juvenilia otherwise mostly display a naughty schoolboy eager
to push against editorial limits, with references to drugs ("I've heard rumors
he takes heroin"), alcohol ("your drunken amigo"), guns (a teacher "carries a
shotgun with him"), and unspecified profanity ("Sid [...] was swearing a blue
streak"). As an adult, Pynchon would sneak other verboten words past readers,
editors, and perhaps censors.

In Pynchon's first two published stories in Cornell University journals,
(what is now considered) low-level profanity apparently typical of the time is
plentiful, but sex scenes are heavily encoded. "The Small Rain" (*Cornell Writer*,
1959) features frequently profane soldiers assisting a rescue and cleanup effort
following a hurricane in Louisiana and exhibits *hell, damn, goddam, ass, bitch,
bastard*, "get laid," and "Jesus Christ" in direct speech and free indirect discourse,
including the name of the protagonist, Nathan "Lardass" Levine. Profanity
directed at agents of power or control are the exception rather than the rule.
A soldier bemoans the Louisiana residents whom they have been deployed to
help: "It's the goddam Cajuns again. They put up all kinds of signs, sure. Dogs
and Army Stay off the Grass and all." Like this open profanity, most scenes in
"The Small Rain" are portrayed directly and unambiguously, with the notable
exception of the sex scene in the cabin, in which oblique but vaguely suggestive
descriptions of sex, such as "a virtuoso duet of small breathings, cries" and "the
performance," are ensconced in descriptions of the noise outside ("frogs intoned
a savage chorus, gradually [...] spasmodic"), a classical allusion ("a never totally
violated Pasiphae"), and a euphemism for orgasm ("the little death"). This beyond
roundabout portrayal of sex was later discussed by Pynchon in his introduction
to *Slow Learner*, which acknowledges the specter of obscenity prosecution
which hovered over the time: "Some kind of sexual encounter appears to take

place, though you'd never know it from the text. The language suddenly gets too fancy," while Pynchon attests to "a general nervousness in the whole college-age subculture. A tendency to self-censorship. It was also the era of *Howl*, *Lolita*, *Tropic of Cancer*, and all the excesses of law enforcement that such works provoked [...] back then it was a felt constraint on folks's writing" (5–6).

Similar patterns regarding profanity and sex are found in "Mortality and Mercy in Vienna" (1959), a far more surreal outing than "The Small Rain" and published in *Epoch*, another literary magazine published by Cornell. This story again features its limited profanity plainly and openly: *bitch, bastard, damn, hell,* as well as "Goddamn all these sex machines." Profane opposition to authority is present in "Screw the Sergeant before He Screweth Thee," although again, this is the exception rather than the rule. The most notable masking in this story is again sexual, in a story about the Ojibwa Native Americans from a lecture delivered by Professor Mitchell: "Before [the Ojibwa youth] can attain to the state of manhood a boy must experience a vision, after starving himself for several days. [...] Out in the wilderness, with nothing but a handful of beaver, deer, moose and bear between him and starvation [...] the Ojibwa becomes highly susceptible to the well-known Windigo psychosis." This Windigo psychosis, Siegel relates, is that "what they see is big fat juicy beavers. And these Indians are hungry. [...] I mean, my gawd. A big mass psychosis. As far as the eye can reach [...] Beavers. Succulent, juicy, fat." Especially in light of a "dirty limerick" earlier in the story involving "young fellow named Cheever who had an affair with a beaver," this reads as a likely encoded description of sex.[44]

In Pynchon's first two stories published in professional literary magazines, "Low-lands" and "Entropy" (both 1960), Pynchon includes the relatively "low" profanity repertoire of his college stories but adds, for the first time, much more explicit profanity "coded" via foreign languages, as well as numerous references to famously banned "obscene" literary works. "Entropy" in the *Kenyon Review* and "Low-lands" in *New World Writing* were big breaks for a young writer, the latter, especially, which was then owned by Lippincott and coedited by Corlies Smith, Pynchon's later publisher and editor. Since its founding in 1951, *New World Writing* had featured a who's who of literary talent including Joseph Heller, Jack Kerouac, and Flannery O'Connor, and these nationally distributed journals provided Pynchon with a platform to engage, for the first time, with a wide American readership. If explicit and profane scenes in *Gravity's Rainbow* can be read as an "in-your-face challenge to existing obscenity and pornography laws, a resistance to governmental dominion over speech," per Herman and Weisenburger, then coded profanity and references to banned literature in

Pynchon's first professional publications may be read as Pynchon's most important first acts of public resistance.

"Low-lands" contains Pynchon's previously used profanity—*damned*, *hell*, *wise-assed*, *screwing up*—but profanity also now appears encoded in foreign languages, such as when Rocco Squarcione bellows "Hey *sfacim*'," Neapolitan slang for *semen* and used as an endearing term (a profane *hey dude*) and when Flange roars "*Chinga tu madre*" (Spanish: *fuck your mother*) to his Hispanic psychologist. In "Low-lands," sex is also described in far more direct and crude language than Pynchon's Cornell stories: sailors "went over the hill and lived off the proceeds of a barmaid, an Armenian refugee named Zenobia, sleeping with her on alternate nights, for two months." Pig Bodine, true to character, utters vulgar statements when Flange hears the mysterious voice of a woman outside the shack: "Great [...] Bring her in and let me have seconds," as well as "if she's any good, like I say, bring her back in and let the enlisted men have a go at it." The profane lexis in "Low-lands" is not particularly presented as in opposition to any authority figure, however.

While profane English lexis is low in Pynchon's other short story published in 1959, "Entropy," strong profanity is again encoded in foreign languages, and the story also contains numerous references to banned works of literature. "Entropy" takes place in two apartments in two storeys of a building; upstairs live an orderly couple, Callisto and Aubade, while downstairs a wild party in "its 40th hour" is being thrown by Meatball Mulligan, in which a number of polyglot, bohemian jazz-loving party guests are "slowly getting wasted on tequila," champagne, benzedrine pills, and cannabis. Within this 1950s bacchanal, strong foreign-language profanity occurs when the Hungarian party guest Sandor Rojas asks Mulligan for a drink, and Mulligan responds, "*Kitchi lofass a segitbe*" (Hungarian: "Shove a little horse-cock into your asshole").[45] Later, a musician at the party utters "*Minghe morte*" in frustration, a phonetic rendering of *minchia*, Sicilian slang for *dick*.[46] Note how in terms of offensive degree, these foreign-language profanities *greatly* exceed the English profanity Pynchon had published thus far, or in these 1960 stories.

"Entropy" contains Pynchon's first published overt reference to a banned book, in the form of an epigraph from Miller's *Tropic of Cancer*, which had been banned in the United States since 1934, and a brief description of its legal journey will inform the following reading. Not only was *Tropic of Cancer* banned, but in 1940, an unauthorized edition was published in New York by one Jacob R. Brussells, who was arrested and served a two-year jail sentence.[47] New Directions and Miller discussed printing the book with blank spaces in offending sentences, which came to nought, and Miller later rebuffed an offer from Penguin to print a bowdlerized version.[48] Testing the law again in 1950, Ernest Besig, the director of the American Civil Liberties Union in San Francisco, imported copies of the novel as a test case; it was seized again and found obscene by a federal district court and the Ninth Circuit Court of Appeals (final decision in 1953).[49] Meanwhile, Miller railed against the censors in essays including "Obscenity and the Law of Reflection" (1945) and "Obscenity and Literature" (1949). What finally turned the tide in the long battle to publish *Tropic of Cancer* were the pair of cases involving *Lady Chatterley's Lover*, the novel and a film adaptation. Lawrence's novel had been banned as obscene since 1929, but sensing a change in the air, Barnet Rosset of Grove Press published a new edition and contested its subsequent seizure by the New York Postmaster. Applying the *Roth* test—"the dominant theme of the material taken as a whole"—a district court held in 1959 that the novel *Lady Chatterley* was not obscene.[50] In the same year, the Supreme Court, also applying the *Roth* test, held that a 1955 French film adaptation of *Lady Chatterley* was also not obscene and noted that "the term 'sexual immorality' [is] a concept entirely different from the concept embraced in words like 'obscenity' or 'pornography.' "[51] Emboldened by these victories, Rosset and Grove Press felt the time was right to finally publish *Tropic of Cancer*, which they did in 1961, to much controversy, including new bannings and lawsuits, a year after Pynchon included the epigraph from *Tropic of Cancer* in "Entropy."

This history supports a new reading of the *Tropic of Cancer* passage Pynchon quotes in "Entropy":

> Boris has just given me a summary of his views. He is a weather prophet. The weather will continue bad, he says. There will be more calamities, more death, more despair. Not the slightest indication of a change anywhere … We must get into step, a lockstep toward the prison of death. There is no escape. The weather will not change. — Tropic of Cancer (*SL*, 80)

David Seed provides a reading of this epigraph as "gloomy fatalism, a chain-gang image for man's future," and states that in *Tropic of Cancer*,

> Miller is summarizing Boris's views. Miller's surrogate narrator does not give in to his friend's apocalyptic gloom and even regards him as comically melodramatic. Indeed, only three lines after the summary of Boris's "prophecies," the narrator comments "I am the happiest man alive," a remarkably cheerful statement for a man preoccupied with universal decline. In Miller's novel the interchange between the narrator and Boris creates a considerable amount of humour, and,

by choosing such a passage for an epigraph, Pynchon leads the unwary reader into a kind of trap. […] the weather metaphor makes the abstract concept of entropy easy to grasp [… and] the prophecies lack authority even in Miller's novel. And so we should not jump to the conclusion that Pynchon is endorsing the metaphor. He is rather introducing one theme, one strand of meaning, which will be taken up in the early stages of the story.[52]

As far as an intertextual reading of *Tropic of Cancer* and "Entropy," Seed's reading is well argued. But the mere act of quoting Miller—even before turning to this passage's content—can be read as an act of defiance of censors, as *Tropic of Cancer* was still a banned novel when Pynchon published this. Especially given Pynchon's later statements about censorship in the introduction to *Slow Learner*, a reading that "the weather will continue to be bad" in terms of censorship of literature may be plausibly ascribed to Pynchon as empirical author, not merely the story's narrator.

In addition to the Arthur Miller epigraph, "Entropy" explicitly references a number of curiously grouped literary works:

> Callisto was trying to confront any idea of the heat-death now, as he nuzzled the feathery lump in his hands. He sought correspondences. Sade, of course. And Temple Drake, gaunt and hopeless in her little park in Paris, at the end of *Sanctuary*. Final equilibrium. *Nightwood*. (SL, 92)

Seed's reading of this passage is that Callisto "variously notes De Sade (for libertinage, perhaps), the last scene from Faulkner's *Sanctuary* where the exhausted and apathetic Temple Drake is listening to music with her father in the Jardin de Luxembourg, and Djuna Barnes' *Nightwood* again perhaps for its presentation of moral and physical decline. Decline does seem to be the theme linking these works."[53] But something other than "decline" connects these three works: two were banned books/authors, while *Nightwood* was an obvious target for censorship. De Sade was the most notorious banned and imprisoned "obscene" writer of his times, Faulkner's *Sanctuary* was the subject of an obscenity trial in 1949, and *Nightwood*, about a lesbian love affair, was a novel chafing at the limits of censorship. The editor of *Nightwood*, none other than T. S. Eliot, was keenly aware that the novel was in danger of being banned, due to the banning of previous lesbian-themed works such as Radclyffe Hall's *The Well of Loneliness*. To preemptively protect the novel from legal troubles, Eliot removed numerous sexual descriptions and profanity words prior to publication.[54] By referencing Sade, Faulkner's *Sanctuary*, and Barnes's *Nightwood* in a short story begun with a Henry Miller epigraph, Pynchon's declared loyalties in the war on "obscene" literature could hardly be clearer. Finally, there is the possibility of one more reference to a famously banned work if one reads the boisterous character Meatball Mulligan as a minor allusion to "Stately, plump Buck Mulligan" in *Ulysses*.

In "Low-lands" and "Entropy," Pynchon largely kept *overt* English profanity in line with his Cornell stories, in terms of frequency and degree of profanity, although my impression (not confirmed with corpora or query) is that "Low-lands" was, even when only considering its English profanity, still the most profane story published in *New World Writing* at the time, based on a perusal of issues from 1958 to 1960. Alongside this, however, are references to famously banned novels and encoded instances of much stronger profanity in foreign languages, sometimes doubly encoded via phonetic or simply misspelled renderings. I happen to speak and read Hungarian fluently, and "*Kitchi lofass a segitbe*" is so far from its correct spelling that I did not immediately recognize that it was meant to be Hungarian! Few readers of the *Kenyon Review* would have understood this, either. "Entropy," meanwhile, contains numerous explicit references to banned literary works, including perhaps the famous book banned at the time of its writing, *Tropic of Cancer*. This textual evidence should be read as acts of defiance against the climate of censorship of the time.

It is unclear how much of a risk Pynchon, as a young unknown writer, was taking with these "defiant" acts. Many established writers had publicly championed Miller over the years, and the editors of the *Kenyon Review* did accept and publish Pynchon's story containing the Miller epigraph. The 1960 issue of *New World Writing* in which "Low-lands" appeared, meanwhile, also contains an article by two liberally minded lawyers on the topic of obscenity and literature, discussing *Lolita* and the 1959 obscenity case of *Lady Chatterley* ("It is significant that *Lolita* has thus far circulated without serious interference from public authorities"), alongside a survey of recent obscenity prosecutions, for the edification of the journal's authors and readers.[55] Pynchon's rebellious textual acts against censorship thus arose from within a milieu of greater or lesser resistance to banning.

Based on these first four Pynchon stories, one hypothesis is that in early Pynchon, overt "lesser" English profanity is fairly high for the time period and complemented by coded "greater" foreign-language profanity, while Pynchon's portrayals of sexual matter slowly liberalized with the times. A counterexample to such trends, however, is Pynchon's next published story, "Under the Rose" (*Noble Savage*, 1961), which Cowart summarizes as "a story of international espionage in the 1890s [… which] concerns two English spies, Porpentine and Goodfellow, who travel to what modern journalists would call 'trouble spots' around the world, attempting to prevent acts of terrorism that might start a major war among Europe's contending imperial powers."[56] In this story, Pynchon's first historical fiction, profanity is very low in both frequency and spirit, containing only three *damn/damned* and "fellow is a perfect ass." As Cowart notes, Porpentine is portrayed "coldly, logically, and dispassionately," as "human feelings are dangerous for a spy,"[57] and Porpentine's coolness extends to his restrained profanity, as well. Although Porpentine's harrowing spy adventures provide many moments where swearing might be expected responses, the narrator repeatedly declines to name Porpentine's specific profane utterances. When Porpentine sneaks out his hotel window and falls off a ledge, "on the way down it occurred to him to him to use an obscene word." Then, when climbing a tree back up toward the windows, Porpentine "ascended puffing and cursing." Finally, climbing back down the tree, Porpentine's lit cigarette burns his fingers "and made him swear softly." A naughty schoolboy would simply have named the words that Porpentine uttered.

"Under the Rose" also features some mild profanity which suggests an interest, if not always a firm grasp, of English dialects and historical orthography. "Under the Rose" takes place in Egypt and liberally draws historical minutiae from Baedeker's 1899 guide to Cairo, as Pynchon admits in *Slow Learner*, and the direct speech of the English protagonists was likewise crafted from Pynchon's limited knowledge of British English speech, "Hence all the pip-pip and jolly-ho business, which to a modern reader comes across as stereotyped" (*SL*, 19). Pynchon hazarded some approximations of mild historical English profanity, the obvious "bloody hell" and, inexplicably, "like a bloody grouse," which Goodfellow states twice and of which I can find no historical antecedent. Interestingly, although the Englishmen Goodfellow and Bongo-Shaftsbury both say "damn" in "Under the Rose," the curmudgeonly Sir Alastair Wren, Victoria's father, says, "Damme […] what are they doing, eloping?" Here, Pynchon applies his Baedeker research approach not only to Cairo streets and hotels but also orthography, as the *OED* lists *damme* as archaic spelling of *damn* with entries from 1791 to 1823[58] (the latest entry by Lord Byron, whom the young Pynchon claimed to admire).[59] The fact that *damme* is thus spelled over forty times in *Mason & Dixon* serves as a reminder that "Under the Rose" contains a (very) minor attempt by Pynchon to engage with historical English spelling, which later grew to book-length language experiments in *Mason & Dixon* and *Against the Day*. In contrast to Pynchon's two previous stories, however, I can detect no "coded" profanity in "Under the Rose,"[60] nor references to banned literature.

The story's sole sexual encounter, meanwhile, appears to terminate without consummation. To a degree, then, "Under the Rose" displays a lifelong trend in Pynchon's historical fiction, to reduce profanity greatly in furtherance of the pastiche of historical forms of English, as the queries for *Mason & Dixon*, *Against the Day*, and, as shown below, the historical chapters of *V.* suggest.

These short stories reveal the early formation of profanity trends in Pynchon's pre-*Gravity's Rainbow* texts: coded profanity, low profanity in historical fiction, and veiled or explicit references to authors banned for "obscenity." The following sections examine whether these trends continue in Pynchon's first two novels and the short story, "The Secret Integration," published between them.

5.4 Profanity in *V.* and "The Secret Integration"

Between the publication of "Under the Rose" in 1961 and *V.* in 1963, literary censorship continued to rage in the United States. Burroughs's *Naked Lunch* was published by Grove Press and banned in Boston in 1962. A Boston bookseller was arrested for its sale in 1963, and a trial date was eventually set for January 1965.[61] It is not unlikely that Pynchon, who admired the Beats and referenced current events in the banning of literature, was aware of this chilling development while authoring his first novel.

The frequency and word selection of profanity in *V.* may be read as charting an uneasy middle ground between freedom and restriction within this uncertain period in American literary history. In both "lesser" and "greater" profanity, *V.* is lower than Pynchon's short stories, although *V.* is the first of Pynchon's text to include the two talismans of modern profanity, *fuck* and *shit* (three and seven times, respectively). Alongside a growing repertoire of profanity, *V.* greatly expands the portrayal of the other target of obscenity prosecutions, sex, and the frequency and explicitness of portrayals of sexual acts in *V.* far eclipses any of Pynchon's previous stories.

Amidst this expansion of profanity and sexual subject matter in *V.*, Pynchon also greatly expands his use of coded profanity, which again hints at an awareness (or paranoia?) of the very real threat of censorship at the time. In *V.*, coded profanity may again be read in silly character names and foreign languages. In addition to Benny Profane, characters include Scheissvogel (German: *shit-bird*), Señor Cuernacabrón (*cabrón*, Spanish: *cuckold*), Bung the Foreman, and an Austrian named Vogt (which, pronounced correctly in German, sounds similarly to *fucked*). As for foreign profanity, there appears

"Un' gazz'!" (Italian: slang for *dick*), "Mierda. Mierda. Mierda" (Spanish: *shit*, *shit*, *shit*), *alter kocker* (Yiddish: "old shitter," someone inept), and five instances of *Coño* (Spanish: vulgar for female genitalia). As for Pynchon's early tendency to reference banned writers, John Dugdale reads the relationship between "nympholeptic novelist" Porcepic and Mélanie L'Heuremaudit in *V.* as a reference to Nabokov's *Lolita*."[62] Max Schulz reads Maxwell Rowley-Brugge in *V.* as a parody of Humbert Humbert,[63] while J. Kerry Grant explores echoes of *Lolita* in Gerfaut and his novel featuring "Doucette."[64] Amidst the relatively restrained use of profanity—three *fucks* and seven *shits*—each of these could be read as fresh acts of resistance.

V. also continued Pynchon's trend of reduced profanity in certain historical fiction, as introduced in the short story "Under the Rose." *V.* contains seventeen chapters which switch back and forth between 1950s scenes featuring Benny Profane and the Whole Sick Crew and historical fictions ranging from 1898 through the Second World War. Most chapters are predominantly part of one storyline—Profane and friends, or historical—but four chapters contain larger elements of both. A hypothesis is that the historical sections contain less profanity (and less "greater" profanity), and a query shows that this is generally true (Figure 5.8).

The Benny Profane chapters are more profane in numerous senses than the purely historical chapters of *V.*, which employ only "lesser" profanity (*hell**, *damn**, *bastard**, *ass**), with the exception of instances of *bitch** in chapter 9, the Kurt Mondaugen story.[65] This general pattern, again, would be repeated in *Mason & Dixon* and *Against the Day*.

Although profanity directed at power may be read in isolated instances in Pynchon's juvenilia and short stories, *V.* marks the first sustained appearance of this theme, which Ames, Herman, and Weisenburger later found so notable in *Gravity's Rainbow*. A good illustration of Pynchon's budding interest in profanity *contra* power is chapter 3 of *V.*, a substantial rewrite of "Under the Rose." As stated above, "Under the Rose" is extremely low in profanity, either explicit or coded. Chapter 3 of *V.* rewrites "Under the Rose" by shifting the narrative from Porpentine's consciousness to seven new characters, or focalizers,[66] reworking previously anonymous background characters such as the waiter, carriage driver, and so on into characters with names and points of view. In the process of rewriting this chapter for *V.*, Pynchon introduces profanity via most of these new characters, profanity often directed at agents of power, in this case the English colonial presence. Aïeul the cafe waiter, in response to loud Englishmen requesting coffee, responds, "Merde, Aïeul thought. At the table: 'M'sieu?'" (60).

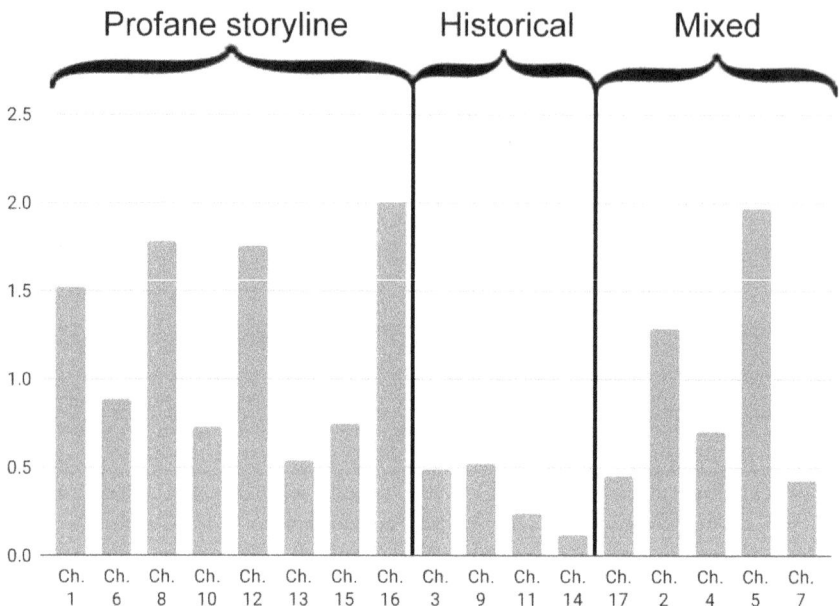

Figure 5.8 Normalized frequency of profanity in chapters of *V.* (per 1,000 word tokens), grouped by chapters that follow the Benny Profane storyline, the historical fiction storyline, and chapters that mix the two.

Yusef the anarchist, upon seeing Victoria, thinks, "Are there any other cavities you wish filled, my English lady" (63). Waldetar the Portuguese train conductor thinks, "Damn some of these English" (78). The carriage driver Gebrail, referring to English tourists, thinks, "You jolly damn right Inglizi" (81). Ralph MacBurgess, as a vaudevillian, "told a number of passable barnyard jokes" (66). The hotel kitchen boss Meknes is unremittingly profane, although never with common profanity words, but rather vulgarities such as "spawn of a homosexual camel" (62). In transforming "Under the Rose" into Chapter 3 of *V.*, the low-profanity short story has thus been reimagined to include a sustained volley of profanity against authority. In the process, Pynchon once again plays the rebel—or perhaps skirts the would-be censor—by abiding by the letter of the law (low profane lexis) but not the spirit.

A brief close reading of *fuck* and *shit* in *V.* yields further examples of profanity *contra* power, as well as shades of the sexism later discussed by critics and admitted by Pynchon himself. In *V.*, *fuck* appears for the first time in Pynchon's oeuvre, although only thrice: once by an inconsequential character, Gouverneur "Roony" Winsome—" 'My wife,' angry all at once, 'is a fucking Fascist, I think you should know that.' " (375); once in a crude "undergraduate adage: 'All the ugly ones fuck'" (102); and when Clyde, Johnny, and Poppy Hod sing a vulgar song during a chase scene:

> Who's the little rodent
>
> That's getting more than me?
>
> F-U-C-K-E-Y Y-O-U-S-E.
>
> A legacy from Pig Bodine, who'd […] composed on the show's theme song an obscene parody of which this variation in spelling was the most palatable part. (*V.*, 475)

"Fucking fascist" could hardly be a more succinct profane rebellion against authority. "F-U-C-K-E-Y Y-O-U-S-E," as the text states, is obviously profane parody but can also be read as directed at power *qua* mainstream America, insofar as it parodies the theme song of *The Mickey Mouse Club* (1955–9), a television show aimed at the children of Baby Boomers and filled with "moralism [and] patriotism," in the words of Howard Chudacoff.[67] Finally, the "unhappy undergraduate adage: 'All the ugly ones fuck'" is an example of the tension between reading sexism in early Pynchon texts as character portrayal vs. indications of sexism in either the empirical author or the times. As Molly Hite writes, "Pynchon too was a product of his era, an era that in many respects he represented satirically but without seriously questioning norms of gender identity and behaviour."[68]

Shit occurs seven times in *V.* (again, for the first time in Pynchon), mostly in direct speech ("Tough shit, Stencil," 481), with one instance in reference to law enforcement: "knocking the shit out of a wise cop" (422). One extended passage contains profane rebellion by Benny Profane against no less an authority figure than the Earth's sun (19). In addition to being an early indication of Pynchon's keen attention to the inanimate, as discussed in Chapter 3, such instances of profane, often youthful rebellion against authority continue in *V.* until the novel's final sentence: "I'd say I haven't learned a goddamn thing" (492), a refutation of novelistic closure, the hero's journey master narrative, and the acquisition or imposition of knowledge that such concepts suggest.

In terms of profanity, then, *V.* marks a turning point in Pynchon's texts: the tentative introduction of harder English profanity, in keeping with the times, the foundations of Pynchon's profanity-*contra*-power *topos*, which would blossom in *Gravity's Rainbow*, and the expansion of coded profanity, which may be read as both eluding the forces of censorship whilst tacitly acknowledging their threat.

There is some indication that Pynchon's private correspondence was more profane than his fiction around the time of *V.*'s publication, in keeping with profanity thriving outside of formal, published discourses. In a letter to his editor, Corlies "Cork" Smith, during the editing of *V.*, Pynchon reportedly wrote, "I do not, frankly, know dick about writing novels yet and need all kinds of help."[69] The offending word, *dick*, appears nowhere in Pynchon's fiction up to this point. Meanwhile, Cork Smith was remembered by a longtime colleague as "idolized by the younger set at Viking for his staggering achievements, his impeccable literary taste, and his dry and sometimes startlingly profane wit ('It does, however, have the best horse-fucking scene I've ever read,' he deadpanned memorably about a novel at one sales conference)."[70] Perhaps Smith's editorship (through *Gravity's Rainbow*) emboldened Pynchon's expanded use of profanity in this time.

Published after *V.*, "The Secret Integration" (1964), a story of a group of boys encountering the realities of racism in small town America, is a unique work by Pynchon in many respects: a foray into politically conscious realist literature and "the closest approximation of either a bildungsroman or an autobiographical story in Pynchon's oeuvre," as well as "the closest Pynchon comes to the classic nineteenth-century narrative mode of the mature, possibly omniscient, and generally trustworthy narrator who vocalizes younger and more naïve characters" per David Witzling's excellent explication in his study of race in Pynchon's texts.[71] "The Secret Integration" is, by the profanity queried, the lowest-profanity fiction Pynchon ever wrote, as only *hell* appears once, but the story does include racial epithets in its portrayal of bigotry. The near lack of profanity unrelated to race and a socially conscious message both suited its publication venue, the *Saturday Evening Post*, the very face of middle-class America, which featured Norman Rockwell paintings on its covers from 1916 to 1962, some of them addressing racial integration.

"Practical jokes" is a central motif of the story, and reading the text with profanity and power in mind reveals that Pynchon may have played some practical jokes of his own, first, by slipping profanity past the editors of the *Saturday Evening Post*. "The Secret Integration" takes place in the oddly named fictional town of Mingeborough, Massachusetts, which may be read as coded profanity as the *OED* lists *minge* meaning female genitalia as early as 1903,[72] there is no actual town in the United States named Mingeborough, and there are plays on *minchia* (Sicilian slang for, granted, male genitalia) in previous Pynchon texts.[73] Mingeborough is first mentioned in a paragraph which emphasizes "thinking up new" practical jokes and "actually playing them":

> [...] from the older part of Mingeborough that Grover and Tim lived in. Like them, and Étienne Cherdlu, Carl was a nut for practical jokes, not just watching

and laughing, but for actually playing them and thinking up new ones, this being one reason the four of them hung around together. (*SL*, 145)

This passage contains another encoded witticism in the name of the newly introduced character, Étienne Cherdlu—encoding the order of keys on linotype typewriters, ETAOIN SHRDLU[74]—and the thematic emphasis on practical jokes and elaborateness of the encoded textual play can strengthen a reading of *Mingeborough* as hidden profanity.

Pynchon seems to have snuck another joke past the editors of the *Saturday Evening Post*, by a sly lampoon of its conservative former editor, George Horace Lorimer. In the story, among the neighborhood boys' pilfered treasures is a "concrete bust of Alf Landon stolen in one of the weekly raids on Mingeborough Park, [... and] one fur overcoat they could hang around the neck of the bust and hide under sometimes, like in a tent" (146). To get the joke, one must first know that Alf Landon (1887–1987) ran for president of the United States as the Republican nominee and lost spectacularly to FDR in 1936. A bust of Alf Landon already suggests parody, as Landon was the loser in an historic landslide election, and I can find no evidence of a bust or statue of Landon in any public park in the United States, in the 1960s or now. The punchline is that Landon was beaten soundly in the election, but championed notably by the *Saturday Evening Post*, "a severe critic of [...] the New Deal," and its longtime editor George Horace Lorimer, who waged a "long and fevered campaign against Roosevelt's reelection in 1936" via the *Post*.[75] Lorimer was so involved in attempting to sway the election that he retired from the *Post* in disgust with American politics after Landon's defeat. Pynchon's later approval of FDR's New Deal may be read in *Vineland*,[76] and Pynchon's cheeky inclusion of the ridiculed Alf Landon bust is reminiscent of his juvenilia, in which the narrator graffitis "a very nasty word in bright orange paint" on the "statue of J. Fattington Woodgrouse."

The ridiculed bust of Alf Landon and the coded name of Étienne Cherdlu appear in a story that is further littered with semantic misunderstanding. The boys struggle over Grover the "boy genius's" vocabulary (e.g., "symmetry" → "Cemetery?"), and Tim must come to understand not only the denotation but also the hateful connotations in the racist epithets employed by the adults. This pattern of encoding in "The Secret Integration," again, lends weight to reading "Mingeborough" as a practical joke played on the wide American readership of the *Saturday Evening Post*, Pynchon's largest audience yet (nearly seven million in 1960).[77] "The Secret Integration" is a criticism or self-criticism of white, middle-class America, even those who fancied themselves progressive (for instance

Doctor Slothrop, considered "progressive" by the boys but who also engages in racial harassment), perhaps like the editors of the *Saturday Evening Post*: liberal enough to print a story decrying racial bigotry, but perhaps too mainstream to escape some veiled criticism from Pynchon. Much like the parody of mainstream America via "F-U-C-K-E-Y Y-O-U-S-E," perhaps Pynchon simply couldn't resist.

5.5 Profanity in *The Crying of Lot 49*

The following years were again marked by important obscenity cases involving literature. In 1964, the Supreme Court reversed a state ban on *Tropic of Cancer*.[78] Miller's novel, the source of Pynchon's 1960 epigraph, was finally able to be legally sold throughout the United States, but Burrough's *Naked Lunch* remained under legal fire. In January 1965, the obscenity trial of *Naked Lunch* commenced in Boston and, despite favorable testimony from authors such as Allen Ginsberg and Norman Mailer, was ruled obscene by the Massachusetts Superior Court in March of that year. Three more obscenity cases were decided by the Supreme Court in 1966, including a case holding that John Cleland's *Memoirs of a Woman of Pleasure*, an eighteenth-century novel popularly known as *Fanny Hill*, was not obscene, in which Justice Brennan reiterated his earlier opinion that obscene material must be "utterly without redeeming social value."[79] Under this new guidance, the Massachusetts Supreme Court held in 1966 that *Naked Lunch* was not obscene,[80] marking the end of an era of censorship of literature in the United States.[81] The same year, Pynchon published *Lot 49*, a novel which featured almost no profanity, depictions of sex which were relatively restrained (in comparison to not only such works as *Naked Lunch* but also Pynchon's previous novel), and Pynchon's now habitual coded profanity.

Lot 49 is the lowest of all Pynchon novels in terms of overall profanity and "greater" profanity, although by certain measures (profanity in direct discourse and narration, as well as "greater" profanity in narration) *Mason & Dixon* is almost equal or a bit lower, still. There are a number of reasons why profanity may be low in *Lot 49*. First, simply, it was published in the mid-1960s, in which profanity in fiction was low, and within the milieu of obscenity prosecutions described above. Nonetheless, *Lot 49* could be called uncommonly tame in terms of profanity, both for the times and Pynchon's work thus far. *Lot 49* features half or less the profane lexis of the Brown Fiction Corpus (1961) and *V*. Just a year later, Barthelme published *Snow White*, which featured 4.5 times the profane lexis, including *fuck* and *shit*. Another reason profanity may be low in *Lot 49* is that it may have been conceived for the magazine market; excerpts were first published in two popular men's magazines, *Esquire* and *Cavalier*, and Pynchon later wrote that *Lot 49* was "marketed as a 'novel,'"[82] suggesting that it originated as a short story or novella. *Esquire* and *Cavalier* were not exactly prudish publications; the cover of the 1966 *Cavalier* issue featuring the excerpt of *Lot 49* trumpets, "Pynchon: Excerpt from His Wild New Novel" in a headline placed above "The New 'Miss World' in a Nude Mood."[83] Pynchon's story excerpts in Esquire also contain sexual content, namely the sex scene between Oedipa and Metzger.

For all of *Lot 49*'s experimental and (in *Cavalier* magazine's adjective) "wild" features, the low profanity in *Lot 49* is nonetheless striking given Pynchon's preceding and following novels. Profane words that appear in both *V.* and *Gravity's Rainbow*, but zero times in *Lot 49*, include *fuck, cock, goddamn, piss*, and *son of a bitch*. *Shit* appears only once in *Lot 49*, in the novel's final pages, which could be read as spillover from *Gravity's Rainbow*. The low use of profanity in *Lot 49* could also allow one to revisit Mendelson's claim that "everything in *Lot 49* participates either in the sacred or the profane,"[84] as ironically very few words in *Lot 49* are explicitly profane.

Although *Lot 49* is low on profane lexis, Pynchon again circumvents this "limitation" with now familiar strategies. Body parts and sexual references may be read in character names: "Slick Dick and the Volkswagens" and Boyd Beaver are the most likely, and scholars have ventured more tenuous etymological readings.[85] *Lot 49* also disguises profanities via euphemism (song lyric "Too fat to Frug"), word scramble (radio station KCUF), and foreign languages: *sfacim* (Italian: literally *semen*, figuratively analogous to "son of a bitch"), *chingado* (Spanish: slang for *fucker*), and when Pierce Inverarity imitates a Mexican-American dialect "full of chingas and maricones" (Spanish: slang for *fuck* and *faggot*).[86] Regarding banned books, Dugdale reads the Tristero in *Lot 49* as representing "a literary tradition of unpublishable desires [...] from incest in Ford [...] to nympholepsy in Nabokov."[87] *Lot 49* also parodies notions of "weird sex," the continual target of censors: Miles "began to narrate for their entertainment a surfer orgy he had been to the week before, involving a five-gallon can of kidney suet, a small automobile with a sun roof, and a trained seal" (28). This notion of "weird sex" taken to the point of absurdity could be read as a veiled acknowledgement or criticism of the censorship milieu.

There are notable textual changes between the magazine excerpts of *Lot 49* and the final published novel, which I am not aware that any scholar has discussed.

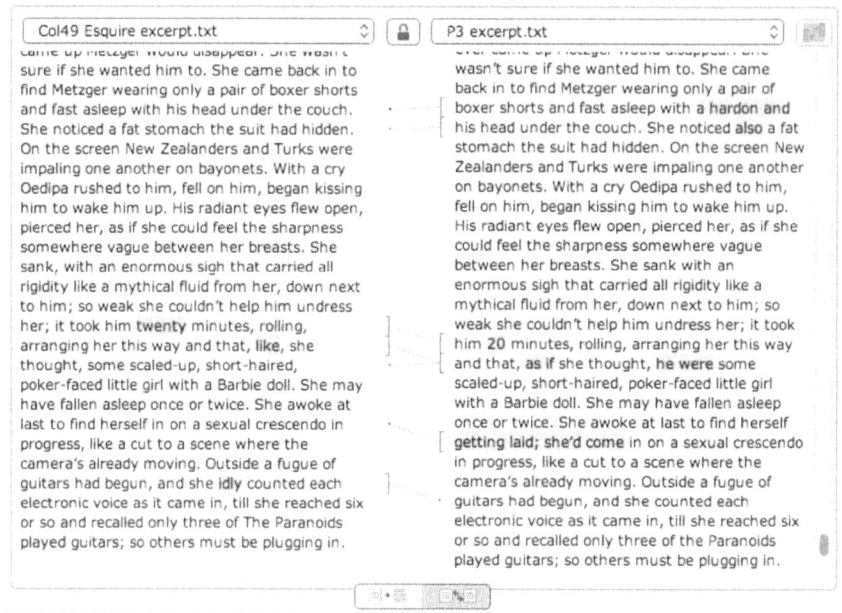

Figure 5.9 Textual variation between the excerpt of *The Crying of Lot 49* published in Esquire (1965) and the published novel (1966).

Some textual changes render the sex scene between Oedipa and Metzger more explicitly (Figure 5.9). The novel is far more direct: Pynchon adds that Metzger has "a hardon" and that Oedipa is "getting laid," which underscore the more oblique approach to sex scenes in the magazine excerpts.

5.6 Pynchon's Profanity: Conclusion

By providing a comparative overview of profanity in the times in which Pynchon has published, to which Pynchon, early in his career, responded more via coded references and profanity than brazen defiance of censors, this chapter contributes the prehistory of profanity in *Gravity's Rainbow* as explored by Ames, Herman, and Weisenburger and traces the origins of features they discuss, most notably profanity directed against power.

The explosion of profanity in *Gravity's Rainbow* benefited from the key legal victories won by authors, publishers, and booksellers in the 1960s. Despite these victories, obscenity law in the United States remained fragmented due to numerous minority and dissenting Supreme Court decisions until *Miller v. California* in 1973, which enshrined the "Miller test" for obscene material, which must meet all three prongs of

1. whether "the average person, applying contemporary community standards," would find that the work, taken as a whole, appeals to the prurient interest;
2. whether the work depicts or describes, in a patently offensive way, sexual conduct specifically defined by applicable state law; and
3. whether the work, taken as a whole, lacks serious literary, artistic, political, or scientific value.[88]

Arguably, the first two prongs would incline courts to hold that *Gravity's Rainbow* is obscene, but the novel would be rescued by the third prong of the test, the novel "taken as a whole." It is actually something of a wonder that *Gravity's Rainbow* has not been banned by some overzealous school board or even country, given some of its content. Probably the dense, difficult nature and length of the novel serve to encode its more shocking content, deflecting the attention of would-be censors.

Benefitting from the legal climate post-Miller, *Gravity's Rainbow* featured astoundingly profane depictions of sex and sadomasochism, and Herman and Weisenburger judge that the coprophagia scene with Brigadier Pudding "runs *Gravity's Rainbow* beyond any other moment in literary history."[89] Pynchon was no longer compelled to mask and code profanity—he could simply write it as he pleased. But attention to profanity in Pynchon's texts may continue to inform readings of his later texts, as well, by contributing to the larger exploration of Pynchon and the political and perhaps, as Samuel Thomas explores in *Pynchon and the Political*, a "rethink[ing of] what the political actually *is*. Pynchon's work places the status and the legitimacy of the political under the microscope— its intimate and public manifestations, its relationships with other systems of influence, its visible and invisible signs."[90] Pynchon's profanity and coded references stand as commentaries on the visible and invisible signs of censorship.

The argument by Ames which is most questioned by this chapter is Ames's exploration of generic roots of profanity in *Gravity's Rainbow*: "*Gravity's Rainbow* belongs to several subgenres of fiction of which obscene language is characteristic."[91] However, as shown, both popular and literary novels published around 1973 feature abundant profanity, giving less force to claims based on genre-dependent profanity. As for profanity in narration, *Gravity's Rainbow* features the highest number in the Pynchon corpus, which confirms the observation by Herman and Weisenburger, that profanity in narration "breaches a long-standing convention. For even as the twentieth-century novel began opening narrative art to forbidden words, it did so by maintaining a membrane of propriety around the narrator's discourse. [… *Gravity's Rainbow*] *profanes* the omniscient narrator's imperial position."[92] As the figures above show, this stylistic tendency was repeated most significantly in Pynchon's later novels set in the 1960s on.

Censored profanity in *Mason & Dixon* was addressed in Chapter 2, and although Pynchon no longer had any need to code profanity to escape censors by the late 1990s, he nonetheless did so, in the form of censored words such as D——'d for *damned*, and double entendres such as "Cock Ale" (119–20) and "Spotted Dick," the British pudding, incorporated into such lines as "ever had a Basin-ful of Spotted Dick slung into your Face?" (56). Clerc correctly observes that "given Pynchon's previous excesses in *Gravity's Rainbow*, this book amazes the reader by how sanitized it is,"[93] although Clerc, without the benefit of text query, misjudges the details of the book's profanity.[94] *Mason & Dixon* can be read to comment on the use of encoded language to evade governments, including, implicitly, censors, in a statement seemingly voiced by Cherrycoke:

> Who claims Truth, Truth abandons. History is hir'd, or coerc'd, only in Interests that must ever prove base. She is too innocent, to be left within the reach of anyone in Power […]. She needs rather to be tended lovingly and honorably by fabulists and counterfeiters, Ballad-Mongers and Cranks of ev'ry Radius, Masters of Disguise to provide her the Costume, Toilette, and Bearing, and Speech nimble enough to keep her beyond the Desires, or even the Curiosity, of Government. As Æsop was oblig'd to tell Fables […]. (*M&D*, 350)

This could be read as a nostalgic reminiscence by Pynchon as empirical author of his own efforts to evade and defy the powers of censorship from 1959 through the 1970s, as well as Pynchon ensconcing the most offensive sections of *Gravity's Rainbow* within a tome that stands impenetrable to impatient readers, as a "Master of Disguise" employing "Speech nimble enough to keep [Truth] beyond the Desires, or even the Curiosity, of Government."

By these experiments *Inherent Vice* is Pynchon's highest-profanity novel, although based on direct discourse alone, it is matched by *Vineland*. It could be hypothesized that *Inherent Vice* features large amounts of profanity not only because it was published in 2009 but because the style it imitates, hard-boiled crime novels, may also feature frequent profanity. Yet in the case of canonical hard-boiled author Raymond Chandler, at least, this is not true; in their digital stylistic examination of Chandler and Chandler pastiches, Sigelman and Jacoby found zero instances of (what they considered) harder profanity such as *fuck*, *cock*, *cunt*, and *asshole* in Chandler (and near-zero in the pastiches), although some use of what these authors considered lesser profanity (*bastard*, *bitch*, *damn*, *hell*, and *shit*), noting that

> Though linguistically adventuresome, Chandler was ever mindful of the puritanical norms of good taste that prevailed in the America of the 1930s, 1940s, and 1950s. *Black Mask* and the other pulps set virtually no limits on graphic portrayal of violence, but explicit sex and strong profanity were taboo. Marlowe, Chandler's knight, never succumbed to the fleshly temptations that surrounded him, and the otherwise authentic-sounding street talk of Chandler's characters was, in the words of Martin Amis (1991, p. 9), "verbally as chaste as *The New York Times.*" To be sure, some sense of hard-boiled authenticity was restored by the presence of an occasional *damn*, *hell*, or *bullshit*, but anything more pungent was "expurgated with pudibund dashes […]."[95]

This tends to discount a hypothesis that *Inherent Vice* or *Bleeding Edge* are high in profanity due to a pastiche of hard-boiled crime fiction.

In *Bleeding Edge*, Pynchon yet again continues his lifelong fondness for foreign language profanity, in the comic duo of Misha and Grisha, for example, "*Po khuy*" (Russian: comparable to "don't give a fuck") and "*Govno*" (Russian: *shit*). Pynchon now takes foreign profanity a step further and even provides translations for his readers, as when Misha (or is it Grisha?) tells Maxine, "We say *khuem grushi okolachivat* […] knocking pears out of pear tree with dick" (139). Over fifty years after Rocco Squarcione bellowed "Hey *sfacim*" in "Low-lands," foreign profanity in Pynchon's recent texts can be read as stubbornly abiding artifacts of mid-twentieth-century censorship, by one stubborn author who chafed against it.

In *Bleeding Edge*, Christian Hänggi locates, among musical references in this novel, "oblique nods to songs that were effectively banned from the airwaves by the Clear Channel corporation in the immediate aftermath of the [9/11] attacks (REM's 'It's the End of the World as We Know It,' Sinatra's 'New York, New York')," as discussed by Thomas.[96] This may be read as yet another continuation of habits from Pynchon's earliest years, coded references to banned art and subtle resistance to the ever-changing laws and standards of censorship, which underscores how this chapter's exploration of coded profanity and references to "obscene" literature may inform larger questions in Pynchon's texts, ever in dialogue with power and control. If Pynchon, despite his subterfuges, can be considered an active resister in the war on censorship, he partakes in a Pynchon family legacy, as William Pynchon (1590–1662), Thomas's ancestor, was a New World colonist and author who famously "wrote the first book banned—and burned—in Boston," per David M. Powers.[97]

There is not only academic but apparently also popular interest in Pynchon's profanity, if Forrest Wickmain's tracing of the phrase "what the fuck" in Pynchon's oeuvre, published in the online magazine, *Slate*, is any indication.[98] Wickman traces the phrase "what the fuck" through Pynchon's works, from its closest approximation "what the hell" in *V.*, to phoneticized instances of "What th' fuck" in *Gravity's Rainbow* through "What the Deuce!" in *Mason & Dixon*, "¿Qué el fuck?" in *Against the Day*, and examples in Pynchon's latest novels. If this is indeed evidence of popular interest in profanity in Pynchon's texts, this chapter may hopefully serve such an audience.

Finally, the centrality of paranoia in Pynchon's texts and commentary is difficult to overstate, and this chapter suggests a possible contributor to Pynchon's fabled paranoia: literary censorship of the 1950s and 1960s, which the young author rebelled against through overt profanity, coded profanity, and veiled and explicit references to banned texts.

As a *denouement*, the next and final chapter explores a seemingly Pynchonesque stylistic feature, the punctuation of trailing off, ellipsis marks...

Notes

1 Peter Kihss, "Pulitzer Jurors Dismayed on Pynchon," *New York Times*, 8 May 1974, http://www.nytimes.com/1974/05/08/archives/pulitzer-jurors-his-third-novel.html?_r=0.

2 Christopher Ames, "Power and the Obscene Word: Discourses of Extremity in Thomas Pynchon's *Gravity's Rainbow*," *Contemporary Literature* 31:2 (1990): 191–207.

3 Ibid., 191.

4 Ibid., 204.

5 J. Dan Rothwell, "Verbal Obscenity: Time for Second Thoughts," *Western Speech* 35 (1971): 233.

6 Tony McEnery, *Swearing in English* (New York: Routledge, 2006), 127.

7 Herman and Weisenburger, Gravity's Rainbow, *Domination, and Freedom*.

8 Ibid., 60.

9 Ibid., 74.

10 Ibid., 52.

11 Ibid., 201.

12 E.g., Ali Chetwynd, Joanna Freer, and Georgios Maragos, eds., *Thomas Pynchon, Sex, and Gender* (Athens: University of Georgia Press, 2018).

13 Roland Barthes, *S/Z* (Oxford: Blackwell, 1996), 11.

14 Anthony McEnery and Zhonghua Xiao, "Swearing in Modern British English: The Case of Fuck in the BNC," *Language and Literature* 13 (2004): 236.

15 McEnery, *Swearing in English*, 30.

16 Luis von Ahn, "Offensive/Profane Word List," accessed September 1, 2019, https://www.cs.cmu.edu/~biglou/resources/.

17 Lee Sigelman and William Jacoby, "The Not-So-Simple Art of Imitation: Pastiche, Literary Style, and Raymond Chandler," *Computers and the Humanities* 30:1 (1996): 18.

18 Mychelle Hadley Smith, "Profanity, Disgust, and Dangerous Literature: A Hermeneutical Analysis of *The Catcher in the Rye* and *The Chocolate War*," PhD diss., Texas A&M University, 2015, 88, 108, https://oaktrust.library.tamu.edu/bitstream/handle/1969.1/155470/SMITH-DISSERTATION-2015.pdf?sequence=1.

19 On race in Pynchon, see e.g., David Witzling, *Everybody's America: Thomas Pynchon, Race, and the Cultures of Postmodernism* (New York: Routledge, 2008). On homophobia in Pynchon, see e.g, Julie C. Sears, "Black and White Rainbows and Blurry Lines: Sexual Deviance/Diversity in *Gravity's Rainbow* and *Mason & Dixon*," in *Thomas Pynchon: Reading From The Margins*, ed. Niran Abbas (Danvers: Rosemont, 2003).

20 Methodological separation: "Lesser" profanity (*ass*, *bastard*, *crap*, *damn*, *hell*, *screw*) and "Greater" profanity (*asshole*, *bitch*, *cock*, *cunt*, *dick*, *fuck*, *goddamn*, *piss*, *pussy*, *shit*).

21 The queries take two approaches: lemma + query for additional characters, then manually isolating profane word forms, and a separate query for hyphenated compounds in which the profanity follows the hyphen. Sample queries: [word="ass.*"]|[word="[A-Za-z]+-ass|[word=".*ass.*"].

22 Ames, "Power and the Obscene Word," 194 ("Studies in obscene language in speech in literature have been surprisingly limited."). McEnery and Xiao, "Swearing in Modern British English," 235 ("To date [swearing] has been infrequently studied, though some recent work […] has addressed the topic. Nonetheless, there is still no systematic account of swear-words in English"). Gretchen McCulloch, "A Linguist Explains the Syntax of 'Fuck,'" *The Toast*, December 9, 2014, http://the-toast.net/2014/12/09/linguist-explains-syntax-f-word/ ("Strange to say, but it doesn't seem like the syntactic study of swear words has really progressed much beyond these obscure, semi-satirical papers from the 60s and 70s.").

23 Michael Adams, *In Praise of Profanity* (Oxford: Oxford University Press, 2016), ix.

24 Geoffrey Hughes, *Swearing: A Social History of Foul Language, Oaths, and Profanity in English* (London: Penguin Books, 1998), 497, 504.

25 Google Ngram Viewer, https://books.google.com/ngrams.

26 *Regina v. Hicklin*, L.R. 3 Q.B. (1868).

27 The contents of this book mostly concern adultery, abortion, the "marriage duty", onan, "carnal sins," and impotence, although "filthy words [...] permitted among married persons" is briefly mentioned. Anonymous, *The Confessional Unmasked: Showing the Depravity of the Romish Priesthood, the Iniquity of the Confessional and the Questions Put to Females in Confession …* (London: Protestant Electoral Union, 1867), 59.

28 Haig A. Bosmajian, "Introduction," in *Obscenity and Freedom of Expression*, ed. Haig A. Bosmajian (New York: Burt Franklin, 1976), ii–v.

29 *United States v. One Book Called "Ulysses,"* 5 F.Supp. 182 (1933).

30 *United States v. One Book Entitled Ulysses*, 72 F.2d 705 (1934).

31 *People v. Dial Press*, 48 N.Y.S.2d 480 (1944).

32 *Commonwealth v. Gordon*, 66 D. & C. 101 (1949).

33 Maurice Girodias, "Lolita, Nabokov and I," *Evergreen Review* 37 (1965): 89–91.

34 *Besig v. United States*, 208 F.2d 142 (1953).

35 *Roth v. United States*, 354 U.S. 476 (1957).

36 Bosmajian, "Introduction," vii.

37 Nancy J. Peters, "Milestones of Literary Censorship," in *Howl on Trial: The Battle for Free Expression*, ed. Bill Morgan and Nancy J. Peters (San Francisco: City Lights Books, 2006), 11.

38 Clayton W. Horn, "From the Decision by Judge Clayton W. Horn," in *Howl on Trial: The Battle for Free Expression*, ed. Bill Morgan and Nancy J. Peters (San Francisco: City Lights Books, 2006), 197.

39 Ibid., 198.

40 Weisenburger, "Thomas Pynchon at Twenty-Two."

41 Sara Solberg, "On Comparing Apples and Oranges: James Joyce and Thomas Pynchon," *Comparative Literature Studies* 56:1 (1979): 33–40.

42 Pynchon's juvenilia are reprinted in Clifford Mead, *Thomas Pynchon: A Bibliography of Primary and Secondary Materials* (Elmwood Park: Dalkey Press Archive, 1989), 155–67.

43 Ames, "Power and the Obscene Word," 191.

44 Illicit beavers also appear decades later in *Bleeding Edge*, which portrays a strip club with a "neon sign depicting a lewdly humanized beaver wearing a beret and winking its eyes alternately at a wiggling stripper" (219).

45 Pynchon's spelling was off or Mulligan, seemingly not a Hungarian speaker, speaks phonetically; the correct Hungarian spelling is "Kisci lófasz a seggedbe."

46 According to a *Pynchon Wiki* contributor, the phrase means "your dick is dead," i.e., impotent. Ware et al., "Minghe," *Pynchon Wiki*, accessed September 1, 2019, https://gravitys-rainbow.pynchonwiki.com/wiki/index.php?title=Minghe.

47 Elisabeth Ladenson, *Dirt for Art's Sake: Books on Trial from* Madame Bovary *to* Lolita (Ithaca: Cornell University Press, 2007), 177.

48 Ibid., 177–8.

49 *Besig v. United States*, 208 F.2d 142 (1953).

50 *Grove Press, Inc. v. Christenberry*, 175 F.Supp. 488 (1959).

51 *Kingsley Pictures v. Regents*, 360 U.S. 684 (1959).

52 David Seed, *The Fictional Labyrinths of Thomas Pynchon* (London: Macmillan, 1988), 38.

53 Ibid., 43.

54 Leigh Gilmore, "Obscenity, Modernity, Identity: Legalizing *The Well of Loneliness* and *Nightwood*," *Journal of the History of Sexuality* 4:4 (1994): 619–20.

55 Harriet F. Pilpel and Nancy F. Wechsler, "The Law and *Lady Chatterley*," *New World Writing* 16 (New York: J. B. Lippincott, 1960), 233.

56 David Cowart, "Love and Death: Variations on a Theme in Pynchon's Early Fiction," *Journal of Narrative Technique* 7:3 (1977): 157.

57 Ibid., 161.

58 "damme, int., n., and adj.," *OED Online*, Oxford University Press, accessed April 26, 2019, http://0-www.oed.com.catalogue.libraries.london.ac.uk/view/Entry/47055?re directedFrom=damme.

59 Weisenburger, "Pynchon at Twenty-Two," 696–7.

60 Cowart, in his reading of this story, states that "according to Eric Partridge's *Dictionary of Slang and Unconventional English*, 'goodfellow' is Covent Garden slang for 'a vigorous fornicator.'" Cowart, "Love and Death," 159. This is highly selective reading, however, as there are many diverse meanings of *Goodfellow* listed in Partridge, including "a roisterer, a boon companion," "a rich man," and "an expert boxer." Eric Partridge, *The Routledge Dictionary of Historical Slang*, 6th ed. (London: Routledge, 2006), 2201. The *OED*'s primary definition, meanwhile, is "an affable or jovial companion; a sociable or convivial person; spec. one who associates with others in feasting, drinking, and merrymaking, esp. habitually or hedonistically; a drinking companion; a reveller, a carouser". "goodfellow, n. and adj.," *OED Online*, Oxford University Press, accessed April 26, 2019, http://0-www. oed.com.catalogue.libraries.london.ac.uk/view/Entry/79938?rskey=6yrLft&result=1 &isAdvanced=false.

61 Ted Morgan, *Literary Outlaw: The Life and Times of William S. Burroughs* (London: Pimlico, 1988), 342–3.

62 John Dugdale, *Thomas Pynchon: Allusive Parables of Power* (Basingstoke: Macmillan, 1990), 181.

63 Max F. Schulz, *Black Humor Fiction of the Sixties* (Athens: Ohio University Press, 1973), 80.

64 J. Kerry Grant, *A Companion to* V. (Athens: University of Georgia Press, 2001), 175.

65 For additional data from this experiment, see the online data appendix at https:// github.com/erikannotations/TPDH.

66 Martínez, "From 'Under the Rose' to *V.*", 633–56.

67 Howard P. Chudacoff, *Children at Play: An American History* (New York: New York University Press, 2007), 154. Pynchon was not the only 1970s counterculture figure to target Mickey Mouse as emblematic of dominant American culture. See e.g., Tom Sito, *Drawing the Line: The Untold Story of the Animation Unions from Bosko to Bart Simpson* (Lexington: University Press of Kentucky, 2006).

68 Molly Hite, "When Pynchon Was a Boys' Club: *V.* and Midcentury Mystifications of Gender," in *Thomas Pynchon, Sex, and Gender*, ed. Ali Chetwynd, Joanna Freer, and Georgios Maragos (Athens: University of Georgia Press, 2018).

69 Howard, "Pynchon From A to V."

70 Ibid.

71 Witzling, *Everybody's America*, 122, 126.

72 "minge, n.," *OED Online*, Oxford University Press, accessed April 28, 2019, http://0-www.oed.com.catalogue.libraries.london.ac.uk/view/Entry/118799?rskey=leFDWs&result=1&isAdvanced=false.

73 These include "minghe morte" in "Entropy," and "Capo di minghe!" and "Signor Mantissa glanced up, startled. 'Minghe,' he said" in V.

74 Slade, *Thomas Pynchon*, 41.

75 Jan Cohn, *Creating America: George Horace Lorimer and* The Saturday Evening Post (Pittsburgh: University of Pittsburgh Press, 1989), 264, 15.

76 "It's the whole Reagan program, isn't it—dismantle the New Deal, reverse the effects of World War II, restore fascism at home and around the world, flee into the past, can't you feel it, all the dangerous childish stupidity" (*Vineland*, 265).

77 Uncredited, "History of *The Saturday Evening Post*," accessed September 1, 2019, https://www.saturdayeveningpost.com/history-saturday-evening-post/.

78 *Grove Press v. Gerstein*, 378 U.S. 577 (1964).

79 *Memoirs v. Massachusetts*, 383 U.S. 413 (1966).

80 Morgan, *Literary Outlaw*, 347.

81 Ibid. Examples of censorship of literature at the level of school boards persists to this day, and material that could be termed as literary has been successfully prosecuted for obscenity since 1966, e.g., Mike Diana for underground comic books in 1994. See e.g., Jean-Paul Gabilliet, *Of Comics and Men: A Cultural History of American Comic Books* (Jackson: University Press of Mississippi, 2010).

82 Pynchon, *Slow Learner*, 22.

83 *Cavalier* 50, March 16, 1966.

84 Mendelson, "The Sacred, The Profane, and *The Crying of Lot 49*," 188.

85 E.g., J. Kerry Grant on Peter Pinguid in *A Companion to* The Crying of Lot 49, 2nd ed. (Athens: University of Georgia Press, 2008), 59–60. And Hollander on Pierce Inverarity, "Pynchon, JFK and the CIA," 69.

86 The Spanish and Italian translations are from *Pynchon Wiki*. Ware et al., *Pynchon Wiki*, accessed September 1, 2019, https://cl49.pynchonwiki.com/wiki/index.php?title=The_Crying_of_Lot_49.

87 Dugdale, *Thomas Pynchon: Allusive Parables of Power*, 181.

88 *Miller v. California*, 413 U.S. 15 (1973).

89 Herman and Weisenburger, Gravity's Rainbow, *Domination, and Freedom*, 79.

90 Samuel Thomas, *Pynchon and the Political* (New York: Routledge, 2007), 152.

91 Ibid., 195.

92 Herman and Weisenburger, Gravity's Rainbow, *Domination, and Freedom*, 174.

93 Clerc, *Mason & Dixon & Pynchon*, 90.

94 Clerc writes that " 'shit' [appears] on a couple of occasions and a dozen or so variants of 'fuck,' " when in fact *shit* has a frequency of eleven while *fuck* has a frequency of twenty-four, with only five derivatives of *fuck* present (*fuck, fucking, fuckin, fuck'd, No-Fuck*; although when one counts the meaning of these words, e.g., literal versus figurative, the number increases). Ibid.

95 Sigelman and Jacoby, "The Not-So-Simple Art of Imitation," 18.

96 Christian Hänggi, "Pynchon's Sonic Fiction" (PhD Diss., University of Basel, 2017). Discussed by Samuel Thomas, "Blood on the Tracks." Hänggi, *Pynchon's Sound of Music*, 175–6.

97 David M. Powers, *Damnable Heresy: William Pynchon, the Indians, and the First Book Banned (and Burned) in Boston* (Eugene: Wipf & Stock, 2015), xv.

98 Forrest Wickman, "Thomas Pynchon and 'WTF': A Love Story," *Slate*, 20 September 2013, https://slate.com/culture/2013/09/thomas-pynchons-favorite-phrase-what-the-fuck-the-writer-is-our-great-poet-of-wtf.html.

6

Pynchon's Ellipsis Marks: Points and Dashes

In place of revelation, Pynchon gives the Ellipses of Uncertainty.
—Peter L. Cooper, *Signs and Symptoms: Thomas Pynchon and the Contemporary World*, 222

This book concludes with an investigation of the smallest, most easily definable and queryable "Pynchonian" stylistic unit yet: ellipsis marks.

Ellipsis marks are punctuation that can achieve both imprecision, through hesitation, interruption, and omission, as well as precision, through more precise rendering of speech and experience, as noted by Anne Toner in *Ellipsis in English Literature*, the most exhaustive study of the subject, which shall be cited extensively in this chapter.[1] *Ellipsis marks* denote not only the familiar series of periods …, but also dashes, hyphens, and asterisks, which over centuries have been used interchangeably in many respects.[2] In this chapter I will use *ellipsis points* to mean …, which quoted sources typically name *ellipsis* or *ellipses*, with *ellipsis marks* to also include dashes/em dashes (—) and asterisks, and *ellipsis* for the broader linguistic concept, "the omission of words, phrases, or clauses that are recoverable from the context."[3]

Critics have noted that Pynchon employs ellipsis marks, mainly ellipsis points and dashes, quite often. Ludovic Hunter-Tilney writes that the "ellipsis is a favourite Pynchonian tool,"[4] James W. Earl writes that ellipsis marks are "another of Pynchon's stylistic signatures,"[5] while Adrian Wisnicki searched for ellipsis marks when attempting to identify which of the uncredited Boeing articles Pynchon must have written.[6] In Laurence Daw's three-page note, "The Ellipsis as Architectonic in *Gravity's Rainbow*," Daw ventured that "such textual tactics [as Pynchon's ellipsis points] in the modern novel probably find their origin in Lawrence [sic] Sterne's *Tristram Shandy*, which contains as many dashes as there are ellipses in Pynchon's novel,"[7] and while this has a basis in truth, it neglects the long and varied history of ellipsis marks in English literature. Sascha Pöhlmann examines silences—achieved by ellipsis marks and unstated history—in texts by Wittgenstein and Pynchon and reads "Pynchon's ellipses as invitations for extrapolation."[8]

Are ellipsis marks truly a "favourite Pynchonian tool" or "stylistic signatures" of Pynchon? The experiments below demonstrate that ellipsis marks *can* credibly be called characteristic of certain major Pynchon novels, but not all of Pynchon's texts employ them significantly more than comparison texts. A brief history of ellipsis marks in English literature shows how ellipsis marks have been considered "characteristic" of a great many genres, writers, and even generations, and that a tendency to consider ellipsis marks as a characteristic feature of postmodern fiction should be questioned or discarded. While critics have paid considerable attention to ellipsis marks in Pynchon's works, with good cause, close examination of their claims demonstrates that, much of the time, these critics have simply described the uses of ellipsis marks in English in general, leading to overinterpretation that does not improve our understanding of Pynchon's stylistics.[9] Despite these cautions against hasty characterizations, some of Pynchon's uses of ellipsis marks are indeed remarkable or novel, including their sheer frequency in certain novels, the high frequency and creative use of ellipsis points in narration, and what could be called "techno-Gothic" ellipsis marks, which evoke the unknown, as in classic Gothic novels, but evoke, in Pynchon's usage, the *technological* unknown.

In the introduction to this book, I quoted Molly Hite's assertion that "ellipses are not a stylistic feature of either *V.* or *The Crying of Lot 49*"[10] as an example where digital methods might correct previous critical impressions. Again, strictly, this is incorrect, as *V.* features more than two hundred ellipsis points, but if Hite meant *foregrounded* or *characteristic* stylistic feature, then her impression was actually correct. As shown below, two hundred ellipsis points were a fairly typical amount for a novel of *V.*'s length and published in the 1960s. In other words, Hite either failed to notice the two hundred ellipsis points in *V.*, or noticed them but guessed that their frequency was not unusual. If the former was the case, Hite's statement thus demonstrates what Toner calls "punctuation's continuing latency on the page, often remaining invisible even to the most observant readers."[11] This latency suggests that more complete data, and more context on ellipsis marks in Pynchon's texts would be a beneficial addition to a groundwork of stylistic Pynchon studies.

6.1 A Brief History of Ellipsis Marks in English Literature

To provide context for the claims and interpretations below, a very brief history of ellipsis marks in English literature is germane, alongside select commentary on ellipsis marks by twentieth-century theorists. A key concept to introduce for this discussion is *aposiopesis*, defined as a "rhetorical artifice, in which the speaker comes to a sudden halt, as if unable or unwilling to proceed,"[12] and which Toner further defines thus: "If the omitted words can be supplied *exactly* from the context, the omission is an ellipsis. If the omission is only paraphrasable or is uncertain it is an aposiopesis."[13]

Ellipsis marks, mostly in the form of dots and dashes, became an increasingly common presence in printed English drama from the late sixteenth century onward, including the works of Ben Jonson and Shakespeare.[14] From drama, "ellipsis marks in their variant forms became a vital and even excessive feature of fictional prose of the eighteenth and early nineteenth centuries."[15] Sterne's *Tristram Shandy*, "English literature's most famous compendium of ellipsis marks," was published in this time, although there were also plenty of ellipsis marks to be found in, for example, works by Samuel Richardson (mostly dashes) and Jonathan Swift's *A Tale of a Tub* (mostly asterisks).[16] Toner notes that "for Sterne, aposiopesis is at the heart of language and of his novel, as his narrator is consistently unable to complete what he wants to say."[17] Generally, in fiction and drama of these periods, ellipsis marks were used in dialogue and first-person narration to capture the pauses and rhythm of the spoken word, as well as omissions of words or phrases to conceal a place name ("in the parish of …") or unprintable words ("does not care to let a man come so near her …").

Ellipsis marks were then notably popular in Gothic fictions which employed them, in a novel fashion, to evoke the supernatural forces typical of that genre, effecting incompleteness, fragments, gaps, unfinished endings ("abrupt narrative termination by means of elliptical punctuation"[18]), as well as "moments of non-rational or non-conscious experience,"[19] including ghosts, visions, fits, swoons, and death. "To say that ellipsis became an excessive presence in Gothic fiction is to put it mildly," writes Toner,[20] and Gothic writers would sometimes fill entire pages with ellipsis marks to evoke the unsettling unknown. This Gothic use of ellipsis marks will be important in discussing Pynchon's texts.

Toner also traces how the dash and ellipsis points "were originally equivalent versions of the same mark. […] In the radical transformation of writing into a commercialized activity that occurred in the early eighteenth century, the dash likewise was seen as the signature of the 'hack journalist.' "[21] In the nineteenth century, the "dash became an accepted and valued mark of punctuation, and some of the typographical idiosyncrasies and obscurities of sentimental and Gothic literature were composed into a more regular and orderly page."[22] Evolving practices of transcribing speech in the nineteenth century, such as shorthand, "facilitated developments in novelistic aspiration toward accurate reporting of speech and 'ordinary' talk,"[23] which influenced how writers such as George Eliot and Dickens employed ellipsis marks to capture the cadence and omissions of the spoken word in dialogue. The Victorian novelist and poet George Meredith "introduce[d] '...' to English fiction of high quality," in the opinion of one contemporary, and Toner writes that "Meredith's experiments with obscurity facilitate the adoption of ... as a signature of modernist prose."[24] For instance, Meredith often omitted "he said" or "she said," "creating a sense of the fragmentary, fleeting nature of conversation and the immediacy of exchange."[25] Additionally, "Meredith was also interested in ellipsis points as a notation not just of incomplete speech, but of incomplete thought [...]. On multiple occasions, ellipsis points are employed to capture the failure of thoughts to materialize fully, and accordingly they puncture narrated thought."[26]

Following Meredith, ellipsis points matured and flowered under Modernism:

> Ellipsis points came to consciousness at the turn of the century. Even though ... had been lurking on the pages of English print for over two hundred years, it suddenly became prominent as a punctuation mark in its own right. The possibilities of Meredith's experiments with ellipsis points were galvanized by a new generation of authors who were committed philosophically and aesthetically to forms of the obscure. The ellipsis was, again, rejuvenated as a force of the modern, this time specifically in the form of dot, dot, dot.

> The ambitious literary aims of Modernist writers cultivated new connotations for ellipsis points [...]. Rupture, fragmentation, and formlessness were invested with generational significance and with increasing existential significance as the century went on, as certainties collapsed at every turn. [...] The expanding volume of ellipsis points, from Conrad to Beckett, provides quantifiable support for th[is] trajectory [...]. Ellipsis points can be seen as a symbol of the century as they articulate its ever-unravelling coherence.[27]

In addition to characterizing ellipsis marks as a "signature of modernism,"[28] Toner mentions numerous roughly contemporary writers who employed ellipsis marks abundantly, such as H. G. Wells, Samuel Beckett, Joseph Conrad, and Ford

Maddox Ford. To this I could add some authors located by querying the Corpus of the Canon of Western Literature;[29] a simple query indicates that ellipsis points are also overrepresented in works by, for example, Rudyard Kipling, Thomas Hardy, and Edith Wharton.

The semantic and symbolic expansion of ellipsis points was touched upon in 1967 by Derrida, who "adopted the ellipsis as the figure of *différance*, the infinite deferral of meaning. In his philosophy, ellipsis *is* meaning, in that meaning only emerges by virtue of its own lack," per Toner.[30] Derrida's short essay "Ellipsis" is typical of his imprecise style; Derrida avoids categorical statements about ellipsis and makes no distinction between the broad linguistic concept of ellipsis and the punctuation marks of ellipsis points. Yet by at least *hinting at* the possibility for ellipsis marks to evoke aspects of deconstructionist philosophy, which centered on the anxiety of language and opposition to logocentrism, Derrida gestured toward concepts that commentators on Pynchon's ellipsis marks would later flesh out.

At the same time as the blossoming of ellipsis marks in the "higher" literature of the nineteenth and twentieth centuries, ellipsis marks were enjoying an equally vibrant life in popular culture, which did not escape the ire of self-appointed cultural arbiters. Toner writes how "ellipsis is repeatedly associated with popular and often debased forms of writing. It is as much a sin as a sign of omission […] an evasion adopted by the hasty and inadequate author or a genre-based cliché."[31] Theodor Adorno likewise associated ellipsis points with "the hack journalist" in 1956, echoing a centuries-old stigma,[32] which can even later be found in a typical example from the genre of "writing advice": Frederick Crews wrote in *The Random House Handbook* that in "general, it is good to avoid the 'stylistic' use of ellipses to connect your own sentences or to link elements within them […]. In these examples the ellipses make a vague and lazy effect."[33] This negative association between ellipsis marks and "hack writers" was alluded to by Umberto Eco, who wrote that a "scientific criterion can be applied to distinguish the professional writer from the Sunday, or non-writer. […] This is the use of suspension points in the middle of a sentence," although as this appears in a humorous essay, the targets of Eco's satire may be not only "bad writers" but also pedantic, prescriptive grammarians.[34]

Ellipsis points, in short, have been sweepingly and confidently dubbed characteristic of an enormous variety of writers, genres, periods, and styles, both "high" and "low." In the present millenium, as ellipsis marks are acquiring yet another life in email, text messaging, and other forms of computer-mediated communication, linguists are beginning to investigate how ellipsis points in these forms of discourse "adhere to the marker's traditional uses within written English [...] or are more innovatively employed by speakers."[35] Once again, there are also indications that ellipsis marks are being claimed by overconfident journalists and bloggers as "typical" of some group, from "old people"[36] to "people over 25"[37] to "valley girls."[38] While ellipsis marks continue to acquire new semantics, the temptation to characterize them as a trademark stylistic feature persists, which suggests that data on Pynchon's ellipsis marks would be beneficial.

6.2 Ellipsis Marks in Pynchon and Comparison Corpora

In Earl's brief examination of ellipsis marks in *Against the Day*, he inquires, "What other novelist uses them so often?"[39] The following figures and tables present ellipsis marks in the Pynchon corpus and comparison corpora (Figures 6.1–6.4).

The clear outlier in ellipsis mark frequency is William Gaddis. For dashes, this is because Gaddis (like Joyce, or certain Romance and Slavic languages) begins dialogue with a dash, for example, "— My dear Mister Cohen" (*J R*, 9). Gaddis is also an outlier in ellipsis points, which litter the text and often end direct

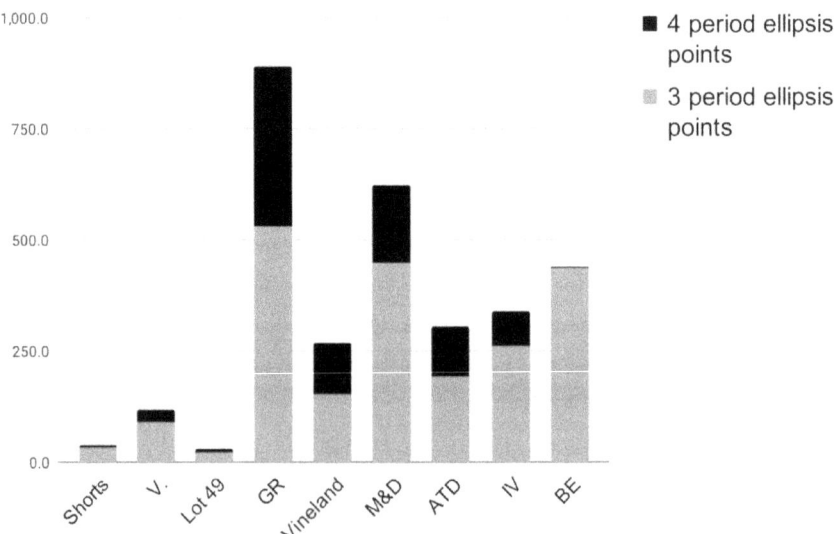

Figure 6.1 Normalized frequency (per 100k word tokens) of ellipsis points in Pynchon corpus.

Ellipsis points ...

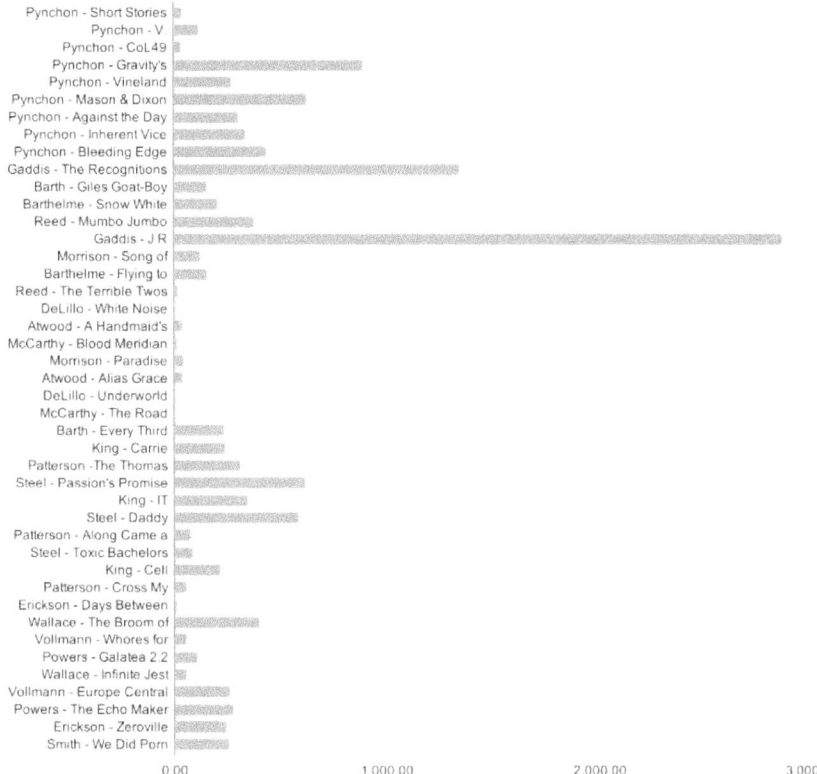

Figure 6.2 Normalized frequency (per 100k word tokens) of ellipsis points in Pynchon and comparison corpora.

Em-dashes —

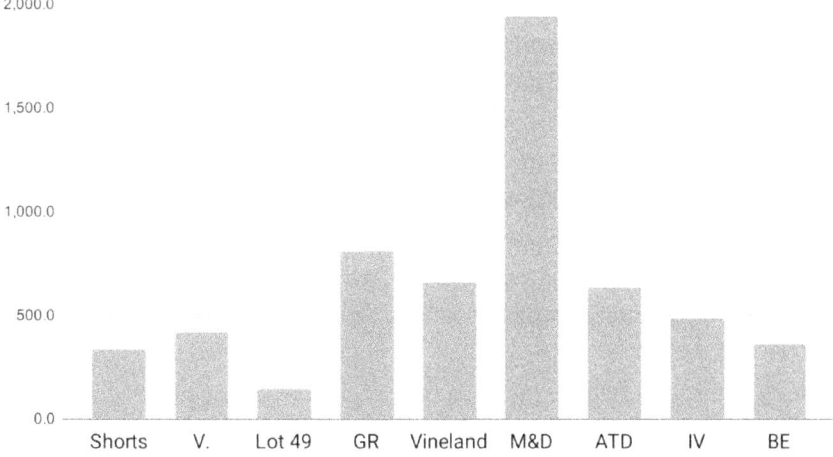

Figure 6.3 Normalized frequency (per 100k word tokens) of em dashes in Pynchon corpus.

Em-dashes —

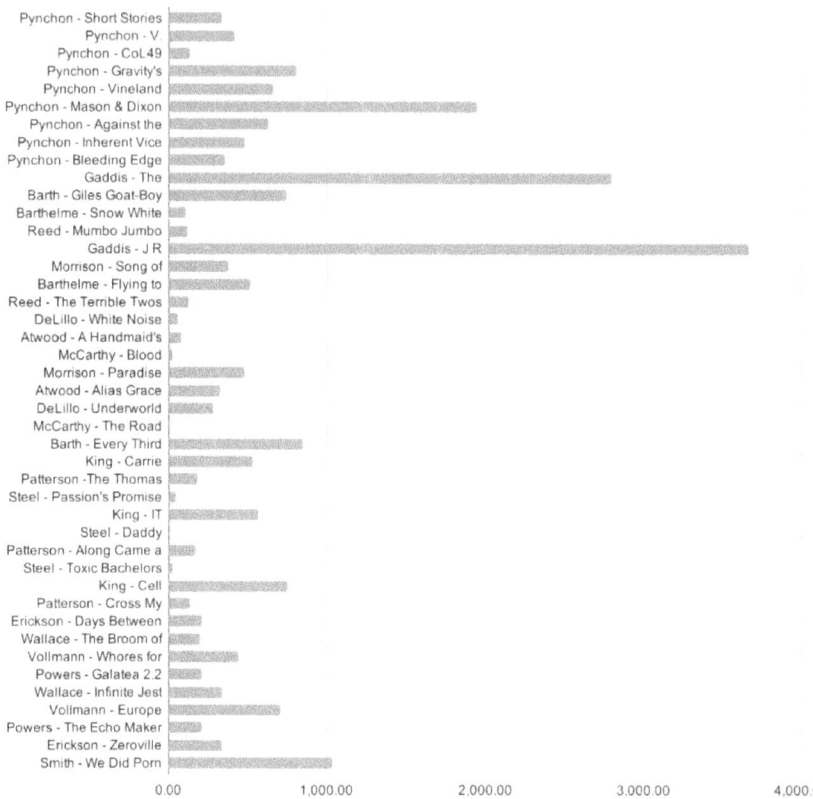

Figure 6.4 Normalized frequency (per 100k word tokens) of em dashes in Pynchon and comparison corpora.

speech. Yet this is an unsurprising result insofar as Gaddis is already known as a stylistic outlier, "Mr. Difficult," as Jonathan Franzen dubbed him, whose *J R* "consist[s] almost entirely of overheard voices, with nary a quotation mark, no conventional narration of any kind, no 'later that same evening,' no 'meanwhile in New York,' not a single chapter break, not even a section break, but thousands of dashes and ellipses."[40]

Gaddis aside, the two novels with the highest relative frequency of ellipsis points and dashes are indeed by Pynchon: *Gravity's Rainbow* greatest in ellipsis points and *Mason & Dixon* greatest in dashes. This overuse is partly what attracted critics, and ellipsis points in *Gravity's Rainbow* were such a conspicuous feature that back in 1983, Laurence Daw manually counted the pages of *Gravity's Rainbow* containing them, finding that 90.3 percent of its pages do.[41] Clearly,

Gravity's Rainbow marked a watershed moment in the use of ellipsis points for Pynchon, with approximately 7 to 29 times greater ellipsis point density than Pynchon's preceding works and 1.5–3.2 times greater than Pynchon's later works. This overuse is very highly statistically significant compared to other works in the corpora.[42] After *Gravity's Rainbow*, ellipsis points were greatly reduced, but then generally increased in a lifelong habit.

The trend for dashes is less clear: a large increase in *Gravity's Rainbow*, but then a steady decline, with the exception of the copious number of dashes in *Mason & Dixon*, which, in its mock eighteenth-century English pastiche, included such unexpected punctuation as dashes after commas (e.g., "Thankee, Jellow,— slow again, I see."; frequency 4,574) and following quotation marks (e.g., " 'We regret it, Sir,' Dixon offers, '— far too much Whim-Wham.' "; frequency 213). This overuse in *Mason & Dixon* is also very highly significant.[43] Keith Houston remarks that "in parodying the literary tropes of earlier works, postmodern writers such as Thomas Pynchon and John Barth have taken up dashes and dash hybrids as the perfect emblems of times past,"[44] which is consistent with the profusion of dashes in *Mason & Dixon,* although less so with Pynchon's later historical novels, which feature the same amount or fewer dashes than, for instance, certain Stephen King novels. Houston also ventured that "if the quantity of dashes seen in the wild is any indication of its future survival, Pynchon may have singlehandedly removed it from the list of endangered marks of punctuation."[45] Yet this speculation goes too far. For instance, *Gravity's Rainbow* features 1.5 times the density of dashes in comparison with Stephen King's *Carrie*, published only a year later, but *Carrie* still featured over three hundred, in a fairly short novel, and undoubtedly sold many more copies than Pynchon's magnum opus. A wider variety of corpora would be needed to investigate this minor question, but my data questions or refutes the claim that Pynchon "saved" the endangered dash. If Houston guesses that Pynchon's dashes influenced the style of his literary descendants, my data provides no general answer. Some of the more clearly Pynchon-influenced writers such as David Foster Wallace employ dashes in low amounts, while the Pynchon-influenced Zak Smith employs them abundantly.

Gaddis aside, the ellipsis points in Pynchon's postmodern peers display a wide range of frequency and semantic and grammatical functions. Ellipsis points are prevalent in Barth's *Every Third Thought* and Reed's *Mumbo Jumbo*, at notable levels in *Giles Goat-Boy* and Barthelme, low in certain works by Morrison and Atwood, and rare to nonexistent in McCarthy. DeLillo employs ellipsis points only once in ~390,000 words queried, and then his narrator spends an entire paragraph remarking upon it:

> And the sexy voice on the radio repeated the Du Pont slogan now. Better Things for Better Living … Through Chemistry. The woman enjoyed the pause. She prolonged the pause. She moaned through the pause. She spoke urgently and excitedly up to the pause and then she paused and moaned slowly and then she finished reciting the slogan, finally, all sated and limp and moaned out, and then she started from the beginning again. (*Underworld*, 602)

The amount of commentary that DeLillo is able to sustain from a single set of ellipsis points serves as a strong reminder that measuring frequency without some close(r) reading of these stylistic devices is extremely limited, which I shall turn to below.

Some romances and horror novels by Danielle Steel and Stephen King, respectively, equal or exceed the ellipsis points of most of Pynchon's novels, even the most recent ones. This recalls the long historical association of ellipsis marks with genre fiction (whether justified by evidence or not) but calls into question the "distinctiveness" of ellipsis points in Pynchon's novels other than *Gravity's Rainbow* and *Mason & Dixon*.

Are ellipsis marks a characteristic of Pynchon's style? In two major novels, the answer is yes. But apart from Gaddis, *Gravity's Rainbow*, and *Mason & Dixon*, the high number of ellipsis points in popular fiction generally and dashes in a variety of authors suggest that further speculation based on frequency alone is unwise. In a Pynchon Wiki discussion, Tore Rye Andersen ventured that "the ellipsis has always been one of Pynchon's favorite rhetorical devices,"[46] yet this is arguably untrue for Pynchon's first two novels, in which the number of ellipsis points is matched or greatly exceeded by a host of comparison novels. Other commenters have associated ellipsis points with not only Pynchon but postmodernism at large, such as Joanna Freer ("postmodern literary techniques [… which] include Pynchon's careful ambiguity, his use of ellipses")[47] and Paul Maltby ("Postmodern writers make frequent use of ellipses").[48] Outside of Pynchon studies, ellipsis marks and postmodernism have been occasionally linked, as well. An obituary for the novelist Tom Wolfe characterized his style thus: "Ridiculously long sentences, sometimes depending on the heavy use of … ellipses … and more ellipses … and complex punctuation like::::. He was probably the first postmodernist on a major metro daily."[49] Due to my findings, the wider history of ellipsis marks in fiction, and the myriad writers and genres associated with them, the notion of frequent ellipsis marks as particularly postmodern should be questioned, if not discarded.

6.3 Ellipsis Words

Textual ellipsis can be achieved not only through ellipsis marks but also through common ellipsis words and phrases such as "and so forth" and "and so on" (a few examples of vagueness words, as discussed in a previous chapter). Pynchon uses these, also, along with as a number of unconventional ellipsis phrases, including *und so weiter* and *u.s.w.* (German: and so forth), as well as the idiomatic *and whatever* (e.g., "shit, connectors, chargers, cables, and whatever," *BE*, 44). But for comparative purposes, Figure 6.5 presents simple queries of *and so on, and so forth*, and *etc./etcetera/et cetera*.

The first observation regarding common ellipsis phrases is how many writers eschew them, with zero instances of "and so on" or "and so forth" in the included works of Gaddis, Morrison, McCarthy, Patterson, and Erickson, who avoid these imprecise expressions. The greatest frequencies may be found in late Pynchon texts and writers most associated with Pynchon's style of postmodernism—Barth, Barthelme—as well as the Pynchon-influenced Wallace and Smith. Recall that Pynchon employs ellipsis points most frequently in *Gravity's Rainbow*, after which the numbers drop in all subsequent novels—this is precisely where Pynchon's frequent use of "and so on" and "and so forth" begins, suggesting that perhaps Pynchon swaps the punctuation mark for phrases which similarly effect ellipsis/aposiopesis.

6.4 From Frequency to Close(r) Reading

Gerald Howard suggests a particular quotation featuring ellipsis points in *Gravity's Rainbow*, "Tantivy…" (*GR*, 252), when Slothrop learns of the death of his friend, as "the most poignant ellipsis in all of fiction."[50] From a humanistic standpoint, the deep impression this lone punctuation mark left on Howard points to the interpretive richness of Pynchon's ellipsis marks. From a cold data standpoint, however, the ellipsis points that Howard found so moving are only one instance out of over three thousand in *Gravity's Rainbow*, which underscores how little of the semantic and functional features may be illuminated by simple frequencies.

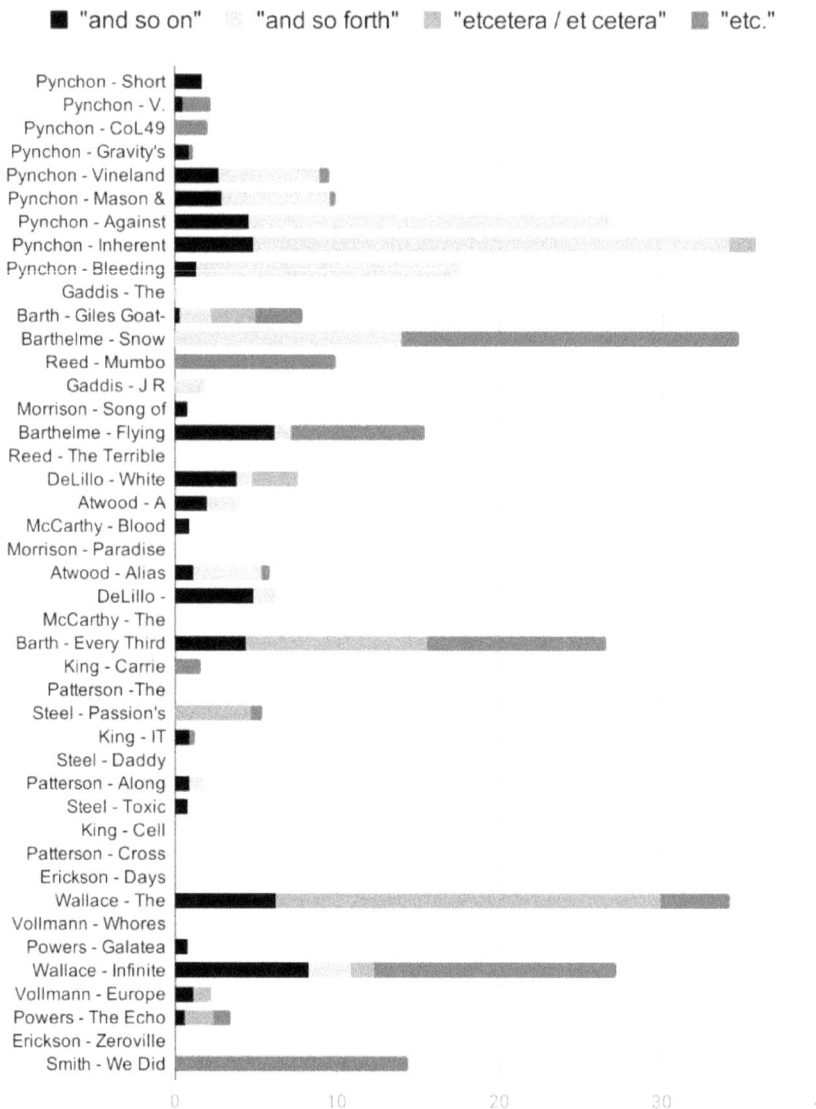

Figure 6.5 Normalized frequency (per 100k word tokens) of ellipsis phrases.

While query may at times seem hopefully imprecise, close reading of Pynchon's ellipsis marks has hardly been free from interpretive pitfalls. For instance, when critics have ventured to describe Pynchon's ellipsis marks in more detail, too often they have simply restated the historical uses of ellipsis marks in English. Charles Clerc provides one summary of ellipsis points in *Gravity's Rainbow*: "Ellipses are liberally used to suspend action, to pause, to suggest prolonged continuance or repetition, to trail off, to interpolate, and conversely to join, ideas."[51] However, most of these are features of ellipsis marks in English, not specific to Pynchon. Hite discusses how "the ellipses [in *Gravity's Rainbow*] imply that an action, description, or train of thought simply goes on, further than the narrative can or will follow,"[52] but this essentially restates aposiopesis, also not unique to Pynchon. Hohmann states that ellipsis points "are instances of aposiopesis, of a speaker's inability to pursue his thoughts because of an inner agitation which, in *Gravity's Rainbow*, is due to apocalyptic intimations," citing seven page numbers.[53] These textual locations do indeed terminate in ellipsis points while invoking apocalypse, yet as *Gravity's Rainbow* contains over three thousand sets of ellipsis points, passages evoking virtually any thematic concern could be found that contain them.

Another minor example of the temptation to overinterpret ellipsis marks in Pynchon is speculation on the significance of three vs. four ellipsis points. In a Pynchon Wiki discussion, Andersen proposed that "the ellipsis has always been one of Pynchon's favorite rhetorical devices, and the way I see it, the number of dots simply signifies how large the ellipsis is meant to be."[54] Another Pynchon Wiki user pointed out that Pynchon uses four periods only at the end of sentences, an observation repeated by Earl: "sometimes three dots, sometimes four dots, always carefully distinguished, three interrupting a sentence, four ending it,"[55] and this rule is mostly consistent within Pynchon's texts.[56]

While many of the analyses of ellipsis marks in Pynchon's texts simply describe common uses in English, scholars have more successfully argued a number of functions which seem unique to or at least representative of Pynchon. Hite discussed how ellipsis points in *Gravity's Rainbow* are an "indication of Pynchon's commitment to incompleteness."[57] Daw writes that Pynchon uses ellipsis points to achieve ambiguity, citing Schaub. Stefan Mattessich notes how Pynchon's "long sentences verg[e] on incoherence through the use of dashes and the heaping on of present participles."[58] Yoichiro Miyamato provides the most linguistically informed description of ellipsis points in *Gravity's Rainbow*:

> On the syntactic level, the structure of sentences [in *Gravity's Rainbow*] tends to be loose: sentences tend to become compounds of fragmentary phrases. The most obvious symptom of this is the frequent use of ellipses. [… Which] also blurs the conjunction between sentences. As if sentences are not quite sure whether they are completed or not, they pause with ellipses, and merge with each other, or with silence.[59]

Pöhlmann essentially repeats many of these scholars' claims but generalizes them to a broader thematic concern in Pynchon, "the problematic relation between language and the world" and "the idea that words cannot represent things fully."[60] The notion that ellipsis marks gesture beyond the limits of language is also stated by Earl, who writes that "ellipses often indicate more than something unexpressed, avoided, implied, or almost implied, but rather something hidden, sometimes […] inexpressible."[61] Ellipsis marks, then, are a component of Pynchon's ambiguous, fragmentary worldview, which encapsulate and are used to convey Pynchon's themes of incompleteness and the difficulty (or impossibility) for language to express ideas or, in other words, the inherent vagueness/ambiguity of language. Much of this is exemplified by a remark by a narrator of *Against the Day*, "But didn't that imply … the tantalizing possibility was just out of reach …" (*ATD*, 436).

Extending these interpretations, commentaries on ellipsis marks in *Gravity's Rainbow* also point to how ellipsis marks suggest not only essential vagueness but also revelation and multiple worlds. In a wide-ranging study of Pynchon's texts within the contexts of literature, science, and epistemology, Peter L. Cooper provides a description of ellipsis marks as loci of vagueness and connotative of myriad worlds:

> What do all the ellipses cover? […] They suggest the inconceivable number of things left unnamed, paths left unexplored, realities left untouched; they demonstrate the pitiful inadequacy language in the face of the endless relation and ramification that is our cosmos; they testify to the insufficiency of the words from which the book is made. This passage describes the approach of Tchitcherine and Džaqzp Qulan to the Kirghiz light: "Waiting, out in the sunlight which is not theirs yet, is the… The…" (*GR*, 343)[62]

Daw similarly suggested that ellipsis points can be found where "characters sense parallels between facets of existence" and that the extreme number of ellipses in *Gravity's Rainbow* may be read as "Pynchon's way of showing us how the imminence of revelation is omnipresent."[63] Jim Neighbors later argued that "Pynchon's ellipses indicate the necessary incapacity of language to capture or contain the immensity of its always dividing and proliferating referent,"[64] while Pöhlmann also further explores the connection between the limits of language, ellipsis marks, and multiple worlds.

What many of these critics describe is partly the Gothic use of ellipsis marks, fits and swoons that invoke the supernatural, and indeed Daw mentions the Gothic in his note on Pynchon's ellipsis points, citing Douglas Fowler's exploration of

Gothic effects in Pynchon. Fowler stated that "more than any other single effect, supernatural terror is what Pynchon works to convey" and that "Gothic effects, especially gothic effects as perceived by witnesses whose sensibilities are too delicate or perverse to deal with them, are fundamental in Pynchon," referring especially to the many mysterious forces and unfinished quests in Pynchon.[65] Discussion of the Gothic in Pynchon was later aided by Pynchon's extended observations on Gothic literature in "Is It O.K. to Be a Luddite?": "The craze for Gothic fiction after 'The Castle of Otranto' was grounded, I suspect, in deep and religious yearnings for that earlier mythical time which had come to be known as the Age of Miracles. [...] Giants, dragons, spells," which Pynchon reads in opposition to science, the Age of Reason, and the "emerging technopolitical order."[66] Interestingly, Gothic literature scholar Allan Lloyd Smith reads the Gothic in Pynchon as a *merger* of Gothic sensibilities with technology, the very forces Pynchon states are in conflict: "Pynchon developed a form of techno-gothic much influenced by science fiction in *V.* and *Gravity's Rainbow*, and his *The Crying of Lot 49* is a controlled exercise in Gothic hysteria."[67] Smith provides no further argument for this claim, but in another essay on "striking parallels" between the Gothic and postmodern that discusses Pynchon, Smith notes how "at some point [...], the development of technology merges with mysticism and superstition: at a sufficiently refined level technology itself becomes uncanny and reopens the symbol system of the Gothic."[68]

Smith's suggested concept and term, "techno-Gothic," aptly describes a particular function of ellipsis points in Pynchon's texts. Bénédicte Chorier-Fryd, in examining scientific subtext in Pynchon, highlights two passages which evoke such a techno-Gothic concept.[69] The first example passage appears in the early Pynchon short story "Under the Rose" and the second in *Inherent Vice*, where a "sentence leading to the revelation of the uncanny is suspended by a dash." The first describes the cyborg-like Bongo Shaftsbury:

> Shiny and black against the unsunned flesh was a miniature electric switch, single-pole, double-throw, sewn into the skin. Thin silver wires ran from its terminals up the arm, disappearing under the sleeve. [...] "The wires run up into my brain. When the switch is closed like this I act the way I do now. When it is thrown the other—" (*SL*, 121)

Another occurrence of "techno-Gothic" ellipsis occurs in *Inherent Vice*, where Doc, per Chorier-Fryd, "catches a ride with one Japonica Fenway, an 'insane' 'Kozmic Traveler' who happens to have a cyborg double [...]; her 'skillful' driving style turns out to be rather out of the ordinary":

Her humming was way too intense. Doc made the mistake of looking over, only to find her staring at him and not the road, eyes glittering ferally through a blond curtain of California-chick hair. No, this was not reassuring. Though hardly a connoisseur of the freakout, he did recognize a wraparound hallucination when he saw one and understood immediately that while she likely didn't see Doc at all, whatever she was seeing was indeed physically out there, in the gathering fog, and just about to— (*IV*, 176–7)

Yet another example from *Against the Day* is noted by Earl:

Descending to the platform at Stuffed Edge, Lew found a prospect bleak and hushed, all but unmodified by vegetation … a scent of daylight oil hung over the scene, as if phantom motor vehicles operated on some other plane of existence, close but just invisible. (*ATD*, 610)

The Gothic ellipsis mark itself was an evolution from previous centuries, from Sterne's aposiopesis and the pauses and omissions of speech to Gothic's evoking of the supernatural and unknown (essentially Pynchon's "Giants, dragons, and spells") via syntactic omission. In the passages above, published almost fifty years apart, we see that Pynchon has updated the Gothic ellipsis mark with heady science and science fiction to arrive at a techno-Gothic function of ellipsis marks. Amongst the comparison corpora I have, the techno-Gothic ellipsis points seem fairly unique to Pynchon's texts and also fit well within Zofia Kolbuszewska's exploration of the Gothic in *Mason & Dixon*: Pynchon "parod[ies] classical Gothic motifs" in *Mason & Dixon* and "extends the boundaries of [Gothic] convention" via Pynchon's subjunctive, possible time, possible worlds.[70]

Many hundreds or probably thousands of ellipsis points in Pynchon's texts function semantically and grammatically in the ways that they normally function in English, but Pynchon employs ellipsis marks in at least two relatively distinct ways. First, ellipsis marks in Pynchon's texts notably effect and symbolize his lifelong stylistic and thematic ambiguity and vagueness, Pynchon's tendency to almost, but not quite, express something directly... Second, whereas ellipsis marks in Gothic fiction often evoked the supernatural, Pynchon sometimes employs them in similar, but updated, fashion to suggest a mélange of the supernatural and the technological—as well as the multiple worlds suggested by twentieth-century science and the flights of imagination of science fiction—merging the "irrational" Gothic with "rational" science in one punctuation mark.

6.5 Ellipsis Marks and Speech

Despite these notable uses of ellipsis marks in Pynchon's texts, the most mundane functions of ellipsis marks, the pauses and omissions of speech, are certainly in abundance in Pynchon and are the rule, rather than the exception. To examine this, I separated the amount of ellipsis marks in direct discourse and narration in the corpora (Figures 6.6 and 6.7).

In this sample, ellipsis points in fiction occur mostly in dialogue, but *Gravity's Rainbow* is an outlier in this regard, containing the most number of ellipsis points in narration, by far. This is probably why ellipsis points are so remarked upon by critics of this novel—within character dialogue, ellipsis points are found in abundance in a variety of postmodern and popular fiction works, and thus seem unremarkable, but ellipsis points in narration (and in such quantities) naturally foregrounds the technique.

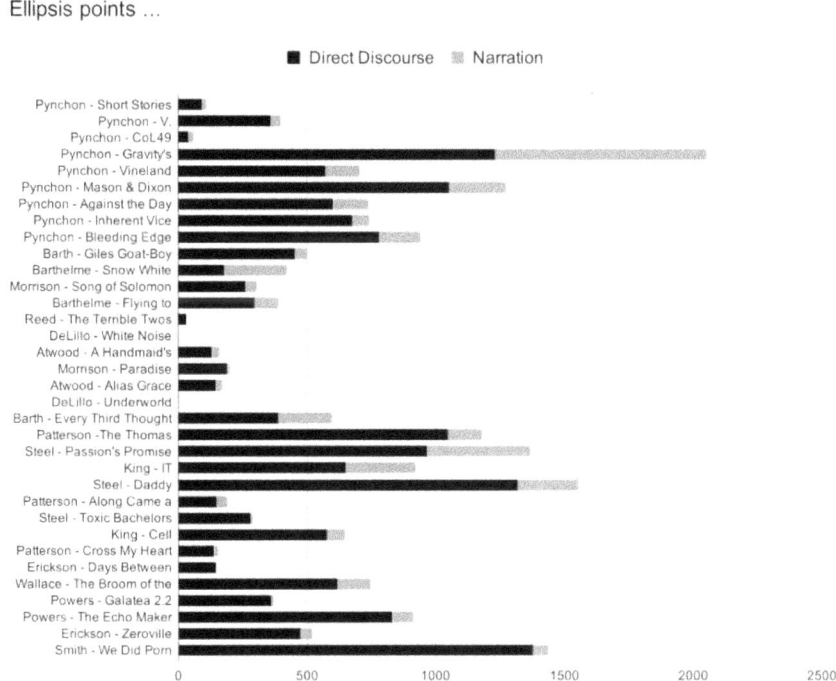

Figure 6.6 Normalized frequency (per 100k word tokens) of ellipsis points in direct discourse and narration.

Em-dashes —

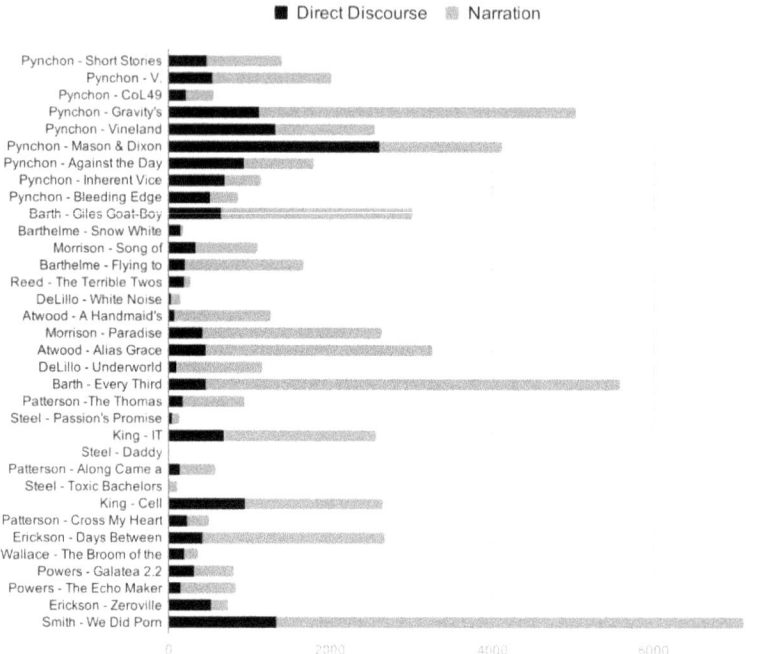

Figure 6.7 Normalized frequency (per 100k word tokens) of em dashes in direct discourse and narration.

Rendering pauses in speech is a fundamental function of ellipsis marks, per Toner: "Ellipses marks have developed in literary dialogue as a means of getting closer to the sounds of spoken language,"[71] and ellipsis points in dialogue thus fall into what Toner described as "punctuation's continuing latency on the page, often remaining invisible even to the most observant readers," as mentioned above. In *Gravity's Rainbow*'s kaleidoscopic narration, featuring shifting and unknown narrative voices, the ellipsis points become notably salient, ripe for interpretation or overinterpretation, in passages such as,

> They dreamed of their orders, of colossal explosions and death—if they even saw her it was sidewise, sly … her Father will tame her … her teeth will bite the pole … someday I will have a herd of them for myself … but first I must find my Captain … somewhere out in the War … first they must deliver me from this little place…. (*GR*, 429)

As for ellipsis marks in direct discourse (i.e., mostly pauses or aposiopesis in the direct speech of characters), this increases markedly with *Gravity's Rainbow* and becomes a lifelong trend in Pynchon's writing, hypothetically in furtherance of Pynchon's increasing attention to rendering speech, as discussed in Chapter 1. As for em dashes, conversely, the frequency of em dashes in Pynchon's dialogue is noticeably higher than most compared texts. The frequent use of em dashes in narration is high in numerous postmodern and popular fiction texts, and most of Pynchon's novels employ em dashes in narration in unremarkable quantities, although, again, *Gravity's Rainbow* is high.

In Pynchon's nonfiction texts such as book reviews, books forewords, and articles, which are not included in the comparison corpora, ellipsis marks appear almost exclusively in the dialogue of characters and figures, real and imagined, to effect the rhythm and aposiopesis of speech, as well as elision when quoting a source. The only exception is from Pynchon's introductory essay on Barthelme, in which Pynchon describes a dreamlike quality to Barthelme's assaults on reality: "The effect each time, at any rate, is to put us in the presence of something already eerily familiar … to remind us that we have lived in these visionary cities and haunted forests, that the ancient faces we gaze into are faces we know.…"[72] Pynchon here employs ellipsis points for their canonical Gothic effects, invoking language that echoes his description of Gothic literature in "Is It O.K. to Be a Luddite?," strengthening a reading of Gothic traces in Pynchon's ellipsis marks.

6.6 Ellipsis Marks and Verse

Some other texts in which ellipsis marks are often common are poems and song lyrics, and ellipsis marks appear in Pynchon's poems and songs, as well (Figures 6.8 and 6.9).

Ellipsis points in verse are a lifelong stylistic feature for Pynchon, with ellipsis points in verse increasing in *Gravity's Rainbow* and greatly increasing in *Vineland*. As for em dashes in verse, these were almost nonexistent in early Pynchon texts but then ballooned in *Gravity's Rainbow*. Of all Pynchon's novels, *Gravity's Rainbow* has attracted the most critical reception, and most critical descriptions of Pynchon's style are focused on this book, unsurprisingly, as Pynchon's widely acknowledged magnum opus. This data suggest that *Gravity's Rainbow* also marks a shift in Pynchon's stylistic use of ellipsis marks, probably related to the novel's fragmentary narration and shifting perspectives but perhaps also related to how Pynchon's style in *Gravity's Rainbow* is sometimes characterized as a prose poem.[73] Verse, ellipsis points, and em dashes all reach new highs for

Ellipsis points in verse/songs

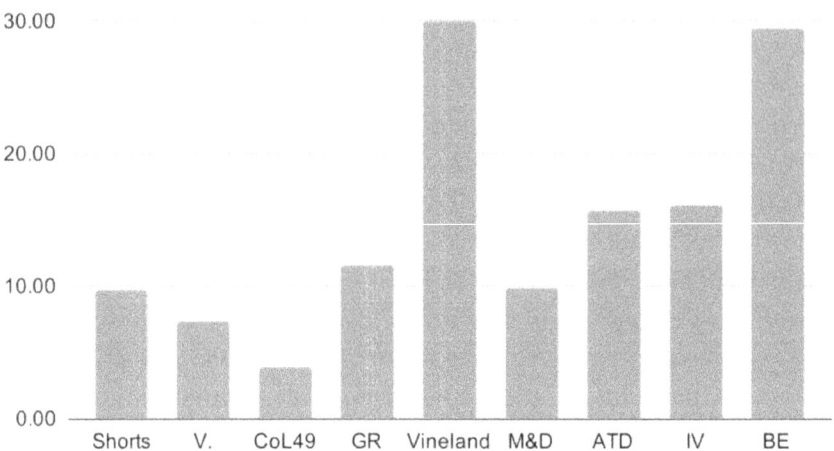

Figure 6.8 Normalized frequency (per 1,000 word tokens) of ellipsis points in verse.

Em-dashes in verse/songs

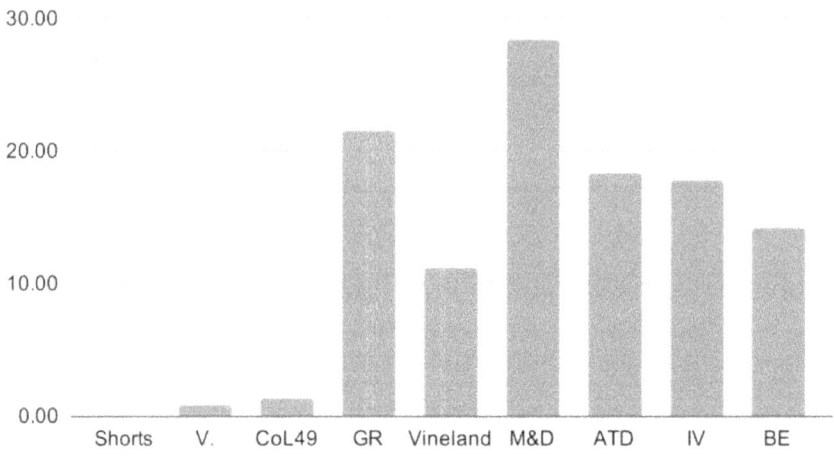

Figure 6.9 Normalized frequency (per 1,000 word tokens) of dashes in verse.

Pynchon in *Gravity's Rainbow*, suggesting that the stylistics of poetry may be worth considering in any investigation of Pynchon's ellipsis marks.

6.6.1 Rilke's Ellipses

The poetry of Rainer Maria Rilke plays an outsized metatextual role in *Gravity's Rainbow*. Rilke is referenced by name nine times in the novel, and a lead character, Enzian, is named after Rilke's "Tenth Elegy," as the text informs the reader. In his 1973 review of *Gravity's Rainbow*, Locke proclaimed Rilke the "most important cultural figure" in the novel, writing that "the book could be read as a serio-comic variation on Rilke's *Duino Elegies* and their German Romantic echoes in Nazi culture."[74] John O. Stark wrote that Pynchon "includes echoes of Rilke's 'Tenth Elegy' so often throughout his novel that it sometimes seems like an expanded version of that poem."[75] Hohmann explored the intertextual relationship between Rilke's and Pynchon's texts at length; as succinctly summarized by Duyfhuizen, "Hohmann shows a complex interrelationship that is both serious and parodic. On the one hand, he shows how Pynchon and Rilke share many elements in their conceptual framework; however, on the other hand, the promises of transcendence that are so crucial to Rilke's transfigurative vision become either sick jokes or targets of sympathetic parody in Pynchon's post-nuclear vision."[76] Given the clear importance of Rilke to Pynchon's magnum opus, one might look for not only thematic allusion but stylistic allusion, as well.

Doug Haynes, in his article on "Pynchon's Rilke," hints that Rilke's influence on *Gravity's Rainbow* may be not only philosophical or thematic but also stylistic.[77] Explicating one of Blicero's Rilke-esque monologues ("Death only rules here. It has never, in love, become one with...," 723), Haynes writes that Blicero's "speech dwindl[es] to *the ellipses it imports from Rilke's verse*" (emphasis added).[78] The notion that Pynchon "imports" ellipsis marks from Rilke—not only once, as Haynes states, but broadly—is extremely tantalizing, but having so repeatedly warned against broad claims of influence and the "charac8teristicness" of ellipsis marks in particular writers or genres, the question must be approached with caution. Although Rilke's *Duino Elegies* and *Sonnets to Orpheus*, the two key Rilke works mentioned in *Gravity's Rainbow*, do not *teem* with ellipsis marks, they are present:

> [...] Tote
> Kinder wollten zu dir ... O leise, leise,
> tu ein liebes vor ihm, ein verläßliches Tagwerk, — führ ihn
> nah an den Garten heran, gieb ihm der Nächte
> Übergewicht ......
> Verhalt ihn ......
> (Rilke, *Duineser Elegien*, Die Dritte Elegie)
>
> Wartet..., das schmeckt ... Schon ists auf der Flucht.
> ... Wenig Musik nur, ein Stampfen, ein Summen—:
> Mädchen, ihr warmen, Mädchen, ihr stummen,

tanzt den Geschmack der erfahrenen Frucht! (Rilke, *Die Sonette an Orpheus*, Erster Teil, XV)

Although much of Pynchon's verse could be characterized as comic/pseudocomic song, the more impressionistic poems do evoke Rilke's style in a number of ways. For instance, late in *Gravity's Rainbow*, a scene in which Slothrop imagines himself as Fay Wray in the 1933 *King Kong* film invokes Carl Denham, the fictional protagonist filmmaker who captures Kong on his island:

> [...] I was thinking
> Of Denham — only him, with gun and camera
> Wisecracking in his best bum actor's way
> Through Darkest Earth, making the unreal reel
> By shooting at it, one way or the other —
> Carl Denham, my director, my undying,
> Carl ...
> Ah, show me the key light, whisper me a line.... (*GR*, 689)

Ellipsis marks break and end lines in both Pynchon's and Rilke's texts sampled here. "Ah, show me" recalls the perennial swooning "Oh"s in Rilke, such as "Oh pure surpassing! Oh Orpheus sings! Oh great tree of sound!" (*Sonnets to Orpheus*, 1:1). Both samples feature variable meter, in which a single word may constitute a line. The imploring tone of Rilke ("Ah, who then can / we make use of? Not Angels: not men," First Elegy) is echoed here in Pynchon's verse: "show me the key light, whisper me a line." Many such simple comparisons can be found in the rich verses of Rilke and Pynchon—and many other poets, as well. But more to the point, in an extended passage where Rilke is cited in *Gravity's Rainbow*, the style of Pynchon's prose adopts the form of ellipsis-laden prose poetry. In one scene, Blicero cites the *Sonnets to Orpheus* and the Tenth Elegy, as related by an indeterminate narrator:

> She appears to have reasons for being in the Party. A woman with some background in mathematics, and with *reasons*.... "Want the Change," Rilke said, "O be inspired by the Flame!" To laurel, to nightingale, to wind ... *wanting* it, to be taken, to embrace, to fall toward the flame growing to fill all the senses and ... not to love because it was no longer possible to act ... but to be helplessly in a condition of love.... (*GR*, 97)

It will come, it will, his Destiny ... not that way—but it will come.... *Und nicht einmal sein Schritt klingt aus dem tonlosen Los*.... Of all Rilke's poetry it's this Tenth Elegy he most loves, can feel the bitter lager of Yearning begin to prickle behind eyes and sinuses at remembering any passage of … the newly-dead youth, embracing his Lament, his last link, leaving now even her marginally human touch forever, climbing all alone, terminally alone, up and up into the mountains of primal Pain, with the wildly alien constellations overhead…. (*GR*, 97)

Pynchon's text becomes more stylistically Rilke-esque as Rilke is repeatedly invoked. This could be read merely as Blicero's figural discourse becoming blended into the narratorial discourse in focalization or free indirect discourse. But the invocation of Rilke inspiring a series of impressionistic, stylistically Rilke-esque riffs, all linked together with ellipsis points, also invokes the phenomenon of *Ansteckung* ("contagion"),[79] also known as the "Uncle Charles Principle" (UCP).[80]

UCP has been defined as the narratorial appropriation of figural idiom,[81] or, per Hägg, "the intrusion of a character's supposed verbal traits into narratorial discourse in situations which do not involve speech and thought representation."[82] As explained more simply by Hägg, UCP is where "the character who at the moment is the subject of narration, or 'on stage', has an effect on the narrator's style." While UCP in fiction is actually more common than one might expect, Hägg writes that "examples of the character-related 'contagion' abound in *Gravity's Rainbow*; the novel makes use of UCP flexibly and often."[83] As examples, Hägg cites the Floundering Four episode, in which the narrator adopts the idiom of each character described, and the Kenosha Kid sequence, in which a series of riffs on the phrase "You never did the Kenosha Kid" are finally revealed to be the daydreams or hallucinations of Slothrop in a chemical haze. As Hägg writes, "there seem to be no restrictions in Pynchon's UCP. All of the aspects of the narration, including the choice of the basic *format* of the narration, are liable to be influenced by the character's presence as the subject of narration."[84] Hägg suggested that this expanded conception of UCP should be christened as the Kenosha Kid Principle: "any feature of the diegetic situation can affect any aspect of the narration."[85] Rilke is not a character in *Gravity's Rainbow*, but Blicero is, and Blicero's direct and indirect discourse include citations of Rilke's verse and imitations of Rilke's style. Could it be that through Blicero, Rilke's ellipsis marks have "infected" the entire text of *Gravity's Rainbow*, and Pynchon's style for the rest of his career, via the Kenosha Kid Principle?

The notion of Rilke's ellipsis points "infecting" Pynchon's prose is more than a bit fanciful. Pynchon had access to, and alludes to, many literary role models from whom he may have taken ellipsis inspiration. It is also incautious to ascribe a single style to Rilke, as Hohmann reminds us that "critical opinion [in Pynchon studies] glosses over the fact that the *Elegies*, the *Sonnets to Orpheus* and the

Notebooks of Malte Laurids Brigge represent different stages in Rilke's evolution as a poet and cannot be drawn upon as a unified textual corpus."[86] But Rilke is as notable a candidate for influencing Pynchon's ellipsis marks as any.

6.6.2 Emily Dickinson's Dashes

Another of the few poets directly cited in *Gravity's Rainbow* is Emily Dickinson, whose poetry is characterized by extremely frequent dashes. Dickinson in Pynchon has received scant scholarly attention, which may be expected, given that she is explicitly referenced only twice, within one page of *Gravity's Rainbow*. Weisenburger simply identifies the source poems of the quoted Dickinson verses.[87] Mattessich draws comparisons between a single Dickinson poem and the treatment of time in *Gravity's Rainbow*.[88] Cowart downplays the significance of Dickinson in Pynchon: "Of course it is one thing to mention a writer, another really to embrace that writer's aesthetic or moral vision. Thus one discerns only a casual connection to, say, the Emily Dickinson quoted in *Gravity's Rainbow*, but real affinities with the Transcendentalists."[89] In the same book, Cowart briefly places his finger on two Dickinson/Pynchon issues relevant here. First, Cowart notes how the speech of Japanese characters in *Vineland* is rendered with "an abundance of dashes and exclamation points (which can lead readers familiar with the eccentric punctuation of a certain nineteenth-century American poet to think they have wandered into a screening of *Emily Dickinson Meets Godzilla*)."[90] Oddly, Cowart chooses this one atypical example to raise the issue of dashes in Pynchon, and connects them with Dickinson, but does not mention the abundant dashes in Pynchon's work *at large*. Cowart also cites Dickinson's famous line of "Tell all the Truth but tell it slant— / Success in Circuit lies" in a discussion of Pynchon's "alternat[ion] between the blunt instrument of satire […] and the extreme subtlety of his more nuanced historical themes."[91] Yet Cowart places this within the context of "the more generalized law [of indirection] observed by thoughtful literati (and their critics) in every age," and that "Pynchon seems to have sprung from the artistic matrix fully aware that effective literary representation cannot dispense with this principle," the principle of "Tell all the Truth but tell it slant."[92] Cowart thus cites Dickinson as an illustration of writing's eternal themes—when to be direct and when to be subtle—rather than argue Dickinson/Pynchon links, which, again, he contends are "casual."

Yet if dashes as signifiers of poetic language in Pynchon's texts are to be examined, a more thorough examination of Pynchon's stylistic affinity to Dickinson is required. Dashes were Dickinson's "stylistic signature" per Gary Lee

Stonum[93] and Dickinson's "primary form of punctuation," per Paul Crumbley.[94] Crumbley is perhaps the most extensive commentator among many scholars who have examined Dickinson's manuscript/editorial history and interpreted Dickinson's voluminous dashes, a scholarly field so crowded that, per Ena Jung, "Dickinson's dashes are among the most widely contested diacriticals in the modern literary canon."[95] An example:

> Read—Sweet—how others—strove—
> Till we—are stouter—
> What they—renounced—
> Till we—are less afraid—
> (Emily Dickinson, Poem 260)[96]

The considerable scholarly commentary on Dickinson's dashes yields a surprising number of parallels to Pynchon studies. Crumbley discusses how "Dickinson's idiosyncratic use of [dashes] challenges, in almost every poem, the search for a particular speaker with a fixed and unitary identity [… the] shifting self and the corrolary [*sic*] shifts in voice," echoing Pynchon's multitude of shifting and unidentifiable narratorial voices, especially in *Gravity's Rainbow*.[97] Crumbley discusses how, in a particular Dickinson poem, "acknowledging the dashes means considering dialogical readings that do not yield to the pressures of binary logic,"[98] echoing the perennial ambiguity in Pynchon and continual exploration of values and meaning between the crisp, definable black and white of 0 and 1. Crumbley cites and supports Margaret Dickie, insofar as she attacked the way that the "problems of interpretation that Dickinson's poetry poses are essentially problems of narrative readability which have usually been resolved by the imposition of a master narrative on the work and the life [… But] Dickinson's lyric speakers have no narrative continuity, no social viability, no steadfast identity."[99] For Crumbley, this means confronting the "maddeningly arcane details of [Dickinson's] work, such as orthography and syntax" and that "the dash is the least accommodating [stylistic detail] to conventional readings that stress linear progression and logical coherence."[100]

Although neither Crumbley nor Dickie evoke the term "postmodern" in these Dickinson readings, this is essentially the postmodern reading of Pynchon, for example, as articulated by Hutcheon: "Postmodernism [...] refuses to posit any structure or [...] master narrative—such as art or myth."[101] Perhaps unsurprisingly, scholars have put forth postmodern readings of Dickinson, for instance Jed Deppman,"[102] but these parallels between the authors' texts raise issues for Pynchon scholars. First, the similarities between Dickinson's and Pynchon's texts—shifting, uncertain narrators, resistance to master narratives, semantic ambiguity, and teeming with dashes that effect them all—support a reading that Pynchon cites Dickinson in recognition of an early progenitor, whether thematic or stylistic. Subsequently, intertextual and even biographical readings could be explored further.

Pynchon and Dickinson share a surprising family history heretofore unmentioned by scholars. Dickinson was born and died in Amherst, Massachusetts, a town which dates to the 1658 purchase of Native American land by John Pynchon of Springfield, Thomas Pynchon's ancestor. Emily Dickinson's ancestors were early settlers, including Nathaniel Dickinson, Emily's great-great-great-grandfather, who surveyed the lands of Amherst. If web genealogy websites are to be trusted, Pynchon and Emily Dickinson are eighth cousins, twice removed.[103]

This genealogical connection between the writers could be interpreted as pointless trivia—many Americans with early settler roots are genealogically related, for example, Barack Obama is distantly related to George W. Bush—except for two facts: Pynchon engages extensively with his own early American ancestry in *Gravity's Rainbow*, and Emily Dickinson is *only* referenced in *Gravity's Rainbow* in a scene that discusses those ancestors. In a vision or flashback to a Massachusetts graveyard full of Slothrop ancestors, the tombstone of Slothrop's grandfather bears an inscription, "bagged" "from Emily Dickinson, without a credit line: Because I could not stop for Death / He kindly stopped for me" (27). This is followed by a history of the Slothrop family that comments not only on the family's fortunes, which "all began to go sour for them around the time Emily Dickinson, never far away, was writing Ruin is formal, devil's work," followed by the verses quoted above. This is one of a number of scenes in which Pynchon "drew on miscellaneous details of his own family history for the background of the Slothrop's in *Gravity's Rainbow*," per Mathew Winston.[104]

Scholars have scoured the biographies and writings of Pynchon ancestors to explore echoes and confluences with Thomas Pynchon,[105] especially William Pynchon, pioneer and "heretic" Puritan writer, a clear analogue for William Slothrop in *Gravity's Rainbow*.[106] By situating Emily Dickinson's verse within the Slothrop graveyard, Dickinson's place as a familial forbear within the extended Slothrop/Pynchon family tree can at least be considered. If biographical parallels are fair game for scholarly musing, it could also be mentioned that Dickinson, like Pynchon, has long borne the unjust epithet of "recluse."

Returning to the dash, although I have stressed that the long history of ellipsis marks cautions against theorizing correlation and causation based on individual genres or writers, it remains a fact that dash-obsessed Dickinson is cited in *Gravity's Rainbow*, the novel in which Pynchon's use of dashes multiplies (with almost double the rate of dashes in *V.* and almost six times the rate of *Lot 49*). There is also evidence that Pynchon associates dashes with poetry in general in *Gravity's Rainbow*, from the simple fact that dashes appear in Pynchon's verse only twice in *V.* and once in *Lot 49*, yet 148 times in *Gravity's Rainbow*, and become a common feature in all of Pynchon's later verse. The dash in Pynchon's texts, then, could be read as a small signifier of poetic language. If Dickinson's style were strongly related to Pynchon's style, one might expect more than two minor mentions of Dickinson in a 760-page novel. However, it can at least be entertained that Dickinson partially inspired Pynchon's newfound affection for dashes in *Gravity's Rainbow*, in verse, prose, and prose poetry.

This conjecture is undermined by the fact that Pynchon quotes Dickinson from apparently early editions of her work, which omitted or replaced many of Dickinson's dashes!

Because I could not stop for death
He kindly stopped for me

(as quoted in *GR*, 27)

— —

Because I could not stop for Death—
He kindly stopped for me—

(Poem 712, in *The Complete Poems of Emily Dickinson*, 1955, Vol. 2, 546).

— —

Ruin is formal, devil's work,
Consecutive and slow—
Fail in an instant no man did,
Slipping is crash's law,

(as quoted in *GR*, 28)

— —

Ruin is formal—Devils work
Consecutive and slow—
Fail in an instant, no man did
Slipping—is Crashe's law.

(Poem 997, in *The Complete Poems of Emily Dickinson*, 1955, Vol. 2, 721).

Pynchon does *not* quote Dickinson's poems with the same punctuation and capitalization as the editions named in *Gravity's Rainbow*'s acknowledgements, edited by Thomas H. Johnson. Pynchon may have changed the punctuation himself or, more likely, quoted from earlier, pre-Johnson editions of Dickinson which tended to omit her dashes or replace them with more common punctuation.[107]

If indeed Pynchon's relation to Dickinson is more than "casual," I leave it to Dickinson experts to explore further. As with Rilke, a scholar could easily—too easily—present any number of stylistic parallels between Dickinson's and Pynchon's rich texts. Consider Poem 508:

> I'm ceded—I've stopped being Theirs—
> The name They dropped upon my face
> With water, in the country church
> Is finished using, now,
> And They can put it with my Dolls,
> My childhood, and the string of spools,
> I've finished threading—too—
>
> Baptized, before, without the choice,
> But this time, consciously, Of Grace—
> Unto supremest name—
> Called to my Full—The Crescent dropped—
> Existence's whole Arc, filled up,
> With one—small Diadem.
> (Dickinson, Poem 508)

Here is fierce defiance of an unnamed, capitalized They (cf. *They* in *Gravity's Rainbow*), Dickinson's "odd, Blakean capitalizations," in the words of Joyce Carol Oates[108] (cf. Pynchon's selective capitalization), a repudiation of an unconsented childhood baptism (cf. Slothrop as child experimentee), and Crescents and Arcs, evoking the rainbows which paranoid Pynchon scholars may discern in all skies. Dickinson's famous Poem 1129, which Cowart briefly referenced, could also extensively be compared to the final hymn of *Gravity's Rainbow*:

Tell all the Truth but tell it slant—	There is a Hand to turn the time,
Success in Circuit lies	Though thy Glass today be run,
Too bright for our infirm Delight	Till the Light that hath brought the Towers low
The Truth's superb surprise	Find the last poor Pret'rite one…
	Till the Riders sleep by ev'ry road,
As Lightning to the Children eased	All through our crippl'd Zone,
With explanation kind	With a face in ev'ry mountainside,
The Truth must dazzle gradually	And a Soul in ev'ry stone….
Or every man be blind—	
(Dickinson, Poem 1129)	Now everybody —
	(*GR*, 760)

First, a number of formal similarities are apparent: both consist of two quatrain stanzas, eight lines total, in which even numbered lines end in a rhyme. Dickinson strictly maintains form, iambic, with alternating eight and six syllables, which Pynchon loosely mirrors in a mix of iambic and anapest meter.[109] Both poems feature selective capitalization and end with ellipsis marks… Thematically, both could be read to equate light/lightning with knowledge, and perhaps divinity, which Anthony Hecht reads in the Dickinson poem ("the poem seems to me to have a good deal of religious significance that such a statement inclines altogether to flout")[110] and for example, Eberhard Alsen reads in Pynchon's ("Written by a heretic, the hymn […] includes a belief in a Janus-like God with both positive and negative attributes").[111] More to the point, Dickinson's poem expresses Pynchon's most enduring stylistic feature, Pynchon's ambiguity, his perpetual habit of stating things obliquely, indirectly, at a tangent, "words on your page only Δt from the things they stand for" (*GR*, 510), captured succinctly by Dickinson's immortal line: "Tell all the truth but tell it slant — / Success in Circuit lies."

6.7 Ellipsis Marks: Conclusion

Such extended attention to the diachronic change in a single writer's punctuation would be fruitful in few contemporary writers, but my exploration of Pynchon's ellipsis marks adds the following to Pynchon studies. Ellipsis marks have been considered to be characteristic, often the "trademark" punctuation of a multitude of writers and periods, which should instill caution when assuming that ellipsis marks are particularly characteristic of Pynchon and postmodernism. Based on frequencies, *Gravity's Rainbow* and *Mason & Dixon* do indeed contain many more ellipsis marks (for ellipsis points and dashes, respectively) than almost all comparison texts, but this does not apply to Pynchon's other novels. There is also evidence that in later Pynchon texts, Pynchon tends to use fewer ellipsis marks and more ellipsis phrases—"and so on," "and so forth"—to evoke ellipsis and aposiopesis.

Reading ellipsis marks in Pynchon has elicited interpretation and overinterpretation, and when critics describe ellipsis marks in Pynchon, too often they simply describe the historical uses of ellipsis marks in English literature. However, Pynchon's ellipsis marks effect and encapsulate broader postmodern concerns of ambiguity and incompleteness, and this chapter presented evidence for "techno-Gothic" ellipsis marks in Pynchon's texts, a concept that is consistent with critical discourse on the Gothic in Pynchon more generally. Apart from their sheer frequency, ellipsis marks are foregrounded in *Gravity's Rainbow* because of their unusual frequency in unquoted text, no longer "hidden" in character dialogue. Both ellipsis points and verse—and dashes *in* verse—increase greatly in *Gravity's Rainbow*, suggesting a possible link, and connections with the ellipsis marks of Rilke and Emily Dickinson have been explored.

In the first work devoted to ellipsis marks in Pynchon, Daw speculated that "the ellipsis is an architectonic for Pynchon," and while "architectonic" is a concept too vague to support or challenge directly with the hope of much success, this chapter connects some of the dots on ellipsis marks in Pynchon's texts. In 2018, Andrew Piper devoted a chapter in *Enumerations: Data and Literary Study* to tracing the use of periods (the punctuation mark) in twentieth-century poetry, writing that "we have never had a history of what Georges Bataille might have called the general economy of punctuation, a study of the norms and excesses of punctuation in a given period."[112] While it could be countered that Toner's monograph constitutes such a work, this chapter has described the "general economy" of ellipsis marks in Pynchon's texts and postmodern American fiction.

Notes

1 Anne Toner, *Ellipsis in English Literature* (Cambridge: Cambridge University Press, 2015), 1.

2 Ibid.

3 Keith Brown and Jim Miller, *The Cambridge Dictionary of Linguistics* (Cambridge: Cambridge University Press, 2013), 150.

4 Ludovic Hunter-Tilney, "Invisible man," *Financial Times*, December 1, 2006, https://www.ft.com/content/9415c2b4-8040-11db-9096-0000779e2340.

5 Earl, "Tom's Longest Sentence," 203.

6 Adrian Wisnicki, "A Trove of New Works by Thomas Pynchon? Bomarc Service News Rediscovered," *Pynchon Notes* 46–9 (2001): 9–34.

7 Laurence Daw, "The Ellipsis as Architectonic in *Gravity's Rainbow*," *Pynchon Notes* 11 (1983): 54.

8 Sascha Pöhlmann, "Silences and Worlds: Wittgenstein and Pynchon," *Pynchon Notes* 56–7 (2009): 163.

9 On overinterpretation, see Umberto Eco, *Interpretation and Overinterpretation* (Cambridge: Cambridge University Press, 1992).

10 Hite, *Ideas of Order in the Novels of Thomas Pynchon*, 138.

11 Toner, *Ellipsis in English Literature*, 2.

12 "aposiopesis, n.," *OED Online*, Oxford University Press, accessed March 5, 2018, http://0-www.oed.com.catalogue.libraries.london.ac.uk/view/Entry/9392?redirected From=Aposiopesis.

13 Toner, *Ellipsis in English Literature*, 7.

14 Ibid., 25.

15 Ibid., 54.

16 Ibid., 54–64.

17 Ibid., 61.

18 Ibid., 98.

19 Ibid., 108.

20 Ibid., 107.

21 Ibid., 3.

22 Ibid., 118.

23 Ibid., 134.

24 Ibid., 138.

25 Ibid., 139.

26 Ibid., 141.

27 Ibid., 151.

28 Ibid., 138.

29 Clarence Green, "Introducing the Corpus of the Canon of Western Literature: A Corpus for Culturomics and Stylistics," *Language and Literature* 26:4 (2017): 282–99.

30 Ibid. Jacques Derrida, "Ellipsis," in *Writing and Difference* (London: Routledge, [1967] 1978).

31 Toner, *Ellipsis in English Literature*, 3.

32 Theodor Adorno, "Punctuation Marks," *Antioch Review* 48:3 (1990): 303.

33 Frederick Crews, *The Random House Handbook*, 4th ed. (New York: Random House, 1984), 332–3.

34 Umberto Eco, *How to Travel with a Salmon and Other Essays* (New York: Harcourt, 1994), 184.

35 Joshua Raclaw, "Punctuation as Social Action: The Ellipsis as a Discourse Marker in Computer-Mediated Communication," in *The Proceedings of the 32nd Annual Berkeley Linguistics Society* (Berkeley, 2006).

36 Paris Martineau, "Why … do old people … text … like this …? An investigation …," *The Outline*, February 8, 2018, https://theoutline.com/post/3333/ why-do-old-people-text-like-this-an-investigation?zd=1&zi=qx76aecq.

37 Mark Liberman, "Generational Punctuation Differences Again," *Language Log*, August 1, 2014, http://languagelog.ldc.upenn.edu/nll/?p=13723.

38 Caleb Melby, "The Generation Gap in Online Punctuation: An Open Letter (and Revised Style Guide) to Digital English," *Forbes*, May 8, 2013, https://www.forbes.

com/sites/calebmelby/2013/05/08/the-generation-gap-in-online-punctuation-an-open-letter-and-revised-style-guide-to-digital-english/#444a61a91876.

39 Earl, "Tom's Longest Sentence," 204.

40 Jonathan Franzen, "Mr. Difficult: William Gaddis and the Problem of Hard-to-Read Books," *New Yorker*, September 30, 2002, https://www.newyorker.com/magazine/2002/09/30/mr-difficult.

41 Daw, "The Ellipsis as Architectonic in *Gravity's Rainbow*," 54.

42 Ellipsis points in *Gravity's Rainbow* compared with various works in the comparison corpora that represent the range of normalized frequency, at the p < 0.0001, 99.99th percentile: *Vineland, Mason & Dixon, Giles Goat Boy, Paradise, The Thomas Berryman Number, Passion's Promise, The Broom of the System*.

43 *Mason & Dixon* compared with various works in the comparison corpora that represent the range of normalized frequency at the p < 0.0001, 99.99th percentile: *Gravity's Rainbow, Giles Goat Boy, The Terrible Twos, Paradise, Passion's Promise, The Broom of the System*.

44 Houston, *Shady Characters*, 164–5.

45 Ibid.

46 Ware et al., "Talk: Errata," *Pynchon Wiki*, accessed September 1, 2019, https://against-the-day.pynchonwiki.com/wiki/index.php?title=Talk:Errata.

47 Freer, *Thomas Pynchon and the American Counterculture*, 81.

48 Paul Maltby, *Dissident Postmodernists: Barthelme, Coover, Pynchon* (Philadelphia: University of Pennsylvania Press, 1991), notes on the text.

49 Christopher Bonanos, "Tom Wolfe, Pioneer of New York and New Journalism, Dies at 88," *New York Magazine*, May 15, 2018, https://www.vulture.com/2018/05/tom-wolfe-new-york-and-new-journalism-legend-dies-at-88.html.

50 Howard, "Pynchon From A to V."

51 Charles Clerc, "Introduction," in *Approaches to* Gravity's Rainbow, ed. Charles Clerc (Columbus: Ohio State University Press, 1983), 17–18.

52 Hite, *Ideas of Order in the Novels of Thomas Pynchon*, 138.

53 Hohmann, *Angel and Rocket*, 126.

54 Ware et al., "Talk: Errata."

55 Earl, "Tom's Longest Sentence," 204.

56 Pynchon does sometimes end sentences with three dot ellipsis points.

57 Hite, *Ideas of Order in the Novels of Thomas Pynchon*, 138.

58 Stefan Mattessich, *Lines of Flight: Discursive Time and Countercultural Desire in the Work of Thomas Pynchon* (Durham: Duke University Press, 2002), 245.

59 Yoichiro Miyamoto, "*Gravity's Rainbow* and the Question of Postmodernism," *Studies in English Literature* 65:2 (1989): 212.

60 Pöhlmann, "Silences and Worlds: Wittgenstein and Pynchon," 158, 160.

61 Earl, "Tom's Longest Sentence," 204.

62 Cooper, *Signs and Symptoms*, 221–2.

63 Daw, "The Ellipsis as Architectonic in *Gravity's Rainbow*," 55.

64 Jim Neighbors, "Kant, Terror and Aporethics in *Gravity's Rainbow*," *Pynchon Notes* 42–3 (1998): 281.

65 Douglas Fowler, *A Reader's Guide to* Gravity's Rainbow (Ann Arbor: Ardis, 1980), 13, 33.

66 Pynchon, "Is It O.K. to Be a Luddite?" *New York Times Book Review*, October 28, 1984, https://archive.nytimes.com/www.nytimes.com/books/97/05/18/reviews/pynchon-luddite.html?.

67 Allan Lloyd Smith, "American Gothic," in *The Handbook of the Gothic*, 2nd ed., ed. Marie Mulvey-Roberts (New York: Palgrave Macmillan, 2009), 275.

68 Allan Lloyd Smith, "Postmodernism/Gothicism," in *Modern Gothic: A Reader*, ed. Victor Sage and Allan Lloyd Smith (Manchester: Manchester University Press, 1996), 16.

69 Bénédicte Chorier-Fryd, "Deadpan to Demonic—Subtextual Uses of Science in Thomas Pynchon's *Inherent Vice*," in *Science and American Literature in the 20th and 21st Centuries*, ed. Claire Maniez, Ronan Ludot-Vlasak, and Frédéric Dumas (Newcastle upon Tyne: Cambridge Scholars, 2012), 24. Although Chorier-Fryd does not employ the word "Gothic" here, she invokes the concept by quoting from Pynchon's discussion of Gothic literature in "Is It O.K. To Be a Luddite?"

70 Zofia Kolbuszewski, *The Poetics of Chronotope in the Novels of Thomas Pynchon* (Lublin: Learned Society of the Catholic University of Lublin, 2000), 184.

71 Toner, *Ellipsis in English Literature*, 5.

72 Thomas Pynchon, "Introduction," in *The Teachings of Don B.*, ed. Kim Herzinger (New York: Turtle Bay, 1992), xvii.

73 Stark, *Pynchon's Fictions*, 37; Aaron Sultanik, *Inventing Orders* (Lanham: University Press of America, 2003), 174.

74 Richard Locke, "One of the Longest, Most Difficult, Most Ambitious Novels in Years"; Uncredited, "Danger: mad professor at work," *The Economist*, November 30, 2006, https://www.economist.com/node/8348701/print?story_id=8348701.

75 Stark, *Pynchon's Fictions*, 151.

76 Bernard Duyfhuizen, "Review: Taking Stock: 26 Years since *V.* (Over 26 Books on Pynchon!)," *NOVEL: A Forum on Fiction* 23:1 (1989): 83.

77 Doug Haynes, "'Gravity Rushes Through Him': *Volk* and Fetish in Pynchon's Rilke," *MFS Modern Fiction Studies* 58:2 (2012): 308–33.

78 Ibid., 317.

79 F. K. Stanzel, *A Theory of Narrative* (Cambridge: Cambridge University Press, 1979).

80 Hugh Kenner, *Joyce's Voices* (Berkeley: University of California Press, 1978).

81 Fludernik, *The Fictions of Language and the Languages of Fiction*, 332–8.

82 Hägg, *Narratologies* of Gravity's Rainbow, 108. Also see Appendix I of this book.

83 Ibid., 108.

84 Ibid., 110.

85 Ibid., 112.

86 Hohmann, *Angel and Rocket*, 9.

87 Mattessich, *Lines of Flight*, 79.

88 Weisenburger, *Gravity's Rainbow Companion*, 34–5.

89 Cowart, *Thomas Pynchon and the Dark Passages of History*, 193.

90 Ibid., 95.

91 Ibid., 169.

92 Ibid., 169–70.

93 Gary Lee Stonum, *The Dickinson Sublime* (Madison: University of Wisconsin Press, 1990), 24.

94 Paul Crumbley, "Dickinson's Dashes and the Limits of Discourse", *The Emily Dickinson Journal* 1:2 (1992): 9.

95 Ena Jung, "The Breath of Emily Dickinson's Dashes," *Emily Dickinson Journal* 24:2 (2015): 1.

96 Emily Dickinson, *The Poems of Emily Dickinson*, ed. Thomas H. Johnson (Cambridge, MA: Belknap Press of Harvard University Press, 1955), 186.

97 See e.g., Hite, *Ideas of Order in the Novels of Thomas Pynchon*, 44: "The world [of *Gravity's Rainbow*] exists as an indefinite number of partial, contingent, and overlapping visions; and by shifting points of view, often with unnerving rapidity, this narrator multiplies angles and opens up new vistas of possibility."

98 Crumbley, "Dickinson's Dashes," 15.

99 Margaret Dickie, "Dickinson's Discontinuous Lyric Self," *American Literature* 60:4 (1988): 553.

100 Crumbley, "Dickinson's Dashes," 8.

101 Linda Hutcheon, *A Poetics of Postmodernism* (New York: Routledge, 1998), 6.

102 Jed Deppman, "Trying to Think with Emily Dickinson," *Emily Dickinson Journal* 14:1 (2005): 87.

103 Uncredited, *Famouskin.com*, accessed September 1, 2019, https://famouskin.com/famous-kin-chart.php?name=33543+emily+dickinson&kin=41896+thomas+pynchon&via=8735+edmund+reade.

104 Mathew Winston, "The Quest for Pynchon," *Twentieth Century Literature* 21:3 (1975): 280.

105 Charles Hollander, "Pynchon's Politics: The Presence of an Absence," *Pynchon Notes* 26–7 (1990): 5–59; Mark Sussman and Martin Paul Eve, "'A Shorthand of Stars': From John to Thomas Pynchon," *Orbit: A Journal of American Literature* 4:2 (2016): 1–7.

106 Deborah L. Madsen, "Family Legacies: Identifying the Traces of William Pynchon in *Gravity's Rainbow*," *Pynchon Notes* 42–3 (1998): 29–48; Philip Storey, "William Slothrop: Gentleman," *Pynchon Notes* 13 (1983): 61–70.

107 Paul Crumbley, *Inflections of the Pen: Dash and Voice in Emily Dickinson* (Louisville: University Press of Kentucky, 1997), 14.

108 Joyce Carol Oates, "Introduction," in *The Essential Emily Dickinson*, ed. Joyce Carol Oates (New York: Ecco, [1996] 2016), xviii.

109 A thorough formal description of the final poem in *Gravity's Rainbow* is in Vesterman, "Pynchon's Poetry," 110.

110 Anthony Hecht, "The Riddles of Emily Dickinson," *New England Review* 1:1 (1978): 18–19.

111 Eberhard Alsen, *Romantic Postmodernism in American Fiction* (Amsterdam: Rodopi B. V., 1996), 181.

112 Andrew Piper, *Enumerations: Data and Literary Study* (Chicago: University of Chicago Press, 2018), 23.

Conclusion

This book has attempted to provide a groundwork of digital investigations of Thomas Pynchon's style, both to contribute new knowledge and support future studies, which I suggested in the introduction should take the form of a "common project," a vast, varied, and continuous scholarly effort to confirm, contest, and improve upon existing Pynchon studies of all kinds, as well as contribute to an understanding of Pynchon's stylistics specifically, which has only begun to be charted. If the reader's response to any of these investigations has been "what about another experiment?" or "what about analyzing this using a different method?," such questions only confirm one claim of this book: that the stylistic study of Pynchon's texts is a rich and largely unmined vein of scholarly study.

Is there an irony in computational analysis of texts by Thomas Pynchon, a writer so deeply associated with the interrogation of science and technology's claims of empiricism and neutrality? Certainly—more than one reader of this book in its earlier incarnations even referred to this as "the elephant in the room" of this project. The complexity of Pynchon's style includes problematic cases for stylistic and narratological inquiries, but that is all the more reason to study it, as McHale, Fludernik, Hägg, and others already have. By ignoring the elephant in the room, I hoped to approach fundamental research of Pynchon's stylistics with pragmatism and an open mind, and thus leave the inherent tensions in digital humanities Pynchon studies for future commentators. The nascent digital Pynchon studies could well benefit more from concrete results than theorizing at this juncture, given how little remains agreed-upon about Pynchon's style.

When threads from this book are brought together, what emerges especially are contours of Pynchon's "late style," although how, and by what period one defines this, remain open questions. The concept of late style has been approached by, *inter alia*, Hermann Broch, Gottfried Benn, Adorno, and Edward Said, rarely in ways that would be recognized as modern stylistics.[1] But a number of scholars have begun to approach late style via digital humanities. Henry James, whose early and later styles are so radically different (especially syntactically), has been the subject of much stylistic and digital stylistic investigation, especially by David L. Hoover.[2] Digital humanities studies of late style are growing, with papers variously confirming and denying the observability of late style in texts. Jonathan P. Reeve tested the corpora of twelve well-known authors via a distinctiveness score, derived from most frequent word vectors and clustering methods, from which Reeve claims that "late style is not a statistically quantifiable phenomenon. Instead, the opposite is true: the novelists tested exhibit very distinctive early styles."[3] Meanwhile, Simone Rebora and Massimo Salgaro, in experiments on the works of Goethe, Robert Musil, and Franz Kafka, report that " 'Late Style' seemed confirmed by our 'internal' studies on semantic areas and through [part-of-speech-based] measurements, but it appeared unsupported by such traditional stylometric methods as network analysis and Zeta analysis."[4] Late style, Rebora and Salgaro suggest, has so far only been observable quantifiably when measuring for specific stylistic features, semantic categories suggested by previous scholars or by attention to classes of words.

But analog Pynchon studies have so far provided few clues in conceptualizing Pynchon's late style. Herman discusses how "the usual association of late style and absolute mastery does not quite apply [to Pynchon], since it is for the climax of his first period that Pynchon has become part of the literary canon."[5] Paul Mason, in a review of *Inherent Vice* titled "Is This Thomas Pynchon's 'Late Style?,' " characterizes the novel's style thus:

> What's gone though are the large swathes of digression, reflection and description that make reading any other Pynchon novel an exercise in hermeneutics. Here the story is boiled down to chunks of movie-style dialogue and chunks of Pynchonesque description. [...] This late turn in his literary style [...] is a move towards form, and closed form at that, towards genre, and towards communication. And it is a move away from subtext.[6]

While Herman highlighted the difficulty of periodizing Pynchon's vast and inconsistently received output, and Mason placed his finger on the increasingly dominant role of dialogue in later Pynchon, this book has presented some quantifiably observable trends in Pynchon's late style. Later works by Pynchon tend to feature more dialogue, which, as Mason alludes to, runs counter to long-held perceptions of Pynchon's "superficial" and "unbelievable" characters and is a marked departure from the relatively scant amount of dialogue in *Gravity's Rainbow*. Later works dramatically reduce the poems/songs, once considered such a notable Pynchonian feature, and the poems that appear in later works are light verse more often than not. Ambiguity/vagueness words, which encapsulate Pynchon's thematic messages, are increasing in later works, perhaps allowing style to convey a *Weltanschauung* that Pynchon previously explored more overtly thematically, and/or increasing the haze of confusion and memory loss in which the later characters increasingly wander. Later texts by Pynchon also feature a rising frequency of acronyms, more profanity, and a reigning in of the ellipsis points which ran so wild in *Gravity's Rainbow*. There is exploratory evidence that, in his two most recent novels, Pynchon has abandoned the sustained attention to the inanimate which was notably found in earlier works. In *Bleeding Edge*, Luc Herman observed that the final part of the novel becomes "much more explicit" and less "ironic,"[7] which may be related to the decrease of vagueness words in *Bleeding Edge*'s later chapters. The exceptions and qualifications to all of these claims are in this book's chapters, but here, at least, is some groundwork for a comprehension of Pynchon's late style.

A final argument that emerges from this book is that close attention to style may sustain readers and scholars of Pynchon's fitfully "unrewarding," "boring," or "difficult" later works. Pynchon's shorter late novels have been dubbed "Pynchon lite," while *Mason & Dixon* and especially *Against the Day* stretch readers' endurance to breaking points, due to seemingly endless digressions and go-nowhere plots, the "cruft" described by David Letzler.[8] *Against the Day* in particular is such a slog that even the eminent Pynchon scholar Herman admitted that he finished reading it for the first time "only because I had to review it."[9] Reading later Pynchon with a close attention to style may be a path for readers to reapproach and re-appreciate some later works.

Having multiple times invoked the dream of a common project devoted to Pynchon's stylistics, I end by suggesting some avenues of future research and methodology which the groundwork in this book may support. While regular expressions and a KWIC interface have been beneficial for the experiments in this book, which mostly required close manual, contextual inspection of query results, myriad computational methods from digital humanities and computational linguistics could shed further light on Pynchon's evolving style. Ideally, a richly annotated Pynchon corpus could be created and distributed among scholars, although the former will require prodigious XML/TEI tagging effort, and the latter is impeded by the copyright laws of most countries in which Pynchon scholarship is vibrant. While I assembled bespoke comparison corpora of over five million word tokens, ever larger corpora can only improve future research, which could include, in addition to more sophisticated measures of the stylistic features I have focused on, thematic vocabulary (such as religious or scientific), the nature and frequency of references, text reuse (Pynchon borrowing from other texts, or others borrowing from Pynchon), syntax, neologism, negation, "and whatever," in one of Pynchon's preferred ellipsis phrases…

Notes

1 Hermann Broch, "Mythos und Altersstil," in *Schriften zur Literatur 2: Theorie*, ed. P. M. Lützeler (Frankfurt: Suhrkamp, 1995); Gottfried Benn, "Altern als Problem für Künstler," in *Gottfried Benn: Sämtliche Werke, Volume 6*, ed. G. Schuster and H. Hof (Stuttgart: Klett, 1989); Theodor Adorno, "'Late Style' in Beethoven," in *Essays on Music by Theodor W. Adorno*, ed. R. Leppert (Berkeley: University of California Press, 2002); Edward Said, *On Late Style* (London: Bloomsbury, 2006).

2 David L. Hoover, "Corpus Stylistics, Stylometry, and the Styles of Henry James," *Style* 41:2 (2007): 174–203; David L. Hoover, "Modes of Composition in Henry James: Dictation, Style, and What Maisie Knew," *Henry James Review* 35:3 (2014): 257–77.

3 Jonathan Pearce Reeve, "Does 'Late Style' Exist? New Stylometric Approaches to Variation in Single-Author Corpora," in *Digital Humanities 2018 Book of Abstracts* (Mexico City: ADHO, 2018), 479.

4 Simone Rebora and Massimo Salgaro, "Is 'Late Style' Measurable? A Stylometric Analysis of Johann Wolfgang Goethe's, Robert Musil's, and Franz Kafka's Late Works," *Elephant & Castle* 18 (2018): 33.

5 Luc Herman, "Early Pynchon," in *The Cambridge Companion to Thomas Pynchon*, ed. Inger H. Dalsgaard, Luc Herman, and Brian McHale (Cambridge: Cambridge University Press, 2012), 19.

6 Paul Mason, "Is This Thomas Pynchon's 'Late Style?'" *BBC News*, July 31, 2009, https://www.bbc.co.uk/blogs/newsnight/paulmason/2009/07/is_this_thomas_ pynchons_late_s.html.

7 Herman, "Reading Pynchon in and on the Digital Age," 204.

8 Letzler, *The Cruft of Fiction*.

9 Herman, "Reading Pynchon in and on the Digital Age," 199.

Appendix I

Corpora, Software, Methods

I.1 Pynchon Corpus

The Pynchon fiction corpus includes Pynchon's eight published novels, the short story collection *Slow Learner*, and the uncollected short story, "Mortality and Mercy in Vienna." There are minor variants in published editions of *V.*, as discussed by Albert Rolls, who compared published versions of *V.* alongside Pynchon's letters to his editors.[1] After *V.* was first published in the United States, Pynchon corrected a number of errata and typos alongside other minor textual changes, but due to a byzantine publishing history (almost straight out of *Lot 49)*, two versions are being sold to this day: the original, uncorrected version in the United States, and Pynchon's corrected version sold in the UK. To investigate the differences between the editions, and whether this variance should be considered in this book's experiments, both the US and UK editions were scanned and loaded into Juxta,[2] an open-source tool for collating variants, which allowed visual comparison with changes highlighted (Figure A.1).

For a more detailed comparison which classifies some of the changes, the .txt files were collated using the Wdiff command line tool[3] and then used a Python script I developed with Christof Schöch for a separate project, which separates the edits between two text files and automatically classified some of the edits.[4] Figure A.2 illustrates the changes to the texts with the highest Levenshtein distance (edit distance in characters).

In the UK paperback, note that "after seven months" and "around midnight" were deleted, which Rolls mentions, and in fact, my experiment confirms that Rolls located and discusses virtually every remarkable substantive change in the texts (aided, certainly, by Rolls's access to Pynchon's letters to his editors).[5] Given that these textual changes are so minor, this book includes only one version of *V.* in the experiments, the recent US edition. Although I do not have access

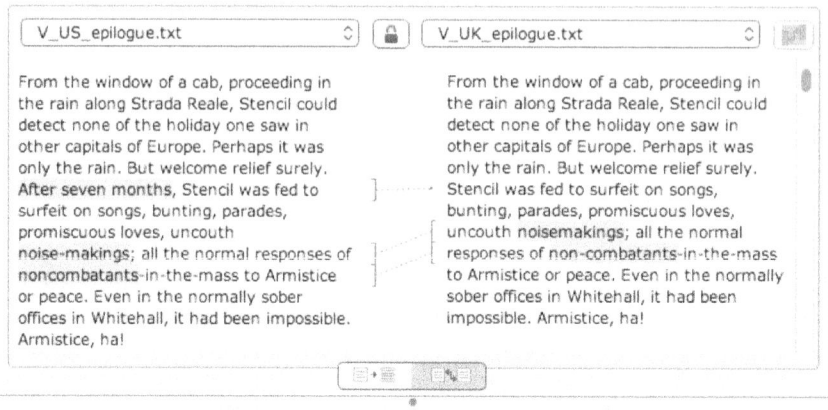

Figure A.1 Comparing variants of *V.* in the Juxta application.

Item-id	Version1	Version2	Levenshtein	Type
71–1	two hundred and fifty	250	21	numbers
699–1	eight hundred dollars	$800	21	numbers
1170–1	one hundred and fifty	150	21	numbers
4322–1	one hundred and forty	140	21	numbers
8044–2	one hundred dollars	$100	19	numbers
8367–3	wind though it was June,	wind,	19	condensation
8377–1	After seven months,		19	deletion
161–1	Levi's with rolled-up	rolled up levi	17	condensation
2436–1	around midnight		15	deletion
465–1	four foot nine	4'10"	14	numbers

Figure A.2 Comparing and classifying edits in variants of *V.* using methodology by Ketzan and Schöch.

to them, future stylistic Pynchon studies may wish to investigate unpublished manuscripts[6] and technical articles written for Boeing.[7]

I.1.1 Normalization of *Mason & Dixon*

For experiments outside of Chapter 2 based on lexical queries, the text of *Mason & Dixon* was normalized to remove certain archaisms, especially orthography. For example, "match'd" was adjusted so that it returns when "matched" is queried, "Musick" for "music," "thee" for "you," and so on. In a sense, this is removing style to study style, but as the lexical experiments consider broad trends in

Pynchon's style across his oeuvre, this normalization was considered necessary for the aims of these experiments. Capitalized words were left unaltered, as no queries outside of Chapter 2 required a distinction between common and proper nouns, nor employed taggers such as part-of-speech or semantic taggers which rely in part on capitalization for classification. Archaic spelling, especially <-ick>, religious censorship, archaic apostrophes, contractions, pronouns and verbs, as well as superscripts (e.g., *Rev^d* for *Reverend* or *Col^O* for *Colonel*) were all normalized with modern orthography for lexical experiments.

I.2 Us vs. Them: Comparison Corpora

It has happened before, but there is nothing to compare it to now.

—*GR*, 1

The choice of appropriate comparison corpora is critical in computational stylistics, and experimental results are commonly compared "off-the-shelf" reference corpora and/or custom-made, "bespoke" comparison corpora.[8] Appropriate comparison corpora for digital Pynchon studies must thus first be chosen.

For American fiction over the period in which Pynchon has published, 1959–2013, no single existing reference corpus is ideal. The Brown University Standard Corpus of Present-Day American English was the first modern corpus of English and provides a snapshot of American English in the year 1961 (five hundred chunks of approximately two thousand-word written texts, approximately one million words in total, of works across fifteen genres published in the United States).[9] While the Brown Corpus has been a de facto standard for the construction of small-scale written corpora in the field of corpus linguistics, it is limited to a single year, before Pynchon's first novel was published, and even at a million words, is not large by modern corpus standards[10] (recall that the Pynchon corpus is over 1.7 million words). Nonetheless, as Brown is contemporary to Pynchon's early short stories, the Fiction subcorpus of Brown (117 texts, 252,000 word tokens) is included as a comparison in experiments. Many of the queries are also compared to the Corpus of Contemporary American English (COCA), a 520 million word token corpus that contains a wide array of texts from 1991 to 2015, evenly balanced across five genres of spoken, fiction, popular magazines, newspapers, and academic journals (Fiction subcorpus: ~100 million word tokens).[11] COCA is an appropriate reference corpus for the years of Pynchon's later work, but not, obviously, as ideal for work before *Vineland* (1990).[12] In one instance, additional context is provided by the Corpus of the Canon of Western Literature, a corpus of 805 plain text files comprising 73 million word tokens of poetry, prose, and theatre works from the *Bible* through the early twentieth century.[13] Existing reference corpora fall well short of ideally supporting stylistic Pynchon studies; Brown provides a snapshot of 1961, COCA covers 1991–2015. A number of bespoke comparison corpora are thus desirable.

Before laying out the rationale and goals of the bespoke comparison corpora creation, it is worth briefly exploring the question: to whom shall Pynchon be compared? Numerous commentators have posited groups of writers who might be considered Pynchon's peer group. Schaub dubbed a group of writers "Pynchon's company," including Richard Fariña, Tom Robbins, and William S. Burroughs, connected, Schaub argued, in that they "present social and psychological views which have dramatic political consequences."[14] In 1976, Gore Vidal reviewed a group of authors that he and others dubbed The New Novel or The New Fiction, including Donald Barthelme, William Gass, John Barth, and Pynchon.[15] Gerald Howard judges that *Gravity's Rainbow* "has no real rival among the novels published since [… although] William Gaddis's *J R* is a virtuoso turn […]. Then there is the special case of Don DeLillo, the other giant figure in postwar American fiction."[16] Another possibility for comparison is contemporary authors that reviewers of Pynchon mention when contextualizing his work. Professional reviewers of *Gravity's Rainbow*, for instance, have mentioned Nabokov, Vonnegut, Barth, and Heller, while amateur reviewers on Amazon (naturally, often writing many years after publication) invoke Burroughs, Wallace, Stephen King, Neal Stephenson, Gaddis, DeLillo, Philip K. Dick, Tom Robbins, William Gass, Umberto Eco, Neil Gaiman, William Vollman, as well as most of those mentioned by the professionals.[17] Yet another choice for a comparison corpus could be the authors that Pynchon himself mentions with approval or overtly as influences. In Pynchon's Ford Foundation application, which he wrote at age twenty-two, these included Eugène Ionesco, Ray Bradbury, Alfred Bester, Thomas Wolfe, F. Scott Fitzgerald, Lord Byron, Henry James, Nelson Algren, William Faulkner, Kerouac, Ginsberg, Voltaire, and T. S. Eliot.[18] In his "Introduction to Slow Learner," Pynchon adds Hemingway, Saul Bellow, Herbert Gold, Philip Roth, Norman Mailer, *The Education of Henry Adams*, and the spy fiction of John Buchan,[19] while many other writers are favorably mentioned throughout Pynchon's fiction and nonfiction.

In *The Tribe of Pyn*, David Cowart explores what he calls generations of postmodernists:

> The careers of Thomas Pynchon, Don DeLillo, and Cormac McCarthy—all born in the 1930s—represent the full flowering of the [postmodern] aesthetic variously contested, interrogated, and carried forward into the new millennium by such younger writers as Richard Powers, William Vollmann, David Foster Wallace, Maxine Hong Kingston, Carole Maso, and Steve Erickson. Postmodern fiction, in other words, already boasts its apostolic succession, its general filiation.[20]

To Pynchon's generation, Cowart adds Toni Morrison and Margaret Atwood as possible additions and sees "considerable continuity" between Barth, Pynchon, Gaddis, DeLillo, and the younger Wallace, Vollmann, and Powers.[21] The choice of any comparison corpora depends on the study, as David L. Hoover writes:

> The need for some kind of comparative norm suggests that counting more than one text will often be required and the nature of the research will dictate the appropriate comparison text. In some cases, other texts by the same author will be selected, or contemporary authors, or a natural language corpus. In other cases, genres, periods, or parts of texts may be the appropriate focus. Counting may be limited to the dialogue or narration of a text, to one or more speakers or narrators, or to specific passages.[22]

The choice of comparison corpora will also inevitably be subjective and imperfect. As Stanford Literary Lab researchers discovered when attempting to select a list of the "canon" to include in their Stanford Corpus of 20th-Century Fiction, there can be no "pretense that the construction of the corpus-as-canon could be an innocent one."[23]

McEnery et al. suggest general guidelines for DIY corpora. As for size, "[o]ne must be clear about one's research question […]. The size of the corpus needed depends upon the purpose for which it is intended as well as a number of practical considerations."[24] For the experiments in this book, bespoke comparison corpora should ideally be at least as large as the Pynchon corpus, ~1.7 million words, bearing in mind the practical difficulty in obtaining large numbers of contemporary texts. Balance and representativeness are key principles of corpus building, although as McEnery et al. note, "corpus-building is of necessity a marriage of perfection and pragmatism," and representativeness "of most corpora is to a great extent determined by two factors: the range of genres included in a corpus," or balance, "and how the text chunks for each genre are selected," or sampling.[25]

The "range of genres" present in Pynchon's texts is manifold, as Pynchon parodies and plays with seemingly dozens of genres throughout his work, as critics have explored.[26] The dizzying variety of genres adopted ironically or otherwise in Pynchon's texts might form the basis for future digital research,[27] but as a pragmatic solution for the experiments in this book, Pynchon's genre is considered to be postmodern American literary fiction (acknowledging that this label is inevitably problematic, perhaps especially for later Pynchon novels).[28] Ultimately, comparison corpora should establish *relative norms* of comparison in stylistic research, as Leech and Short write: "There are manifest dangers in the way a relative norm is chosen, but once it is accepted that relative validity is all we can aim at these need not worry us unduly [...]. What counts as 'the same category of writing,' however, can be defined to different degrees of narrowness."[29] The subjectivity of comparison corpora creation is therefore unavoidable, as McEnery et al. state that the notions of balance and representativeness of a corpus (or comparison corpus) "are *per se* open to question," and "conclusions drawn from a particular corpus must be treated as deductions rather than facts."[30]

With those potential avenues and cautions for comparison corpora in mind, the bespoke comparison corpora assembles for this book's experiments are:

- Pynchon's Peers: North American postmodern literary fiction, published 1959–2013 (~2.4 million word tokens). The choice of prominent writers and the desire to balance the corpus with diversity in race and gender led to the inclusion of writers who are contemporary to Pynchon within fifteen years of his birth (in 1937) and one Canadian writer. Includes two novels or short story collections each by Margaret Atwood, John Barth, Donald Barthelme, Don DeLillo, William Gaddis, Cormac McCarthy, Toni Morrison, and Ishmael Reed, including one earlier- and one later-career text.
- Popular fiction: American popular fiction published 1974–2013 (~1.2 million word tokens). Includes novels by Stephen King, Danielle Steel, and James Patterson, representing the genres of horror, romance, and thriller, respectively. Again, this includes one earlier- and one later-career novel.
- Pynchon-influenced: American fiction and one literary memoir by younger American authors whom critics have claimed as notable postmodernists or Pynchon-influenced (~1.6 million word tokens). Includes two novels

each by Steve Erickson, Richard Powers, William Vollmann, David Foster Wallace, and a literary memoir by Zak Smith.

I.2.1 Influence Corpus

The authors included in the Peers and Pop corpora require no introduction, but the Influence corpus authors and their relation to Pynchon may. To compare Pynchon with works of later generations, authors have been selected whom critics state have been influenced by Pynchon and/or are considered major figures of relatively recent postmodernism and experimental fiction. Influence has attracted substantial critical attention, especially following the landmark *The Anxiety of Influence* by Harold Bloom, who declared that "strong poets make [poetic] history by misreading one another, so as to clear imaginative space for themselves."[31] The Influence corpus serves as a comparative point of reference and context, as well as an exploratory springboard for future work on these authors *vis-a-vis* Pynchon and on their own, as some chapters present intriguing results for these younger authors' texts which are not explored further in this book.

To begin selecting the Influence authors, Tom LeClair wrote that Powers, Vollmann, and Wallace are "our new prodigies" after Pynchon, noting especially the rise of science and technical language in novels following *Gravity's Rainbow*.[32] Regarding influence, LeClair wrote that

> Powers, William Vollmann, and David Foster Wallace all admit within their novels their filial debt to "Pop" Pynchon. A major character in Powers's *The Gold Bug Variations* has Pynchon as his "favorite living novelist" [...], several references to *Gravity's Rainbow* appear in Vollmann's *You Bright and Risen Angels*, and a major character in Wallace's *Infinite Jest* is constructed from the obsessions of Pynchon's biggest book. Of the three younger writers, Wallace is the most ambivalent toward Pynchon: Wallace praises *Gravity's Rainbow* as generous in its gift-giving but also calls Pynchon, along with Nabokov, "a patriarch for my patricide" [...].[33]

Powers may be the least problematic of the three when discussing Pynchon's influence. In *The Tribe of Pyn*, Cowart wrote that Pynchon "may plausibly be said to inspire Richard Powers,"[34] and notes that Powers has "repeatedly expressed his admiration for Pynchon. He rereads *Gravity's Rainbow* every five years or so, and annually revisits one particularly moving passage."[35] The inclusion of works by Steve Erickson is similarly unproblematic, as his texts have often been discussed in terms of their relation to Pynchon.[36] Erickson, for his part, stated in an interview that he had somehow absorbed Pynchon's influence even before reading his works: "I saw that people were absolutely right, that I had been influenced by Pynchon. Kind of like Joyce, Pynchon's influence was so pervasive, it was so much in the literary air, I had breathed it without knowing it."[37]

Pynchon and Wallace's fiction has, at least, many formal and stylistic similarities: esoteric vocabulary, silly names, acronyms, endless references, and daunting length. Wallace's first novel, *The Broom of the System*, has been widely regarded as influenced by *Lot 49*. Michiko Kakutani noted the connections in her review ("from its opening pages onward through its enigmatic ending, *The Broom of the System* will remind readers of *The Crying of Lot 49*").[38] Meanwhile, Wallace's biographer D. T. Max writes that the "overwhelming influence is Pynchon," that "Pynchon saturates [*The Broom of the System*'s] DNA," and that "dozens" of authors passed on providing a blurb for the novel's cover, presumably because most "likely saw the book as derivative of Pynchon."[39] There is also evidence that Wallace harbored a considerable anxiety of influence. Although Wallace had been an avid reader and admirer of Pynchon, according to Max, Wallace "told a friend he hid in his room for two days and cried after reading yet another paragraph devoted to parallels between [*Broom*] and Pynchon's most popular novel."[40] The later "patricidal" comment by Wallace that LeClair quotes is, more fully,

> If I have a real enemy, a patriarch for my patricide, it's probably Barth and Coover and Burroughs, even Nabokov and Pynchon. Because, even though their self-consciousness and irony and anarchism served valuable purposes, were indispensable for their times, their aesthetic's absorption by the U.S. commercial culture has had appalling consequences for writers and everyone else.[41]

Andersen characterized this much-quoted statement as an "unambiguous statement of aesthetic intent—or provocative declaration of war—[which] laid down a clear set of guidelines for the literary critic wishing to tackle Wallace's work […] with often fruitful results."[42] Andersen argued further, however, that while there are "many advantages in following Wallace's own lead from [this] interview and focusing on the many differences between Wallace and his postmodern predecessors, a discussion of these differences should be tempered by an awareness of the many similarities between Wallace and those authors."[43] In some chapters of this book, some of these many similarities between Pynchon and Wallace are illustrated, as the two are outliers in a number of experiments.

Although early critics of Vollmann compared him with Pynchon, and LeClair read allusions to *Gravity's Rainbow* in Vollmann's 1987 novel, *You Bright and Risen Angels*, such claims are not standing the test of time. Vollmann has denied the possibility of intentional references and downplayed any connection between his own writing and Pynchon: "I hadn't read *Gravity's Rainbow* until after *Angels* came out, even though I'd read other Pynchon books. But I don't think my stuff is much like Pynchon's."[44] While scholars are not obliged to follow Vollmann's statements when reading his work in relation to Pynchon, critics such as Alexander Nazaryan have also challenged the comparison: "though [Vollmann] is often compared in the press to the postmodernist trickster Thomas Pynchon, that's just critical laziness."[45] Influence aside, Cowart argues that he "see[s] considerable continuity between the David Foster Wallaces, the William Vollmanns […] and such older writers as Barth, Pynchon, Gaddis, and DeLillo."[46]

Zak Smith requires an introduction here as his writings have not yet received literary academic attention. Smith (b. 1976) has demonstrated a special relationship with Pynchon's texts through his massive illustrated project, published as *Pictures Showing What Happens on Each Page of Thomas Pynchon's Novel* Gravity's Rainbow, with 760 drawings and paintings that depict each page of Pynchon's magnum opus and were exhibited together at the 2004 Whitney Biennial.[47] This work is not unknown in Pynchon communities, and Smith's illustration of Slothrop in a Hawaiian shirt adorns the cover of *The Cambridge Companion to Thomas Pynchon*.[48] Certainly no visual artist has engaged more with Pynchon's texts than Smith, and it should be unsurprising that Smith's memoir engages with Pynchon, as well. Smith's 2009 *We Did Porn: Memoirs and Drawings*,[49] a memoir of Smith's contrapuntal experiences in the fine art and pornography *milieux*, contains much evidence of Pynchon's influence. Amidst its digressive style and melange of high and low language and subject matter, Smith references Pynchon explicitly numerous times, and its text contains a number of suspiciously *Gravity's Rainbow*-esque thematic and stylistic elements, including frequent acronyms, riffs on paranoia, the tarot, scientific language (including parabolas), Hawaiian shirts, and repeated references to cause and effect inverted or broken down.

I.3 Software

The experiments in this book are mostly based on corpus query using regular expressions, and results would be identical or very similar using a variety of coding languages or software applications, such as R, Python, AntConc, LancsBox, and

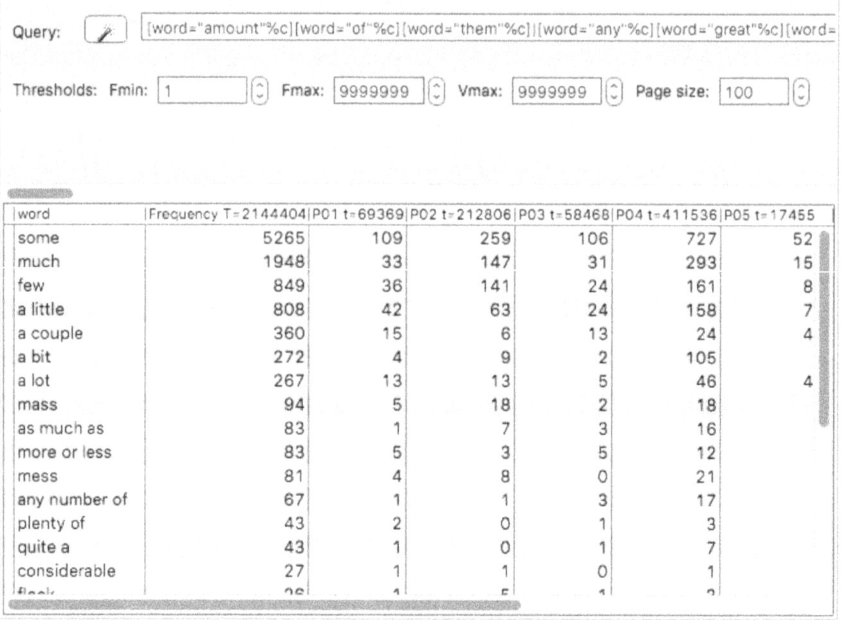

| Query: | [word="amount"%c][word="of"%c][word="them"%c]|[word="any"%c][word="great"%c][word= |

Thresholds: Fmin: `1` Fmax: `9999999` Vmax: `9999999` Page size: `100`

word	Frequency T=2144404	P01 t=69369	P02 t=212806	P03 t=58468	P04 t=411536	P05 t=17455
some	5265	109	259	106	727	52
much	1948	33	147	31	293	15
few	849	36	141	24	161	8
a little	808	42	63	24	158	7
a couple	360	15	6	13	24	4
a bit	272	4	9	2	105	
a lot	267	13	13	5	46	4
mass	94	5	18	2	18	
as much as	83	1	7	3	16	
more or less	83	5	3	5	12	
mess	81	4	8	0	21	
any number of	67	1	1	3	17	
plenty of	43	2	0	1	3	
quite a	43	1	0	1	7	
considerable	27	1	1	0	1	
flock	26	1	5	1	2	

Figure A.3 TXM display of query across Pynchon corpus.

so on. I mostly used TXM, a free, open-source text/corpus analysis environment developed at the ENS Lyon, designed for linguistic or literary text analysis,[50] due to its use of the CQP query processing language, which was designed for querying large text corpora with linguistic annotations,[51] incorporation of a widely-used part of speech tagger (TreeTagger, developed by Helmut Schmid,[52] which employs the part of speech tags of the Penn Treebank Project[53]), and its graphical interface, which combines query with convenient KWIC (keyword-in-context) views of the texts, so that queries could be manually checked quickly and efficiently (Figures A.3 and A.4).

Occasional use is also made of Natural Language Toolkit (NLTK), a leading Python-based platform for natural language processing which is widely used in corpus linguistics, stylistics, and digital humanities.[54]

I.4 Statistics

Log-likelihood (LL) is a widely used standard statistic in corpus stylistics to compare the statistical significance of overuse and underuse of frequencies of words and phrases between target corpora and reference corpora, and leading

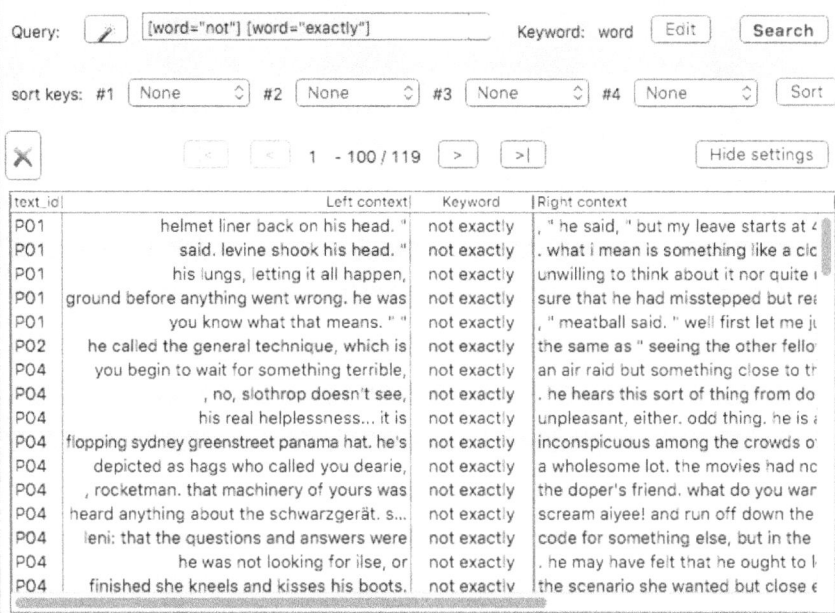

Figure A.4 TXM keyword-in-context (KWIC) view.

researchers often[55] make use of Paul Rayson's online LL calculator.[56] The experiments in this book employ log-likelihood, but future work could consider evolving work on statistical measures in corpus linguistics.[57]

I.5 Shared Data

Output data from the experiments is shared online at GitHub for reusability and reproducibility: https://github.com/erikannotations/TPDH.

Notes

1 Albert Rolls, "The Two *V.*s of Thomas Pynchon, or From Lippincott to Jonathan Cape and Beyond," *Orbit: Writing Around Pynchon*, 1:1 (2012).

2 Juxta, accessed September 1, 2019, http://www.juxtasoftware.org/about/.

3 For the original diff algorithm, see J. W. Hunt and M. D. McIlroy, "An Algorithm for Differential File Comparison," *Bell Laboratories Computing Science Technical Report* 41 (1976): 1–9. Wdiff is currently maintained by Martin von Gagern, accessed September 1, 2019, https://www.gnu.org/software/wdiff/.

4 Erik Ketzan and Christof Schöch, "What Changed When Andy Weir's *The Martian* Got Edited?" *Digital Humanities 2017, Conference Book of Abstracts* (Montréal: McGill University and Université de Montréal, 2017). Erik Ketzan and Christof Schöch, "Classifying and Contextualizing Edits in Variants with *Coleto*: Three Versions of Andy Weir's *The Martian*," *Digital Humanities Quarterly*, publication forthcoming.

5 Minor differences in the current UK paperback not specifically mentioned by Rolls include one song in which a *Chorus* is changed to a *Refrain* (*V*. UK, 351), minor stylistic changes such as "making noises at one another" (*V*. US, 13) → "making noises at each other" (*V*. UK, 20) and "North African merchant-ships" (*V*. US,506) → "North African merchantmen" (*V*. UK, 468), and changes to numbers (e.g., "eight hundred dollars" → "$800"). Rolls notes the introduction of diacritical marks in the recent UK edition, and there are errata involving non-English languages, e.g., "Mondaugen's doppelgänger" (*V*. US, 256) → "Mondaugen's doubleganger" (*V*. UK, 242), presumably the mistakes of editors and typesetters. In addition, British spelling was applied inconsistently in the UK edition, e.g., *recognise* and *recognized* appearing within the same paragraph (*V*. UK, 341).

6 Luc Herman and John M. Krafft, "Fast Learner: The Typescript of Pynchon's *V.* at the Harry Ransom Center in Austin," *Texas Studies in Literature and Language* 49:1 (2007): 1–20. Rodney Gibbs, "A Portrait of the Luddite as a Young Man," *Denver Quarterly* 39:1 (2004): 35–42. Lee Konstantinou, *Cool Characters, Irony and American Fiction* (Cambridge: Harvard University Press, 2016), 76–8.

7 Wisnicki, "A Trove of New Works by Thomas Pynchon?"; Muth, "The Grammars of the System: Thomas Pynchon at Boeing."

8 See e.g., Gareth Twose, "What's in a Clause? Milton's Participial Style Revisited," *Language and Literature* 17:1 (2008): 77–9.

9 Henry Kučera and W. Nelson Francis, *Computational Analysis of Present-Day English* (Providence: Brown University Press, 1967). Licensed through International Computer Archive of Modern and Medieval English (ICAME), accessed September 1, 2019, http://clu.uni.no/icame/.

10 "The Brown family of corpora (Brown, Frown, LOB, FLOB) is neither large nor recent." Mark Davies, "Looking at Recent Changes in English with the Corpus of Contemporary American English (COCA)," *The 21st Century Text* 1 (2011), accessed September 1, 2019, https://21centurytext.wordpress.com/2012/06/15/changes-in-english-with-coca/.

11 Mark Davies, "The Corpus of Contemporary American English: 520 Million Words, 1990–2015," 2008, accessed September 1, 2019, http://corpus.byu.edu/coca/.

12 Note that COCA has been criticized for the messiness of its data. Eve, *Close Reading with Computers*, 116.

13 Green, "Introducing the Corpus of the Canon of Western Literature," 282–99.

14 Schaub, *Pynchon: Voice of Ambiguity*, 139

15 Gore Vidal, "American Plastic: The Matter of Fiction," *New York Review of Books*, July 15, 1976, 31–9.

16 Howard, "Pynchon From A to *V*."

17 Finn, "The Social Lives of Books," 60–4.

18 Weisenburger, "Thomas Pynchon at Twenty-Two," 694–7.

19 Pynchon, *Slow Learner*.

20 David Cowart, *The Tribe of Pyn* (Ann Arbor: University of Michigan Press, 2015), 1.

21 Ibid., 9, 20.

22 David L. Hoover, "Quantitative Analysis and Literary Studies," in *A Companion to Digital Literary Studies*, ed. Ray Siemens and Susan Schreibman (Oxford: Blackwell, 2013), 520.

23 Mark Algee-Hewitt and Mark McGurl, "Between Canon and Corpus: Six Perspectives on 20th-Century Novels," *Pamphlets of the Stanford Literary Lab* 8 (2015): 5.

24 McEnery, Xiao, and Tono, *Corpus-Based Language Studies*, 71.

25 Ibid., 73, 13.

26 Birger Vanwesenbeeck, "*Gravity's Rainbow*: A Portrait of the Artist as Engineer," *Pynchon Notes* 56–7 (2009): 144–57; Brian McHale, "Genre as History: Pynchon's Genre-Poaching," in *Pynchon's* Against the Day: *A Corrupted Pilgrim's Guide*, ed. Jeffrey Severs and Christopher Leise (Maryland: University of Delaware Press, 2011), 25.

27 Pynchon's texts might be excellent test cases for recent work in the detection of "microgenres," or fragments within texts which display linguistic similarity with particular genres. See J. D. Porter, Mark Algee-Hewitt, Erik Fredner, Michaela Bronstein, Alexander Manshel, Nichole Nomura, and Abigail Droge, "Microgenres," *DH2019 Conference Book of Abstracts* (Utrecht: 2019).

28 See Sascha Pöhlmann, "Pynchon and Post-postmodernism," in *The New Pynchon Studies*, ed. Joanna Freer (Cambridge: Cambridge University Press, 2019), 17–32.

29 Leech and Short, *Style in Fiction*, 42.

30 McEnery, Xiao, and Tono, *Corpus-Based Language Studies*, 73.

31 Bloom, *The Anxiety of Influence*, 5.

32 LeClair, "The Prodigious Fiction," 12–13.

33 Ibid., 12.

34 Cowart, *The Tribe of Pyn*, 20.

35 Ibid., 91.

36 Ibid., 81–90.

37 Rob Trucks, *The Pleasure of Influence: Conversations with American Male Fiction Writers* (West Lafayette: Purdue University Press, 2002), 61.

38 Michiko Kakutani, "Books of the Times; Life in Cleveland, 1990," *New York Times*, December 27, 1986, https://www.nytimes.com/1986/12/27/books/books-of-the-times-life-in-cleveland-1990.html.

39 D. T. Max, *Every Love Story is a Ghost Story: A Life of David Foster Wallace* (London: Granta, 2012), 47, 48, 77.

40 Ibid., 82.

41 Larry McCaffery, "An Interview with David Foster Wallace," *Review of Contemporary Fiction* 13:2 (1993): 15.

42 Tore Rye Andersen, "Pay Attention! David Foster Wallace and his Real Enemies," *English Studies* 95:1 (2014): 9.

43 Ibid., 22.

44 Larry McCaffery, "A Conversation with William T. Vollmann," in *William T. Vollmann: Selected Interviews*, ed. Scott Rhodes (Self-published, 2015), 41.

45 Alexander Nazaryan, "The Lush Life of William T. Vollmann," *Newsweek*, November 6, 2013, http://www.newsweek.com/2013/11/08/lush-life-william-t-vollmann-243896.html.

46 Cowart, *The Tribe of Pyn*, 20.

47 Zak Smith, *Pictures Showing What Happens on Each Page of Thomas Pynchon's Novel* Gravity's Rainbow (New York: Tin House Books, 2006).

48 Inger H. Dalsgaard, Luc Herman, and Brian McHale, eds., *The Cambridge Companion to Thomas Pynchon* (Cambridge: Cambridge University Press, 2012).

49 Zak Smith, *We Did Porn: Memoir and Drawings* (New York: Tin House Books, 2009).

50 TXM 0.7.8 desktop software, accessed September 1, 2019, http://textometrie.ens-lyon.fr/?lang=en. Serge Heiden, "The TXM Platform: Building Open-Source Textual Analysis Software Compatible with the TEI Encoding Scheme," in *24th Pacific Asia Conference on Language, Information and Computation* (Tokyo: Waseda University, 2010).

51 "The IMS Open Corpus Workbench (CWB)," accessed September 1, 2019, http://cwb.sourceforge.net; Stefan Evert and Andrew Hardie, "Twenty-First Century Corpus Workbench: Updating a Query Architecture for the New Millennium," in *Proceedings of the Corpus Linguistics 2011 Conference* (University of Birmingham, 2011).

52 Helmut Schmid, "TreeTagger - a Part-of-Speech Tagger for Many Languages," accessed September 1, 2019, http://www.cis.uni-muenchen.de/~schmid/tools/TreeTagger/; Helmut Schmid, "Probabilistic Part-of-Speech Tagging Using Decision Trees," in *Proceedings of International Conference on New Methods in Language Processing* (Manchester: 1994); Helmut Schmid, "Improvements in Part-of-Speech Tagging with an Application to German," in *Proceedings of the ACL SIGDAT-Workshop* (Dublin: 1995). For accuracy of TreeTagger, see Eugenie Giesbrecht and

Stefan Evert, "Part-of-Speech (POS) Tagging - a solved task? An evaluation of POS taggers for the Web as corpus," *Proceedings of the Fifth Web as Corpus Workshop (WAC5)* (Donostia, San Sebastian: 2009), 27–35.

53 Beatrice Santorini, "Part of Speech Tagging Guidelines for the Penn Treebank Project," 1991, http://www.cis.uni-muenchen.de/~schmid/tools/TreeTagger/data/Penn-Treebank-Tagset.pdf.

54 See Steven Bird, Edward Loper, and Ewan Klein, *Natural Language Processing with Python* (Sebastopol, CA: O'Reilly Media, 2009).

55 E.g., McEnery, *Swearing in English*.

56 Rayson, "Matrix: A Statistical Method and Software Tool." Rayson's Log-likelihood calculator available at http://ucrel.lancs.ac.uk/llwizard.html.

57 E.g., Vaclav Brezina, *Statistics in Corpus Linguistics* (Cambridge: Cambridge University Press, 2018).

Literature Review of Digital Pynchon Studies

Digital approaches to Pynchon's texts comprise such a relatively small body of work that its entirety may be discussed here. I have been inspired by the publications of all the authors discussed below, and hope that criticisms of method and interpretation will be received in the constructive spirit in which they are intended, as steps toward a common project of digital Pynchon studies in which results are vigorously confirmed and challenged.

In the first digital study of Pynchon's texts in 2003, Luc Herman, Robert Hogenraad, and Wim van Mierlo attempted "a first and modest step towards the quantification of postmodernism" via a number of experiments on *Gravity's Rainbow*: lexical change over the course of the novel, an early form of topic modeling, and a dictionary-based approach to determine, though an early form of sentiment analysis, whether a "night journey" trend may be found in the novel.[1] These authors must be acknowledged as the original pioneers of digital Pynchon studies, as well as for advancing earlier methodologies for topic modeling and sentiment analysis. In their best experiment, Herman et al. traced the rate of lexical change in the novel—when new words appear in the text and previously appearing words no longer appear—and reported that "the rate of replacement of old words by new ones is quite marked from section 31 on, and subsides only toward the end." This is an interesting result, but difficult to interpret due to an absence of comparison corpora (only *Gravity's Rainbow* was analyzed in this paper's experiments).

Herman et al.'s next experiment was an early form of topic modeling. The authors grouped three bags of words, traced them over the course of the text, and ventured to interpret the associations of, for instance in one topic, "*Slothrop, head, sun, little, tree*," and so on. Given advances in the understanding of interpreting topic models (and, again, the total absence of comparison texts), some of the authors' claims should now be rejected, especially that this experiment "corroborates the connective nature of a postmodern text like *GR*" and "corroborates the idea of a connectedness that seems to belie, in part, the pervasive presence of a paranoid hermeneutic."[2] Herman et al.'s study advanced the state of the art of what eventually became known as topic modeling, most of which now uses Latent Dirichlet Allocation, which was only first described in the same year by David Blei et al.[3] It is now more widely discussed that topic models should be approached with certain cautions. As Benjamin Schmidt suggests, topic models are known for creating "unexpected juxtapositions,"[4] and apparently disconnected groups of words are common in topic models applied to many literary texts, not only Pynchon's. Andrew Goldstone and Ted Underwood argue that "interpreters really need to survey a topic model as a whole, instead of considering single topics in isolation,"[5] as Herman et al. did here. Schmidt writes further that topic models are "messy, ambiguous, and elusive. When humanists examine the output from MALLET (the most widely used topic-modeling tool), they need to be aware of the ways that topics may not be as coherent as they assume."

Herman et al.'s third experiment applied a 2,483-word dictionary of words indicating "primordial" and "conceptual" content across twenty-nine categories—Martindale's Regressive Imagery Dictionary—to score the textual progression of *Gravity's Rainbow* in a form of sentiment analysis, with the goal of determining whether a "night journey" pattern, as defined by earlier work by Colin Martindale, emerges. As comparisons, this "night journey" experiment cites Martindale's 1979 results for only three other novels—*Ulysses*, *Heart of Darkness*, and (presumably a translation of) Dante[6]—but these linguistically heterogeneous texts are extremely poor comparison texts for any experiment on a twentieth-century American author such as Pynchon.[7] Herman et al. report a sentiment-based "inverse night journey" pattern when dividing *Gravity's Rainbow* by episode, and as the methods and application of sentiment analysis have shown impressive results in recent years,[8] it is possible that this result could someday inform further sentiment analysis of Pynchon's texts. On its own, the experiments of Herman et al., which claimed evidence of an amorphously defined "night journey" based on a methodologically questionable dictionary of words and trialed on only a handful of mismatched novels, remains deficient in both method and interpretation. With the benefit of hindsight, this study should be acknowledged as creative but exploratory work.

In 2016, Letzler explored *Gravity's Rainbow* via three experiments operationalized by existing software: word frequency/keyness, social network analysis, and topic modeling.[9] Keywords in text are identified by software as unusually frequent compared to a comparison corpus, and of the highly ranked keywords in *Gravity's Rainbow* (compared to the Brown corpus), Letzler reports that many are present tense verbs, for example, *is*, *are*, and *knows*. Letztler correctly identifies that these results are partially explained by the fact that *Gravity's Rainbow* is written in the present tense, unlike his comparison corpus. Letzler then interprets textual instances of the keywords *here* and *now* to argue "that the novel is peculiarly concerned with the concept of the present moment," contributing to what Letzler interprets as a "phenomenology of the present" in *Gravity's Rainbow*. One issue with this approach, however, is that *here* and *now* may not be as notably frequent in *Gravity's Rainbow* as Letzler's results lead him to believe. While Letzler acknowledges the issue of tense, he nonetheless proceeds with a close reading of *here* and *now* in *Gravity's Rainbow* without appropriate comparisons. For such a comparison, I queried *here* and *now* in the Pynchon corpus and comparison corpora and report the following results in Table A.1.[10]

These new data indicate that *here* may be highly frequent in *all* texts written in the present tense, not only *Gravity's Rainbow*, and, among Pynchon's novels, *Gravity's Rainbow* is hardly unique in its frequent use of *here*. As for *now*, while *Gravity's Rainbow*'s frequency is the highest of any novel tested, it is not statistically significantly higher than such disparate works as a juicy romance novel by Danielle Steel, a postmodern fairy tale by Donald Barthelme, and a dark, historical war novel by William Vollmann. The frequencies of *here* and

Table A.1 Normalized frequency (per 100k word tokens) of "here" and "now" in corpora. Statistical significance in log-likelihood.

here (normalized frequency)	*now (normalized frequency)*
286.8 in *Gravity's Rainbow*.	344.1 in *Gravity's Rainbow*, highest result among all corpora.
Statistically significantly much higher than COCA ($p < 0.0001$).	Statistically significantly much higher than COCA ($p < 0.0001$).
For Pynchon, is close, matched or exceeded in frequency by *Mason & Dixon* (250.4), *Against the Day* (287.8), *Inherent Vice* (259.5) and *Bleeding Edge* (318.3, present tense).	No significant difference (below $p < 0.05$) compared to Barthelme's *Snow white*, Danielle Steel's *Passion's Promise*, and Vollmann's *Europe Central*.
In comparison corpora, matched or exceeded only by Gaddis's *J R* (728.1, written in the present tense) and Wallace's *The Broom of the System* (284.8).	

now in *Gravity's Rainbow* thus present weak evidence for the interpretation of a "phenomenology of the present" in the novel.

Letzler's second experiment impressively creates a social network of 260 characters in *Gravity's Rainbow*, which may aid a variety of future research as Letzler shares his data. Letzler's third experiment explores topic modeling in *Gravity's Rainbow*, but Letzler admits that "the overall experiment was too inconsistent to claim much in the way of global results." Like Herman et al., Letzler ventures an interpretation of one bag of seemingly disconnected words grouped by the software as a topic (body parts such as *back*, *head*, etc., colors, evaluating adjectives e.g., *great*, *good*, etc.), which Letzler suggests could be interpreted as "romanticism." While Letzler offers a well-written possible reading of this topic in *Gravity's Rainbow*, the criticisms of topic modeling applied to literary texts discussed above are relevant here, and it is difficult for any reader of Letzler's paper to build on or contest this reading.

Another data-driven Pynchon study is Eve's blog post "Visualizing *Gravity's Rainbow*," in which Eve inputted *Gravity's Rainbow* into David McClure's Textplot program,[11] which visualizes all the types of words in a text based on distances.[12] Eve accompanies the outputted word cloud of *Gravity's Rainbow* with a number of "critical observations," and the blog post is presented as exploratory in nature ("I want to do much more playing with this"). But some of Eve's "critical observations" demonstrate the questionable "leaps" from data to interpretation discussed in this book's introduction. For instance, Eve writes that "compared to running the same process on, say, *War and Peace*, as has David, the groupings are incredibly dense, for the most part. This probably structurally contributes to the paranoid associations of connectedness that is the novel's desired aesthetic effect." The main problem is that this claim is based on a comparison of a data visualization of merely two novels, perhaps also aided by other texts presented in person by McClure (whose project website displays data for fewer than ten other texts). Just as importantly, Eve does not entertain alternate explanations for why the words are visualized so densely. One explanation could simply be that there are more types of words in *Gravity's Rainbow* than an English translation of Tolstoy, resulting in words grouped more closely visually. Again, Eve's work is clearly labeled as exploratory (which, Professor Eve told me, was written "over a 45 minute period at an airport while I was waiting for a flight"), but Eve's blog post, if expanded, would greatly benefit from more corpus texts, including all of Pynchon's.

Christos Iraklis Tsatsoulis applied topic modeling and a range of other technical approaches—a number of clustering methods using a variety of distance functions, visualized both as nodes in a network graph and in a hierarchy—to explore how these digital approaches group the chapters of *V*.[13] The chapters in *V*. present a classification problem, as most can be clearly grouped as one of the two novel's main storylines: the story of Benny Profane and the Whole Sick Crew (chapters 1, 6, 8, 10, 12, 13, 15, 16) and the historical fictions (chapters 3, 9, 11, 14, 17), but four chapters feature a mix of storylines (chapters 2, 4, 5, 7). Tsatsoulis demonstrates that various methods consistently group the chapters from the main storylines together, while different methods group the mixed chapters in different ways.

These early assays in digital Pynchon studies share a number of features: two are data-driven, all focus on a single Pynchon novel, all make self-admittedly exploratory and limited interpretations, and all would benefit from comparison corpora (or, in Letzler's case, larger ones). This book has attempted to advance digital Pynchon studies by, rather, hypothesis-based inquiry, which crafts experiments based on textual features already identified in analog Pynchon studies, and by larger and more comprehensive comparison corpora, including Pynchon's entire body of fiction.

The computational linguist Mark Liberman occasionally investigates stylistic issues in Pynchon in his *Language Log* blog, and once mentioned rereading *Inherent Vice* "for purely phonetic reasons."[14] Liberman's brief but intriguing experiments include the number of masculine and feminine pronouns in novels, including some of Pynchon's,[15] explicating Pynchon's use of UNIX terminology in *Inherent Vice*,[16] unearthing the Unicode character of the New Turkic Alphabet letter that Tchitcherine is assigned to in *Gravity's Rainbow*,[17] the phonetics of Pynchon's rendering of a New York dialect,[18] and proportion of dialogue in novels, including Pynchon's,[19] which I addressed in Chapter 1.

In 2018, Christian Hänggi published a database of 927 musical references in Pynchon compiled from print guides, *Pynchon Wiki*, and his own observations and presented visualizations of raw and normalized frequencies to aid such questions as the following: "Which musicians or works does Pynchon reference most frequently? Which genres occur most often? Which novels contain most references? Are there any notable anachronisms?"[20] Hänggi's work is largely a model of formal Pynchon studies: clearly described methodology, shared data, and interesting results. Although Hänggi writes that he provides "a statistical overview" to this data, no statistics are present, merely normalized frequency. But examining Hänggi's data in Rayson's log-likelihood calculator, I can find no instance of statistical significance that calls any of Hänggi's assertions into question. In 2020, Hänggi released his monograph, *Pynchon's Sound of Music*, which adroitly expands upon the topic of musical references in Pynchon's texts and adds visualizations such as the gender of musicians referenced and the distribution of Pynchon's original verse within his texts (which may be compared with my Figure 1.2, which includes verse within Pynchon's texts also authored by others).[21] Hänggi's experiments would still benefit from a statistic such as log-likelihood to compare relative frequencies (to question whether variation of results from book to book might be attributable to chance), but Hänggi's work must be acknowledged as the first book-length mixed method Pynchon study, and a fine one, at that.

A number of quantitative formal analyses of Pynchon reception and the *Pynchon Wiki* itself have been published. In 2011, Ed Finn approached Pynchon reception digitally by examining a dataset of books "linked" to Pynchon's novels through Amazon and LibraryThing recommendations, to analyze the "networks of cultural consumption" that surround Pynchon's novels.[22] Finn also visualized the temporality of Pynchon reception via a timeline of academic publications on Pynchon (according to MLA data and *Pynchon Notes* contributions), Pynchon-L mailing list contributions, and Amazon reviews. Finn reported, for instance, "major spikes [in academic publications] frequently occurring approximately six years after the appearance of a new novel."[23] *Pynchon Wiki*, meanwhile, has been the subject of formal studies by Ralph Schroeder and Matthijs L. den Besten in 2008 and Simon Rowberry in 2012.[24]

Pynchon's texts have been the subject of three stylometric studies. In the first, Eve investigated the rumor that Pynchon had secretly authored a novel titled *Cow Country*, published by an author listed on the book jacket as "Adrian Jones Pearson."[25] Eve employed the established workhorse of stylometry, Delta, in the widely used Stylo package to present evidence that Pynchon did not write *Cow Country*, confirming the denial by Pynchon's publisher, Penguin. Eve's comparison corpus was relatively small, consisting of only eight novels by Don DeLillo, but as no evidence, digital or otherwise, exists that would challenge this result, the case that Pynchon may have written *Cow Country* may safely be considered closed.[26]

The journalist Ben Blatt examined a wide range of stylistic features in contemporary and twentieth-century fiction in *Nabokov's Favorite Color is Mauve* (2017) and included Pynchon's texts in his large corpus.[27] Blatt conducted a stylometric analysis to test the hypothesis that Pynchon and J. D. Salinger were the same empirical author, based on (what then, as now seem) fairly silly rumors in the 1970s, and unsurprisingly found no stylometric evidence for this.[28] In another section on cliché phrases in fifty authors, Blatt employed a dictionary of four thousand clichés published in 2013 to score fifty authors from various time periods, from Jane Austen to contemporary, in their cliché use.[29] Blatt acknowledged the main problem with his approach: that by including authors from diverse time periods, a dictionary-based approach based on a 2013 cliché dictionary is partly a dictionary-based score of contemporary English. And indeed, the older the writer, the lower they tended to score in Blatt's cliché measure. Pynchon, as a recent author, unsurprisingly scored fairly high on Blatt's list, but Blatt devoted no subsequent discussion to clichés in Pynchon. Blatt also investigated n-gram anaphora at the beginning of sentences (in other words, n-grams at the beginning of a sentence that are identical to the n-gram that began the previous sentence), and reported that among all the novels by these fifty writers, *Bleeding Edge* contains the least amount of one-word anaphora, with five Pynchon novels in the lowest ten novels among the whole corpus. This is an interesting result, and Blatt reported that Pynchon and Joyce display the lowest percentage of sentences that begin with three-gram anaphor, indicating the variety by which these authors begin sentences.[30]

In an experiment from which Blatt drew the title of his book, *Nabokov's Favorite Word is Mauve*, Blatt attempted to identify some "favorite" words in these fifty authors by comparing word frequency in the texts and the Corpus of Historical American English (COHA), a corpus of works from 1810 to 2009.[31] Blatt created two measures, "cinnamon" words, or "favorite" words by which authors add spice to their prose, and "nod words," "tic words that writers end up leaning on *a lot*, to the point where they appear hundreds of times in a book"[32] and then measured the highest relative frequencies of these compared with COHA using a keyness score. Pynchon's "cinnamon words" are reported as "someplace, paranoia, freeway," and "nod words" as "here, around, back." For digital Pynchon scholars, these are tantalizing results for "Pynchon's favorite words," as Letzler previously noted the keyness of *here* and *back* in *Gravity's Rainbow*, *someplace* is exemplary of the vagueness words I explored in Chapter 3, and *paranoia* is a ubiquitous theme in Pynchon's works and criticism. However, the methodology and results of Blatt's experiment should be strongly questioned, due to Blatt's choice of comparison corpus. By selecting COHA (works from 1810 to 2009) to compare the idiolects of writers from Jane Austen to Pynchon, the keyness is greatly affected by diachronic change in English over two centuries. In Blatt's experiment, the keyness of Pynchon's words is calculated not in comparison with American writers who are Pynchon's contemporaries, but almost a century of nineteenth-century American English texts, as well. Meanwhile, Jane Austen, James Joyce, Ian Fleming, and many other English and Irish writers are compared to a Corpus of Historical *American* English. Differences in American and British lexis thus readily explain many of Blatt's results for writers' "favorite" words: *trouser* for *James Bond* author Ian Fleming (Americans say "pants"), *tram* for James Joyce (Americans say "trolley"), *freeway* for Pynchon (nonexistent in most of nineteenth-century American English, first *OED* instance in 1890),[33] *laptop* for three contemporary writers, and profanity such as *fucked/fucking* in a number of other recent writers—these words did not exist or were little used in most of Blatt's comparison corpus.

Katie Muth's "The Grammars of the System: Thomas Pynchon at Boeing" attempts to correctly attribute the technical articles which may have been written by Pynchon while an employee at Boeing, writing for a periodical called *Bomarc Service News*.[34] Muth provides an excellent history and context of these rare Boeing articles and advances our understanding of Pynchon's early technical writing, although one wishes that Muth's comparison corpus were larger; Muth includes only six articles (seven thousand word tokens) of Bomarc articles written by staff writers, despite access to many issues of the *Bomarc Service News*. Also regarding word count, Muth employs the Jstylo stylometry application[35] to assess authorship attribution in technical texts of seemingly one thousand to two thousand word tokens that may have been written by Pynchon, but Maciej Eder (one of the creators of the widely used *Stylo* stylometry package) has argued that authorship attribution for modern novels requires a minimum sample size of some five thousand word tokens,[36] which suggests that Muth's results may at least be questioned.

In 2019, Ted Underwood devoted two sentences to Pynchon in *Distant Horizons*, his impressive large-scale digital investigation of genre classification over centuries of English literature, and these contain both an intriguing result and what Stanley Fish might call a "leap" from data to interpretation. Underwood writes that his computer model "strongly (and persuasively) misclassifies" Pynchon's *Lot 49* as science fiction,[37] the noteworthy result. In a single-sentence interpretation of this result, however, Underwood leaps straight to thematic cliches of Pynchon criticism without considering linguistic or computational explanations: "It may not be Pynchon's explicit concern with entropy but his paranoid fascination with the sheer scale of mass society that this model sees as connected to the tradition of science fiction." While this sentence should probably be read as, simply, a colorful hyperbole by Underwood, there are simpler alternative explanations for Underwood's result which can be suggested. Underwood's genre classification model relies on content words: the "words most predictive of detective fiction reveals the themes we would expect: *police, murder, investigation*, and *crime*."³⁸ The simple presence of scientific lexis in *Lot 49*—including, for example, *electronic, molecules*, and *information* in its most frequent one thousand words—likely contributed more to *Lot 49*'s classification as science fiction than a computer model recognizing a "paranoid fascination with the sheer scale of mass society."

In 2019, a chapter on "Digital Readings" by Muth was published in a new volume of collected essays, *The New Pynchon Studies*.³⁹ Following Eve, Muth inputs *Gravity's Rainbow* into Textplot and improves upon Eve's blog post by, first, adding more comparison texts. Muth notes that Textplot includes a stop-word list of highly frequent words, some of which may be highly indicative of tense, for example, "have," "be," "is," "was," and so on, and Muth attempts to reintroduce tense detection into Textplot by reinserting some of these words. This supports an exploration of tense in *Gravity's Rainbow*, which is mostly, but not always, written in the present tense, and Muth reports "some forty to fifty past-tense flashbacks" in the novel. Muth reports that after running Textplot with more tense-indicative verbs included, the visualization of *Gravity's Rainbow* visually expands, with a peninsula of sorts appearing which contains words from the Franz Pökler chapter, which is the greatest sustained span of past-tense text in the novel. Muth presents the interpretation that this visualization of *Gravity's Rainbow* "doesn't just visualize the conceptual and thematic content of the novel; it visualizes the novel's treatment of history and its complex handling of time. [...] The map's polarity—bawdy immediacy versus historical weight—matches our general sense of the novel's thematic hierarchies."⁴⁰ Muth supports this partly by listing words from the various sections of the Textplot graph, but any such argument may be highly selective; whichever words Muth lists as examples of "bawdy immediacy" and "historical weight," it can be questioned how many hundreds or even thousands are excluded. Muth then provides a fine close reading of tense and historical themes in the Franz Pökler chapter and elsewhere in *Gravity's Rainbow*, before concluding that "past tense, unevenly distributed over *Gravity's Rainbow*'s novelistic time, clusters around Pökler's narrative—itself an allegory of complicity with historical atrocity—as well as with words such as 'pattern,' 'structure,' 'truth,' and 'history.'"⁴¹ Even though these words resonate with Pynchon scholars, this could again be a selective list of four words plucked from hundreds in the Pökler cluster of Textplot's visualization. Nonetheless, I suspect that Muth has identified something very observable in *Gravity's Rainbow*: a correlation of tense with thematic and broader stylistic shifts.

In 2019, Paul Razzell published "*Inherent Vice* Diagrammed" online, which impressively maps all of the novel's characters in a series of network graphs, with edges between characters such as "son of" and "lovers."[42] Along with Letzler's network of characters in *Gravity's Rainbow*, this could contribute to a richly annotated Pynchon knowledge graph in the future

In conclusion, the newly emerging digital Pynchon studies should place increasing emphasis on comparison corpora, methodological criticism, and shared data, so that we can avoid some of the missteps long discussed by digital humanists in other domains. Perhaps the greatest challenge to existing and future stylistic Pynchon studies remains the "leap" from data to interpretation, particularly as Pynchon studies provides such an attractive set of *topoi* to leap *to*. It is all too tempting to analogize a messy graph of dots to "entropy" or "paranoia." But beyond individual experiments and arguments, I hope that this book will further the notion of digital Pynchon studies as a large, common project, in which studies will be continuously challenged, confirmed, or adapted by scholars.

Notes

1 Luc Herman, Robert Hogenraad, and Wim van Mierlo, "Pynchon, Postmodernism and Quantification: An Empirical Content Analysis of Thomas Pynchon's *Gravity's Rainbow*," *Language and Literature* 12:1 (2003): 27–41.

2 Ibid., 37, 27.

3 David M. Blei, Andrew Ng, Michael Jordan, "Latent Dirichlet Allocation," *Journal of Machine Learning Research* 3 (2003): 993–1022.

4 Benjamin M. Schmidt, "Words Alone: Dismantling Topic Models in the Humanities," *Journal of Digital Humanities* 2:1 (2012), online, http://journalofdigitalhumanities. org/2-1/words-alone-by-benjamin-m-schmidt/.

5 Andrew Goldstone and Ted Underwood, "What Can Topic Models of PMLA Teach Us about the History of Literary Scholarship?" *Journal of Digital Humanities* 2:1 (2012), online, http://journalofdigitalhumanities.org/2-1/what-can-topic-models-of-pmla-teach-us-by-ted-underwood-and-andrew-goldstone/.

6 Colin Martindale, "The Night Journey: Trends in the Content of Narratives Symbolizing Alteration of Consciousness," *Journal of Altered States of Consciousness* 4:4 (1979): 321–43.

7 Comparing texts by Conrad, Joyce, a translation of Dante, and Pynchon based on Martindale's Regressive Imagery Dictionary, a psychological dictionary developed in the 1970s by an American professor, especially suggests that heterogeneity in English dialect and time period should be accounted for. Colin Martindale, *Romantic Progression: The Psychology of Literary History* (Washington, DC: Hemisphere, 1975).

8 E.g., Jodie Archer and Matthew L. Jockers, *The Bestseller Code* (New York: St. Martin's Press, 2016).

9 David Letzler, "A Phenomenology of the Present: Toward a Digital Understanding of *Gravity's Rainbow*," *Orbit: A Journal of American Literature* 4:2 (2016): 1–32.

10 Word frequencies calculated by TXM, total word counts by AntWordProfiler, significance by Rayson's Log Likelihood calculator, as described in Chapter 2.

11 David McClure, "(Mental) Maps of Texts," *DClure.org*, September 24, 2014, http://dclure.org/essays/mental-maps-of-texts/.

12 Martin Paul Eve, "Visualizing *Gravity's Rainbow*," *Martineve.com*, June 7, 2015, https://eve.gd/2015/06/07/visualizing-gravitys-rainbow/.

13 Christos Iraklis Tsatsoulis, "Unsupervised Text Mining Methods for Literature Analysis: A Case Study for Thomas Pynchon's *V.*," *Orbit: A Journal of American Literature* 1:2 (2013): 1–34, https://doi.org/10.7766/orbit.v1.2.44.

14 Liberman, "The Price of Wisdom."

15 Mark Liberman, "The G.K. Chesterton Prize for Ignoring Women," *Language Log*, October 6, 2015, http://languagelog.ldc.upenn.edu/nll/?p=21536.

16 Mark Liberman, "CD tilde home," *Language Log*, October 1, 2013, http://languagelog.ldc.upenn.edu/nll/?p=7420.

17 Mark Liberman, "How Alphabetic Is the Nature of Molecules," *Language Log*, September 27, 2004, http://itre.cis.upenn.edu/~myl/languagelog/archives/001498.html.

18 Liberman, "The Syntonic Phonetics of Pynchon's Pitchuhv."

19 Liberman, "Proportion of Dialogue in Novels."

20 Christian Hänggi, "The Pynchon Playlist: A Catalogue and Its Analysis," *Orbit: A Journal of American Literature* 6:1 (2018): 1–35. https://doi.org/10.16995/orbit.487.

21 Hänggi, *Pynchon's Sound of Music*, 211, 219.

22 Finn, "The Social Lives of Books," 80.

23 Ibid., 84.

24 Ralph Schroeder and Matthijs L. den Besten, "Literary Sleuths Online: E-Research Collaboration on the Pynchon Wiki," *Information, Communication & Society* 11:2 (2008): 25–45; Simon Rowberry, "Reassessing the *Gravity's Rainbow* Pynchon Wiki: a new research paradigm?," *Orbit: A Journal of American Literature* 1:1 (2012): 1–25, https://doi.org/10.7766/orbit.v1.1.24.

25 Martin Paul Eve, "Did Thomas Pynchon Write Cow Country? Stylistic Affinities and Divergences," *Martineve.com*, June 11, 2017, https://eve.gd/2017/06/11/did-thomas-pynchon-write-cow-country-stylistic-affinities-and-divergences/.

26 The similar suspicion that Pynchon may have authored the so-called "Wanda Tinasky Letters" was debunked by some analog stylistic analysis but mostly biographical detective work. Don Foster, *Author Unknown* (New York: Holt, 2001), 188–219.

27 Ben Blatt, *Nabokov's Favourite Word Is Mauve* (London: Simon & Schuster, 2017).

28 Ibid., 69–70.

29 Ibid., 154–61.

30 Blatt, *Nabokov's Favourite Word*, 148–54.

31 Mark Davies, *The Corpus of Historical American English (COHA): 400 Million Words, 1810–2009* (2010–), accessed September 1, 2019, https://www.english-corpora.org/coha/.

32 Blatt, *Nabokov's Favourite Word*, 167.

33 "freeway, n.," *OED Online*, Oxford University Press, accessed April 13, 2019, http://www.oed.com/view/Entry/74436?redirectedFrom=freeway.

34 Katie Muth, "The Grammars of the System: Thomas Pynchon at Boeing," *Textual Practice* 33:3 (2019): 473–93. https://doi.org/10.1080/0950236X.2019.1580514.

35 Andrew W. E. McDonald, Sadia Afroz, Aylin Caliskan, Ariel Stolerman, and Rachel Greenstadt, "Use Fewer Instances of the Letter 'i': Toward Writing Style Anonymization," *Lecture Notes in Computer Science* 7384 (2012): 299–318.

36 Maciej Eder, "Does Size Matter? Authorship Attribution, Small Samples, Big Problem," *Digital Scholarship in the Humanities* 30:2 (2015): 167–82.

37 Underwood, *Distant Horizons*, 59.

38 Ibid., 48.

39 Katie Muth, "Digital Readings," in *The New Pynchon Studies*, ed. Joanna Freer (Cambridge: Cambridge University Press, 2019).

40 Ibid., 187.

41 Ibid., 190.

42 Paul Razzell, "*Inherent Vice* Diagrammed," accessed July 1, 2021, https://inherent-vice.com.

Bibliography

Works by Thomas Pynchon

Against the Day. New York: Penguin, 2006.

"A Journey into the Mind of Watts." *New York Times Magazine*, June 12, 1966. https://archive.nytimes.com/www.nytimes.com/books/97/05/18/reviews/pynchon-watts.html?_.

Bleeding Edge. New York: Penguin, 2013.

The Crying of Lot 49. New York: Lippincott, 1966.

"Entropy." *Kenyon Review* 22 (1960): 277–92.

Foreword to *Nineteen Eighty-Four*, by George Orwell. New York: Plume, 2003, vii–xxvi.

Gravity's Rainbow. New York: Viking, 1973.

"The Heart's Eternal Vow." *New York Times Book Review*, April 10, 1998. https://www.nytimes.com/1988/04/10/books/the-heart-s-eternal-vow.html.

Inherent Vice. New York: Penguin, 2009.

Introduction to *Been Down So Long It Looks Like Up to Me*, by Richard Fariña. New York: Penguin, 1983, v–xiv.

Introduction to *Stone Junction*, by Jim Dodge. Edinburgh: Rebel, 1997, vii–xii.

Introduction to *The Teachings of Don B.*, by Donald Barthelme. New York: Turtle Bay, 1992, xv–xxii.

"Is It O.K. to Be a Luddite?" *New York Times Book Review*, October 28, 1984. https://archive.nytimes.com/www.nytimes.com/books/97/05/18/reviews/pynchon-luddite.html?.

"Letter to the Editor." *New York Times Book Review*, July 17, 1966, 22, 24.

"Low-Lands." *New World Writing* 16 (1960): 85–108.

Mason & Dixon. New York: Henry Holt, 1997.

"Mortality and Mercy in Vienna." *Epoch* 9:4 (1959): 195–213.

"Nearer, My Couch to Thee." *New York Times Book Review*, June 6, 1993. https://archive.nytimes.com/www.nytimes.com/books/97/05/18/reviews/pynchon-sloth.html.

Slow Learner. New York: Little, Brown, 1984.

"The Secret Integration." *Saturday Evening Post* (December 19–26, 1964): 36–7, 39, 42–4, 46–9, 51.

"The Shrink Flips." *Cavalier* 16 (March 1966): 32–3, 88–92.

"The World (This One), The Flesh (Mrs. Oedipa Maas), and the Testament of Pierce Inver-arity." *Esquire* 64 (December 1965): 170–3, 296, 298–303.

"Under the Rose." *Noble Savage* 3 (1961): 223–51.

V. New York: Harper Perennial Classics, [1963]1999.

V. London: Vintage Books, [1963] 2000.

Vineland. New York: Little, Brown, 1990.

Comparison Corpora Texts

Peers Corpus

Atwood, Margaret. *Alias Grace*. New York: Anchor, [1996] 2011.

Atwood, Margaret. *The Handmaid's Tale*. New York: Anchor, [1985] 1998.

Barth, John. *Every Third Thought*. New York: Counterpoint, [2011] 2012.

Barth, John. *Giles Goat-Boy*. New York: Doubleday, 1966.

Barthelme, Donald. *Flying to America: 45 More Stories*. New York: Counterpoint, 2007.

Barthelme, Donald. *Snow White*. New York: Touchstone, [1967] 1996.

DeLillo, Don. *Underworld*. New York: Scribner, 1997.

DeLillo, Don. *White Noise*. New York: Viking, 1985.

Gaddis, William. J R. New York: Penguin, [1975] 1993.

Gaddis, William. *The Recognitions*. Normal, IL: Dalkey Archive Press, [1955] 1999.

McCarthy, Cormac. *Blood Meridian*. New York: Vintage, [1985] 1992.

McCarthy, Cormac. *The Road*. New York: Vintage, [2006] 2009.

Morrison, Toni. *Paradise*. New York: Vintage, [1997] 2014.

Morrison, Toni. *Song of Solomon*. New York: Vintage, [1977] 2004.

Reed, Ishmael. *Mumbo Jumbo*. New York: Scribner, [1972] 1996.

Reed, Ishmael. *The Terrible Twos*. Normal, IL: Dalkey Archive Press, [1982] 1999.

Popular Fiction Corpus

King, Stephen. *Carrie*. New York: Anchor, [1974] 2011.

King, Stephen. *Cell*. New York: Hodder & Stoughton, [2006] 2011.

King, Stephen. *IT*. New York: Signet, [1986] 1987.

Patterson, James. *Along Came a Spider*. New York: Little, Brown, [1993] 2001.

Patterson, James. *Cross My Heart*. New York: Grand Central, [2013] 2014.

Patterson, James. *The Thomas Berryman Number*. New York: Grand Central, [1976] 2015.

Steel, Danielle. *Daddy*. New York: Dell, [1989] 2009.

Steel, Danielle. *Passion's Promise*. New York: Dell, [1977] 1985.

Steel, Danielle. *Toxic Bachelors*. New York: Dell, [2005] 2008.

Influence Corpus

Erickson, Steve. *Days Between Stations*. New York: Simon & Schuster, 1985.

Erickson, Steve. *Zeroville*. New York: Europa Editions, 2007.

Powers, Richard. *Galatea 2.2*. New York: Farrar Straus & Giroux, 1995.

Powers, Richard. *The Echo Maker*. New York: Picador, 2006.

Smith, Zak. *We Did Porn: Memoir and Drawings*. New York: Tin House Books, 2009.

Vollmann, William T. *Europe Central*. New York: Viking, 2005.

Vollmann, William T. *Whores for Gloria*. New York: Pantheon, 1991.

Wallace, David Foster. *Infinite Jest*. New York: Back Bay Books, [1996] 2006.

Wallace, David Foster. *The Broom of the System*. New York: Penguin Classics, [1987] 2016.

Bibliography

Abbas, Niran Bahjat. "Introduction." In *Thomas Pynchon: Reading from the Margins*, edited by Niran Bahjat Abbas, 17–34. Cranbury, NJ: Associated University Presses, 2003.

Adams, Michael. *In Praise of Profanity*. Oxford: Oxford University Press, 2016.

Adorno, Theodor. "'Late Style' in Beethoven." In *Essays on Music by Theodor W. Adorno*, edited by R. Leppert, 564–8. Berkeley: University of California Press, 2002.

Adorno, Theodor. "Punctuation Marks." *Antioch Review* 48:3 (1990): 300–5.

Algee-Hewitt, Mark, and Mark McGurl. "Between Canon and Corpus: Six Perspectives on 20th-Century Novels." *Pamphlets of the Stanford Literary Lab* 8 (2015): 1–27. https://litlab.stanford.edu/LiteraryLabPamphlet8.pdf.

Alsen, Eberhard. *Romantic Postmodernism in American Fiction*. Amsterdam: Rodopi B. V., 1996.

Ames, Christopher. "Power and the Obscene Word: Discourses of Extremity in Thomas Pynchon's *Gravity's Rainbow*." *Contemporary Literature* 31:2 (1990): 191–207.

Andersen, Tore Rye. "Mapping the World: Thomas Pynchon's Global Novels." *Orbit: A Journal of American Literature* 4:1 (2016): 1–40.

Andersen, Tore Rye. "Pay Attention! David Foster Wallace and his Real Enemies." *English Studies* 95:1 (2014): 7–24.

Anonymous. *The Confessional Unmasked: Showing the Depravity of the Romish Priesthood, the Iniquity of the Confessional and the Questions Put to Females in Confession*. London: Protestant Electoral Union, 1867.

Anthony, Laurence. *AntWordProfiler* (Version 1.4.1). Tokyo: Waseda University, 2018. http://www.laurenceanthony.net/software.

Archer, Jodie, and Matthew L. Jockers. *The Bestseller Code*. New York: St. Martin's Press, 2016.

Baldwin, James. *The Fire Next Time*. New York: Vintage International, 1993.

Baron, Alistair, and Paul Rayson. "VARD 2: A Tool for Dealing with Spelling Variation in Historical Corpora." In *Proceedings of the Postgraduate Conference in Corpus Linguistics*. Birmingham: Aston University, 2008.

Barthes, Roland. *S/Z*. Oxford: Blackwell, 1996.

Bell, Robert, and William Dowling. *A Reader's Companion to* Infinite Jest. Self-published, 2005.

Benea, Diana. "Post-modernist Sensibility in Thomas Pynchon's *Bleeding Edge.*" *British and American Studies* 21 (2015): 143–51.

Benn, Gottfried. "Altern als Problem für Künstler." In *Gottfried Benn: Sämtliche Werke, Volume 6*, edited by G. Schuster and H. Hof, 123–51. Stuttgart: Klett, 1989.

Bird, Steven, Edward Loper, and Ewan Klein. *Natural Language Processing with Python.* Sebastopol, CA: O'Reilly Media, 2009.

Blakeborough, Richard. *Wit, Character, Folklore and Customs of the North Riding of Yorkshire.* London: Henry Frowde, 1898.

Blatt, Ben. *Nabokov's Favourite Word Is Mauve.* London: Simon & Schuster, 2017.

Blei, David M., Andrew Ng, and Michael Jordan. "Latent Dirichlet allocation." *Journal of Machine Learning Research* 3 (2003): 993–1022.

Bloom, Harold. *The Anxiety of Influence: A Theory of Poetry*, 2nd ed. Oxford: Oxford University Press, 1975.

Bonanos, Christopher. "Tom Wolfe, Pioneer of New York and New Journalism, Dies at 88." *New York Magazine*, May 15, 2018. https://www.vulture.com/2018/05/tom-wolfe-new-york-and-new-journalism-legend-dies-at-88.html.

Bosmajian, Haig A. "Introduction." In *Obscenity and Freedom of Expression*, edited by Haig A. Bosmajian, ii–v. New York: Burt Franklin, 1976.

Brezina, Vaclav. *Statistics in Corpus Linguistics.* Cambridge: Cambridge University Press, 2018.

Britton, W. Earl. "Effects of Science and Technology upon Our Language." *College Composition and Communication* 21:5 (1970): 342–6.

Broch, Hermann. "Mythos und Altersstil." In *Schriften zur Literatur 2: Theorie*, edited by P. M. Lützeler, 212–34. Frankfurt: Suhrkamp, 1995.

Brontë, Charlotte. "Editor's Preface to the New Edition of *Wuthering Heights.*" *Wuthering Heights.* Edinburgh: Turnbull and Spears, 1850.

Brown, Keith, and Jim Miller. *The Cambridge Dictionary of Linguistics.* Cambridge: Cambridge University Press, 2013.

Brunner, Annelen. "Automatic Recognition of Speech, Thought, and Writing Representation in German Narrative Texts." *Literary and Linguistic Computing* 28:4 (2013): 563–75.

Brunner, Annelen. *Automatische Erkennung von Redewiedergabe: Ein Beitrag zur quantitativen Narratologie.* Berlin: De Gruyter, 2015.

Burke, Michael. "Stylistics: From Classical Rhetoric to Cognitive Neuroscience." In *The Routledge Handbook of Stylistics*, edited by Michael Burke, 1–7. London: Routledge, 2014.

Burke, Michael, ed. *The Routledge Handbook of Stylistics.* London: Routledge, 2014.

Burke, Michael, and Kristy Evans. "Formalist Stylistics." In *The Routledge Handbook of Stylistics*, edited by Michael Burke, 31–44. London: Routledge, 2014.

Burrows, John F. *Computation into Criticism: A Study of Jane Austen's Novels and an Experiment in Method*. Oxford: Clarendon Press, 1987.

Burrows, John F. "Not Unless You Ask Nicely: The Interpretative Nexus between Analysis and Information." *Literary and Linguistic Computing* 7:2 (1992): 91–109.

Carroll, Sean M. "Review of *Bleeding Edge*." *Nature* 501 (2013): 312–13.

Carswell, Sean M. "The *Vineland* Guide to Contemporary Rebellion." *Orbit: Writing Around Pynchon* 1:1 (2012): 1–27.

Celmer, Paul W., Jr. "Pynchon's *V.* and the Rhetoric of the Cold War." *Pynchon Notes* 32–3 (1993): 5–32.

Chen, Tsung O. "Acronymophilia: The Exponential Growth of the Use of Acronyms Should Be Resisted." *BMJ: British Medical Journal* 309:6956 (1994): 683–4.

Chetwynd, Ali, Joanna Freer, and Georgios Maragos, eds. *Thomas Pynchon, Sex, and Gender*. Athens: University of Georgia Press, 2018.

Chorier-Fryd, Bénédicte. "Deadpan to Demonic—Subtextual Uses of Science in Thomas Pynchon's *Inherent Vice*." In *Science and American Literature in the 20th and 21st Centuries*, edited by Claire Maniez, Ronan Ludot-Vlasak, and Frédéric Dumas, 19–30. Newcastle upon Tyne: Cambridge Scholars, 2012.

Chudacoff, Howard P. *Children at Play: An American History*. New York: New York University Press, 2007.

Clerc, Charles. "Introduction." In *Approaches to* Gravity's Rainbow, edited by Charles Clerc, 3–30. Columbus: Ohio State University Press, 1983.

Clerc, Charles. Mason & Dixon & *Pynchon*. Lanham: University Press of America, 2000.

Clinton, Alan Ramón. *Intuitions in Literature, Technology, and Politics*. New York: Palgrave MacMillan, 2012.

Clubb, Merrel D., Jr, "The Second Personal Pronoun in *Moby-Dick*." *American Speech* 35:4 (1960): 252–60.

Cohn, Jan. *Creating America: George Horace Lorimer and* The Saturday Evening Post. Pittsburgh: University of Pittsburgh Press, 1989.

Collins, Cornelius. "A Discussion of Thomas Pynchon's New Novel at MLA 2014." *Pynchon at the Bleeding Edge*, August 20, 2013. https://bleedingedge.mla.hcommons.org/2013/08/20/panel-description/.

Cooper, Peter L. *Signs and Symptoms: Thomas Pynchon and the Contemporary World*. Berkeley: University of California Press, 1983.

Cowart, David. "Love and Death: Variations on a Theme in Pynchon's Early Fiction." *Journal of Narrative Technique* 7:3 (1977): 157–69.

Cowart, David. *The Tribe of Pyn: Literary Generations in the Postmodern Period*. Ann Arbor: University of Michigan Press, 2015.

Cowart, David. *Thomas Pynchon: The Art of Allusion*. Carbondale: Southern Illinois University Press, 1980.

Cowart, David. *Thomas Pynchon and the Dark Passages of History*. Athens: University of Georgia Press, 2011.

Crews, Frederick. *The Random House Handbook*, 4th ed. New York: Random House, 1984.

Crumbley, Paul. "Dickinson's Dashes and the Limits of Discourse." *Emily Dickinson Journal* 1:2 (1992): 8–29.

Crumbley, Paul. *Inflections of the Pen: Dash and Voice in Emily Dickinson*. Louisville: University Press of Kentucky, 1997.

Crystal, David. *Language and the Internet*, 2nd ed. Cambridge: Cambridge University Press, 2006.

Crystal, David. *The Cambridge Encyclopedia of the English Language*, 2nd ed. Cambridge: Cambridge University Press, 2003.

Crystal, David, and Derek Davy. *Investigating English Style*. London: Longman, 1969.

Dalsgaard, Inger H. "Readers and Trespassers: Time Travel, Orthogonal Time, and Alternative Figurations of Time in *Against the Day*." In *Pynchon's* Against the Day: *A Corrupted Pilgrim's Guide*, edited by Jeffrey Severs and Christopher Leise, 115–37. Newark: University of Delaware Press, 2006.

Dalsgaard, Inger H., Luc Herman, and Brian McHale, eds. *The Cambridge Companion to Thomas Pynchon*. Cambridge: Cambridge University Press, 2012.

Dandala, Bharath, Rada Mihalcea, and Razvan Bunescu. "Multilingual Word Sense Disambiguation Using Wikipedia." In *Proceedings of the 6th International Joint Conference on Natural Language Processing*. Asian Federation of Natural Language Processing, 2013.

Dannells, Dana. "Automatic Acronym Recognition." In *EACL '06 Proceedings of the 11th Conference of the European Chapter of the Association for Computational Linguistics*, 167–70. Stroudsburg: Association for Computational Linguistics, 2006.

Darby, David. "Form and Context: An Essay in the History of Narratology." *Poetics Today* 22:4 (2001): 829–52.

Davies, Mark. "Looking at Recent Changes in English with the Corpus of Contemporary American English (COCA)." *The 21st Century Text* 1 (2011). https://21centurytext.wordpress.com/2012/06/15/changes-in-english-with-coca/.

Davies, Mark. "Making Google Books N-Grams Useful for a Wide Range of Research on Language Change." *International Journal of Corpus Linguistics* 19:3 (2014): 401–16.

Davies, Mark. "The Corpus of Contemporary American English: 520 Million Words, 1990–2015." Accessed September 1, 2019. http://corpus.byu.edu/coca/.

Davies, Mark. "*The Corpus of Historical American English (COHA): 400 million words, 1810–2009* (2010–)." Accessed September 1, 2019. https://www.english-corpora.org/coha/.

Davies, Mark. "The Corpus of Historical American English (COHA), Google Books (Standard), and the Google Books (BYU / Advanced) corpus." Accessed September 1, 2019. https://googlebooks.byu.edu/compare-googleBooks.asp.

Davis, Christina, and Toni Morrison. "Interview with Toni Morrison." *Présence Africaine* 145 (1988): 141–50.

Daw, Laurence. "The Ellipsis as Architectonic in *Gravity's Rainbow*." *Pynchon Notes* 11 (1983): 54–6.

de Bourcier, Simon. *Pynchon and Relativity: Narrative Time in Thomas Pynchon's Later Novels*. London: Continuum Literary Studies, 2012.

de Bourcier, Simon. "Representations of Sexualized Children and Child Abuse in Thomas Pynchon's Fiction." In *Thomas Pynchon, Sex, and Gender*, edited by Ali Chetwynd, Joanna Freer, and Georgios Maragos, 145–61. Athens: University of Georgia Press, 2018.

Defoe, Daniel. *Robinson Crusoe*, edited by J. W. Clark. London: MacMillan, 1866.

Deppman, Jed. "Trying to Think with Emily Dickinson." *Emily Dickinson Journal* 14:1 (2005): 84–103.

Derrida, Jacques. *Writing and Difference*. London: Routledge and Kegan Paul, 1978.

Dickie, Margaret. "Dickinson's Discontinuous Lyric Self." *American Literature* 60:4 (1988): 537–553.

Dickinson, Emily. *The Poems of Emily Dickinson*, edited by Thomas H. Johnson. Cambridge, MA: Belknap Press of Harvard University Press, 1955.

Dodson, Steve. "David Foster Wallace Demolished." *Language Hat*, April 12, 2002. http://languagehat.com/david-foster-wallace-demolished/.

Doody, Terrence. "*Against the Day* by Thomas Pynchon." *Houston Chronicle*, December 3, 2006. https://www.chron.com/life/books/article/Against-the-Day-by-Thomas-Pynchon-1560368.php.

Dugdale, John. *Thomas Pynchon: Allusive Parables of Power*. Basingstoke: Macmillan, 1990.

Duyfhuizen, Bernard. "A Suspension Forever at the Hinge of Doubt: The Reader-Trap of Bianca in *Gravity's Rainbow*." *Postmodern Culture* 2:1 (1991). https://muse.jhu.edu/article/27320.

Duyfhuizen, Bernard. "'God Knows, Few of Us Are Strangers to Moral Ambiguity': Thomas Pynchon's *Inherent Vice*." *Postmodern Culture* 19:2 (2009). https://muse.jhu.edu/article/366239/.

Duyfhuizen, Bernard. "Review: Taking Stock: 26 Years since *V.* (Over 26 Books on Pynchon!)." *NOVEL: A Forum on Fiction* 23:1 (1989): 75–88.

Duyfhuizen, Bernard. "Review: Thomas H. Schaub, *Pynchon: The Voice of Ambiguity*." *Journal of American Studies* 16:2 (1982): 314–15.

Duyfhuizen, Bernard. "'The Exact Degree of Fictitiousness': Thomas Pynchon's *Against the Day*." *Postmodern Culture* 17:2 (2007). doi:10.1353/pmc.2007.0018.

Dyer, Geoff. "My literary allergy." *Prospect*, March 23, 2011. https://www.prospectmagazine.co.uk/magazine/geoff-dyer-david-foster-wallace-pale-king-literary-allergy.

Earl, James W. "Tom's Longest Sentence." *Literary Imagination* 14:2 (2012): 197–210.

Eco, Umberto. *How to Travel with a Salmon and Other Essays*. New York: Harcourt, 1994.

Eco, Umberto. *Interpretation and Overinterpretation*. Cambridge: Cambridge University Press, 1992.

Eco, Umberto. *The Infinity of Lists: From Homer to Joyce*. London: McLehose
    Press, 2009.
Eder, Maciej. "Does Size Matter? Authorship Attribution, Small Samples, Big Problem."
    Digital Scholarship in the Humanities 30:2 (2015): 167–82.
Editors of N+1. "The Novel: The Way Out Is In." *N+1* 2 (2005). https://nplusonemag.
    com/issue-2/the-intellectual-situation/way-out/.
Edwards, Brian. "Surveying 'America': In *The Mnemonick Deep Of Thomas Pynchon's
    Mason & Dixon*." *Australasian Journal of American Studies* 23 (2004): 21–30.
Eichner, Hans. *"Romantic" and Its Cognates: The European History of a Word*.
    Toronto: University of Toronto Press, 1972.
Elias, Amy J. *Sublime Desire: History and Post-1960s Fiction*. Baltimore: Johns Hopkins
    University Press, 2001.
Empson, William. *Seven Types of Ambiguity*. London: Chatto and WIndus, 1930.
Eve, Martin Paul. *Close Reading with Computers: Textual Scholarship, Computational
    Formalism, and David Mitchell's* Cloud Atlas. Stanford: Stanford University
    Press, 2019.
Eve, Martin Paul. "Did Thomas Pynchon Write Cow Country? Stylistic Affinities
    and Divergences." *Martineve.com*, June 11, 2017. https://eve.gd/2017/06/11/
    did-thomas-pynchon-write-cow-country-stylistic-affinities-and-divergences/.
Eve, Martin Paul. *Pynchon and Philosophy: Wittgenstein, Foucault and Adorno*.
    Basingstoke: Palgrave Macmillan, 2014.
Eve, Martin Paul. "Visualizing *Gravity's Rainbow*." *Martineve.com*, June 7, 2015. https://
    eve.gd/2015/06/07/visualizing-gravitys-rainbow/.
Evert, Stefan, and Andrew Hardie. "Twenty-First Century Corpus
    Workbench: Updating a Query Architecture for the New Millennium." In
    Proceedings of the Corpus Linguistics 2011 Conference. Birmingham: University of
    Birmingham, 2011.
Faraone, Mario. "Traveling and Spying into Baedeker's Land." In *Dream Tonight of
    Peacock Tails: Essays on the Fiftieth Anniversary of Thomas Pynchon's V.*, edited by
    Paolo Simonetti and Umberto Rossi, 53–74. Newcastle upon Tyne: Cambridge
    Scholars, 2015.
Finn, Ed. "The Social Lives of Books: Literary Networks in Contemporary American
    Fiction." PhD diss., Stanford University, 2011.
Fish, Stanley. *Is There a Text in This Class: The Authority of Interpretive Communities*,
    Cambridge, MA: Harvard University Press, [1973] 1980.
Fischer, Andreas, and Peter Schneider. "The Dramatick Disappearance of the
    <-ick> Spelling." In *Text Types and Corpora: Studies in Honor of Udo Fries*,
    edited by Andreas Fischer, Gunnel Tottie, and Hans Martin Lehmann, 139–50.
    Tübingen: Gunter Narr Verlag, 2002.
Fludernik, Monika. *The Fictions of Language and the Languages of Fiction*.
    London: Routledge, 1993.
Foster, Don. *Author Unknown: On the Trail of Anonymous*. New York: Holt, 2001.

Fowler, Douglas. *A Reader's Guide to* Gravity's Rainbow. Ann Arbor: Ardis, 1980.

Franzen, Jonathan. "Mr. Difficult: William Gaddis and the Problem of Hard-to-Read Books." *New Yorker*, September 30, 2002, 100–11.

Freer, Joanna. *Thomas Pynchon and the American Counterculture*. Cambridge: Cambridge University Press, 2014.

Gabilliet, Jean-Paul. *Of Comics and Men: A Cultural History of American Comic Books*. Jackson: University Press of Mississippi, 2010.

Gandolfo, Anita. *Faith and Fiction: Christian Literature in America Today*. London: Praeger, 2007.

Gazi, Jeeshan. "Mapping the Metaphysics of the Multiverse in Pynchon's *Against the Day*." *Critique: Studies in Contemporary Fiction* 57:1 (2016): 80–93.

Gelder, Ken. *Popular Fiction: The Logics and Practices of a Literary Field*. London: Routledge, 2004.

Getelman, Lisa. *Paper Knowledge: Toward a Media History of Documents*. Durham: Duke University Press, 2014.

Gibbs, Rodney. "A Portrait of the Luddite as a Young Man." *Denver Quarterly* 39:1 (2004): 35–42.

Giesbrecht, Eugenie, and Stefan Evert, "Part-of-Speech (POS) Tagging—a Solved Task? An Evaluation of POS Taggers for the Web as Corpus." *Proceedings of the Fifth Web as Corpus Workshop (WAC5)*, 27–35. Donostia, San Sebastian, 2009.

Gilmore, Leigh. "Obscenity, Modernity, Identity: Legalizing *The Well of Loneliness* and *Nightwood*." *Journal of the History of Sexuality* 4:4 (1994): 603–24.

Girodias, Maurice. "Lolita, Nabokov and I." *Evergreen Review* 37 (1965): 44–7, 89–91.

Goldstone, Andrew, and Ted Underwood. "What Can Topic Models of PMLA Teach Us about the History of Literary Scholarship?" *Journal of Digital Humanities* 2:1 (2012). http://journalofdigitalhumanities.org/2-1/what-can-topic-models-of-pmla-teach-us-by-ted-underwood-and-andrew-goldstone/.

Grant, J. Kerry. *A Companion to* The Crying of Lot 49, 2nd ed. Athens: University of Georgia Press, 2008.

Grant, J. Kerry. *A Companion to* V. Athens: University of Georgia Press, 2001.

Green, Clarence. "Introducing the Corpus of the Canon of Western Literature: A Corpus for Culturomics and Stylistics." *Language and Literature* 26:4 (2017): 282–99.

Grose, Francis. *A Classical Dictionary of the Vulgar Tongue*, 2nd ed. London: S. Hooper, 1788.

Gula, Marianna. *A Tale of the Pub: Re-Reading the "Cyclops" of James Joyce's "Ulysses" in the Context of Irish Cultural Nationalism* (Debrecen: DU Press, 2012).

Gussow, Mel. "Pynchon's Letters Nudge His Mask." *New York Times*, March 4, 1998. http://www.nytimes.com/1998/03/04/books/pynchon-s-letters-nudge-his-mask.html.

Hägg, Samuli. *Narratologies of* Gravity's Rainbow. Joensuu: University of Joensuu, 2005.

Hänggi, Christian. "The Pynchon Playlist: A Catalogue and Its Analysis." *Orbit: A Journal of American Literature* 6:1 (2018): 1–35.

Hänggi, Christian. "Pynchon's Sonic Fiction." PhD diss., University of Basel, 2017.

Hänggi, Christian. *Pynchon's Sound of Music.* Zurich: Diaphenes, 2020.

Hardack, Richard. "Consciousness without Borders: Narratology in *Against the Day* and the Works of Thomas Pynchon." *Criticism* 52:1 (2010): 91–128.

Hardack, Richard. "'From Whaling to Armaments to Food': Melville's, Pynchon's, and Wedde's Economies of the Pacific." *Critique: Studies in Contemporary Fiction* 54:2 (2013): 161–80.

Harley, Heidi. "Why Is It *The* CIA but Not *The NASA? Acronyms, Initialisms, and Definite Description." *American Speech* 79:4 (2004): 368–99.

Hawthorne, Mark D. "A 'Hermaphrodite Sort of Deity': Sexuality, Gender, and Gender Blending in Thomas Pynchon's *V.*" *Studies in the Novel* 29:1 (1997): 74–93.

Haynes, Doug. "'Gravity Rushes through Him': *Volk* and Fetish in Pynchon's Rilke." *MFS Modern Fiction Studies* 58:2 (2012): 308–33.

Hecht, Anthony. "The Riddles of Emily Dickinson." *New England Review* 1:1 (1978): 1–24.

Heiden, Serge. "The TXM Platform: Building Open-Source Textual Analysis Software Compatible with the TEI Encoding Scheme." In *24th Pacific Asia Conference on Language, Information and Computation*, 389–98. Tokyo: Waseda University, 2010.

Herman, Luc. "Early Pynchon." In *The Cambridge Companion to Thomas Pynchon*, edited by Inger H. Dalsgaard, Luc Herman, and Brian McHale, 19–29. Cambridge: Cambridge University Press, 2012.

Herman, Luc. "Narratology." In *Thomas Pynchon in Context*, edited by Inger H. Dalsgaard, 273–80. Cambridge: Cambridge University Press, 2019.

Herman, Luc. "Reading Pynchon in and on the Digital Age." In *The New Pynchon Studies*, edited by Joanna Freer, 196–209. Cambridge: Cambridge University Press, 2019.

Herman, Luc, and John M. Krafft. "Fast Learner: The Typescript of Pynchon's *V.* at the Harry Ransom Center in Austin." *Texas Studies in Literature and Language* 49:1 (2007): 1–20.

Herman, Luc, and John M. Krafft. "Race in Early Pynchon: Rewriting Sphere in *V.*" *Critique: Studies in Contemporary Fiction* 52:1 (2011): 17–29.

Herman, Luc, and Steven Weisenburger. Gravity's Rainbow, *Domination, and Freedom.* Athens: University of Georgia Press, 2013.

Herman, Luc, Robert Hogenraad, and Wim van Mierlo. "Pynchon, Postmodernism and Quantification: An Empirical Content Analysis of Thomas Pynchon's *Gravity's Rainbow.*" *Language and Literature* 12:1 (2003): 27–41.

Herrmann, J. Berenike. "In a Test Bed with Kafka. Introducing a Mixed-Method Approach to Digital Stylistics." *Digital Humanities Quarterly* 11:4 (2017). http://www.digitalhumanities.org/dhq/vol/11/4/000341/000341.html.

Hermann, J. Berenike, Karina van Dalen-Oskam, and Christof Schöch. "Revisiting Style, a Key Concept in Literary Studies." *Journal of Literary Theory* 9:1 (2015): 25–52.

Hess, John Joseph. "Music in Thomas Pynchon's *Gravity's Rainbow*." *Orbit: A Journal of American Literature* 2:2 (2014): 1–36.

Hill, Logan. "Pynchon's Cameo, and Other Surrealities." *New York Times*, September 26, 2014. https://www.nytimes.com/2014/09/28/movies/paul-thomas-anderson-films-inherent-vice.html.

Hiller, Jack H. "Verbal Response Indicators of Conceptual Vagueness." *American Educational Research Journal* 8:1 (1971): 151–61.

Hiller, Jack H., Donald R. Marcotte, and Timothy Martin. "Opinionation, Vagueness, and Specificity-Distinctions: Essay Traits Measured by Computer." *American Educational Research Journal* 6:2 (1969): 271–86.

Hinds, Elizabeth Jane Wall. "Sari, Sorry, and the Vortex of History: Calendar Reform, Anachronism, and Language Change in *Mason & Dixon*." *American Literary History* 12:1–2 (2000): 187–215.

Hinds, Elizabeth Jane Wall, ed. *The Multiple Worlds of Pynchon's* Mason & Dixon. New York: Camden House, 2005.

Hite, Molly. *Ideas of Order in the Novels of Thomas Pynchon*. Columbus: Ohio State University Press, 1983.

Hite, Molly. "When Pynchon Was a Boys' Club: *V.* and Midcentury Mystifications of Gender." In *Thomas Pynchon, Sex, and Gender*, edited by Ali Chetwynd, Joanna Freer, and Georgios Maragos, 3–16. Athens: University of Georgia Press, 2018.

Hogenraad, Robert. "Smoke and Mirrors: Tracing Ambiguity in Texts." *Digital Scholarship in the Humanities* 33:2 (2018): 297–315.

Hohmann, Charles. *Angel and Rocket: Pynchon's* Gravity's Rainbow *and Rilke's* Duino Elegies. Norderstedt: Books on Demand GmbH, 2009.

Hohmann, Charles. *Thomas Pynchon's* Gravity's Rainbow, *A Study of Its Conceptual Structure and of Rilke's Influence*. New York: Peter Lang, 1986.

Holland, Mary K. *Succeeding Postmodernism: Language and Humanism in Contemporary American Literature*. London: Bloomsbury, 2013.

Hoover, David L. "Another Perspective on Vocabulary Richness." *Computers and the Humanities* 37 (2003): 151–78.

Hoover, David L. "Corpus Stylistics, Stylometry, and the Styles of Henry James." *Style* 41:2 (2007): 174–203.

Hoover, David L. "Modes of Composition in Henry James: Dictation, Style, and What Maisie Knew." *Henry James Review* 35:3 (2014): 257–77.

Hoover, David L. *Language and Style in* The Inheritors. Lanham: University Press of America, 1999.

Hoover, David L. "The Microanalysis of Style Variation." *Digital Scholarship in the Humanities* 32:2 (2017): ii17—ii18.

Hoover, David L. "Quantitative Analysis and Literary Studies." In *A Companion to Digital Literary Studies*, edited by Ray Siemens and Susan Schreibman, 517–33. Oxford: Blackwell, 2013.

Hollander, Charles. "Pynchon's Politics: The Presence of an Absence." *Pynchon Notes* 26–7 (1990): 5–59.

Horn, Clayton W. "From the Decision by Judge Clayton W. Horn." In *Howl on Trial: The Battle for Free Expression*, edited by Bill Morgan and Nancy J. Peters, 197–9. San Francisco: City Lights Books, 2006.

Horvath, Brooke, and Irving Malin, eds. *Pynchon and* Mason & Dixon. Newark: University of Delaware Press, 2000.

Houston, Keith. *Shady Characters: Ampersands, Interrobangs and Other Typographical Curiosities*. London: Particular Books, 2013.

Howard, Gerald. "Pynchon From A to V: Gerald Howard on *Gravity's Rainbow*." *Bookforum* 12:2 (Summer 2005): 29–40. http://www.bookforum.com/archive/sum_05/pynchon.html.

Hughes, Geoffrey. *Swearing: A Social History of Foul Language, Oaths, and Profanity in English*. London: Penguin Books, 1998.

Hume, Kathryn. *Pynchon's Mythography: An Approach to* Gravity's Rainbow. Carbondale: Southern Illinois University Press, 1987.

Hume, Kathryn. "Repetition and Construction of Character in *Gravity's Rainbow*." *Critique: Studies in Contemporary Fiction* 33:4 (1992): 243–54.

Hume, Kathryn, and Thomas J. Knight. "Pynchon's Orchestration of *Gravity's Rainbow*." *Journal of English and Germanic Philology* 85:3 (1986): 366–85.

Hunt, J. W., and M. D. McIlroy. "An Algorithm for Differential File Comparison." *Bell Laboratories Computing Science Technical Report* 41 (1976): 1–9.

Hurley, Patrick. *Pynchon Character Names*. Jefferson, NC: McFarland, 2008.

Ikeo, Reiko. "An Analysis of Viewpoints by the Use of Frequent Multi-Word Sequences in DH Lawrence's *Lady Chatterley's Lover*." *Language and Literature* 25:2 (2016): 159–84.

Indeherberg, Lindsay. "What You Cannot Avoid: Thomas Pynchon's *Inherent Vice* as a Pastiche of Hard-boiled Detective Fiction." Master's thesis, University of Antwerp, 2015.

Jakobson, Roman. "Closing Statement: Linguistics and Poetics." In *Style in Language*, edited by T. A. Sebeok, 350–77. Cambridge, MA: MIT. Press, 1960.

James, Caryn. "Wittgenstein Is Dead and Living in Ohio." *New York Times*, March 1, 1987. https://www.nytimes.com/1987/03/01/books/wittgenstein-is-dead-and-living-in-ohio.html.

Jameson, Frederick. *DM's Opera Site*, accessed September 1, 2019. http://www.murashev.com/opera/opera.php?opera_id=35.

Jannidis, Fotis. "On the Perceived Complexity of Literature. A Response to Nan Z. Da." *Journal of Cultural Analytics*, June 17, 2019. https://culturalanalytics.org/article/11829-on-the-perceived-complexity-of-literature-a-response-to-nan-z-da.

Jarvis, Michael. "Pynchon's Deep Web." *Los Angeles Review of Books*, September 10, 2013. https://lareviewofbooks.org/article/pynchons-deep-web/.

Jeffries, Lesley, and Dan McIntyre, eds. *Stylistics*. Cambridge: Cambridge University Press, 2010.

Joyce, James. *Ulysses*. New York: Modern Library, 1992.

Jung, Ena. "The Breath of Emily Dickinson's Dashes." *Emily Dickinson Journal* 24:2 (2015): 1–23.

Kachka, Boris. "On the Thomas Pynchon Trail: From the Long Island of His Boyhood to the 'Yupper West Side' of His New Novel." *New York Magazine*, August 25, 2013. http://www.vulture.com/2013/08/thomas-pynchon-bleeding-edge.html.

Käkelä-Puumala, Tina. *Other Side of This Life: Death, Value and Social Being in Thomas Pynchon's Fiction*. Helsinki: Yliopistopaino, 2007.

Kakutani, Michiko. "Another Doorway to the Paranoid Pynchon Dimension." *New York Times*, August 3, 2009. https://www.nytimes.com/2009/08/04/books/04kaku.html.

Kakutani, Michiko. "Books of the Times; Life in Cleveland, 1990." *New York Times*, December 28, 1986. https://www.nytimes.com/1986/12/27/books/books-of-the-times-life-in-cleveland-1990.html.

Kane, Thomas S. *The Oxford Essential Guide to Writing*. Oxford: Oxford University Press, 2000.

Keesey, Douglas. "*Mason & Dixon* on the Line: A Reception Study." *Pynchon Notes* 36–9 (1996): 165–78.

Kenner, Hugh. *Joyce's Voices*. Berkeley: University of California Press, 1978.

Ketzan, Erik, and Christof Schöch. "Classifying and Contextualizing Edits in Variants with Coleto: Three Versions of Andy Weir's *The Martian*." *Digital Humanities Quarterly*, publication forthcoming.

Ketzan, Erik, and Christof Schöch. "What Changed When Andy Weir's *The Martian* Got Edited?" In *Digital Humanities 2017, Conference Book of Abstracts*. Montréal: McGill University and Université de Montréal, 2017.

Ketzan, Erik, Jens Stegmann, and Andreas Witt. "Building a Pynchon Corpus: Technical and Legal Issues." *Pynchon Week 2015*. Athens, Greece, June 11, 2015.

Kihss, Peter. "Pulitzer Jurors Dismayed on Pynchon." *New York Times*, May 8, 1974. http://www.nytimes.com/1974/05/08/archives/pulitzer-jurors-his-third-novel.html?_r=0.

Kolbuszewski, Zofia. *The Poetics of Chronotope in the Novels of Thomas Pynchon*. Lublin: Learned Society of the Catholic University of Lublin, 2000.

Konstantinou, Lee. *Cool Characters, Irony and American Fiction*. Cambridge: Harvard University Press, 2016.

Kučera, Henry, and W. Nelson Francis. *Computational Analysis of Present-Day English*. Providence: Brown University Press, 1967.

Ladenson, Elisabeth. *Dirt for Art's Sake: Books on Trial from* Madame Bovary *to* Lolita. Ithaca: Cornell University Press, 2007.

Lakoff, Robin. "Remarks on This and That." In *Papers from the Tenth Regional Meeting, Chicago Linguistic Society*, edited by Michael W. La Gary, Robert A. Fox, and Anthony Bruck, 345–56. Chicago: Chicago Linguistic Society, 1974.

Lambrou, Marina, and Peter Stockwell. "Introduction: The State of Contemporary Stylistics." In *Contemporary Stylistics*, edited by Marina Lambrou and Peter Stockwell, 1–4. New York: Continuum, 2007.

Larkey, Leah S., Paul Ogilvie, M. Andrew Price, and Brenden Tamilio. "Acrophile: An Automated Acronym Extractor and Server." In *DL '00 Proceedings of the fifth ACM conference on Digital libraries* , 205–214. (2000). https://dl.acm.org/doi/pdf/10.1145/336597.336664.

Lass, Roger. "Phonology and Morphology." In *The Cambridge History of the English Language*, Volume III, edited by Roger Lass, 149–53. Cambridge: Cambridge University Press, 2008.

LeClair, Tom. "The Prodigious Fiction of Powers, William Vollmann, and David Foster Wallace." *Critique* 38:1 (1996): 12–37.

Leech, Geoffrey N. *Language in Literature: Style and Foregrounding*. London: Pearson Education, 2008.

Leech, Geoffrey N., and Mick Short. *Style in Fiction: A Linguistic Introduction to English Fictional Prose*, 2nd ed. New York: Pearson Longman, 2007.

Leland, John P. "Pynchon's Linguistic Demon." *Critique: Studies in Contemporary Fiction* 16:2 (1974): 45–53.

Lemee, Scott. "You Hide, They Seek." *Inside Higher Ed*, November 15, 2006. https://www.insidehighered.com/views/2006/11/15/you-hide-they-seek.

Letzler, David. "A Phenomenology of the Present: Toward a Digital Understanding of *Gravity's Rainbow*." *Orbit: A Journal of American Literature* 4:2 (2016): 1–32.

Letzler, David. "Crossed-Up Disciplinarity: What Norbert Wiener, Thomas Pynchon, and William Gaddis Got Wrong about Entropy and Literature." *Contemporary Literature* 56:1 (2015): 23–55.

Letzler, David. *The Cruft of Fiction: Mega-Novels and the Science of Paying Attention*. Lincoln: University of Nebraska Press, 2017.

Levine, George. "Risking the Moment: Anarchy and Possibility in Pynchon's Fiction." In *Mindful Pleasures: Essays on Thomas Pynchon*, edited by George Levine and David Leverenz, 113–36. Boston: Little, Brown, 1976.

Liberman, Mark. "CD Tilde Home." *Language Log*, October 1, 2013. http://languagelog.ldc.upenn.edu/nll/?p=7420.

Liberman, Mark. "Comment to 'Moar Verbs.'" *Language Log*, March 24, 2015. http://languagelog.ldc.upenn.edu/nll/?p=18398.

Liberman, Mark. "Generational Punctuation Differences Again." *Language Log*, August 1, 2014. http://languagelog.ldc.upenn.edu/nll/?p=13723.

Liberman, Mark. "How Alphabetic Is the Nature of Molecules." *Language Log*, September 27, 2004. http://itre.cis.upenn.edu/~myl/languagelog/archives/001498.html.

Liberman, Mark. "Proportion of Dialogue in Novels." *Language Log*, December 29, 2017. http://languagelog.ldc.upenn.edu/nll/?p=35968.

Liberman, Mark. "The G.K. Chesterton Prize for Ignoring Women." *Language Log*, October 6, 2015. http://languagelog.ldc.upenn.edu/nll/?p=21536.

Liberman, Mark. "The Google Books Settlement." *Language Log*, August 28, 2009. http://languagelog.ldc.upenn.edu/nll/?p=1698.

Liberman, Mark. "The Price of Wisdom." *Language Log*, December 16, 2014. http://languagelog.ldc.upenn.edu/nll/?p=16498.

Liberman, Mark. "The Syntonic Phonetics of Pynchon's Pitchuhv." *Language Log*, January 9, 2007. http://itre.cis.upenn.edu/~myl/languagelog/archives/004023.html.

Lin, Yuri, Jean-Baptiste Michel, Erez Lieberman Aiden, Jon Orwant, William Brockman, and Slav Petrov. "Syntactic Annotations for the Google Books Ngram Corpus." In *Proceedings of the 50th Annual Meeting of the Association for Computational Linguistics* Volume 2: Demo Papers (Jeju Island, Korea: 2012).

Locke, Richard. "One of the Longest, Most Difficult, Most Ambitious Novels in Years." *New York Times Book Review*, March 11, 1973. https://archive.nytimes.com/www.nytimes.com/books/97/05/18/reviews/pynchon-rainbow.html.

Logan, William. "On the Connections between Poetry and Fiction." In *Thomas Pynchon: Bloom's Major Novelists*, edited by Harold Bloom, 138–42. Broomall, PA: Chelsea House, 2003.

Logan, Willam. "Pynchon in the Poetic." *Southwest Review* 83:4 (1998): 424–37.

Luce, Dianne C. "On the Trail of History in McCarthy's *Blood Meridian*." *Mississippi Quarterly* 49:4 (1996): 843–9.

Lynd, Margaret. "Situated Fictions. Reading the California Novels against Thomas Pynchon's Narrative World." In *Pynchon's California*, edited by Scott McClintock and John Miller, 15–34. Iowa City: University of Iowa Press, 2014.

Madsen, Deborah L. "Ambiguity." In *Thomas Pynchon in Context*, edited by Inger H. Dalsgaard, 298–306. Cambridge: Cambridge University Press, 2019.

Madsen, Deborah L. "Family Legacies: Identifying the Traces of William Pynchon in *Gravity's Rainbow*." *Pynchon Notes* 42–3 (1998): 29–48.

Maguire, Michael P. "September 11 and the Question of Innocence in Thomas Pynchon's *Against the Day* and *Bleeding Edge*." *Critique: Studies in Contemporary Fiction* 58:2 (2017): 95–107.

Mahlberg, Michaela. *Corpus Stylistics and Dickens's Fiction*. London: Routledge, 2013.

Mahlberg, Michaela. "Corpus stylistics." In *The Routledge Handbook of Stylistics*, edited by Michael Burke, 378–92. London: Routledge, 2014.

Mallegg, Kristen, ed. *Acronyms, Initialisms & Abbreviations Dictionary*, 49th ed. Detroit: Cengage Gale, 2015.

Maltby, Paul. *Dissident Postmodernists: Barthelme, Coover, Pynchon*. Philadelphia: University of Pennsylvania Press, 1991.

Manning, Christopher D., and Hinrich Schütze. *Foundations of Natural Language Processing*. Cambridge, MA: MIT Press, 1999.

Martindale, Colin. *Romantic Progression: The Psychology of Literary History.*
    Washington, DC: Hemisphere, 1975.

Martindale, Colin. "The Night Journey: Trends in the Content of Narratives
    Symbolizing Alteration of Consciousness." *Journal of Altered States of Consciousness*
    4:4 (1979): 321–43.

Martineau, Paris. "Why ... Do Old People ... Text ... Like This ...? An Investigation
    ..." *The Outline*, February 8, 2018, https://theoutline.com/post/3333/
    why-do-old-people-text-like-this-an-investigation?zd=1&zi=qx76aecq.

Martínez, M. Angeles. "From 'Under the Rose' to *V.*: A Linguistic Approach to Human
    Agency in Pynchon's Fiction." *Poetics Today* 23:4 (2002): 633–56.

Mason, A. Hughlett. *The Journal of Charles Mason and Jeremiah Dixon.*
    Philadelphia: American Philosophical Society, 1969.

Mason, Fran. *Historical Dictionary of Postmodernist Literature and Theater*, 2nd ed.
    New York: Rowman & Littlefield, 2017.

Mason, Paul. "Is This Thomas Pynchon's 'Late Style?'" *BBC News*, July 31, 2009. https://
    www.bbc.co.uk/blogs/newsnight/paulmason/2009/07/is_this_thomas_pynchons_
    late_s.html.

Mattessich, Stefan. *Lines of Flight: Discursive Time and Countercultural Desire in the
    Work of Thomas Pynchon.* Durham: Duke University Press, 2002.

Matthews, P. H. *The Concise Oxford Dictionary of Linguistics*, 2nd ed. Oxford: Oxford
    University Press, 2007.

Max, D. T. *Every Love Story is a Ghost Story: A Life of David Foster Wallace.*
    London: Granta, 2012.

McCaffery, Larry. "A Conversation with William T. Vollmann." In *William
    T. Vollmann: Selected Interviews*, edited by Scott Rhodes, 10–50. Self-
    published, 2015.

McCaffery, Larry. "An Interview with David Foster Wallace." *Review of Contemporary
    Fiction* 13:2 (1993): 127–50.

McCarthy, Cormac. *The Crossing.* New York: Vintage, 1995.

McClure, David. "(Mental) Maps of Texts." *Dclure.org*, September 24, 2014. http://
    dclure.org/essays/mental-maps-of-texts/.

McCulloch, Gretchen. "A Linguist Explains the Syntax of 'Fuck.'" *The Toast*, December
    9, 2014, http://the-toast. net/2014/12/09/linguist-explains-syntax-f-word/.

McDonald, Andrew W. E., Sadia Afroz, Aylin Caliskan, Ariel Stolerman, and
    Rachel Greenstadt. "Use Fewer Instances of the Letter 'i': Toward Writing Style
    Anonymization." *Lecture Notes in Computer Science* 7384 (2012): 299–318.

McEnery, Anthony, and Zhonghua Xiao. "Swearing in Modern British English: The
    Case of Fuck in the BNC." *Language and Literature* 13 (2004): 235–68.

McEnery, Tony. *Swearing in English: Bad Language, Purity, and Power from 1586 to the
    Present.* London: Routledge, 2006.

McEnery, Tony, Paul Baker, and Andrew Hardie. "Swearing and Abuse in Modern British English." In *Practical Applications of Language Corpora*, edited by Barbara Lewandowska-Tomaszczyk and Patrick Melia, 37–48. Hamburg: Peter Lang, 2000.

McEnery, Tony, Richard Xiao, and Yukio Tono. *Corpus-Based Language Studies: An Advanced Resource Book*. London: Routledge, 2006.

McGirr, Elaine. "Interiorities." In *The Cambridge History of the English Novel*, edited by Robert L. Caserio and Clement Hawes, 80–96. Cambridge: Cambridge University Press, 2012.

McHale, Brian. *Constructing Postmodernism*. New York: Routledge, 1992.

McHale, Brian. "Genre as History: Pynchon's Genre-Poaching." In *Pynchon's* Against the Day: *A Corrupted Pilgrim's Guide*, edited by Jeffrey Severs and Christopher Leise, 15–28. Maryland: University of Delaware Press, 2011.

McHale, Brian. "Mason & Dixon in the Zone, or, a Brief Poetics of Pynchon-Space." In *Pynchon and Mason & Dixon*, edited by Brooke Horvath and Irving Malin, 43–62. Newark: University of Delaware Press, 2000.

McHale, Brian. "Pynchon's Postmodernism." In *The Cambridge Companion to Thomas Pynchon*, edited by Inger H. Dalsgaard, Luc Herman, and Brian McHale, 97–111. Cambridge: Cambridge University Press, 2012.

McHale, Brian. "Slade Revisited, or, The End(s) of Pynchon Criticism." *Pynchon Notes* 26–7 (1990): 139–52.

McHale, Brian. "Whatever Happened to Descriptive Poetics." In *The Point of Theory: Practices in Cultural Analysis*, edited by Mieke Bal and Inge E. Boer, 56–65. Amsterdam: Amsterdam University Press, 1994.

McHoul, Alec, and David Wills. *Writing Pynchon*. London: Macmillan, 1990.

McLaughlin, Robert L. "Movie Music in *Gravity's Rainbow*." *Pynchon Notes* 28–9 (1991): 143–5.

McLaughlin, Robert L. "Wallace's Aesthetic." In *The Cambridge Companion to David Foster Wallace*, edited by Ralph Clare, 159–72. Cambridge: Cambridge University Press, 2018.

Mead, Clifford. *Thomas Pynchon: A Bibliography of Primary and Secondary Materials*. Elmwood Park: Dalkey Press Archive, 1989.

Medoro, Dana. "Traces of Blood and the Matter of a Paraclete's Coming: The Menstrual Economy of Pynchon's *V.*" *Pynchon Notes* 44–5 (1999): 14–34.

Meister, Jan Christoph. "Narratology." In *The Living Handbook of Narratology*, edited by Peter Hühn, Jan Christoph Meister, John Pier, and Wolf Schmid, University of Hamburg, January 19, 2014, https://www.lhn.uni-hamburg.de/index.html.

Melby, Caleb. "The Generation Gap in Online Punctuation: An Open Letter (and Revised Style Guide) to Digital English." *Forbes*, May 8, 2013. https://www.forbes.com/sites/calebmelby/2013/05/08/the-generation-gap-in-online-punctuation-an-open-letter-and-revised-style-guide-to-digital-english/.

Mendelson, Edward. "Encyclopedic Narrative: From Dante to Pynchon." *MLN* 91:6 (1976): 1267–75.

Mendelson, Edward. "Gravity's Encyclopedia." In *Mindful Pleasures: Essays on Thomas Pynchon*, edited by George Levine and David Leverenz, 161–95. Boston: Little, Brown, 1976.

Mendelson, Edward. "The Sacred, the Profane, and *The Crying of Lot 49*." In *Individual and Community: Variations on a Theme in American Fiction*, edited by Kenneth H. Baldwin and David K. Kirby, 183–222. Durham: Duke University Press, 1975.

Merryweather, L. W. "Hell in American Speech." *American Speech* 6:6 (1931): 433–5.

Metcalf, Allan A. *OK: The Improbable Story of America's Greatest Word*. Oxford: Oxford University Press, 2011.

Michel, Jean-Baptiste, Yuan Kui Shen, Aviva Presser Aiden, Adrian Veres, Matthew K. Gray, William Brockman, The Google Books Team, Joseph P. Pickett, Dale Hoiberg, Dan Clancy, Peter Norvig, Jon Orwant, Steven Pinker, Martin A. Nowak, and Erez Lieberman Aiden. "Quantitative Analysis of Culture Using Millions of Digitized Books." *Science* 331:6014 (2011): 176–82.

Millard, Bill. "Pynchon's Coast: *Inherent Vice* and the Twilight of the Spatially Specific." In *Pynchon's California*, edited by Scott McClintock and John Miller, 65–90. Iowa City: University of Iowa Press, 2014).

Millard, William B. "Delineations of Madness and Science: *Mason & Dixon*, Pynchonian Space and the Snovian Disjunction." In *American Postmodernity: Essays on the Recent Fiction of Thomas Pynchon*, edited by Ian D. Copestake, 83–127. New York: Peter Lang, 2003.

Mitchell, David. "Interview with David Mitchell." Interview by Carolyn Kellogg. *Goodreads*, July 5, 2019. https://www.goodreads.com/interviews/show/537. David_Mitchell.

Miyamoto, Yoichiro. "*Gravity's Rainbow* and the Question of Postmodernism." *Studies in English Literature* 65:2 (1989): 209–27.

Mobili, Giorgio. *Irritable Bodies and Postmodern Subjects in Pynchon, Puig, Volponi*. New York: Peter Lang, 2008.

Morgan, Ted. *Literary Outlaw: The Life and Times of William S. Burroughs*. London: Pimlico, 1988.

Mozart, Wolfgang Amadeus. *Don Giovanni*, translated by Norman Platt and Laura Salti. Surrey: Alma Books, 2017.

Muth, Katie. "Digital Readings." In *The New Pynchon Studies*, edited by Joanna Freer, 175–94. Cambridge: Cambridge University Press, 2019.

Muth, Katie. "The Grammars of the System: Thomas Pynchon at Boeing." *Textual Practice* 33:3 (2019): 473–93.

Nazaryan, Alexander. "The Lush Life of William T. Vollmann." *Newsweek*, November 6, 2013. http://www.newsweek.com/2013/11/08/lush-life-william-t-vollmann-243896.html.

Nazaryan, Alexander. "The Turbulent Genius of David Foster Wallace." *Newsweek*, January 8, 2015. http://www.newsweek.com/2015/01/16/turbulent-genius-david-foster-wallace-297688.html.

Neighbors, Jim. "Kant, Terror and Aporethics in *Gravity's Rainbow*." *Pynchon Notes* 42–3 (1998): 275–91.

Nelson, Michael. "Pynchon's *Bleeding Edge* a Challenging, Rewarding Read." *Post and Courier*, February 15, 2014. http://www.postandcourier.com/features/arts_and_travel/pynchon-s-bleeding-edge-a-challenging-rewarding-read/article_8f5ae3f1-27fb-5f57-a836-15103f9a424a.html.

Newton, Maud. "Another Thing to Sort of Pin on David Foster Wallace." *New York Times*, August 19, 2011. https://www.nytimes.com/2011/08/21/magazine/another-thing-to-sort-of-pin-on-david-foster-wallace.html?src=tp.

Norvig, Peter. "English Letter Frequency Counts: Mayzner Revisited or ETAOIN SRHLDCU." 2013. http://norvig.com/mayzner.html.

Oates, Joyce Carol. "Introduction." In *The Essential Emily Dickinson*, edited by Joyce Carol Oates, ix–xxv. New York: Ecco, [1996] 2016.

Ochsner, Robert. "Rhythm in Literature and Low Style." *Style* 19:2 (1985): 258–81.

OED Online. Oxford: Oxford University Press, 2019. http://www.oed.com/.

Ohge, Christopher. "Introduction: Computation and Digital Text Analysis at Melville's Marginalia Online." *Leviathan: A Journal of Melville Studies* 20:2 (2018): 1–16.

Ohmann, Richard. "Generative Grammars and the Concept of Literary Style." *Word: Journal of the Linguistic Circle of New York* 20:3 (1964): 423–39.

Osgood, Charles E. "Some Effects of Motivation on Style of Encoding." In *Style in Language*, edited by T. A. Sebeok, 293–306. Cambridge, MA: Technology Press of MIT, 1960.

Palmer, Alan. "Attribution Theory: Action and Emotion in Dickens and Pynchon." In *Contemporary Stylistics*, edited by Marina Lambrou and Peter Stockwell, 81–92. New York: Continuum, 2007.

Palmer, Alan. *Fictional Minds*. Lincoln: University of Nebraska Press, 2004.

Partridge, Eric. *The Routledge Dictionary of Historical Slang*, 6th ed. London: Routledge, 2006.

Pascal, Roy. *The Dual Voice. Free Indirect Speech and Its Functioning in the Nineteenth-Century European Novel*. Manchester: Manchester University Press, 1977.

Pechenick, Eitan Adam, Christopher M. Danforth, and Peter Sheridan Dodds. "Characterizing the Google Books Corpus: Strong Limits to Inferences of Socio-Cultural and Linguistic Evolution." *PLoS ONE* 10:10 (2015): 1–24.

Peck, Dale. *Hatchet Jobs*. New York: New Press, 2004.

Peters, Nancy J. "Milestones of Literary Censorship." In *Howl on Trial: The Battle for Free Expression*, edited by Bill Morgan and Nancy J. Peters, 5–13. San Francisco: City Lights Books, 2006.

Phillips, Forest. "The Star Wars Franchise, Fan Edits, and Lucasfilm." In *Fan/Remix Video*, edited by Francesca Coppa and Julie Levin Russo. https://doi.org/10.3983/twc.2012.0385.

Pilpel, Harriet F., and Nancy F. Wechsler. "The Law and *Lady Chatterley*." *New World Writing* 16, edited by Stewart Richardson and Corlies M. Smith, 231–40. New York: J. B. Lippincott Company, 1960.

Pinkal, Manfred. *Logic and Lexicon*. London: Kluwer Academic, 1995.

Piper, Andrew. *Enumerations: Data and Literary Study*. Chicago: University of Chicago Press, 2018.

Plater, William M. *The Grim Phoenix: Reconstructing Thomas Pynchon*. Bloomington: Indiana University Press, 1978.

Poelitz, Christian, and Thomas Bartz. "Enhancing the Possibilities of Corpus-Based Investigations: Word Sense Disambiguation on Query Results of Large Text Corpora." In *Proceedings of the 8th Workshop on Language Technology for Cultural Heritage, Social Sciences, and Humanities (LaTeCH)*, 42–6. Gothenburg, 2014.

Pöhlmann, Sascha. "Pynchon and Post-postmodernism." In *The New Pynchon Studies*, edited by Joanna Freer, 17–32. Cambridge: Cambridge University Press, 2019.

Pöhlmann, Sascha. "Silences and Worlds: Wittgenstein and Pynchon." *Pynchon Notes* 56–7 (2009): 158–80.

Poirier, Richard. "Cook's Tour." *New York Review of Books*, June 1, 1963. https://www.nybooks.com/articles/1963/06/01/cooks-tour/.

Porter, J. D., Mark Algee-Hewitt, Erik Fredner, Michaela Bronstein, Alexander Manshel, Nichole Nomura, and Abigail Droge. "Microgenres." In *DH2019 Conference Book of Abstracts*. Utrecht, 2019.

Powers, David M. *Damnable Heresy: William Pynchon, the Indians, and the First Book Banned (and Burned) in Boston*. Eugene: Wipf & Stock, 2015.

Pütz, Manfred. "The Art of the Acronym in Thomas Pynchon." *Studies in the Novel* 23:3 (1991): 371–82.

Pütz, Manfred. "John Barth's *The Sot-Weed Factor*: The Pitfalls of Mythopoesis." *Twentieth Century Literature* 22:4 (1976): 454–66.

Quilligan, Maureen. *The Language of Allegory: Defining the Genre*. Ithaca: Cornell University Press, 1979.

Raclaw, Joshua. "Punctuation as Social Action: The Ellipsis as a Discourse Marker in Computer-Mediated Communication." In *The Proceedings of the 32nd Annual Berkeley Linguistics Society*. Berkeley: 2006.

Ramsay, Stephen. *Reading Machines: Toward an Algorithmic Criticism*. Urbana: University of Illinois Press, 2011.

Rayson, Paul. "Matrix: A Statistical Method and Software Tool for Linguistic Analysis through Corpus Comparison." PhD diss., Lancaster University, 2003.

Rayson, Paul. "Wmatrix: A Web-Based Corpus Processing Environment, Computing Department." Lancaster: Lancaster University, 2009. Accessed May 12, 2017. http://ucrel.lancs.ac.uk/wmatrix/.

Razzell, Paul. "*Inherent Vice* Diagrammed." Accessed July 1, 2021. https://inherent-vice.com.

Rebora, Simone, and Massimo Salgaro, "Is 'Late Style' Measurable? A Stylometric Analysis of Johann Wolfgang Goethe's, Robert Musil's, and Franz Kafka's Late Works." *Elephant & Castle* 18 (2018): 1–40.

Reeve, Jonathan Pearce. "Does 'Late Style' Exist? New Stylometric Approaches to Variation in Single-Author Corpora." In *Digital Humanities 2018 Book of Abstracts*. Mexico City: AHDO, 2018, 478–81.

Rich, Nathaniel. "The Thomas Pynchon Novel for the Edward Snowden Era." *The Atlantic*, October 2013. https://www.theatlantic.com/magazine/archive/2013/10/losing-the-plot/309450/.

Rolls, Albert. "The Two *V*.s of Thomas Pynchon, or from Lippincott to Jonathan Cape and Beyond." *Orbit: Writing Around Pynchon* 1:1 (2012): 1–6.

Ronneberger-Sibold, Elke. "Word Creation." In *Variation and Change in Morphology: Selected Papers from the 13th International Morphology Meeting, Vienna, February 2008*, edited by Franz Rainer, Wolfgang U. Dressler, Dieter Kastovsky, and Hans Christian Luschützky, 201–16. Philadelphia: John Benjamins, 2010.

Rosenbaum, Jonathan. "Pynchon on the Beach." *Slate.com*, August 2, 2009. https://slate.com/culture/2009/08/thomas-pynchon-s-inherent-vice.html.

Rothfork, John. "Cormac McCarthy as Pragmatist." *Critique: Studies in Contemporary Fiction* 47:2 (2006): 201–16.

Rothwell, J. Dan. "Verbal Obscenity: Time for Second Thoughts." *Western Speech* 35 (1971): 231–42.

Rouyan, Anahita. "Singing Thomas Pynchon's *Gravity's Rainbow*." *Journal of Literature and the History of Ideas* 15:1 (2017): 117–33.

Rovit, Earl. "The Novel as Parody: John Barth." *Critique: Studies in Contemporary Fiction* 6:2 (1963): 77–85.

Rowberry, Simon. "Reassessing the *Gravity's Rainbow* Pynchon Wiki: A New Research Paradigm?" *Orbit: A Journal of American Literature* 1:1 (2012): 1–25.

Ruggiero, Salvatore. "The Closed Circuit Game: A Hippie Noir." *Critical Flame: A Journal of Literature & Culture* 3 (2009). http://criticalflame.org/the-closed-circuit-game-a-hippie-noir/.

Rushdie, Salman. "Still Crazy after All These Years." *New York Times*, January 14, 1990. http://www.nytimes.com/books/97/05/18/reviews/pynchon-vineland.html.

Ryckx, Michel. "Thomas Pynchon (1937–): A Bibliography of Secondary Materials." *Vheissu.net*. Accessed September 1, 2019. http://www.vheissu.net/biblio/.

Said, Edward. *On Late Style*. London: Bloomsbury, 2006.

Salmon, Vivian. "Orthography and Punctuation." In *The Cambridge History of the English Language*, Volume III, edited by Roger Lass. Cambridge: Cambridge University Press, 2008.

Saltzmann, Arthur. "'Cranks of Ev'ry Radius': Romancing the Line in *Mason & Dixon*." In *Pynchon and* Mason & Dixon, edited by Brooke Horvath and Irving Malin, 63–72. Cransbery, NJ: Associated University Presses, 2000.

Santorini, Beatrice. "Part-of-Speech Tagging Guidelines for the Penn Treebank Project." 1991. http://www.cis.uni-muenchen.de/~schmid/tools/TreeTagger/data/Penn-Treebank-Tagset.pdf.

Sawyer, Thomas W. "*J R*: The Narrative of Entropy." *International Fiction Review* 10:2 (1983): 117–22.

Schaub, Thomas. *Pynchon: The Voice of Ambiguity*. Urbana: University of Illinois Press, 1981.

Schmid, Helmut. "Improvements in Part-of-Speech Tagging with an Application to German." In *Proceedings of the ACL SIGDAT-Workshop*. Dublin, 1995.

Schmid, Helmut. "Probabilistic Part-of-Speech Tagging Using Decision Trees." In *Proceedings of International Conference on New Methods in Language Processing*. Manchester, 1994.

Schmid, Helmut. "TreeTagger—a part-of-speech tagger for many languages." Accessed May 12, 2017. http://www.cis.uni-muenchen.de/~schmid/tools/TreeTagger/.

Schmidt, Benjamin M. "Words Alone: Dismantling Topic Models in the Humanities." *Journal of Digital Humanities* 2:1 (2012). http://journalofdigitalhumanities.org/2-1/words-alone-by-benjamin-m-schmidt/.

Schreibman, Susan, Ray Siemens, and John Unsworth. "The Digital Humanities and Humanities Computing: An Introduction." In *A Companion to Digital Humanities*, edited by Susan Schreibman, Ray Siemens, and John Unsworth. Oxford: Blackwell, 2004. http://www.digitalhumanities.org/companion/.

Schroeder, Ralph, and Matthijs L. den Besten. "Literary Sleuths Online: E-Research Collaboration on the Pynchon Wiki." *Information, Communication & Society* 11:2 (2008): 25–45.

Schulz, Max F. *Black Humor Fiction of the Sixties*. Athens: Ohio University Press, 1973.

Scragg, D. G. *A History of English Spelling*. Manchester: Manchester University Press, 1974.

Searle, John R. *The Rediscovery of the Mind*. Cambridge: MIT Press, 1992.

Sears, Julie C. "Black and White Rainbows and Blurry Lines: Sexual Deviance/Diversity in *Gravity's Rainbow* and *Mason & Dixon*." In *Thomas Pynchon: Reading from the Margins*, edited by Niran Abbas, 108–21. Danvers: Rosemont, 2003.

Seed, David. *The Fictional Labyrinths of Thomas Pynchon*. London: Macmillan Press, 1988.

Shen, Dan. "How Stylisticians Draw on Narratology: Approaches, Advantages and Disadvantages." *Style* 39:4 (2005): 381–95.

Shen, Dan. "Stylistics and Narratology." In *The Routledge Handbook of Stylistics*, edited by Michael Burke, 191–205. New York: Routledge, 2014.

Siegel, Jason. "Meatspace Is Cyberspace: The Pynchonian Posthuman in *Bleeding Edge*." *Orbit: A Journal of American Literature* 4:2 (2016): 1–27.

Siegel, Jules. "Who Is Thomas Pynchon … and Why Did He Take Off with My Wife?" *Playboy*, March 1977, 97, 122, 168–74.

Siegel, Mark Richard. *Pynchon: Creative Paranoia in* Gravity's Rainbow. Port Washington: Kennikat Press, 1978.

Sigelman, Lee, and William Jacoby. "The Not-So-Simple Art of Imitation: Pastiche, Literary Style, and Raymond Chandler." *Computers and the Humanities* 30:1 (1996): 11–28.

Sigvardson, Joakim. *Immanence and Transcendence in Thomas Pynchon's* Mason & Dixon: *A Phenomenological Study*. Stockholm: Almquist & Wiksell, 2002.

Simpson, Paul. *Stylistics: A Resource Book for Students*. London: Routledge, 2004.

Sito, Tom. *Drawing the Line: The Untold Story of the Animation Unions from Bosko to Bart Simpson*. Lexington: University Press of Kentucky, 2006.

Slade, Joseph W. *Thomas Pynchon*. New York: Warner, 1974.

Smetak, Jacqueline R. "Who's Talking Here: Finding the Voice in *Gravity's Rainbow*." *Pynchon Notes* 20–1 (1987): 93–103.

Smith, Allan Lloyd. "American Gothic." In *The Handbook of the Gothic*, 2nd ed., edited by Marie Mulvey-Roberts, 267–75. New York: Palgrave Macmillan, 2009.

Smith, Allan Lloyd. "Postmodernism/Gothicism." In *Modern Gothic: A Reader*, edited by Victor Sage and Allan Lloyd Smith, 6–19. Manchester: Manchester University Press, 1996.

Smith, Mychelle Hadley. "Profanity, Disgust, and Dangerous Literature: A Hermeneutical Analysis of *The Catcher in the Rye* and *The Chocolate War*." PhD diss., Texas A&M University, 2015.

Smith, Shawn. *Pynchon and History: Metahistorical Rhetoric and Postmodern Narrative Form in the Novels of Thomas Pynchon*. New York: Routledge, 2005.

Smith, Zak. *Pictures Showing What Happens on Each Page of Thomas Pynchon's Novel* Gravity's Rainbow. New York: Tin House Books, 2006.

Snyder, Phillip A., Delys W. Snyder, and Jeremy Browne. "All Novels 1.0 in Sentence Structure Search (Experimental)." *The Cormac McCarthy Corpus Project*. Last modified November 14, 2019. http://cmcp.byu.edu/index.php/corpus-and-tool/all-novels-in-sentence-structure-search/.

Solberg, Sara. "On Comparing Apples and Oranges: James Joyce and Thomas Pynchon." *Comparative Literature Studies* 56:1 (1979): 33–40.

Somers, James. "Torching the Modern-Day Library of Alexandria." *The Atlantic*, April 20, 2017. https://www.theatlantic.com/technology/archive/2017/04/the-tragedy-of-google-books/523320/.

Sotirova, Violeta, ed. *A Bloomsbury Companion to Stylistics*. London: Bloomsbury, 2016.

Stark, John O. *Pynchon's Fictions: Thomas Pynchon and the Literature of Information*. Athens: Ohio University Press, 1980.

St. Clair, Justin. "Borrowed Time: Thomas Pynchon's *Against the Day* and the Victorian Fourth Dimension." *Science Fiction Studies* 38:1 (2011): 46–66.

Stanzel, F. K. *A Theory of Narrative*. Cambridge: Cambridge University Press, 1979.

Stockwell, Peter, and Sara Whitely, eds. *The Cambridge Handbook of Stylistics*. Cambridge: Cambridge University Press, 2014.

Stonehill, Brian. "Pynchon's Prophecies of Cyberspace." *Pynchon Notes* 34–5 (1994):13–14.

Stonum, Gary Lee. *The Dickinson Sublime*. Madison: University of Wisconsin Press, 1990.

Storey, Philip. "William Slothrop: Gentleman." *Pynchon Notes* 13 (1983): 61–70.

Strunk, William Jr., and E. B. White. *The Elements of Style*. New York: Macmillan, 1959.

Stubbs, Michael. "Conrad, Concordance, Collocation: Heart of Darkness or Light at the End of the Tunnel?" 2003. https://www.uni-trier.de/fileadmin/fb2/ANG/Linguistik/Stubbs/stubbs-2003-conrad-lecture.pdf.

Stubbs, Michael. "Conrad in the Computer: Examples of Quantitative Stylistic Methods." *Language and Literature* 14:1 (2005): 5–24.

Stubbs, Michael. *Words and Phrases: Corpus Studies of Lexical Semantics*. Oxford: Oxford University Press, 2001.

Sultanik, Aaron. *Inventing Orders*. Lanham: University Press of America, 2003.

Sussman, Mark, and Martin Paul Eve. "'A Shorthand of Stars': From John to Thomas Pynchon." *Orbit: A Journal of American Literature* 4:2 (2016): 1–7.

Swanson, Roy Arthur. "The Putative Second Edition of Slade's *Pynchon*." *Science Fiction Studies* 18 (1991): 262–6.

Tate, J. O. "*Gravity's Rainbow*: The Original Soundtrack." *Pynchon Notes* 13 (1983): 3–24.

Terras, Melissa, Julianne Nyhan, and Edward Vanhoutte, eds. *Defining Digital Humanities: A Reader*. London: Routledge, 2016.

Thomas, Samuel. *Pynchon and the Political*. New York: Routledge, 2007.

Thoreen, David. "The Economy of Consumption: The Entropy of Leisure in Pynchon's *Vineland*." *Pynchon Notes* 30–1 (1992): 53–62.

Toner, Anne. *Ellipsis in English Literature*. Cambridge: Cambridge University Press, 2015.

Trollope, Anthony. *The Bertrams*, Vol. III. London: Chapman & Hall, 1859.

Trollope, Anthony. *The Way We Live Now*. New York: Harper & Brothers, 1875.

Trucks, Rob. *The Pleasure of Influence: Conversations with American Male Fiction Writers*. West Lafayette, Indiana: Purdue University Press, 2002.

Tsatsoulis, Christos Iraklis. "Unsupervised Text Mining Methods for Literature Analysis: A Case Study for Thomas Pynchon's *V*." *Orbit: A Journal of American Literature* 1:2 (2013): 1–34.

Turner, Edwin. "Blog about Thomas Pynchon's Novel, *Bleeding Edge*." *Biblioklept.org*, May 8, 2020. https://biblioklept.org/2020/05/08/blog-about-thomas-pynchons-novel-bleeding-edge/.

Twose, Gareth. "What's in a Clause? Milton's Participial Style Revisited." *Language and Literature* 17:1 (2008): 77–9.

Uncredited. "Danger: Mad Professor at Work." *The Economist*, November 30, 2006. https://www.economist.com/node/8348701/print?story_id=8348701.

Uncredited. *Famouskin.com*. Accessed September 1, 2019. https://famouskin.com/famous-kin-chart.php?name=33543+emily+dickinson&kin=41896+thomas+pynchon&via=8735+edmund+reade.

Uncredited. "History of *The Saturday Evening Post*." Accessed September 1, 2019. https://www.saturdayeveningpost.com/history-saturday-evening-post/.

Uncredited. "Where's Thomas Pynchon?" *CNN.com*, June 5, 1997. http://edition.cnn.com/US/9706/05/pynchon/.

Underwood, Ted. *Distant Horizons: Digital Evidence and Literary Change*. Chicago: University of Chicago Press, 2019.

van Deemter, Kees. *Not Exactly: In Praise of Vagueness*. Oxford: Oxford University Press, 2010.

Vanwesenbeeck, Birger. "*Gravity's Rainbow*: A Portrait of the Artist as Engineer." *Pynchon Notes* 56–7 (2009): 144–57.

Vesterman, William. "Pynchon's Poetry." In *Mindful Pleasures: Essays on Thomas Pynchon*, edited by George Levine and David Leverenz, 101–12. Boston: Little, Brown, 1976.

Vidal, Gore. "American Plastic: The Matter of Fiction." *New York Review of Books*, July 15, 1976, 31–9.

von Ahn, Luis. "Offensive/Profane Word List." Accessed September 1, 2019. https://www.cs.cmu.edu/~biglou/resources/.

Wales, Katie. *A Dictionary of Stylistics*. Harlow: Pearson Education, 2011.

Ware, Tim, et al. *Pynchon Wiki*. Accessed September 1, 2019. https://pynchonwiki.com/.

Ware, Tim, and Andrew E. Mathis, et al. *Wallacewiki.com*. Accessed September 1, 2019. http://www.wallacewiki.com.

Weisenburger, Steven. *A* Gravity's Rainbow *Companion*, 2nd ed. Athens: University of Georgia Press, 2006.

Weisenburger, Steven. "Pynchon at Twenty-Two: A Recovered Autobiographical Sketch." *American Literature* 62:4 (1990): 692–7.

Weiss, Antonio, and Harold Bloom. "Harold Bloom, The Art of Criticism No. 1." *Paris Review* 118 (1991). https://www.theparisreview.org/interviews/2225/harold-bloom-the-art-of-criticism-no-1-harold-bloom.

Wickman, Forrest. "Thomas Pynchon and 'WTF: A Love Story.'" *Slate*, September 20, 2013. https://slate.com/culture/2013/09/thomas-pynchons-favorite-phrase-what-the-fuck-the-writer-is-our-great-poet-of-wtf.html.

Williams, C. B. "Sentence-Length as a Criterion of Literary Style." *Biometrika* 31:3–4 (1940): 356–61.

Winston, Mathew. "The Quest for Pynchon." *Twentieth Century Literature* 21:3 (1975): 278–87.

Wisnicki, Adrian. "A Trove of New Works by Thomas Pynchon? Bomarc Service News Rediscovered." *Pynchon Notes* 46–9 (2001): 9–34.

Witzling, David. *Everybody's America: Thomas Pynchon, Race, and the Cultures of Postmodernism*. London: Routledge, 2008.

Wood, James. "All Gravity, No Rainbow." *New Republic*, March 5, 2007. https:// newrepublic.com/article/63049/all-rainbow-no-gravity.

Wood, James. *The Irresponsible Self: On Laughter and the Novel*. London: Jonathan Cape, 2004.

Woodson, Thomas. "Ahab's Greatness: Prometheus as Narcissus." *ELH* 33:3 (1966): 351–69.

Wynne, Martin. "Stylistics: Corpus Approaches." In *The Encyclopedia of Language and Linguistics*, 2nd ed., edited by Keith Brown, 223–6. Oxford: Elsevier, 2006.

Wynne, Martin. "Review of *Corpus Stylistics in Principles and Practice. A Stylistic Exploration of John Fowles'* The Magus." *Literary and Linguistic Computing* 27:4 (2012): 474–6.

Yeates, Stuart. "Automatic Extraction of Acronyms from Text." In *Proceedings of Third New Zealand Computer Science Research Students' Conference*, 117–24. Hamilton, New Zealand, 1999.

Index

Adams, Henry 214
Adams, Michael 140
Adorno, Theodor 175, 207
Against the Day (Pynchon)
  acronyms 7, 115–21, 125
  archaic language 63
  characterization 25–6
  ellipsis marks 186
  the inanimate 102
  profanity 137–40
Algren, Nelson 214
Alias Grace (Atwood) 141
Alighieri, Dante 228
Along Came a Spider (Patterson) 127
Alsen, Eberhard 199
Ames, Christopher 134, 141, 145,
  153, 160–1
Amis, Martin 163
Andersen, Tore Rye 180, 183, 218
Atwood, Margaret 22, 81, 141, 179,
  215, 216
Austen, Jane 233

Baldwin, James 44
Barnes, Djuna 149
Barth, John
  acronyms 121–3, 126, 128
  ambiguity 81, 116
  comparison with Pynchon 214–16,
    218–19
  ellipsis marks 179, 181
  profanity 141
  stylistics 67
Barthelme, Donald
  acronyms 121, 125–6
  comparison with Pynchon 214,
    216, 229
  ellipsis marks 179, 181, 189
  profanity 158
Barthes, Roland 135
Bataille, Georges 200

Beach Boys, The 19
Beckett, Samuel 174
Bellow, Saul 214
Benn, Gottfried 207
Besig, Ernest 148
Bester, Alfred 214
Blatt, Ben 232–4
Bleeding Edge (Pynchon)
  acronyms 117–19, 124–5
  archaic language 63–4
  capitalization 47
  characterization 25–6, 28
  the inanimate 102
  least vague passages 104–7
  profanity 137–41, 163–4
  vagueness 7
Blei, David 228
Blood Meridian (McCarthy) 81
Bloom, Harold 75, 217
Bosmajian, Haig 142–3
Boswell, James 51–2, 59
Bradbury, Ray 214
Brennan, William J., Jr. 158
British Apollo, The 51
Broch, Hermann 207
Brontë, Charlotte 52
Brontë, Emily 52
Brussells, Jacob R. 147
Buchan, John 214
Burroughs, William S. 141, 152, 158,
  214, 218
Burrows, John F. 10
Byron, George, Lord 19, 151, 214

*Cambridge Encyclopedia of the English
  Language, The* 36
Cantos (Pound) 19
Carrie (King) 22, 179
Carroll, Lewis 18
Carroll, Sean M. 25
Carswell, Sean 47

Carter, Dale 6
Castle of Otranto, The (Walpole) 185
Chandler, Raymond 136, 162–3
Chen, Tsung O. 124
"Childe Harold's Pilgrimage" (Byron) 19
Chorier-Fryd, Bénédicte 185, 203 n.69
Christie, Agatha 22
Chudacoff, Howard 155
Cleland, John 158
Clerc, Charles 36–7, 162, 182–3
Clinton, Alan Ramón 41
Cloud Atlas (Mitchell) 65
Clubb, Merrel D., Jr. 66–7
CNN 73, 78
Cockburn, Alexander 142
Collins, Cornelius 16
Conrad, Joseph 3, 85–6, 174
Constructing Postmodernism (McHale) 4
Cooke, Ebenezer 67
Cooper, Peter L. 171, 184
Coover, Robert 218
Cormier, Robert 136
Cow Country (Jones) 232
Cowart, David 76, 150–1, 167 n. 60, 194,
      198, 214, 219
Crews, Frederick 175
Crumbley, Paul 195
Crystal, David 124

Daddy (Steel) 88
Das Rheingold (Wagner) 20
Daw, Laurence 171, 178, 183–4, 200
de Cervantes, Miguel 18
DeLillo, Don 8
   acronyms 126
   ambiguity 81–5
   comparison with Pynchon 214–16,
      219, 232
   ellipsis marks 179–80
den Besten, Matthijs 232
Deppman, Jed 195
Derrida, Jacques 175
Dick, Philip K. 214
Dickens, Charles 174
Dickie, Margaret 195
Dickinson, Emily 194–200
Dodge, Jim 78–9
Dugdale, John 153
Duino Elegies (Rilke) 191–2

Duyfhuizen, Bernard 25–6, 28, 115, 191
Dyer, Geoff 95

Earl, James W. 8, 176, 184, 186
Echo Maker, The (Powers) 127
Eco, Umberto 8, 175, 214
Eder, Maciej 234
Elias, Amy J. 67
Eliot, George 174
Eliot, T. S. 149, 214
"Entropy" (Pynchon) 44, 76, 146–50
Erickson, Steve 181, 215, 217–18
Europe Central (Vollmann) 229
Eve, Martin Paul 30, 67, 102, 230, 232
Every Third Thought (Barth) 179

Fanny Hill (Cleland) 158
Fariña, Richard 214
Faulkner, William 142–4, 214
Ferlinghetti, Lawrence 144
Fielding, Henry 52, 67
Finn, Ed 232
Fischer, Andreas 49
Fish, Stanley 9–10, 234
Fitzgerald, F. Scott 214
Flaubert, Gustave 87–8
Fleming, Ian 233–4
Fludernik, Monika 4, 207
Ford Foundation 20
Ford, Ford Maddox 174
Fowler, Douglas 184–5
Franzen, Jonathan 178
Freer, Joanna 75, 180

Gaddis, William 10
   acronyms 125
   ambiguity 81, 87, 95
   comparison with Pynchon 214–16,
      219, 229
   direct discourse 22
   ellipsis marks 176–81
Gaiman, Neil 214
Galatea 2.2 (Powers), 83
Gandolfo, Anita 82
Gass, William 214
Gelder, Ken 82
Giles Goat-Boy (Barth) 121–2, 126,
      128, 179
Ginsberg, Allen 144, 158, 214

Goethe, Johann Wolfgang von 208
Gold, Herbert 214
Golding, William 65
Goldstone, Andrew 228
Google Ngram Viewer 141
Gothic fiction 172–4, 184–5, 189,
     199–200
Grant, J. Kerry 153
Gravity's Rainbow (Pynchon)
    acronyms 117–19
    archaic language 61–2
    characterization 24–5
    early criticism 3–6
    ellipsis marks 178–9, 182–4, 187–94,
         199–200
    the inanimate 98, 101
    linguistic and textual studies 4–5
    profanity 137–41, 161–2
    style 3
    vagueness 104
    word frequencies 5

Hägg, Samuli 4, 193, 207
Hall, Radclyffe 149
Hänggi, Christian 11 n.3, 20, 163, 231–2
Hardy, Thomas 175
Harley, Heidi 117
Hart, John 36, 38
Hawthorne, Mark D. 77
Haynes, Doug 191
Heart of Darkness (Conrad) 3, 85–7, 228
Hecht, Anthony 199
Heller, Joseph 121, 126, 146, 214
Hemingway, Ernest 214
Herman, Luc 43, 57, 106, 134–5, 141, 146,
     153, 160–2, 208–9, 227–8, 230
Herrmann, J. Berenike 2, 10
Hess, John Joseph 30
Hiller, Jack H. 86–97, 107–8
Hinds, Elizabeth Jane Wall 65
History of English Spelling (Scragg) 49
Hite, Molly 5, 155, 172, 183
Hogenraad, Robert 73, 86–97, 107–8,
     227–8, 230
Hohmann, Charles 43, 183, 191, 193–4
Hoover, David L. 208, 215
Horn, Clayton W. 144
Houston, Keith 179
Howard, Gerald 181, 214

Howl (Ginsberg) 144, 146
Hughes, Geoffrey 140
Hunter-Tilney, Ludovic 171
Hutcheon, Linda 195
Hyman, Stanley Edgar 57

Indeherberg, Lindsay 24
Infinite Jest (Wallace)
    acronyms 115–16, 121–3, 127–8
    ambiguity 84, 95
    comparison with Pynchon 217
    direct discourse 22
Inherent Vice (Pynchon)
    acronyms 117–19, 124–5
    archaic language 63
    capitalization 47
    ellipsis marks 185–6
    the inanimate 102
    profanity 137–41, 162–3
Ionesco, Eugène 214
IT (King) 22

J R (Gaddis) 95, 125, 176, 178, 214, 229
Jacoby, William 136
James, Henry 8, 87, 207–8, 214
Jarvis, Michael 105
Jefferson, Thomas 51, 102
Johnson, Samuel 59
Johnson, Thomas H. 197–8
Jonson, Ben 173
*Journal of Charles Mason & Jeremiah
     Dixon, The* 36, 49
Joyce, James 1
    compared with Pynchon 25,
         65–6, 218
    lists 8
    modernism 87
    sentence style 233–4
Jung, Ena 195

Kachka, Boris 57
Kafka, Franz 208
Käkelä-Puumala, Tina 46
Kakutani, Michiko 28, 218
Keats, John 19
Keesey, Douglas 25, 64–5
Kenyon Review 146, 150
Kerouac, Jack 146, 214
King, Stephen 8, 22, 179–80, 214, 216

Kingston, Maxine Hong 215
Kipling, Rudyard 18, 175
Kolbuszewska, Zofia 186

Lady Chatterley's Lover (Lawrence) 143,
        148, 150
Lakoff, Robin 4
Larkey, Leah S. 124
Lawrence, D. H. 143, 148
LeClair, Tom 129, 217–18
Leech, Geoffrey 2, 216
Leonard, Elmore 22
Letzler, David 209, 228–31,
        233, 236
Levine, George 3
Liberman, Mark 3, 18, 22, 29, 231
Locke, Richard 3, 24, 191
Lodge, David 121
Lolita (Nabokov) 143, 146, 150, 153
Love in the Time of Cholera (García
        Márquez) 77
"Low-Lands" (Pynchon) 44, 146–7,
        150, 163

MacAdam, Alfred 25
Madsen, Deborah L. 73, 75
Mailer, Norman 158, 214
Maltby, Paul 180
Marlowe, Christopher 75
Martindale, Colin 228
Martínez, M. Angeles 4–5
Maso, Carole 215
Mason & Dixon (Pynchon)
    acronyms 7, 116–21, 129
    archaic pronouns and verbs 58–9
    archaic spelling 48–51
    archaic use of apostrophes 54–8
    capitalized nouns 35–40
    characterization 25
    ellipsis marks 178–9, 186, 199
    profanity 137–40, 162
    religious/profane censorship 51–3
    vagueness 103
Mason, Paul 208
Mattessich, Stefan 183, 194
Max, D. T. 218
McCarthy, Cormac 10
    ambiguity 81, 95
    comparison with Pynchon 215–16

direct discourse 22
    ellipsis marks 179, 181
McClure, David 230
McEnery, Tony 134–6, 215–16
McHale, Brian 4, 6, 25–6, 47, 64, 75,
        106, 207
McHoul, Alec 4–5
Meister, Jan Christoph 9
Melville, Herman 65–7
Mendelson, Edward 3, 65, 159
Meredith, George 174
Millard, William (Bill) 25, 38–9, 41
Miller v. California 141, 161
Miller, Henry 135, 142–3, 147–8, 150
Minstral Island (Pynchon) 20
Mitchell, David 58, 65
Miyamoto, Yuichiro 183
Moby-Dick (Melville) 65–7
Moore, Alan 65
Morrison, Toni 8
    acronyms 125
    ambiguity 81, 111 n.40
    comparison with Pynchon 215–16
    ellipsis marks 179, 181
    profanity 141
"Mortality and Mercy in Vienna"
        (Pynchon) 211
    accents in 33 n.42
    ambiguity 77
    archaisms 44, 60–1, 64
    profanity 146
Mumbo Jumbo (Reed) 125, 128, 179
Musil, Robert 208
Muth, Katie 234–5

Nabokov, Vladimir 135, 143–4, 153, 159,
        214, 217–18
Naked Lunch (Burroughs) 141, 152, 158
Narratology 9–10, 12 n.30
Nazaryan, Alexander 219
Neighbors, Jim 184
New World Writing 146, 150
Newton, Maud 95
Nightwood (Barnes) 149
Not Exactly
    In Praise of Vagueness (van
        Deemter) 108

O'Connor, Flanners 146

Oates, Joyce Carol 198
Ochnser, Robert 4

Palmer, Alan 27
Passion's Promise (Steel) 88, 229
Patterson, James 8, 216
  acronyms 121, 127
  ambiguity 82
  direct discourse 22
  ellipsis marks 181
  profanity 141
Pearson, Adrian Jones 232
Peck, Dale 116
Pet Sounds (The Beach Boys) 19
Pinkal, Manfred 74
Piper, Andrew 200
Plater, William 1
Pöhlmann, Sascha 172, 184
Pope, Alexander 36
Postmodernist Fiction (McHale) 75–6
Pound, Ezra 19
Powers, David M. 164
Powers, Richard 8, 83–4, 127
Proust, Marcel 8
Pulitzer Prize 133
Pütz, Manfred 67, 115–16, 119, 121–2,
  124–5, 128
Pynchon Wiki 43, 167 n 46, 169 n.86,
  180, 183, 231–2
Pynchon, Thomas
  authorship of Mason & Dixon 56–7
  descriptions of style 3
  juvenilia 60
  "late style" 207–9
  "messages" 108
  musical aspirations 20
  productivity 15–17. *See also* texts by
    Pynchon
Pynchon, William 164, 196
Pynchon
  The Voice of Ambiguity (Schaub) 7,
    73–6, 89

Rabelais, François 75
Rayson, Paul 220–1
Razzell, Paul 235–6
Rebora, Simone 208
Reed, Ishmael 81, 125, 128, 179, 216
Reeve, Jonathan P. 208

Regina v. Hicklin 142–3
Rich, Nathaniel 106
Richardson, Samuel 173
Richer, Carol 25
Rilke, Rainer Maria 190–4, 200
Robbins, Tom 214
Robinson Crusoe (Defoe) 52
Rolls, Albert 211, 222 n.5
Rosset, Barnet 148
Roth v. United States 143–4, 148
Roth, Philip 214
Rothfork, John 95
Rothwell, J. Dan 134
Rouyan, Anahita 19–20
Rovit, Earl 67
Rowberry, Simon 232
Rushdie, Salman 57

Said, Edward 207
Salgaro, Massimo 208
Salinger, J. D. 136, 232
Sanctuary (Faulkner) 143, 149
Schaub, Thomas 3, 5, 7, 42, 65, 73–6, 89,
  107, 183, 214
Schmid, Helmut 220
Schmidt, Benjamin 228
Schneider, Peter 49
Schöch, Christof 2, 211
Schroeder, Ralph 232
Schulz, Max 153
Scragg, D. G. 49
"Secret Integration, The" (Pynchon) 57,
  76–7, 156–8
Seed, David 148
Shakespeare, William 75, 173
Shen, Dan 9
Short, Mick 2, 216
Siegel, Jason 105–6
Sigelman, Lee 136
Slade, Joseph W. 4–6, 26
Slow Learner (Pynchon) 29, 145, 149,
  151, 214
"Small Rain, The" (Pynchon) 33
  n.42, 144–5
Smith, Allan Lloyd 185
Smith, Corlies "Cork" 44–5, 146, 156
Smith, Zak
  acronyms 121–2, 124, 127
  ambiguity 84–5, 88, 95

ellipsis marks 179, 181
  Pynchon influence 219
Snow White (Barthelme) 125–6, 158, 229
Song of Solomon (Morrison) 111
  n.40, 125
Sonnets to Orpheus (Rilke) 191–2
Stark, John O. 191
Steel, Danielle 8, 88
Steer, Martin 31 n.9
Stephenson, Neal 214
Sterne, Laurence 51, 171–3
Stone Junction (Dodge) 78–9
Stonhill, Brian 98
Stonum, Gary Lee 194–5
Strunk, William 97
Stubbs, Michael 3, 85–7
Swearing in English (McEnery) 136
Swift, Jonathan 36, 51, 53, 173

Tale of a Tub, A (Swift) 173
The Bostonians (James) 87
The Broom of the System (Wallace) 22,
  83–4, 110 n.28, 128, 218, 229
The Crying of Lot 49 (Pynchon)
  acronyms 117–19, 128
  archaic language 62
  capitalization 46
  characterization 27
  classification as science
      fiction 100, 234–5
  its 100
  profanity 137–40, 158–60
  word frequencies 5
The Elements of Style (Strunk and
  White) 97
The Fire Next Time (Baldwin) 44
The Inheritors (Golding) 65
The Sot-Weed Factor (Barth) 67
The Well of Loneliness (Hall) 149
Tom Jones (Fielding) 52
Toner, Anne 171–5, 188, 200
Toxic Bachelors (Steel) 88
Traherne, Thomas 36
Tristram Shandy (Sterne) 171–3
Tropic of Cancer (Miller) 143, 146–9,
  150, 158
Tsatsoulis, Christos 230–1
Turner, Edwin 105

TXM (software) 44, 111 n.37, 116,
  136, 220

Ulysses (Joyce) 1, 228
  banning 142–3, 150
  comparison with Pynchon 25, 65–6
  lists in 13 n.49
"Under the Rose" (Pynchon) 5, 45,
  150–4, 185
Underwood, Ted 100, 228, 234–5
Underworld (DeLillo) 81, 126,
  179–80

V. (Pynchon)
  acronyms 117–19
  archaic language 61–2
  capitalization 45–6
  ellipsis marks 5
  profanity 137–40, 152–6
  word frequencies 5
van Dalen-Oskam, Karina 2
van Deemter, Kees 108
van Mirlo, Wim 227–8, 230
Vesterman, William 19
Vidal, Gore 214
Vineland (Pynchon)
  acronyms 117–19
  archaic language 62–3
  capitalization 47
  ellipsis marks 189
  estimated composition time 6, 16–17
  profanity 137–41
Voice of the Fire (Moore) 65
Vollmann, William 22, 215, 217–19, 229
Voltaire 214
von Ahn, Luis 136
Vonnegut, Kurt 214

Wagner, Richard 20
Wales, Katie 2
Wallace, David Foster 8, 10
  acronyms 116, 121–3, 127–8
  ambiguity 83–4, 95, 110 n.28
  capitalization 48, 70 n.28
  comparison with Pynchon 214–19, 229
  direct discourse 22
  ellipsis marks 179, 181
  on Pynchon 16

War and Peace (Tolstoy) 230
Washington, George 39
We Did Porn (Smith) 84–5, 88, 95, 121–2, 124, 219
Weisenburger, Steven 43, 57, 104, 134–5, 141, 146, 153, 160–2, 194
Wells, H. G. 174
Wharton, Edith 175
White Noise (DeLillo) 81–2
White, E. B. 97
Whitman, Walt 8
Wickmain, Forrest 164
Wilde, Oscar 143

Wills, David 4–5
Winston, Mathew 196
Wisnicki, Adrian 171
Witzling, David 156
Wolfe, Thomas 214
Wolfe, Tom 180
Wood, James 25–6
Woodson, Thomas 66
Woolf, Virginia 87
Woolsey, John M. 142–3
Wuthering Heights (Brontë) 52

Xiao, Zhonghua 135

Ingram Content Group UK Ltd.
Milton Keynes UK
UKHW020752140323
418545UK00006B/794